NEGIMA!

6

Ken Akamatsu

TRANSLATED BY
Toshifumi Yoshida

ADAPTED BY
Trish Ledoux

LETTERING AND RETOUCH BY
Steve Palmer

BALLANTINE BOOKS · NEW YORK

A Word from the Author

In this volume, the long "student trip" story arc finally comes to an end. What can be the ultimate technique of the woman in the monkey suit?! What is Konoka's secret, and why can't Setsuna Sakurazaki be honest about her own feelings...?

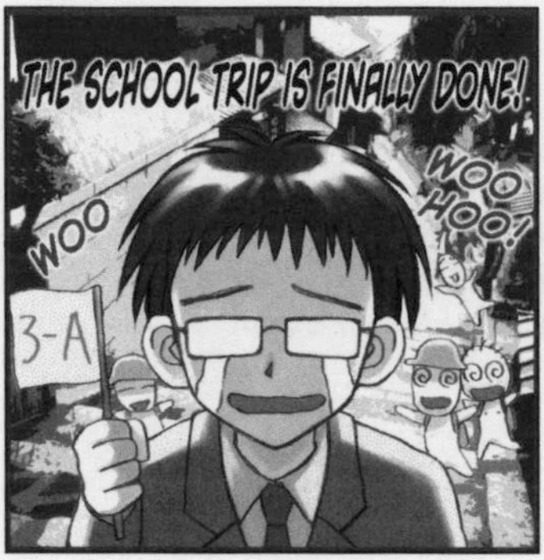
THE SCHOOL TRIP IS FINALLY DONE!
WOO HOO!
WOO
3-A

In Volume 6, all of Kansai's secrets will be made clear. As with Volume 3, ten chapters' worth of story has been packed into these 200 pages, so dig in! We'll be going back for more Mahora Academy wacky love-comedy in Volume 7, so if that's more your thing, you'll be able to look forward to that.

Ken Akamatsu
www.ailove.net

Translator —Toshifumi Yoshida
Adaptor—Trish Ledoux
Lettering and retouch—Steve Palmer
Cover Design—David Stevenson

Negima is a work of fiction. Any resemblance to actual persons, living or dead, is unintentional and purely coincidental.

2005 Del Rey Books Trade Paperback Edition
Published in the United States by Del Rey Books, an imprint of The Random House Publishing Group, a division of Random House, Inc., New York.

First published in serial form by Shonen Magazine Comics and subsequently published in book form by Kodansha, Ltd., Tokyo in 2004.

www.delreymanga.com

Library of Congress Control Number: 2004090830

ISBN 0 345 47786 3

Printed in the United States of America

First Edition: July 2005

5 6 7 8 9

Honorifics

Throughout the Del Rey Manga books, you will find Japanese honorifics left intact in the translations. For those not familiar with how the Japanese use honorifics and, more importantly, how they differ from American honorifics, we present this brief overview.

Politeness has always been a critical facet of Japanese culture. Ever since the feudal era, when Japan was a highly stratified society, use of honorifics—which can be defined as polite speech that indicates relationship or status—has played an essential role in the Japanese language. When addressing someone in Japanese, an honorific usually takes the form of a suffix attached to one's name (example: "Asuna-san"), or as a title at the end of one's name or in place of the name itself (example: "Negi-sensei," or simply "Sensei!").

Honorifics can be expressions of respect or endearment. In the context of manga and anime, honorifics give insight into the nature of the relationship between characters. Many translations into English leave out these important honorifics, and therefore distort the "feel" of the original Japanese. Because Japanese honorifics contain nuances that English honorifics lack, it is our policy at Del Rey not to translate them. Here, instead, is a guide to some of the honorifics you may encounter in Del Rey Manga.

-*san:* This is the most common honorific and is equivalent to Mr., Miss, Ms., or Mrs. It is the all-purpose honorific and can be used in any situation where politeness is required.

-*sama:* This is one level higher than "-san" and is used to confer great respect.

-*dono:* This comes from the word "tono," which means "lord." It is an even higher level than "-sama" and confers utmost respect.

-kun: This suffix is used at the end of boys' names to express familiarity or endearment. It is also sometimes used by men among friends, or when addressing someone younger or of a lower station.

-chan: This is used to express endearment, mostly towards girls. It is also used for little boys, pets, and even among lovers. It gives a sense of childish cuteness.

Bozu: This is an informal way to refer to a boy, similar to the English term "kid" or "squirt."

Sempai: This title suggests that the addressee is one's senior in a group or organization. It is most often used in a school setting, where underclassmen refer to their upperclassmen as "sempai." It can also be used in the workplace, such as when a newer employee addresses an employee who has seniority in the company.

Kohai: This is the opposite of "sempai" and is used toward underclassmen in school or newcomers in the workplace. It connotes that the addressee is of a lower station.

Sensei: Literally meaning "one who has come before," this title is used for teachers, doctors, or masters of any profession or art.

[blank]:   Usually forgotten in these lists, but perhaps the most significant difference between Japanese and English. The lack of honorific means that the speaker has permission to address the person in a very intimate way. Usually, only family, spouses, or very close friends have this kind of permission. Known as *yobisute,* it can be gratifying when someone who has earned the intimacy starts to call one by one's name without an honorific. But when that intimacy hasn't been earned, it can also be very insulting.

魔法先生(まほうせんせい)ネギま!

MAGISTER NEGI MAGI

6

K
Akamats

赤松(あかまつ) 健(け)

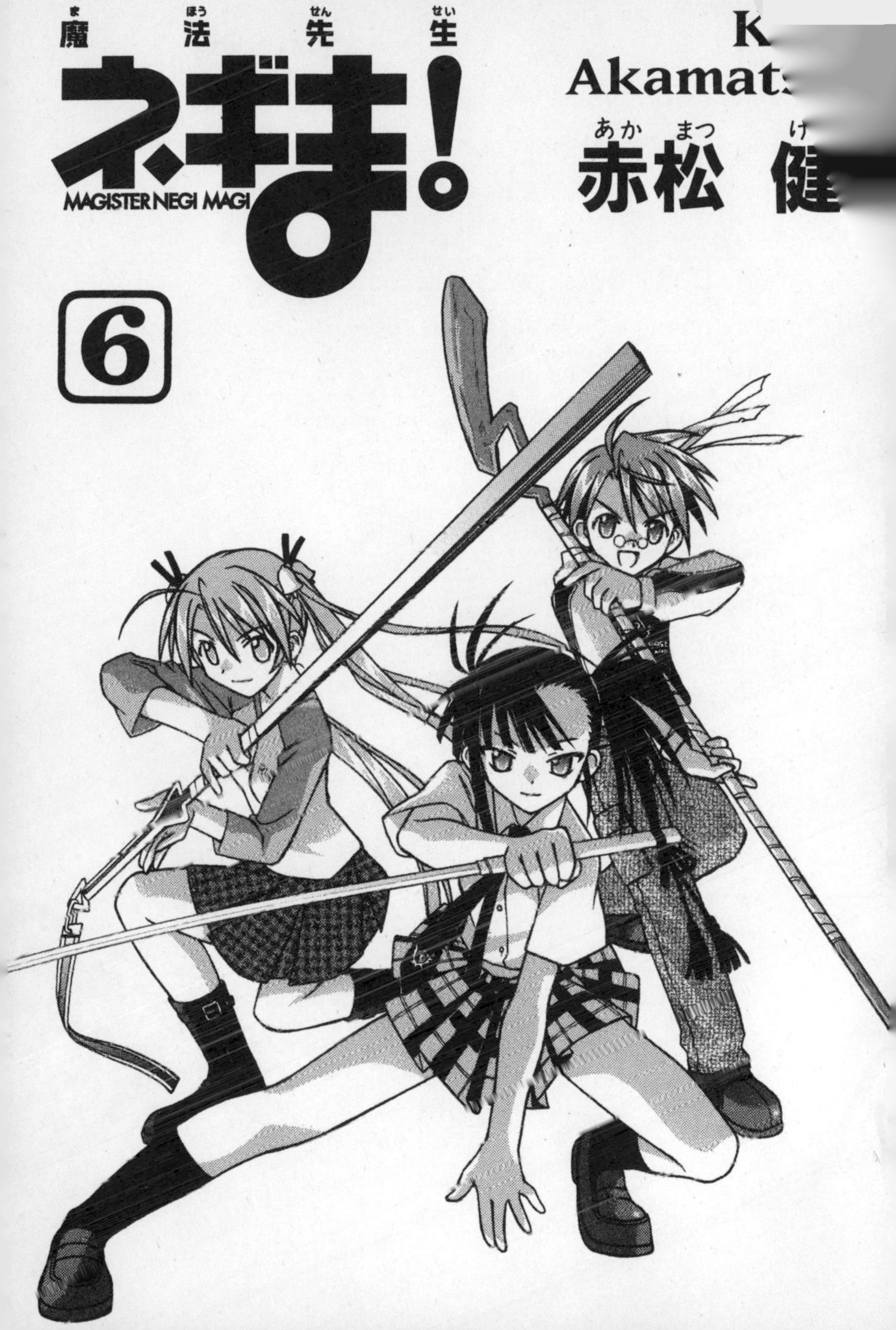

CONTENTS

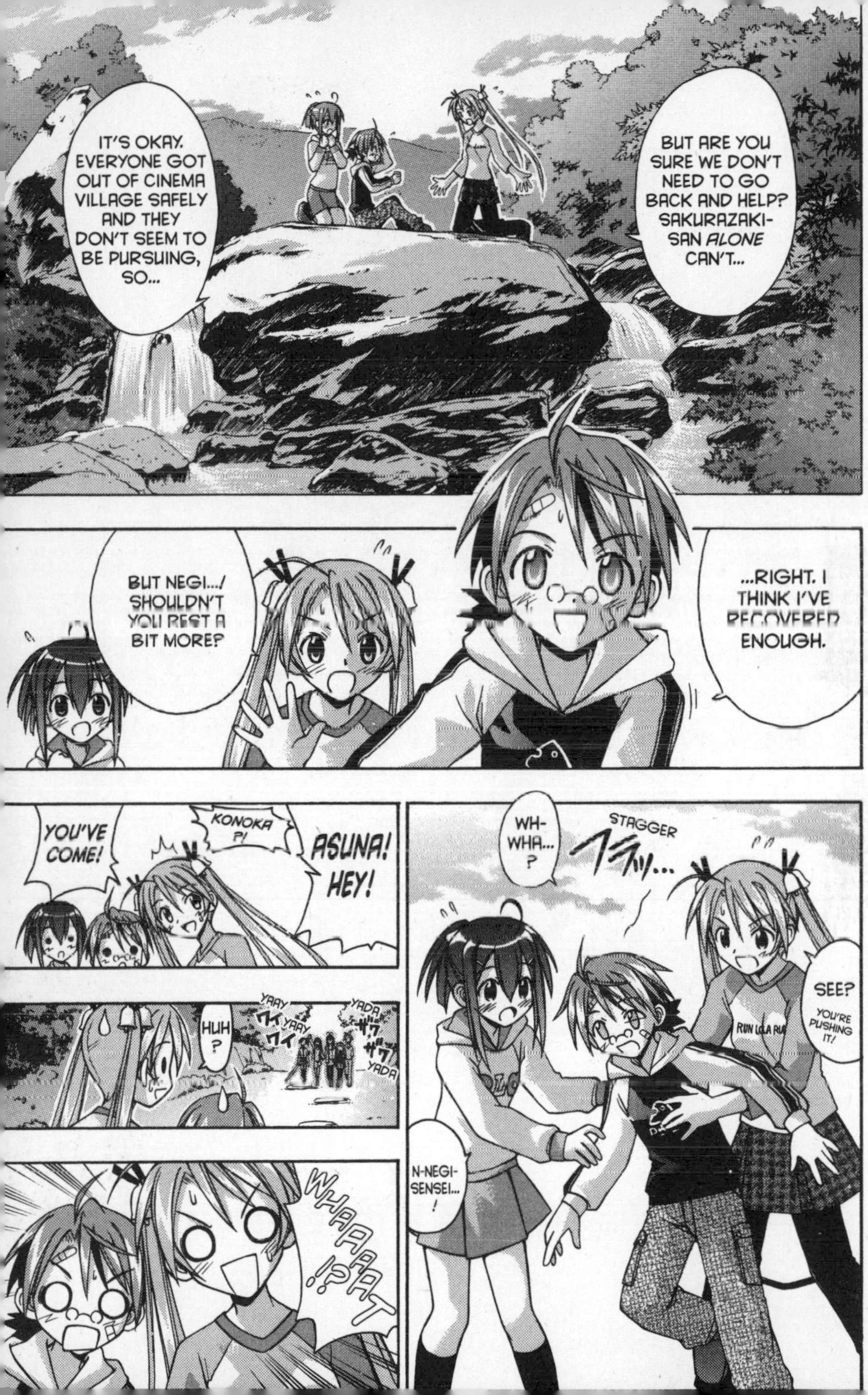
BUT ARE YOU SURE WE DON'T NEED TO GO BACK AND HELP? SAKURAZAKI-SAN *ALONE* CAN'T...
IT'S OKAY. EVERYONE GOT OUT OF CINEMA VILLAGE SAFELY AND THEY DON'T SEEM TO BE PURSUING, SO...
...RIGHT. I THINK I'VE RECOVERED ENOUGH.
BUT NEGI...! SHOULDN'T YOU REST A BIT MORE?
WH-WHA...?
STAGGER
SEE? YOU'RE PUSHING IT!
N-NEGI-SENSEI...!
ASUNA! HEY!
KONOKA?!
YOU'VE COME!
YADA YADA YADA
YAAY YAAY YAAY
HUH?
WHAAAAT!?

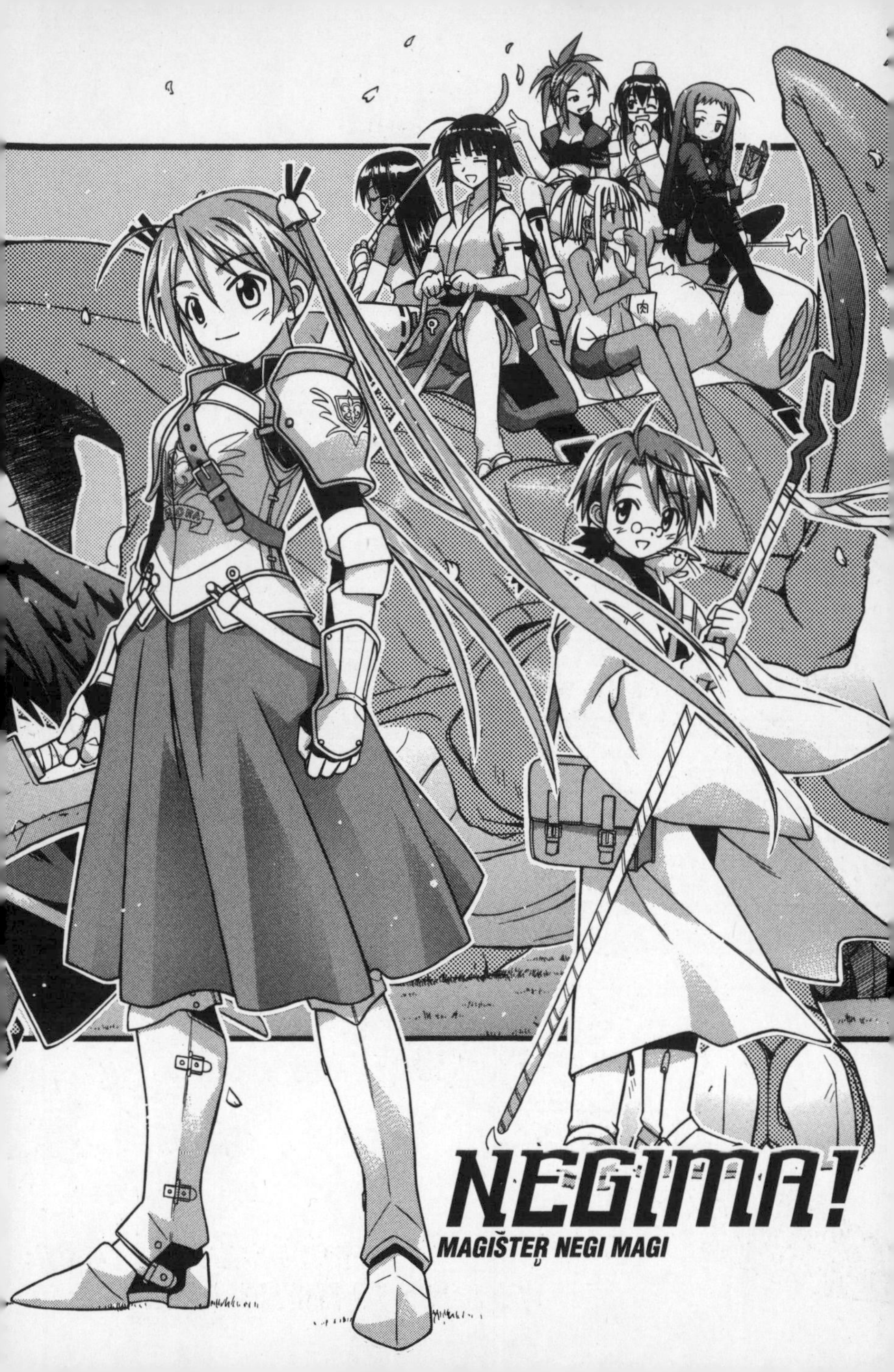
NEGIMA!
MAGISTER NEGI MAGI

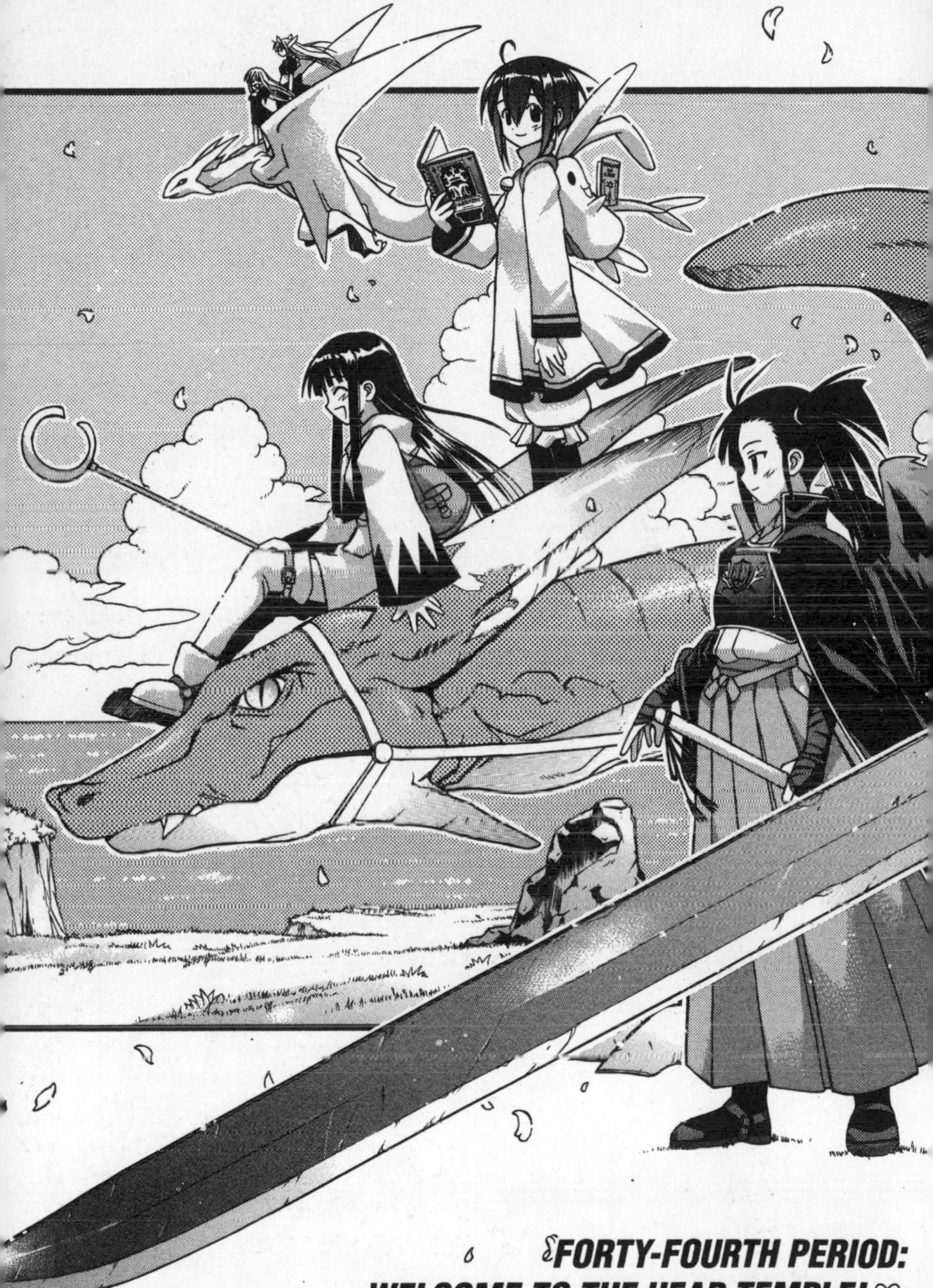

FORTY-FOURTH PERIOD: WELCOME TO THE HEAD TEMPLE! ♡

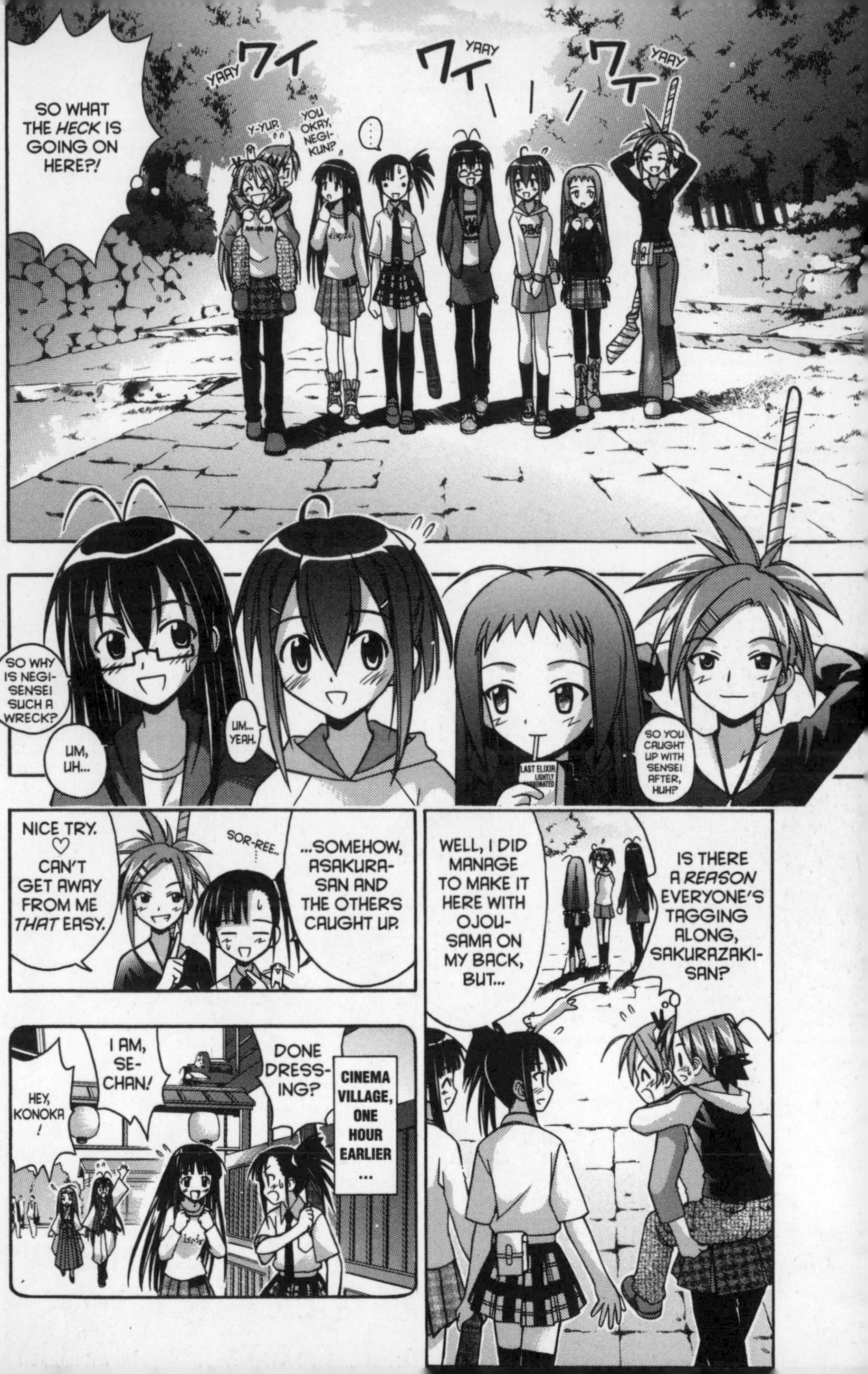
YAAY ワイ
YAAY ワイ
YAAY ワイ
...
YOU OKAY, NEGI-KUN?
Y-YUP.
SO WHAT THE *HECK* IS GOING ON HERE?!
SO YOU CAUGHT UP WITH SENSEI AFTER, HUH?
LAST ELIXIR LIGHTLY CARBONATED
UM... YEAH.
SO WHY IS NEGI-SENSEI SUCH A WRECK?
UM, UH...
IS THERE A *REASON* EVERYONE'S TAGGING ALONG, SAKURAZAKI-SAN?
WELL, I DID MANAGE TO MAKE IT HERE WITH OJOU-SAMA ON MY BACK, BUT...
...SOMEHOW, ASAKURA-SAN AND THE OTHERS CAUGHT UP.
SOR-REE...
NICE TRY. ♡ CAN'T GET AWAY FROM ME *THAT* EASY.
CINEMA VILLAGE, ONE HOUR EARLIER...
DONE DRESS-ING?
I AM, SE-CHAN!
HEY, KONOKA!

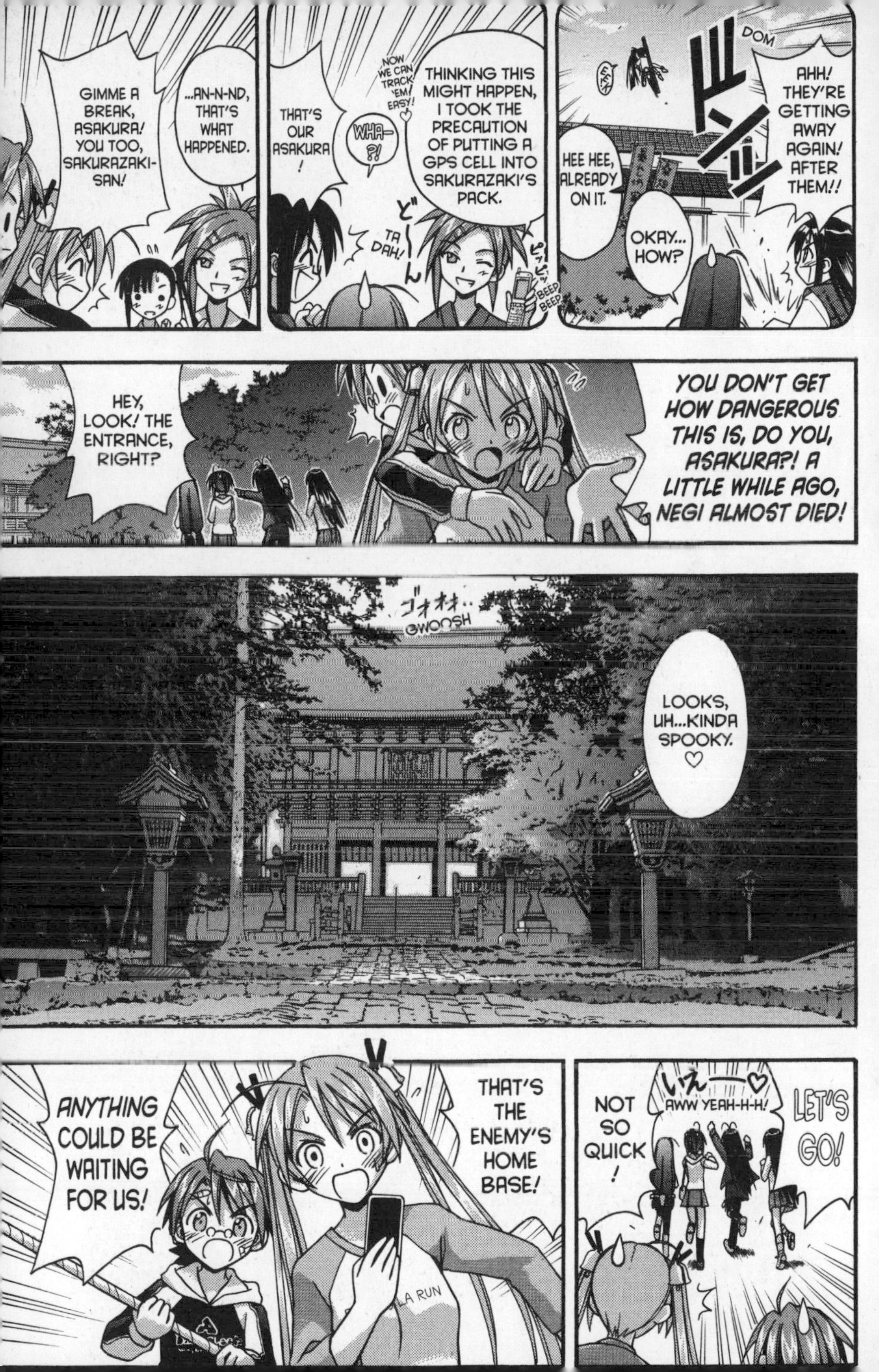
DOM
AHH! THEY'RE GETTING AWAY AGAIN! AFTER THEM!!
HEE HEE, ALREADY ON IT.
OKAY... HOW?
THINKING THIS MIGHT HAPPEN, I TOOK THE PRECAUTION OF PUTTING A GPS CELL INTO SAKURAZAKI'S PACK.
NOW WE CAN TRACK 'EM EASY! ♡
WHA—?!
THAT'S OUR ASAKURA!
TA DAH!
BEEP BEEP
...AN-N-ND, THAT'S WHAT HAPPENED.
GIMME A BREAK, ASAKURA! YOU TOO, SAKURAZAKI-SAN!
YOU DON'T GET HOW DANGEROUS THIS IS, DO YOU, ASAKURA?! A LITTLE WHILE AGO, NEGI ALMOST DIED!
HEY, LOOK! THE ENTRANCE, RIGHT?
GWOOSH
LOOKS, UH...KINDA SPOOKY. ♡
LET'S GO!
AWW YEAH-H-H!
NOT SO QUICK!
THAT'S THE ENEMY'S HOME BASE!
ANYTHING COULD BE WAITING FOR US!

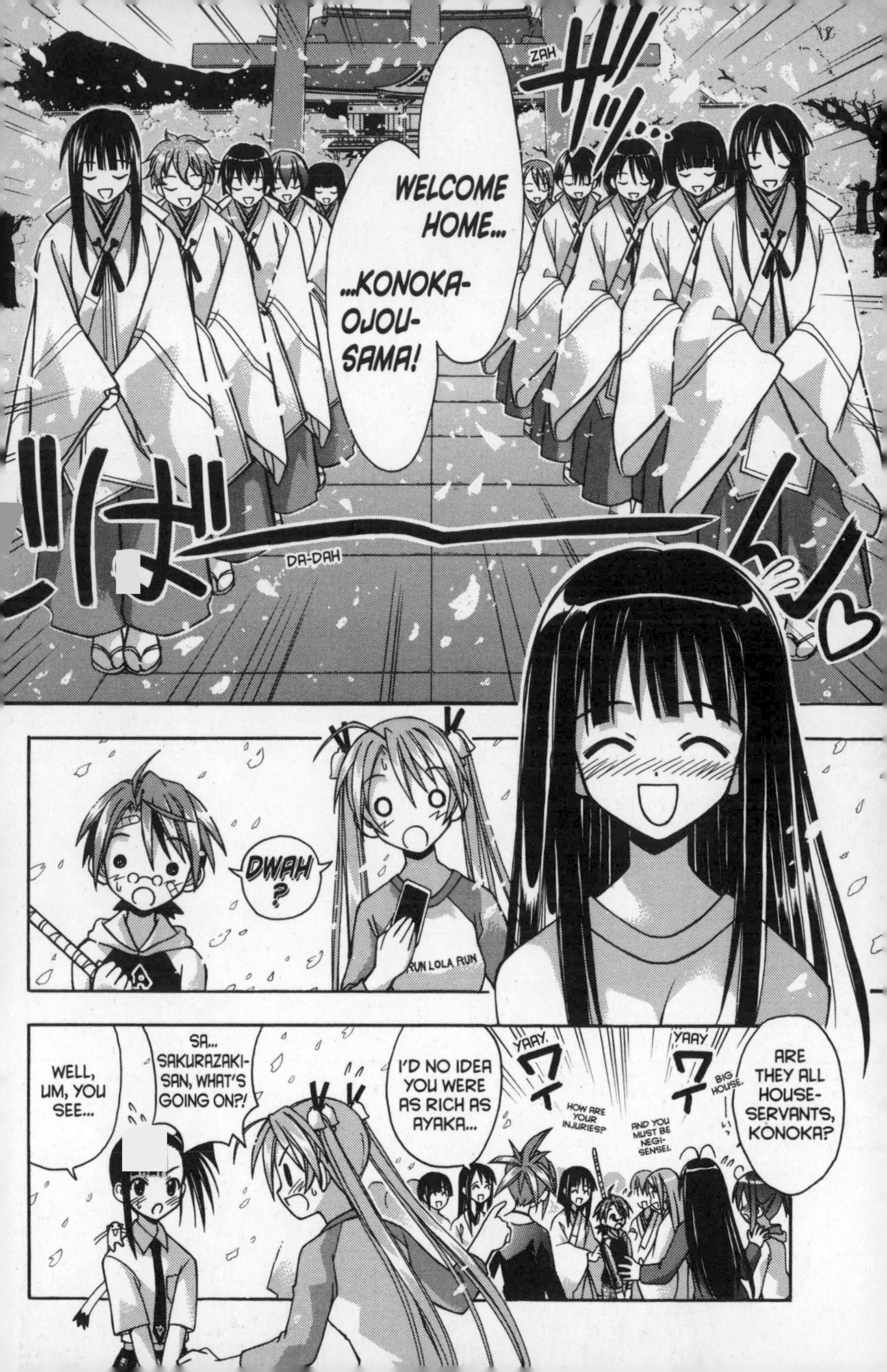
ZAH
WELCOME HOME...
...KONOKA-OJOU-SAMA!
DA-DAH
DWAH?
RUN LOLA RUN
ARE THEY ALL HOUSE-SERVANTS, KONOKA?
BIG HOUSE.
YAAY
AND YOU MUST BE NEGI-SENSEI.
HOW ARE YOUR INJURIES?
YAAY.
I'D NO IDEA YOU WERE AS RICH AS AYAKA...
SA... SAKURAZAKI-SAN, WHAT'S GOING ON?!
WELL, UM, YOU SEE...

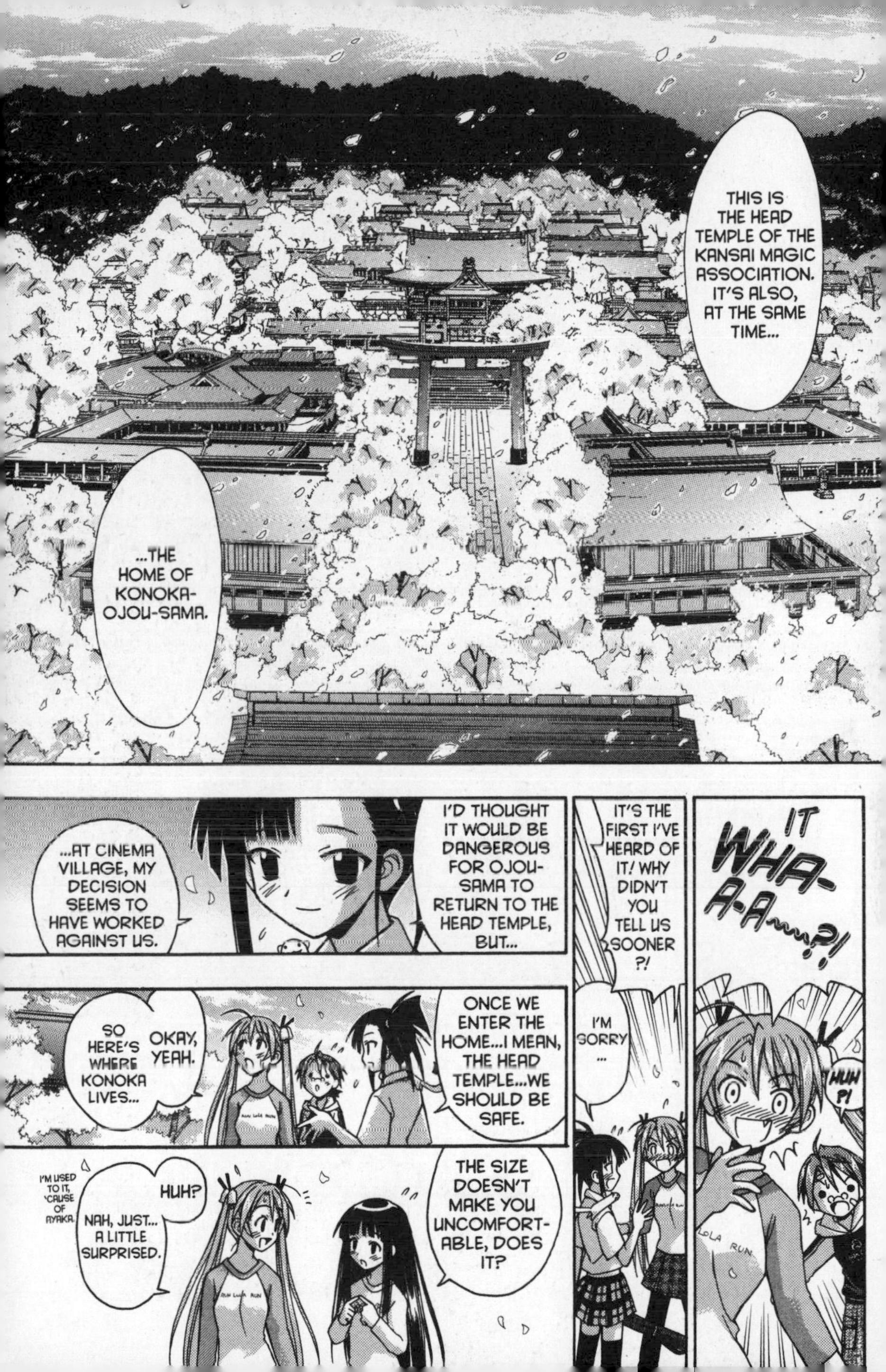
THIS IS THE HEAD TEMPLE OF THE KANSAI MAGIC ASSOCIATION. IT'S ALSO, AT THE SAME TIME...
...THE HOME OF KONOKA-OJOU-SAMA.
IT WHA-A-A~~?!
HUH ?!
IT'S THE FIRST I'VE HEARD OF IT! WHY DIDN'T YOU TELL US SOONER ?!
I'M SORRY ...
I'D THOUGHT IT WOULD BE DANGEROUS FOR OJOU-SAMA TO RETURN TO THE HEAD TEMPLE, BUT...
...AT CINEMA VILLAGE, MY DECISION SEEMS TO HAVE WORKED AGAINST US.
ONCE WE ENTER THE HOME...I MEAN, THE HEAD TEMPLE...WE SHOULD BE SAFE.
OKAY, YEAH.
SO HERE'S WHERE KONOKA LIVES...
THE SIZE DOESN'T MAKE YOU UNCOMFORTABLE, DOES IT?
HUH?
NAH, JUST... A LITTLE SURPRISED.
I'M USED TO IT, 'CAUSE OF AYAKA.

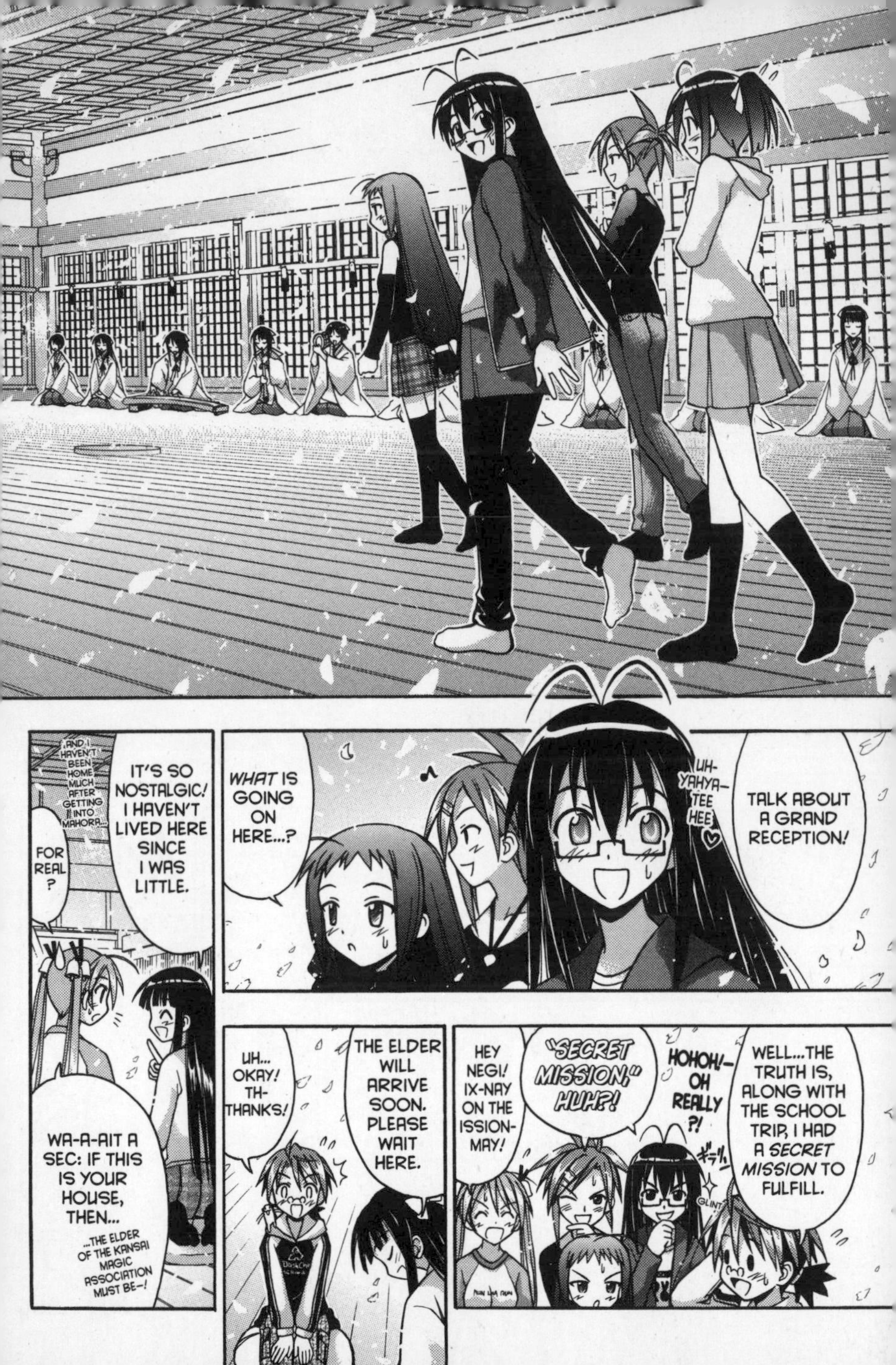
TALK ABOUT A GRAND RECEPTION!
UH-YAHYA-TEE HEE ♡
WHAT IS GOING ON HERE...?
WELL...THE TRUTH IS, ALONG WITH THE SCHOOL TRIP, I HAD A SECRET MISSION TO FULFILL.
HOHOH!—OH REALLY?!
"SECRET MISSION," HUH?!
HEY NEGI! IX-NAY ON THE ISSION-MAY!
THE ELDER WILL ARRIVE SOON. PLEASE WAIT HERE.
UH... OKAY! TH-THANKS!
IT'S SO NOSTALGIC! I HAVEN'T LIVED HERE SINCE I WAS LITTLE.
...AND I HAVEN'T BEEN HOME MUCH AFTER GETTING INTO MAHORA...
FOR REAL?
WA-A-AIT A SEC: IF THIS IS YOUR HOUSE, THEN...
...THE ELDER OF THE KANSAI MAGIC ASSOCIATION MUST BE—!

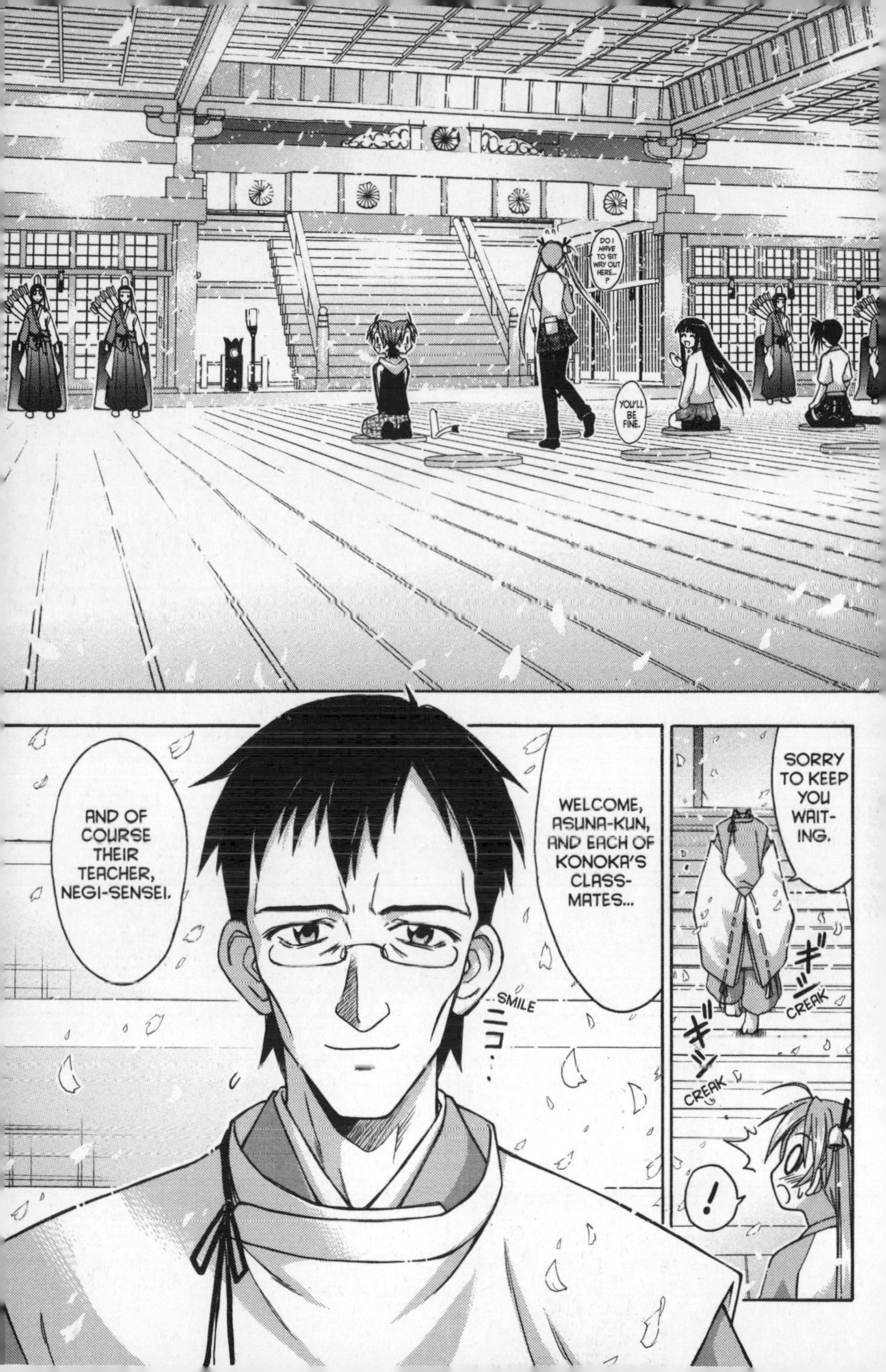
DO I HAVE TO SIT WAY OUT HERE...?
YOU'LL BE FINE.
SORRY TO KEEP YOU WAIT-ING.
CREAK
CREAK
!
WELCOME, ASUNA-KUN, AND EACH OF KONOKA'S CLASS-MATES...
AND OF COURSE THEIR TEACHER, NEGI-SENSEI.
SMILE

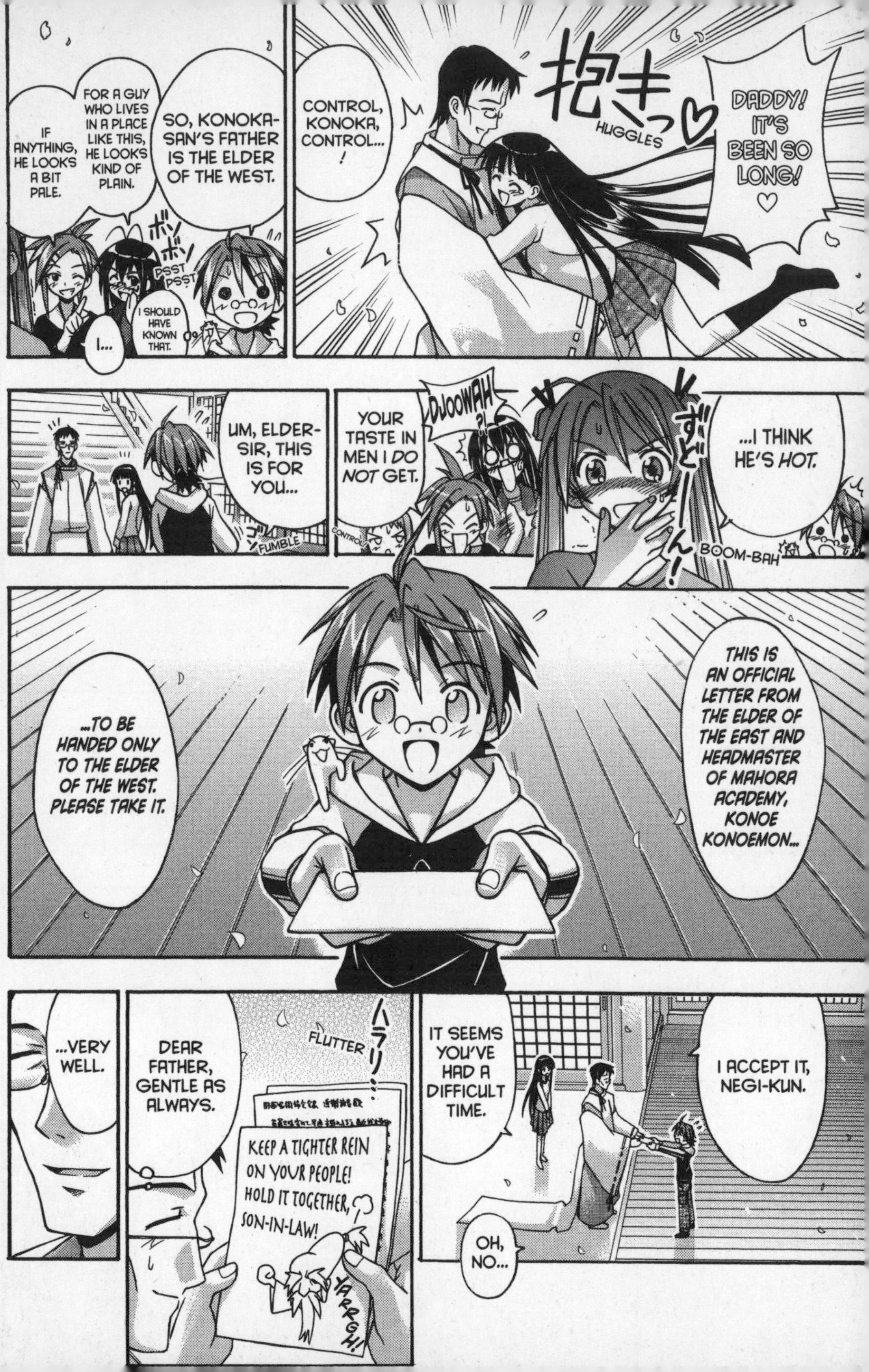
抱きっ
HUGGLES
DADDY! IT'S BEEN SO LONG! ♥
CONTROL, KONOKA, CONTROL...!
SO, KONOKA-SAN'S FATHER IS THE ELDER OF THE WEST.
FOR A GUY WHO LIVES IN A PLACE LIKE THIS, HE LOOKS KIND OF PLAIN.
IF ANYTHING, HE LOOKS A BIT PALE.
ボソボソ
PSST PSST
I SHOULD HAVE KNOWN THAT.
I...
...I THINK HE'S *HOT.*
ずどーん!
BOOM-BAH
DJOOWAH?!
YOUR TASTE IN MEN I *DO NOT* GET.
CONTROL
UM, ELDER-SIR, THIS IS FOR YOU...
FUMBLE
THIS IS AN OFFICIAL LETTER FROM THE ELDER OF THE EAST AND HEADMASTER OF MAHORA ACADEMY, KONOE KONOEMON...
...TO BE HANDED ONLY TO THE ELDER OF THE WEST. PLEASE TAKE IT.
I ACCEPT IT, NEGI-KUN.
IT SEEMS YOU'VE HAD A DIFFICULT TIME.
OH, NO...
ハラリ…
FLUTTER
DEAR FATHER, GENTLE AS ALWAYS.
KEEP A TIGHTER REIN ON YOUR PEOPLE! HOLD IT TOGETHER, SON-IN-LAW!
YARRGH!
...VERY WELL.

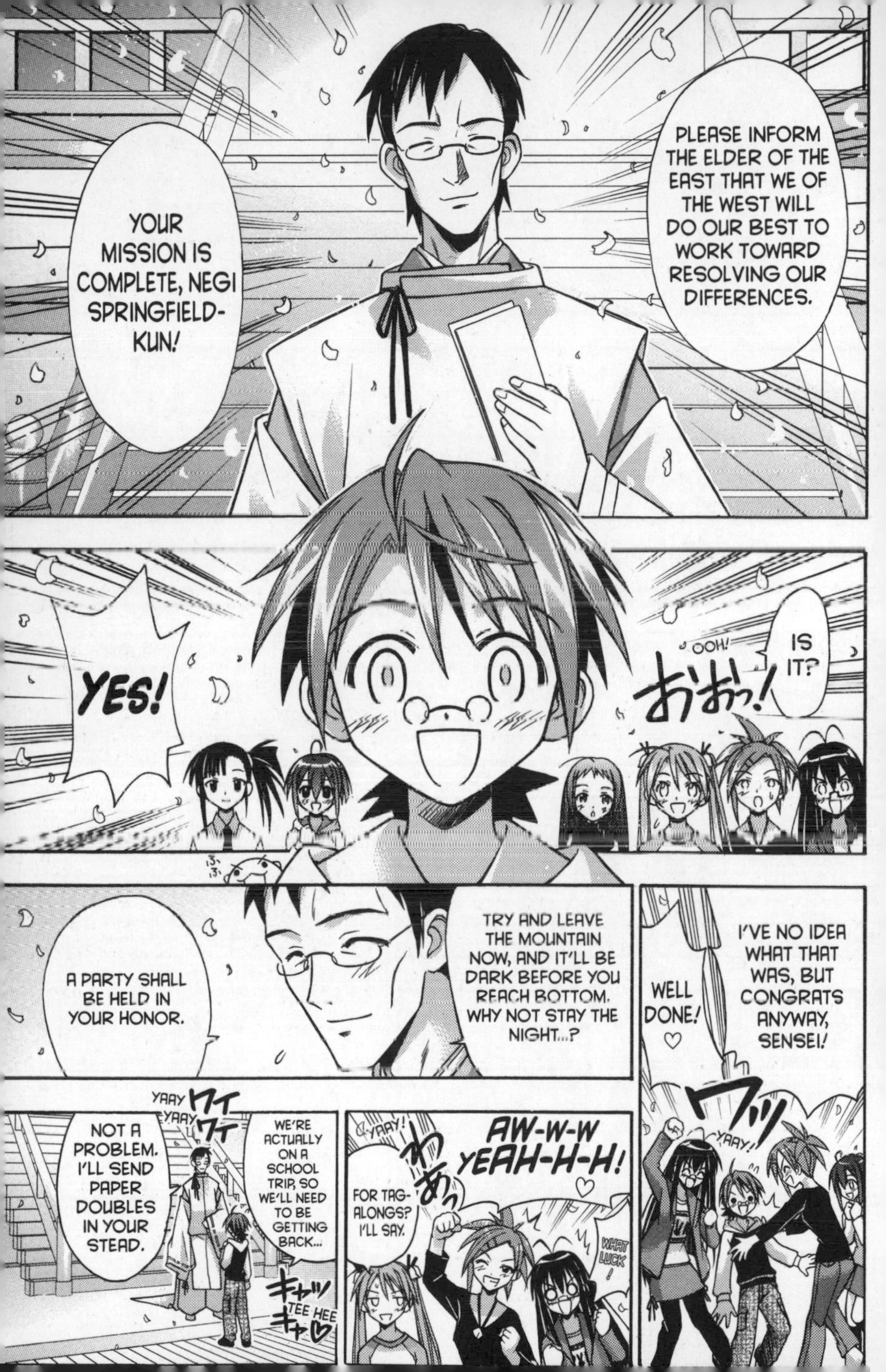
PLEASE INFORM THE ELDER OF THE EAST THAT WE OF THE WEST WILL DO OUR BEST TO WORK TOWARD RESOLVING OUR DIFFERENCES.
YOUR MISSION IS COMPLETE, NEGI SPRINGFIELD-KUN!
IS IT?
OOH!
おおっ!
YES!
ふふ
I'VE NO IDEA WHAT THAT WAS, BUT CONGRATS ANYWAY, SENSEI!
WELL DONE! ♡
TRY AND LEAVE THE MOUNTAIN NOW, AND IT'LL BE DARK BEFORE YOU REACH BOTTOM. WHY NOT STAY THE NIGHT...?
A PARTY SHALL BE HELD IN YOUR HONOR.
ワッ
YAAY!
AW-W-W YEAH-H-H!
わあっ
YAAY!
FOR TAG-ALONGS? I'LL SAY.
WHAT LUCK!
WE'RE ACTUALLY ON A SCHOOL TRIP, SO WE'LL NEED TO BE GETTING BACK...
NOT A PROBLEM. I'LL SEND PAPER DOUBLES IN YOUR STEAD.
YAAY YAAY
ワイワイ
キャッ キャ♡
TEE HEE

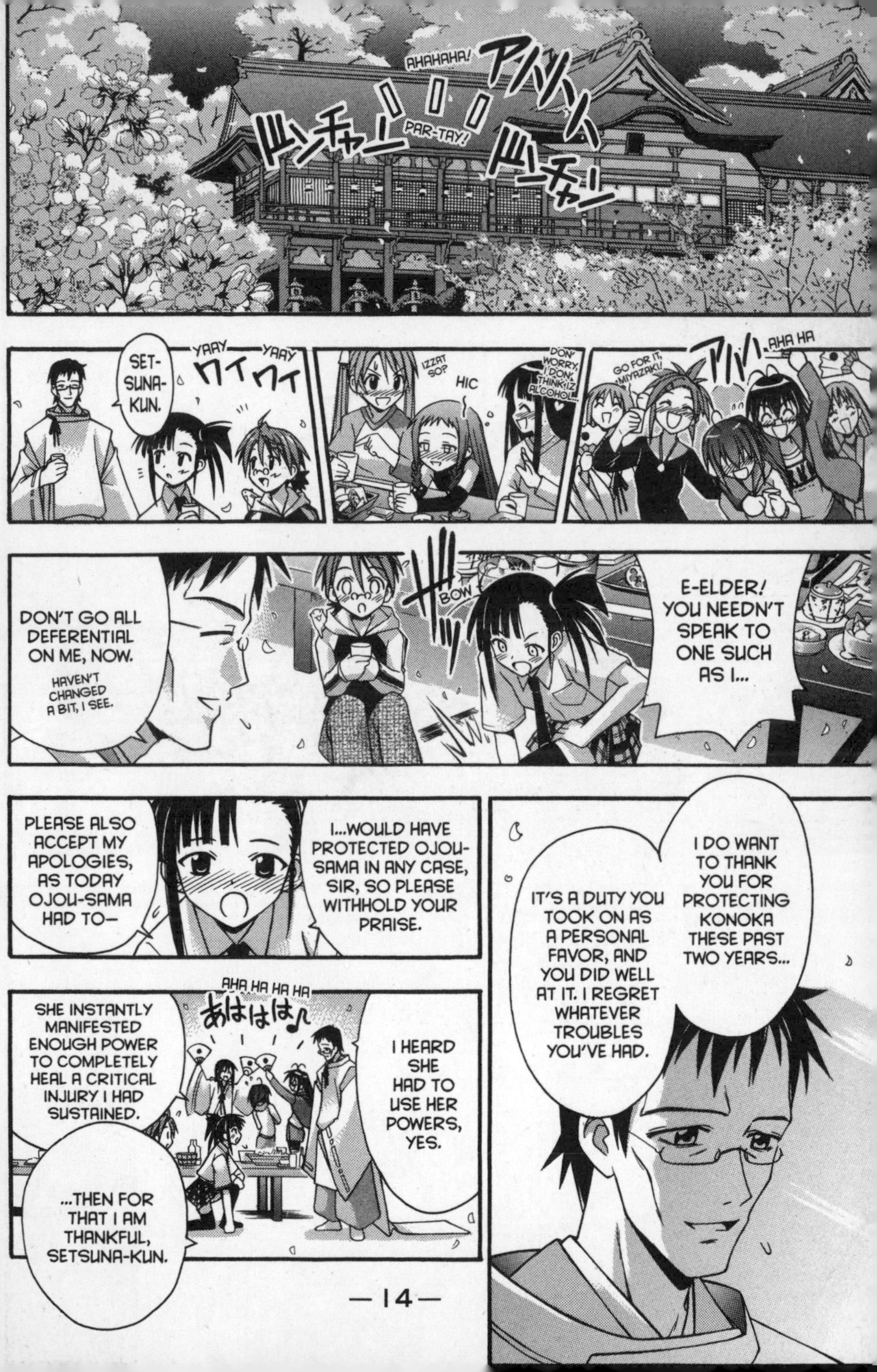
AHAHAHA!
アハハハ
PAR-TAY!
ドンチャン
ドンチャン
GO FOR IT, MIYAZAKI!
アハハ AHA HA
IZZAT SO?
HIC
DON' WORRY, I DON' THINK IZ ALCOHOL...
SET-SUNA-KUN.
ワイ YAAY
ワイ YAAY
E-ELDER! YOU NEEDN'T SPEAK TO ONE SUCH AS I...
BOW
DON'T GO ALL DEFERENTIAL ON ME, NOW.
HAVEN'T CHANGED A BIT, I SEE.
I DO WANT TO THANK YOU FOR PROTECTING KONOKA THESE PAST TWO YEARS...
IT'S A DUTY YOU TOOK ON AS A PERSONAL FAVOR, AND YOU DID WELL AT IT. I REGRET WHATEVER TROUBLES YOU'VE HAD.
I...WOULD HAVE PROTECTED OJOU-SAMA IN ANY CASE, SIR, SO PLEASE WITHHOLD YOUR PRAISE.
PLEASE ALSO ACCEPT MY APOLOGIES, AS TODAY OJOU-SAMA HAD TO—
あははは♪ AHA HA HA HA
I HEARD SHE HAD TO USE HER POWERS, YES.
SHE INSTANTLY MANIFESTED ENOUGH POWER TO COMPLETELY HEAL A CRITICAL INJURY I HAD SUSTAINED.
...THEN FOR THAT I AM THANKFUL, SETSUNA-KUN.

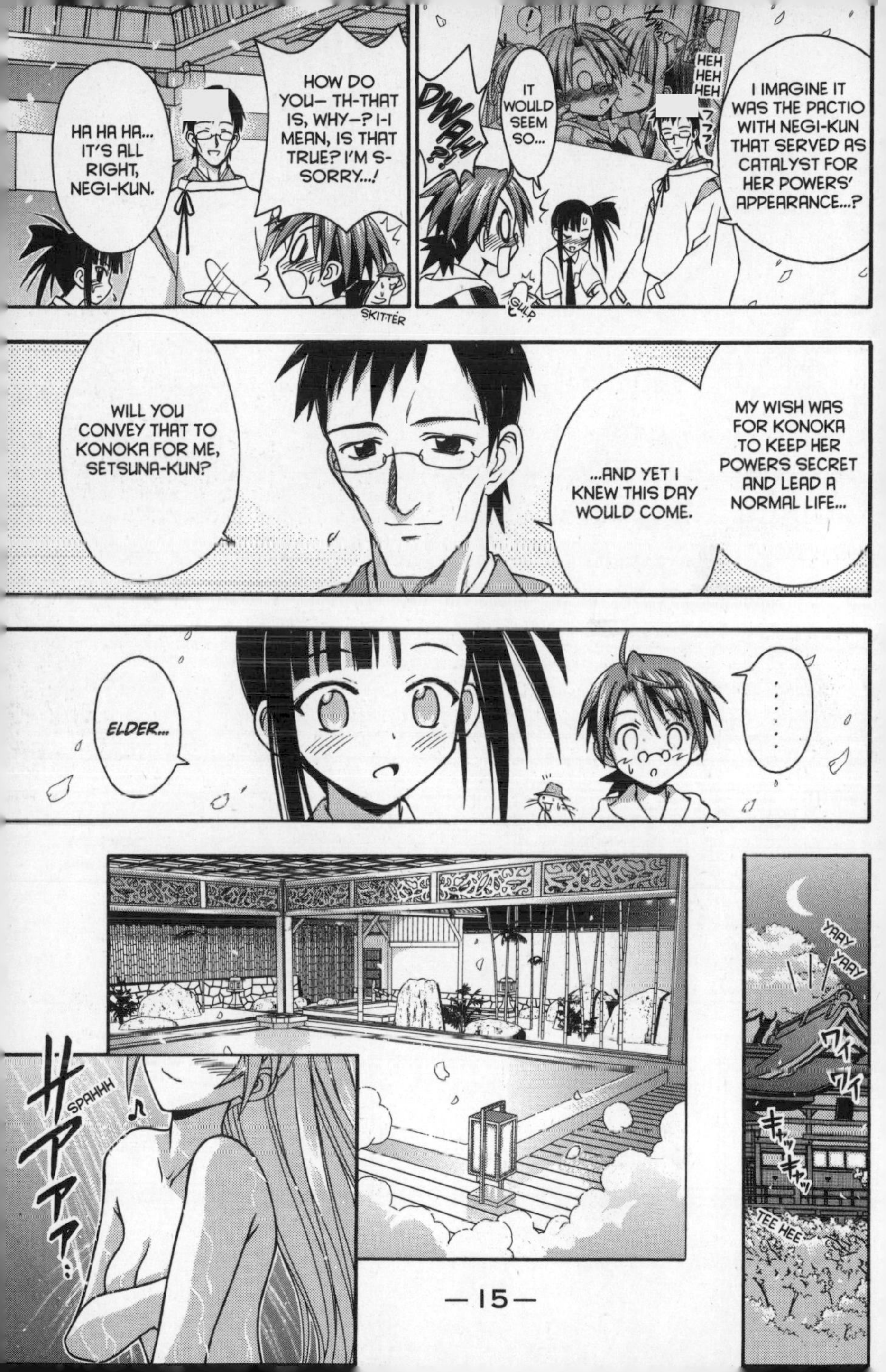
I IMAGINE IT WAS THE PACTIO WITH NEGI-KUN THAT SERVED AS CATALYST FOR HER POWERS' APPEARANCE...?
HEH HEH HEH
フフフ
IT WOULD SEEM SO...
DWAH?!
GULP
HOW DO YOU— TH-THAT IS, WHY–? I-I MEAN, IS THAT TRUE? I'M S-SORRY...!
HA HA HA... IT'S ALL RIGHT, NEGI-KUN.
SKITTER
MY WISH WAS FOR KONOKA TO KEEP HER POWERS SECRET AND LEAD A NORMAL LIFE...
...AND YET I KNEW THIS DAY WOULD COME.
WILL YOU CONVEY THAT TO KONOKA FOR ME, SETSUNA-KUN?
......
ELDER...
YAAY
YAAY
ワイワイ
キャッキャッ
TEE HEE
SPAHHH
ザァァ

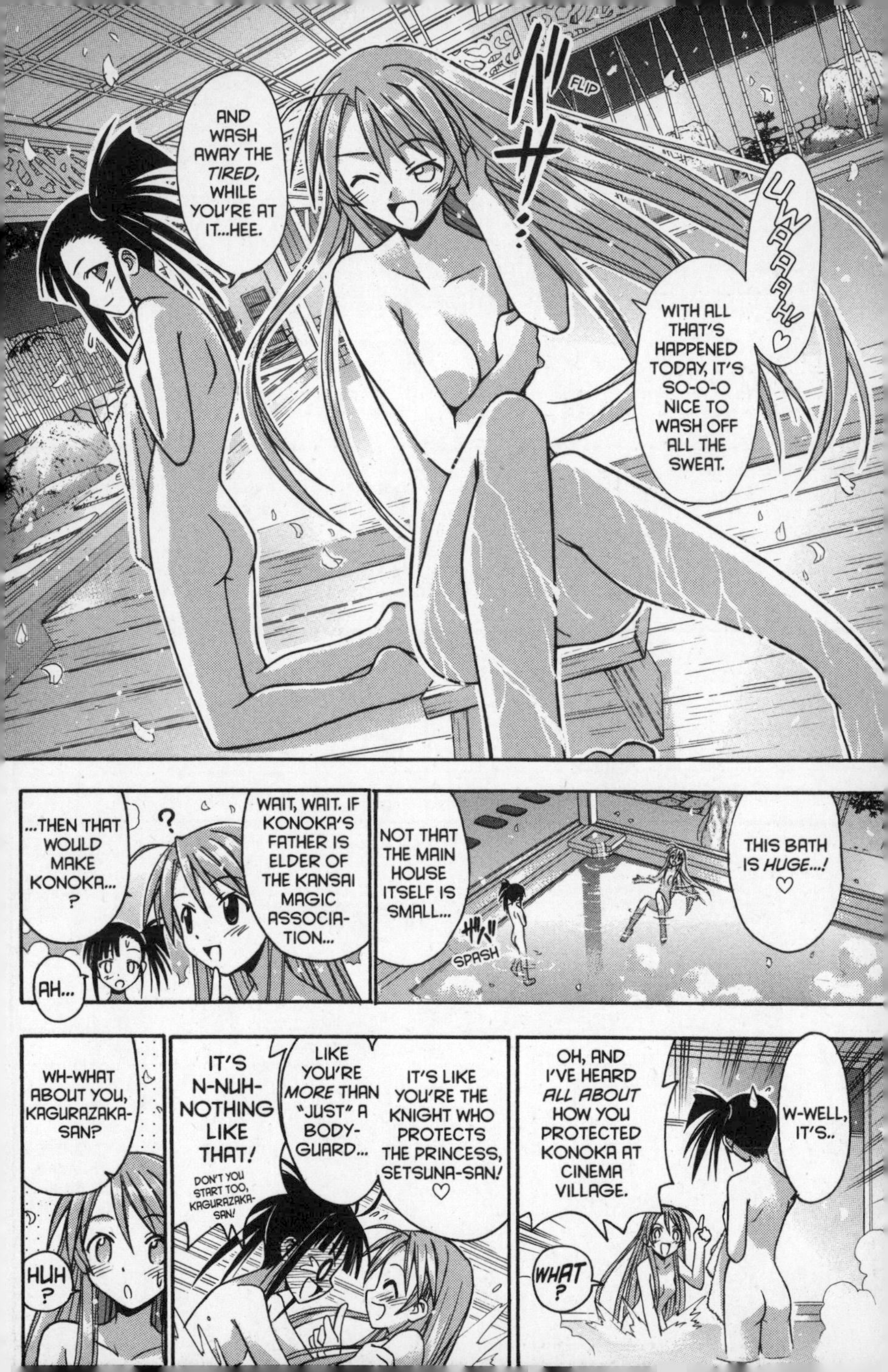
UWAAAAH! ♡
WITH ALL THAT'S HAPPENED TODAY, IT'S SO-O-O NICE TO WASH OFF ALL THE SWEAT.
FLIP
AND WASH AWAY THE *TIRED*, WHILE YOU'RE AT IT...HEE.
THIS BATH IS *HUGE*...! ♡
NOT THAT THE MAIN HOUSE ITSELF IS SMALL...
SPASH
WAIT, WAIT. IF KONOKA'S FATHER IS ELDER OF THE KANSAI MAGIC ASSOCIATION...
?
...THEN THAT WOULD MAKE KONOKA...?
AH...
W-WELL, IT'S..
OH, AND I'VE HEARD *ALL ABOUT* HOW YOU PROTECTED KONOKA AT CINEMA VILLAGE.
WHAT?
IT'S LIKE YOU'RE THE KNIGHT WHO PROTECTS THE PRINCESS, SETSUNA-SAN! ♡
LIKE YOU'RE *MORE* THAN "JUST" A BODY-GUARD...
IT'S N-NUH-NOTHING LIKE THAT!
DON'T YOU START TOO, KAGURAZAKA-SAN!
WH-WHAT ABOUT YOU, KAGURAZAKA-SAN?
HUH?

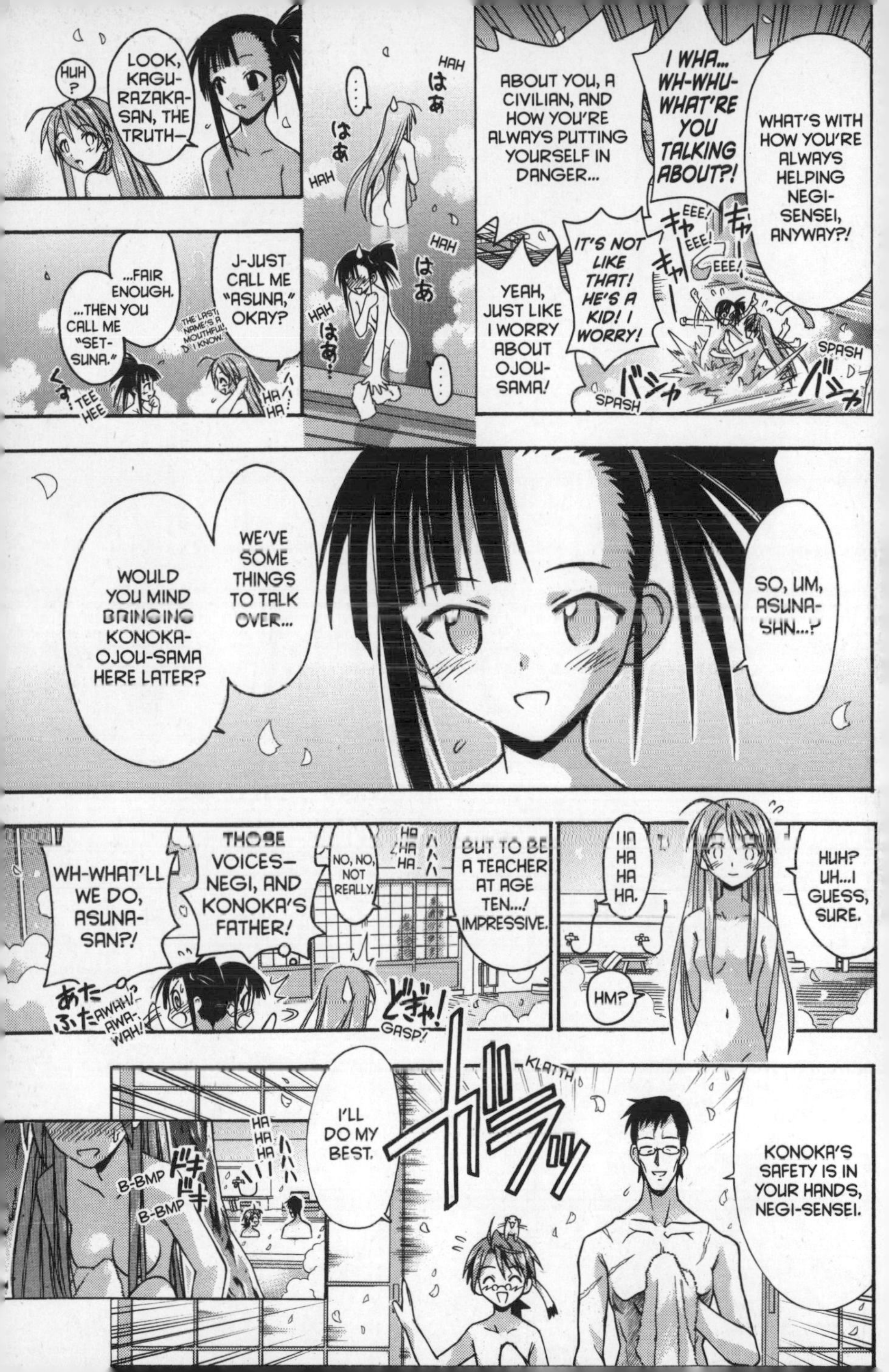
WHAT'S WITH HOW YOU'RE ALWAYS HELPING NEGI-SENSEI, ANYWAY?!
I WHA... WH-WHU-WHAT'RE YOU TALKING ABOUT?!
ABOUT YOU, A CIVILIAN, AND HOW YOU'RE ALWAYS PUTTING YOURSELF IN DANGER...
ギャ EEE!
キャ EEE!
キャ EEE!
IT'S NOT LIKE THAT! HE'S A KID! I WORRY!
YEAH, JUST LIKE I WORRY ABOUT OJOU-SAMA!
バシャ SPASH
バシャ SPASH
はぁ HAH
はぁ HAH
...
はぁ HAH
はぁ HAH
...
LOOK, KAGURAZAKA-SAN, THE TRUTH—
HUH ?
J-JUST CALL ME "ASUNA," OKAY?
THE LAST NAME'S A MOUTHFUL, I KNOW.
...FAIR ENOUGH. ...THEN YOU CALL ME "SETSUNA."
ハハ HA HA
くす TEE HEE
SO, UM, ASUNA-SAN...?
WE'VE SOME THINGS TO TALK OVER...
WOULD YOU MIND BRINGING KONOKA-OJOU-SAMA HERE LATER?
HUH? UH...I GUESS, SURE.
HM?
HA HA HA HA.
BUT TO BE A TEACHER AT AGE TEN...! IMPRESSIVE.
ハハハ HA HA HA
NO, NO, NOT REALLY.
THOSE VOICES— NEGI, AND KONOKA'S FATHER!
どぎゃ! GASP!
WH-WHAT'LL WE DO, ASUNA-SAN?!
あたふた AWAH! AWA-WAH!
KONOKA'S SAFETY IS IN YOUR HANDS, NEGI-SENSEI.
ガロロ KLATTH
I'LL DO MY BEST.
ハハハ HA HA HA
ドキドキ B-BMP B-BMP

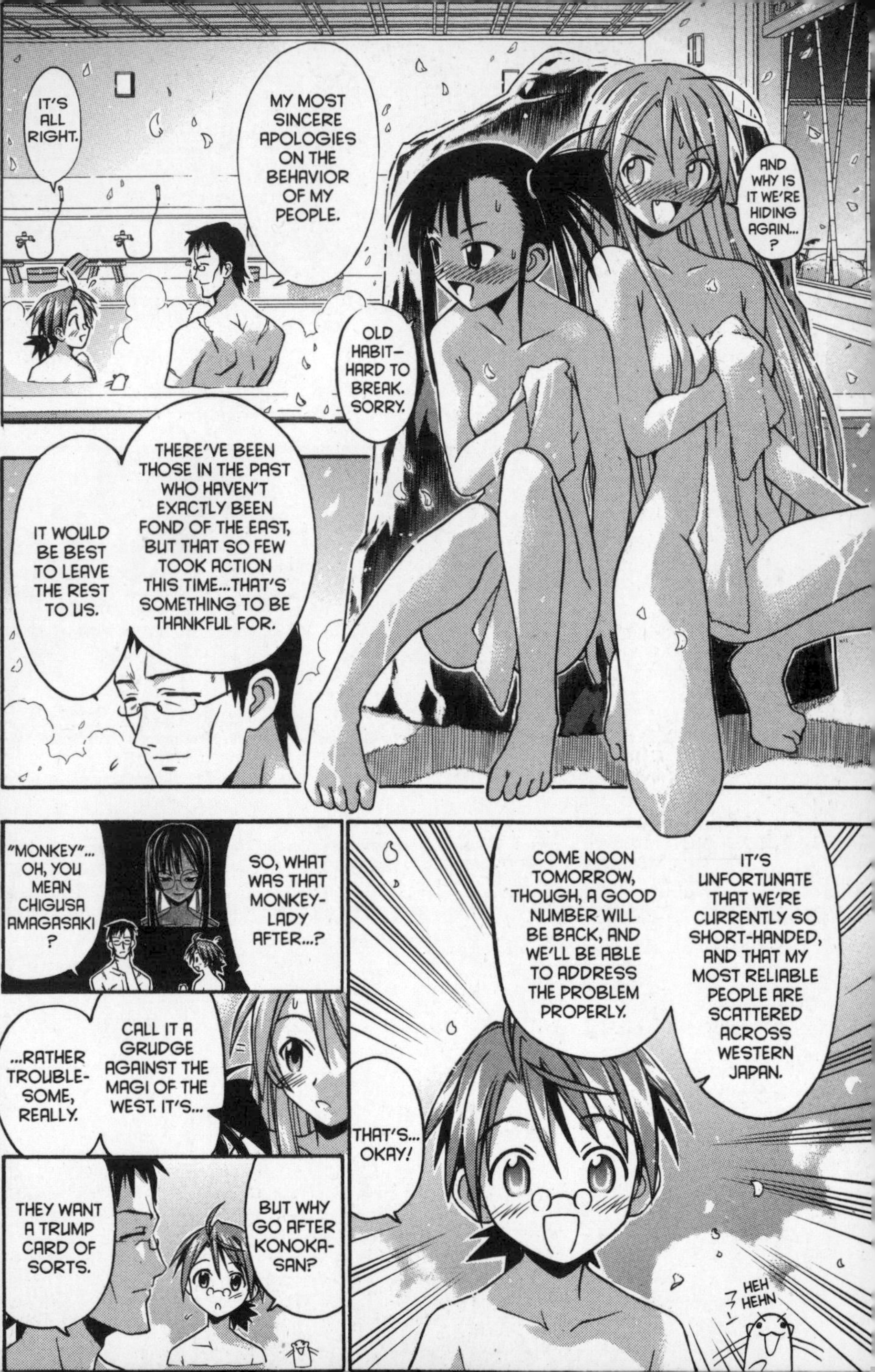
AND WHY IS IT WE'RE HIDING AGAIN...?
MY MOST SINCERE APOLOGIES ON THE BEHAVIOR OF MY PEOPLE.
IT'S ALL RIGHT.
OLD HABIT— HARD TO BREAK. SORRY.
THERE'VE BEEN THOSE IN THE PAST WHO HAVEN'T EXACTLY BEEN FOND OF THE EAST, BUT THAT SO FEW TOOK ACTION THIS TIME...THAT'S SOMETHING TO BE THANKFUL FOR.
IT WOULD BE BEST TO LEAVE THE REST TO US.
IT'S UNFORTUNATE THAT WE'RE CURRENTLY SO SHORT-HANDED, AND THAT MY MOST RELIABLE PEOPLE ARE SCATTERED ACROSS WESTERN JAPAN.
COME NOON TOMORROW, THOUGH, A GOOD NUMBER WILL BE BACK, AND WE'LL BE ABLE TO ADDRESS THE PROBLEM PROPERLY.
THAT'S... OKAY!
HEH HEHN
SO, WHAT WAS THAT MONKEY-LADY AFTER...?
"MONKEY"... OH, YOU MEAN CHIGUSA AMAGASAKI?
CALL IT A GRUDGE AGAINST THE MAGI OF THE WEST. IT'S...
...RATHER TROUBLE-SOME, REALLY.
BUT WHY GO AFTER KONOKA-SAN?
THEY WANT A TRUMP CARD OF SORTS.

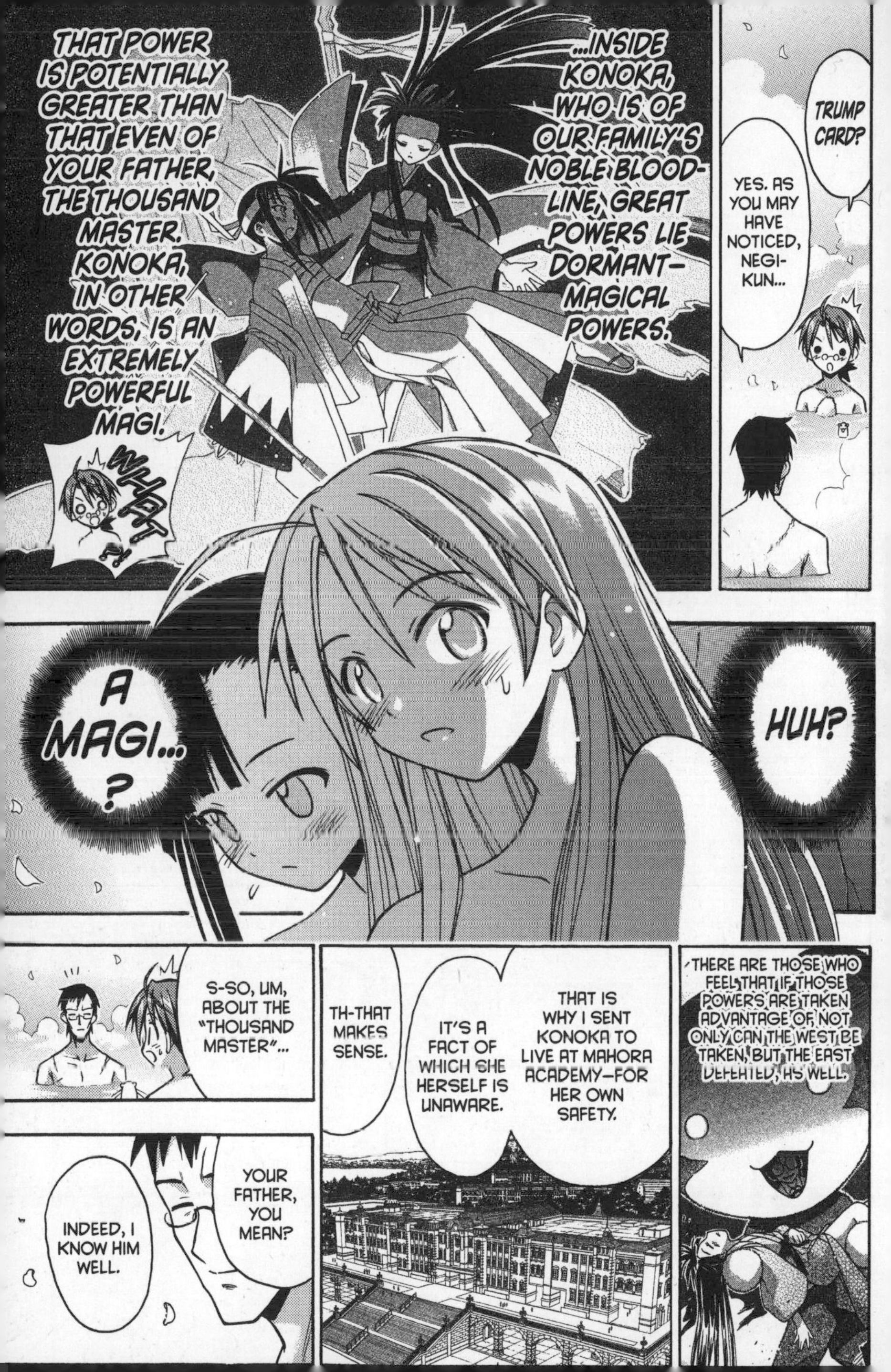
TRUMP CARD?
YES. AS YOU MAY HAVE NOTICED, NEGI-KUN...
...INSIDE KONOKA, WHO IS OF OUR FAMILY'S NOBLE BLOOD-LINE, GREAT POWERS LIE DORMANT—MAGICAL POWERS.
THAT POWER IS POTENTIALLY GREATER THAN THAT EVEN OF YOUR FATHER, THE THOUSAND MASTER. KONOKA, IN OTHER WORDS, IS AN EXTREMELY POWERFUL MAGI.
WHAT?!
HUH?
A MAGI...?
THERE ARE THOSE WHO FEEL THAT IF THOSE POWERS ARE TAKEN ADVANTAGE OF, NOT ONLY CAN THE WEST BE TAKEN, BUT THE EAST DEFEATED, AS WELL.
THAT IS WHY I SENT KONOKA TO LIVE AT MAHORA ACADEMY—FOR HER OWN SAFETY.
IT'S A FACT OF WHICH SHE HERSELF IS UNAWARE.
TH-THAT MAKES SENSE.
S-SO, UM, ABOUT THE "THOUSAND MASTER"...
YOUR FATHER, YOU MEAN?
INDEED, I KNOW HIM WELL.

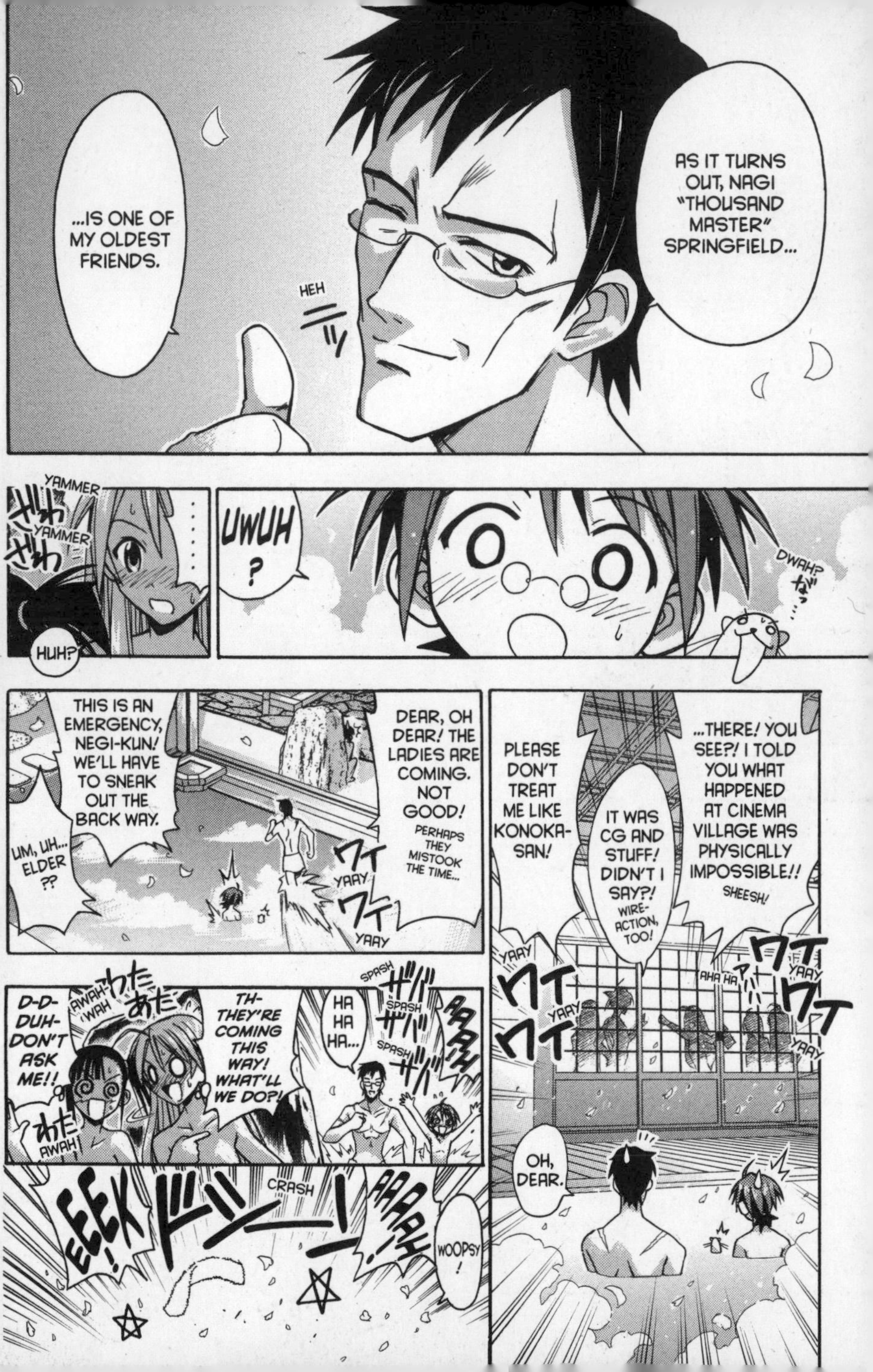
AS IT TURNS OUT, NAGI "THOUSAND MASTER" SPRINGFIELD...
HEH
...IS ONE OF MY OLDEST FRIENDS.
DWAH?
UWUH ?
YAMMER
YAMMER
HUH?
...THERE! YOU SEE?! I TOLD YOU WHAT HAPPENED AT CINEMA VILLAGE WAS PHYSICALLY IMPOSSIBLE!!
SHEESH!
IT WAS CG AND STUFF! DIDN'T I SAY?!
WIRE-ACTION, TOO!
PLEASE DON'T TREAT ME LIKE KONOKA-SAN!
YAAY
AHA HA
YAAY
YAAY
YAAY
YAAY
OH, DEAR.
DEAR, OH DEAR! THE LADIES ARE COMING. NOT GOOD!
PERHAPS THEY MISTOOK THE TIME...
THIS IS AN EMERGENCY, NEGI-KUN! WE'LL HAVE TO SNEAK OUT THE BACK WAY.
UM, UH... ELDER ??
YAAY
YAAY
SPASH
SPASH
SPASH
AAAAH
HA HA HA...
TH-THEY'RE COMING THIS WAY! WHAT'LL WE DO?!
AWAH-WAH
D-D-DUH-DON'T ASK ME!!
AWAH
WOOPSY!
AAAAH
CRASH
EEEK!

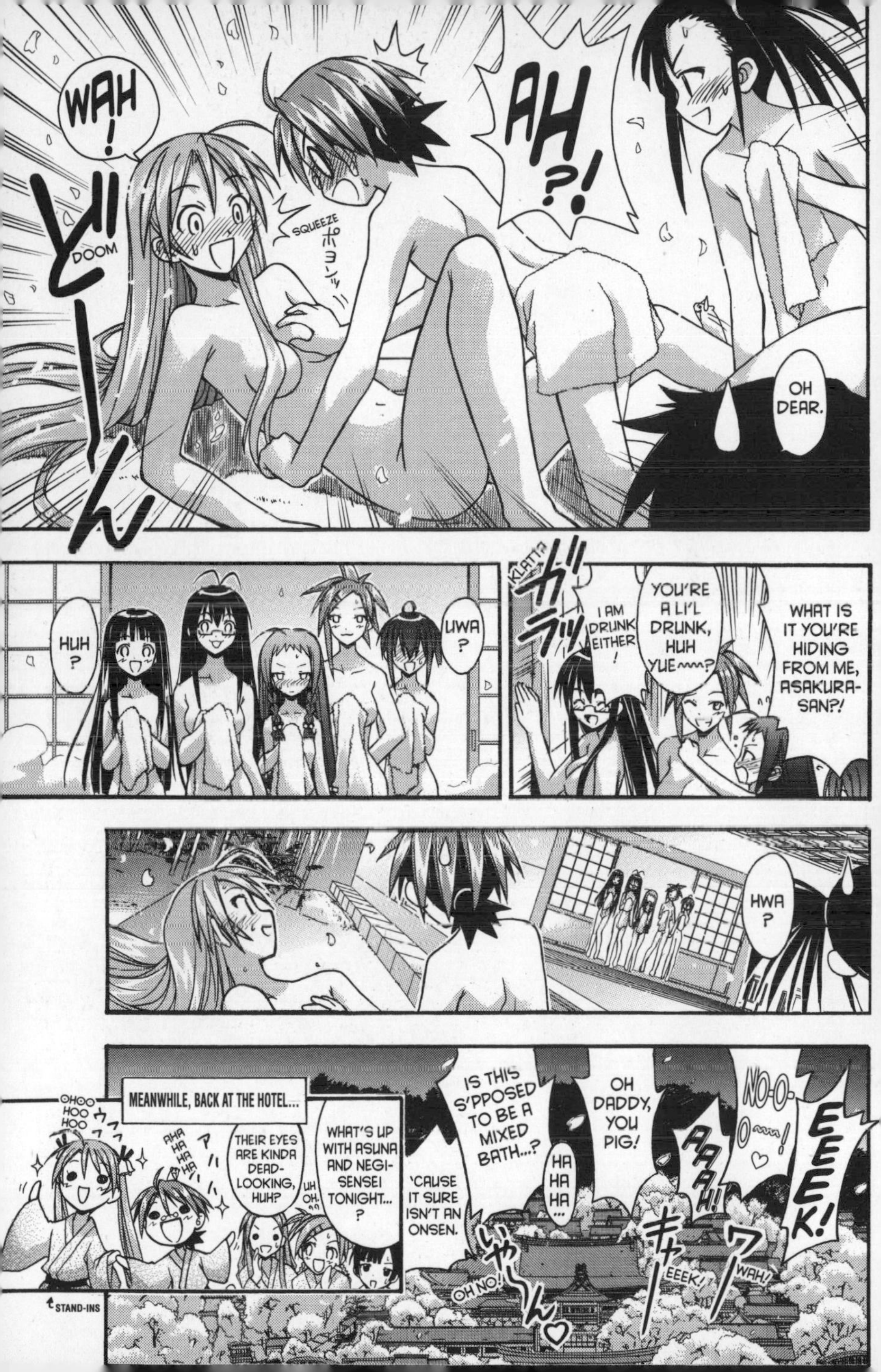
AH ?!
OH DEAR.
SQUEEZE
ポヨンッ
WAH !
DOOM
どーーん
WHAT IS IT YOU'RE HIDING FROM ME, ASAKURA-SAN?!
YOU'RE A LI'L DRUNK, HUH YUE~~~?
I AM DRUNK EITHER !
KLATTA
ガラッ
UWA ?
HUH ?
HWA ?
NO-O-O~~~!
EEEEK!
AAAAH!
OH DADDY, YOU PIG!
IS THIS S'PPOSED TO BE A MIXED BATH...?
HA HA HA...
'CAUSE IT SURE ISN'T AN ONSEN.
WAH!
EEEK!
OH NO!
MEANWHILE, BACK AT THE HOTEL...
WHAT'S UP WITH ASUNA AND NEGI-SENSEI TONIGHT...?
THEIR EYES ARE KINDA DEAD-LOOKING, HUH?
UH OH.
AHA HA HA
OHOO HOO HOO
STAND-INS

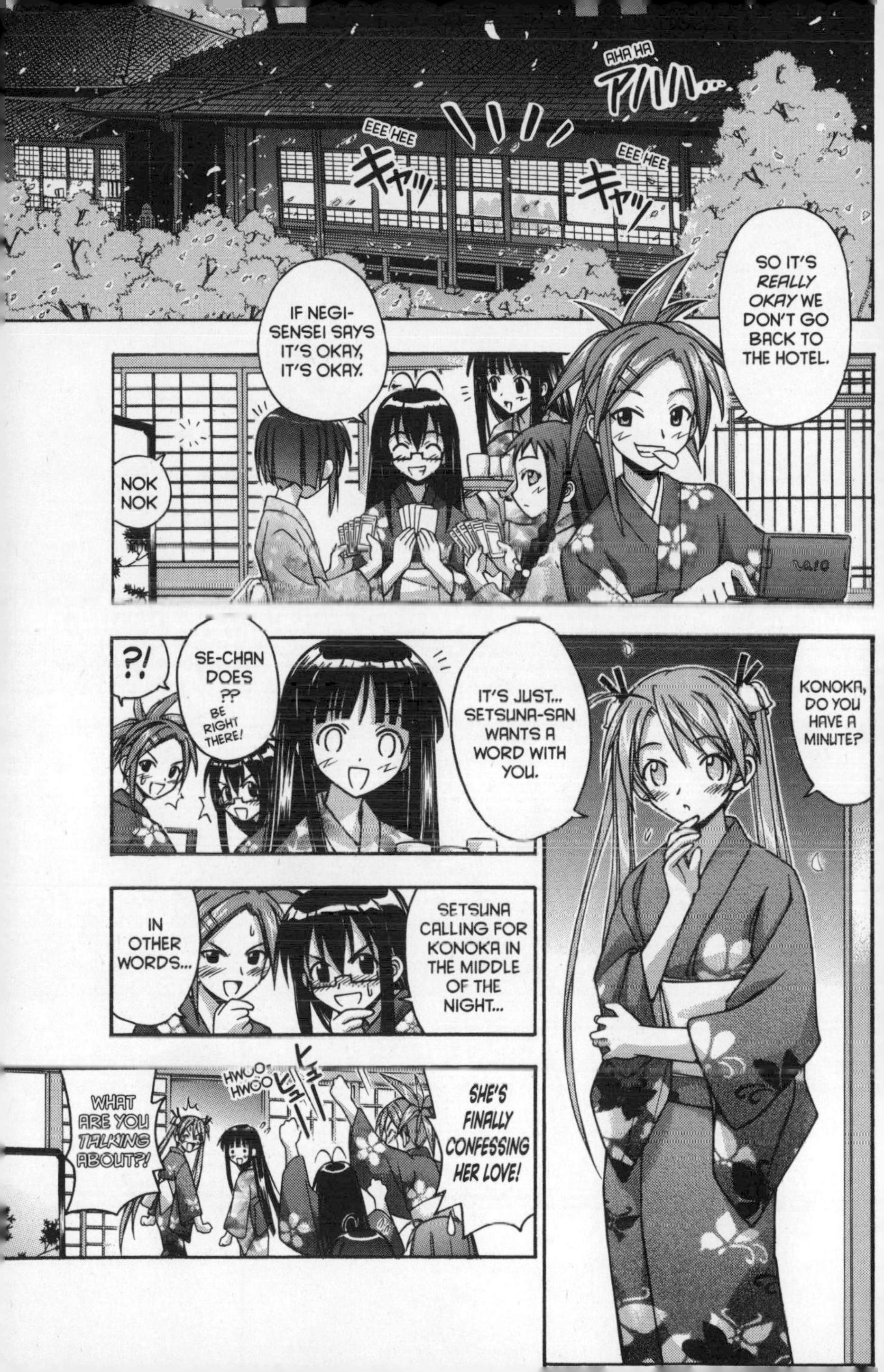
AHA HA
アハハ...
EEE HEE
キャッ
EEE HEE
キャッ
SO IT'S *REALLY OKAY* WE DON'T GO BACK TO THE HOTEL.
IF NEGI-SENSEI SAYS IT'S OKAY, IT'S OKAY.
NOK NOK
KONOKA, DO YOU HAVE A MINUTE?
IT'S JUST... SETSUNA-SAN WANTS A WORD WITH YOU.
SE-CHAN DOES?? BE RIGHT THERE!
?!
SETSUNA CALLING FOR KONOKA IN THE MIDDLE OF THE NIGHT...
IN OTHER WORDS...
SHE'S FINALLY CONFESSING HER LOVE!
HWOO HWOO
WHAT ARE YOU *TALKING* ABOUT?!

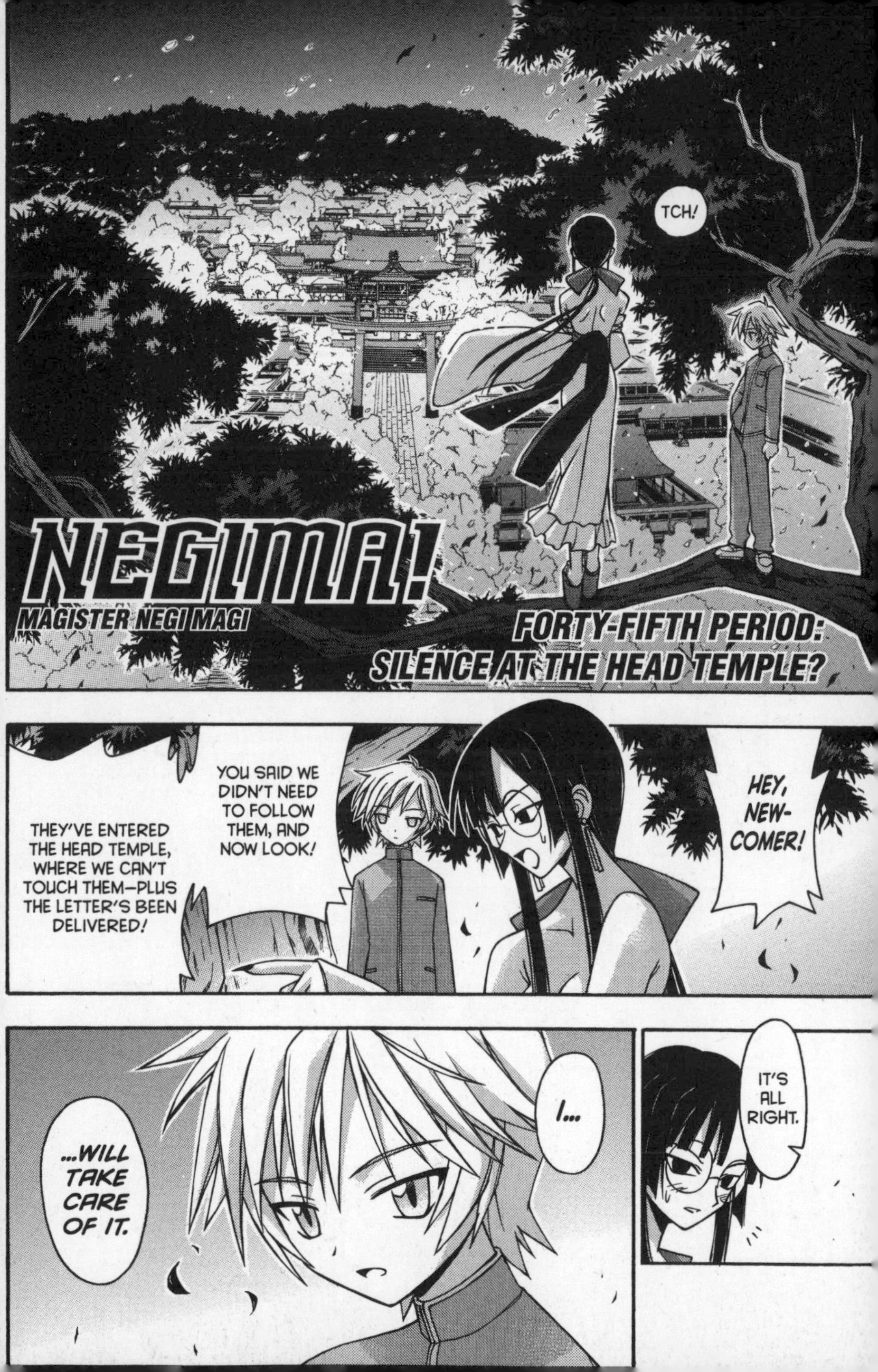
TCH!
NEGIMA!
MAGISTER NEGI MAGI
FORTY-FIFTH PERIOD: SILENCE AT THE HEAD TEMPLE?
HEY, NEW-COMER!
YOU SAID WE DIDN'T NEED TO FOLLOW THEM, AND NOW LOOK!
THEY'VE ENTERED THE HEAD TEMPLE, WHERE WE CAN'T TOUCH THEM—PLUS THE LETTER'S BEEN DELIVERED!
IT'S ALL RIGHT.
I...
...WILL TAKE CARE OF IT.

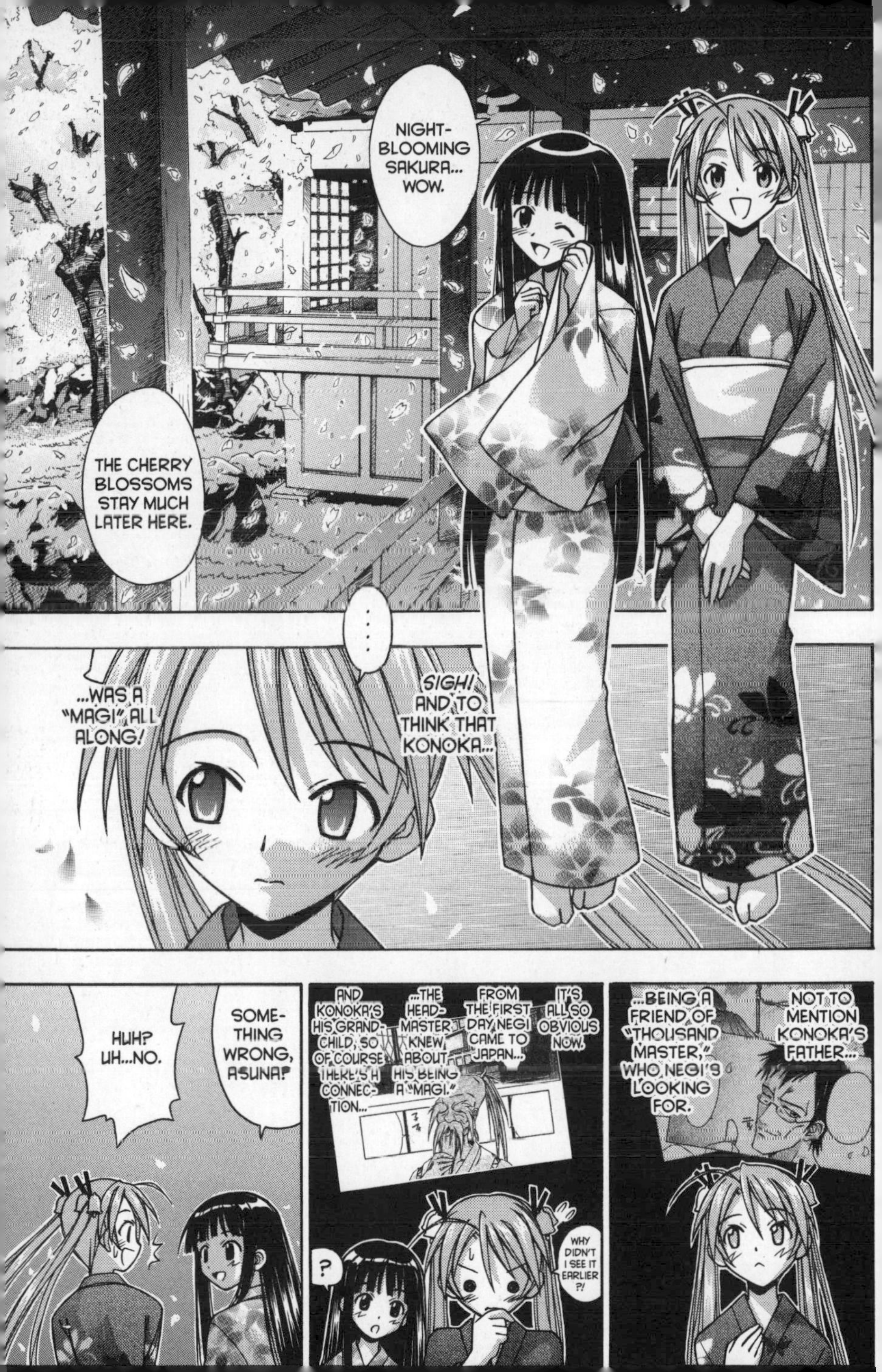
NIGHT-BLOOMING SAKURA... WOW.
THE CHERRY BLOSSOMS STAY MUCH LATER HERE.
....
SIGH! AND TO THINK THAT KONOKA...
...WAS A "MAGI" ALL ALONG!
NOT TO MENTION KONOKA'S FATHER...
...BEING A FRIEND OF "THOUSAND MASTER," WHO NEGI'S LOOKING FOR.
IT'S ALL SO OBVIOUS NOW.
FROM THE FIRST DAY NEGI CAME TO JAPAN...
...THE HEAD-MASTER KNEW ABOUT HIS BEING A "MAGI."
AND KONOKA'S HIS GRAND-CHILD, SO OF COURSE THERE'S A CONNEC-TION...
WHY DIDN'T I SEE IT EARLIER?!
?
SOME-THING WRONG, ASUNA?
HUH? UH...NO.

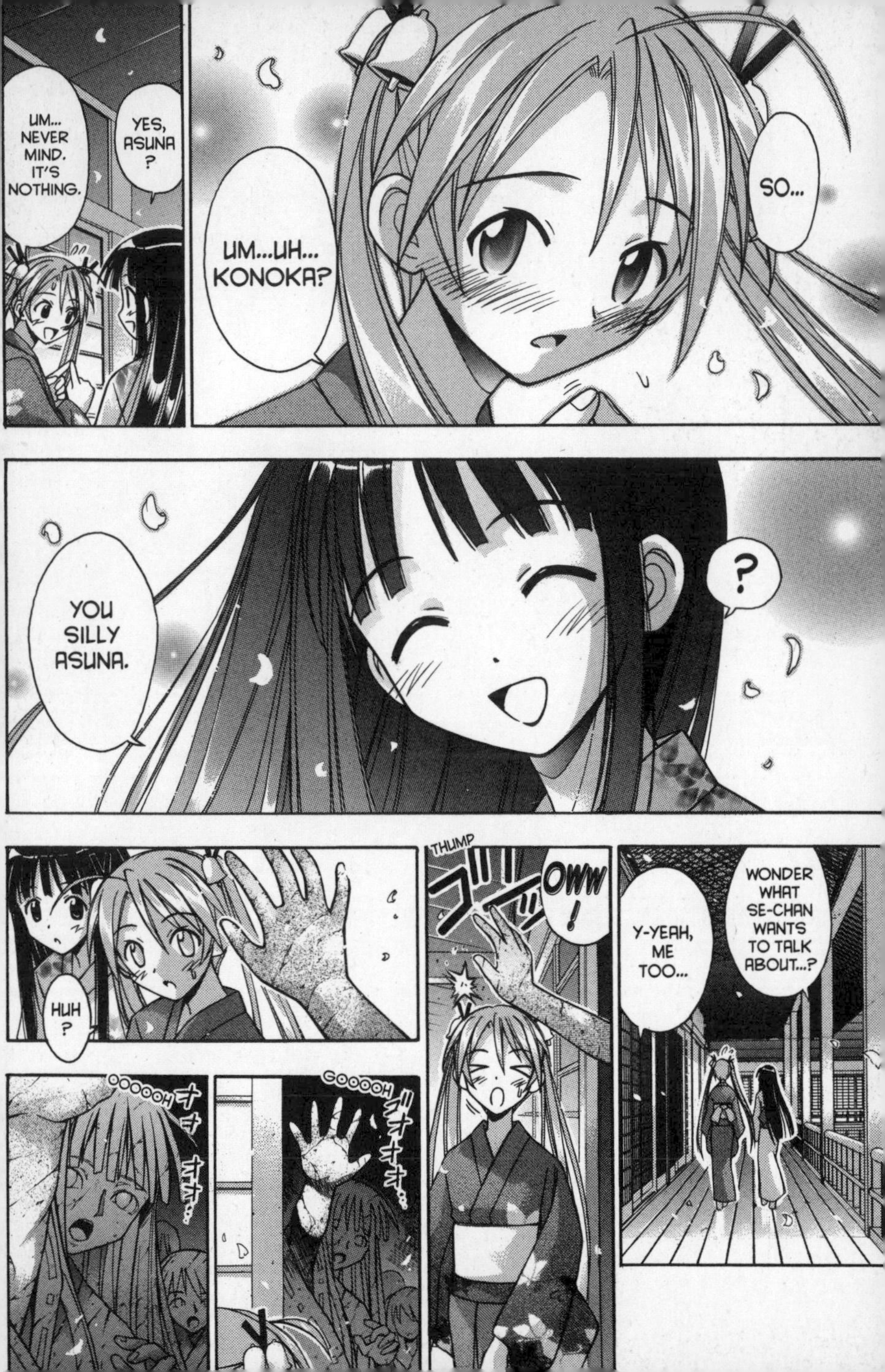
SO...
UM...UH... KONOKA?
YES, ASUNA?
UM... NEVER MIND. IT'S NOTHING.
?
YOU SILLY ASUNA.
WONDER WHAT SE-CHAN WANTS TO TALK ABOUT...?
Y-YEAH, ME TOO...
THUMP
OWW!
HUH?
GOOOOOH
OOOOOOH

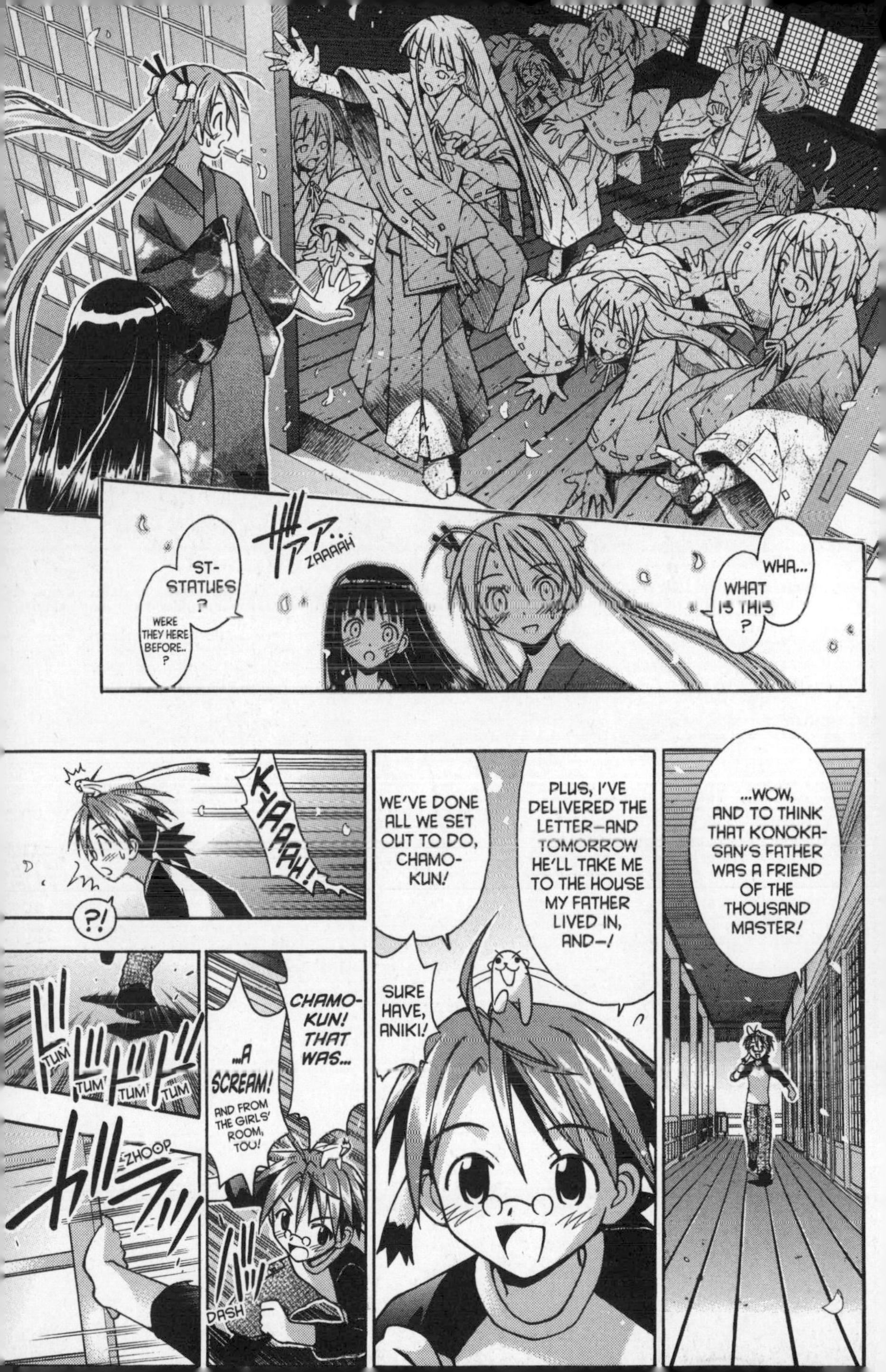
WHA... WHAT IS THIS?
ZAAAAAH
ST-STATUES?
WERE THEY HERE BEFORE..?
...WOW, AND TO THINK THAT KONOKA-SAN'S FATHER WAS A FRIEND OF THE THOUSAND MASTER!
PLUS, I'VE DELIVERED THE LETTER—AND TOMORROW HE'LL TAKE ME TO THE HOUSE MY FATHER LIVED IN, AND—!
WE'VE DONE ALL WE SET OUT TO DO, CHAMO-KUN!
SURE HAVE, ANIKI!
KYAAAAH!
?!
CHAMO-KUN! THAT WAS...
...A SCREAM!
AND FROM THE GIRLS' ROOM, TOO!
DASH
TUM TUM TUM TUM
ZHOOP

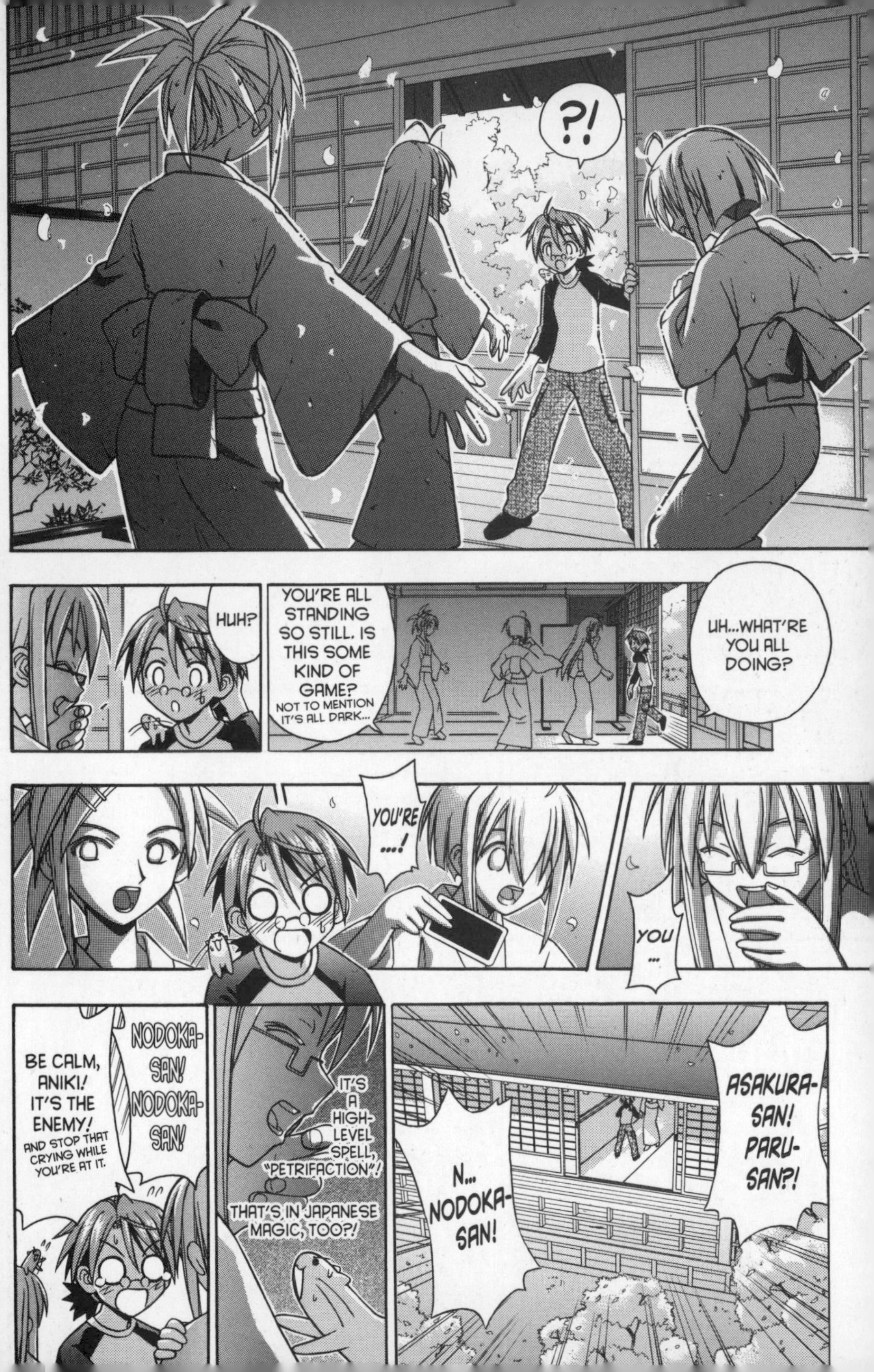
?!
UH...WHAT'RE YOU ALL DOING?
YOU'RE ALL STANDING SO STILL. IS THIS SOME KIND OF GAME?
NOT TO MENTION IT'S ALL DARK...
HUH?
YOU ...
YOU'RE ...!
ASAKURA-SAN! PARU-SAN?!
N... NODOKA-SAN!
IT'S A HIGH-LEVEL SPELL, "PETRIFACTION"!
THAT'S IN JAPANESE MAGIC, TOO?!
NODOKA-SAN! NODOKA-SAN!
BE CALM, ANIKI! IT'S THE ENEMY!
AND STOP THAT CRYING WHILE YOU'RE AT IT.

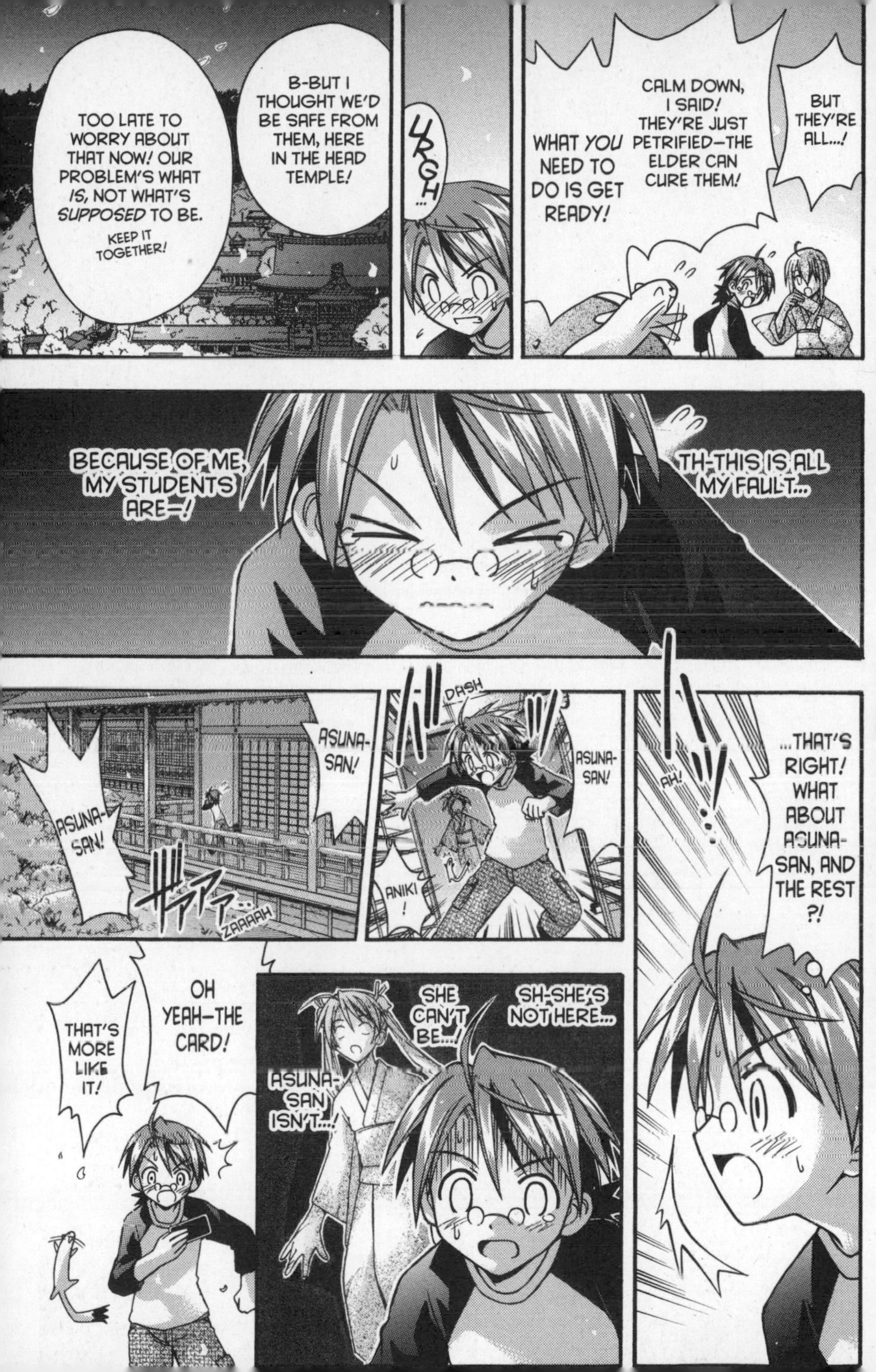
BUT THEY'RE ALL...!
CALM DOWN, I SAID! THEY'RE JUST PETRIFIED—THE ELDER CAN CURE THEM!
WHAT YOU NEED TO DO IS GET READY!
URGH...
B-BUT I THOUGHT WE'D BE SAFE FROM THEM, HERE IN THE HEAD TEMPLE!
TOO LATE TO WORRY ABOUT THAT NOW! OUR PROBLEM'S WHAT IS, NOT WHAT'S SUPPOSED TO BE.
KEEP IT TOGETHER!
TH-THIS IS ALL MY FAULT...
BECAUSE OF ME, MY STUDENTS ARE—!
AH!
...THAT'S RIGHT! WHAT ABOUT ASUNA-SAN, AND THE REST?!
DASH
ASUNA-SAN!
ASUNA-SAN!
ANIKI!
ASUNA-SAN!
ASUNA-SAN!
ZAAAAH
SH-SHE'S NOT HERE...
SHE CAN'T BE...!
ASUNA-SAN ISN'T...!
OH YEAH—THE CARD!
THAT'S MORE LIKE IT!

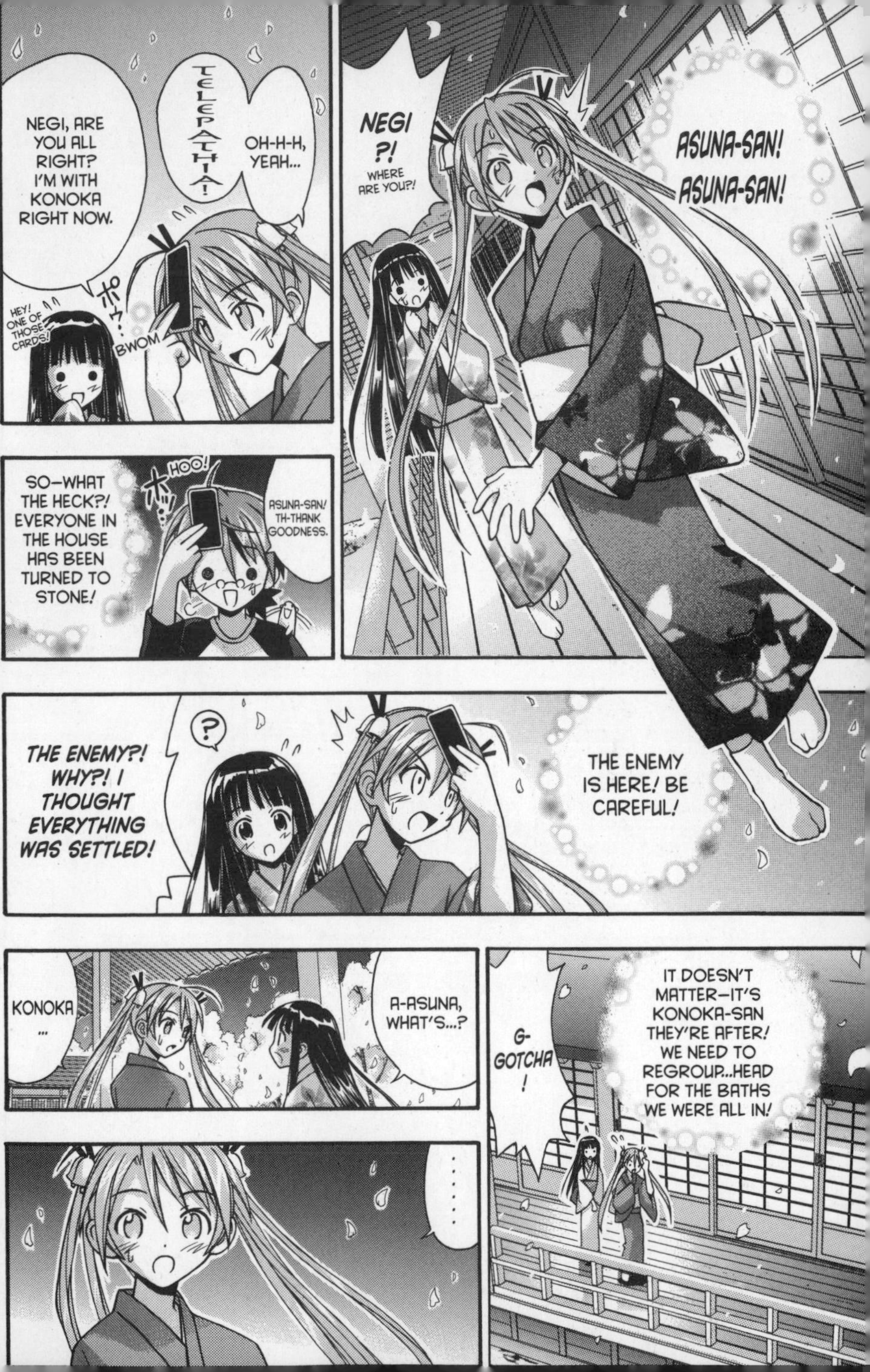
ASUNA-SAN! ASUNA-SAN!
NEGI ?!
WHERE ARE YOU?!
TELEPATHIA!
OH-H-H, YEAH...
NEGI, ARE YOU ALL RIGHT? I'M WITH KONOKA RIGHT NOW.
ポウ・・
BWOM
HEY! ONE OF THOSE CARDS!
ASUNA-SAN! TH-THANK GOODNESS.
ホッ
HOO!
SO—WHAT THE HECK?! EVERYONE IN THE HOUSE HAS BEEN TURNED TO STONE!
THE ENEMY IS HERE! BE CAREFUL!
?
THE ENEMY?! WHY?! I THOUGHT EVERYTHING WAS SETTLED!
IT DOESN'T MATTER—IT'S KONOKA-SAN THEY'RE AFTER! WE NEED TO REGROUP...HEAD FOR THE BATHS WE WERE ALL IN!
G-GOTCHA!
A-ASUNA, WHAT'S...?
KONOKA ...
......

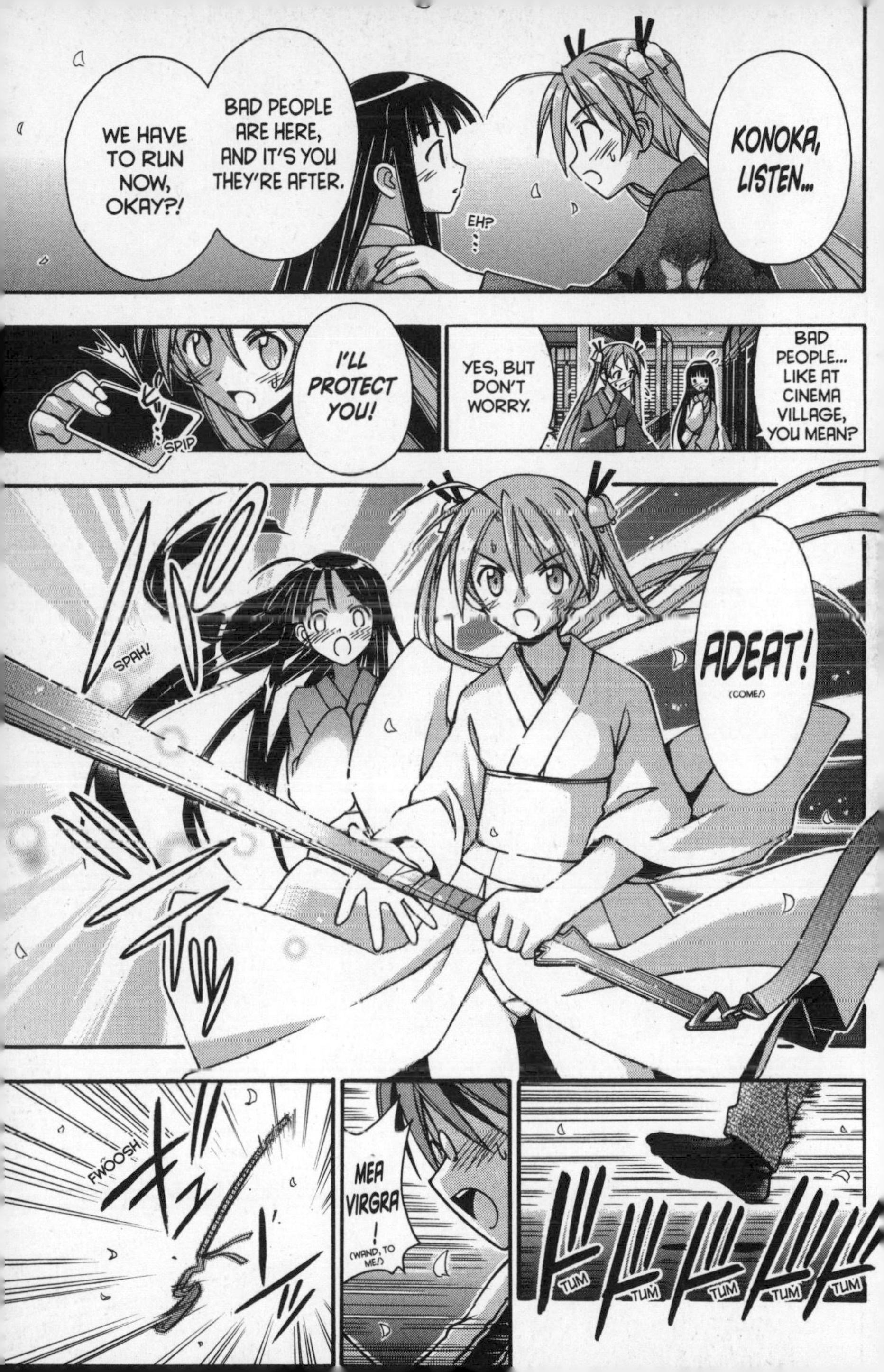
KONOKA, LISTEN...
EH? ...
BAD PEOPLE ARE HERE, AND IT'S YOU THEY'RE AFTER.
WE HAVE TO RUN NOW, OKAY?!
BAD PEOPLE... LIKE AT CINEMA VILLAGE, YOU MEAN?
YES, BUT DON'T WORRY.
I'LL PROTECT YOU!
SPIP
ADEAT!
(COME!)
SPAH!
TUM
TUM
TUM
TUM
TUM
MEA VIRGRA!
(WAND, TO ME!)
FWOOSH

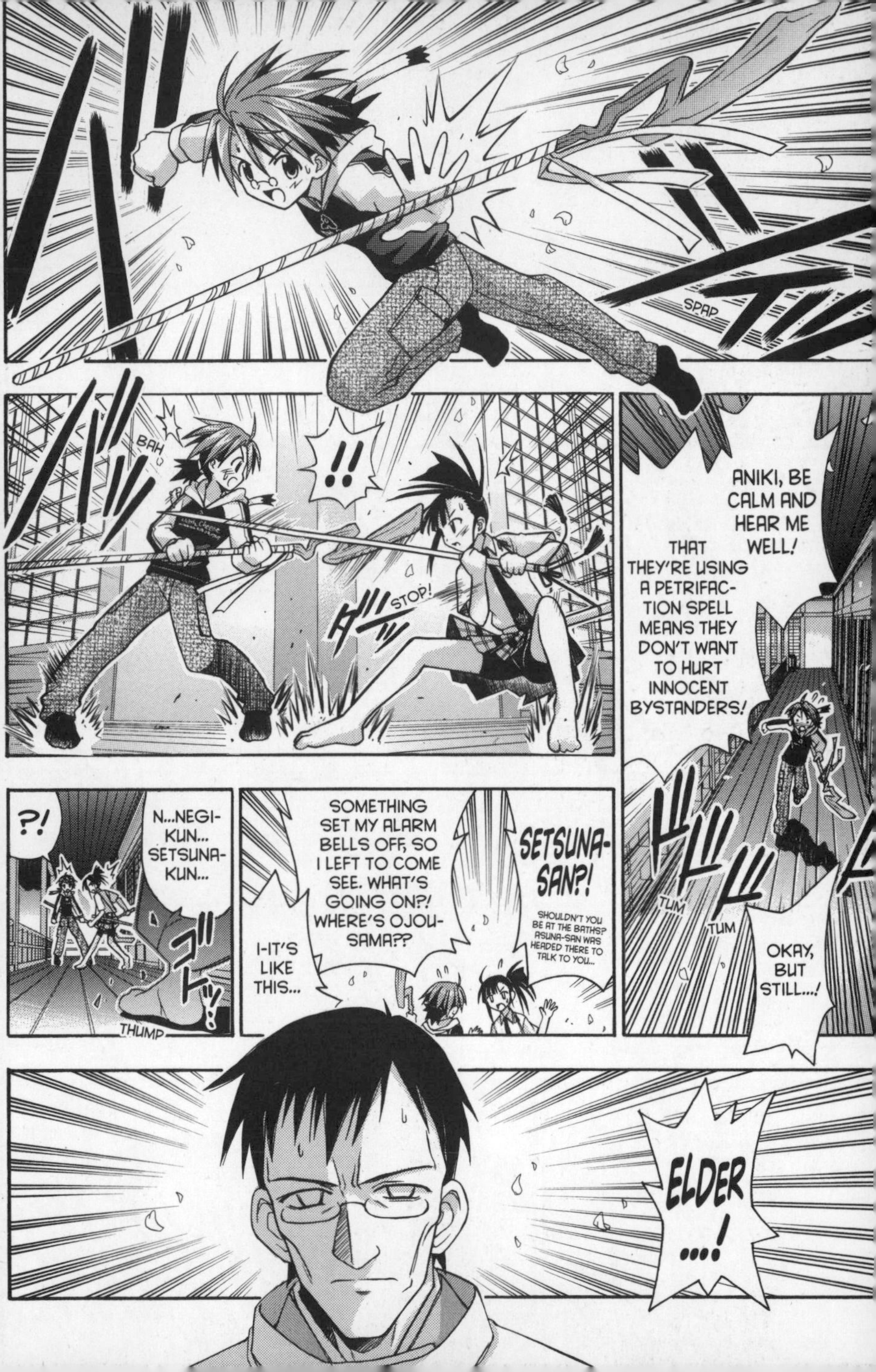
SPAP
ANIKI, BE CALM AND HEAR ME WELL!
THAT THEY'RE USING A PETRIFACTION SPELL MEANS THEY DON'T WANT TO HURT INNOCENT BYSTANDERS!
TUM
TUM
OKAY, BUT STILL...!
!!
BAH
STOP!
SETSUNA-SAN?!
SHOULDN'T YOU BE AT THE BATHS? ASUNA-SAN WAS HEADED THERE TO TALK TO YOU...
SOMETHING SET MY ALARM BELLS OFF, SO I LEFT TO COME SEE. WHAT'S GOING ON?! WHERE'S OJOU-SAMA??
I-IT'S LIKE THIS...
N...NEGI-KUN... SETSUNA-KUN...
?!
THUMP
ELDER ...!

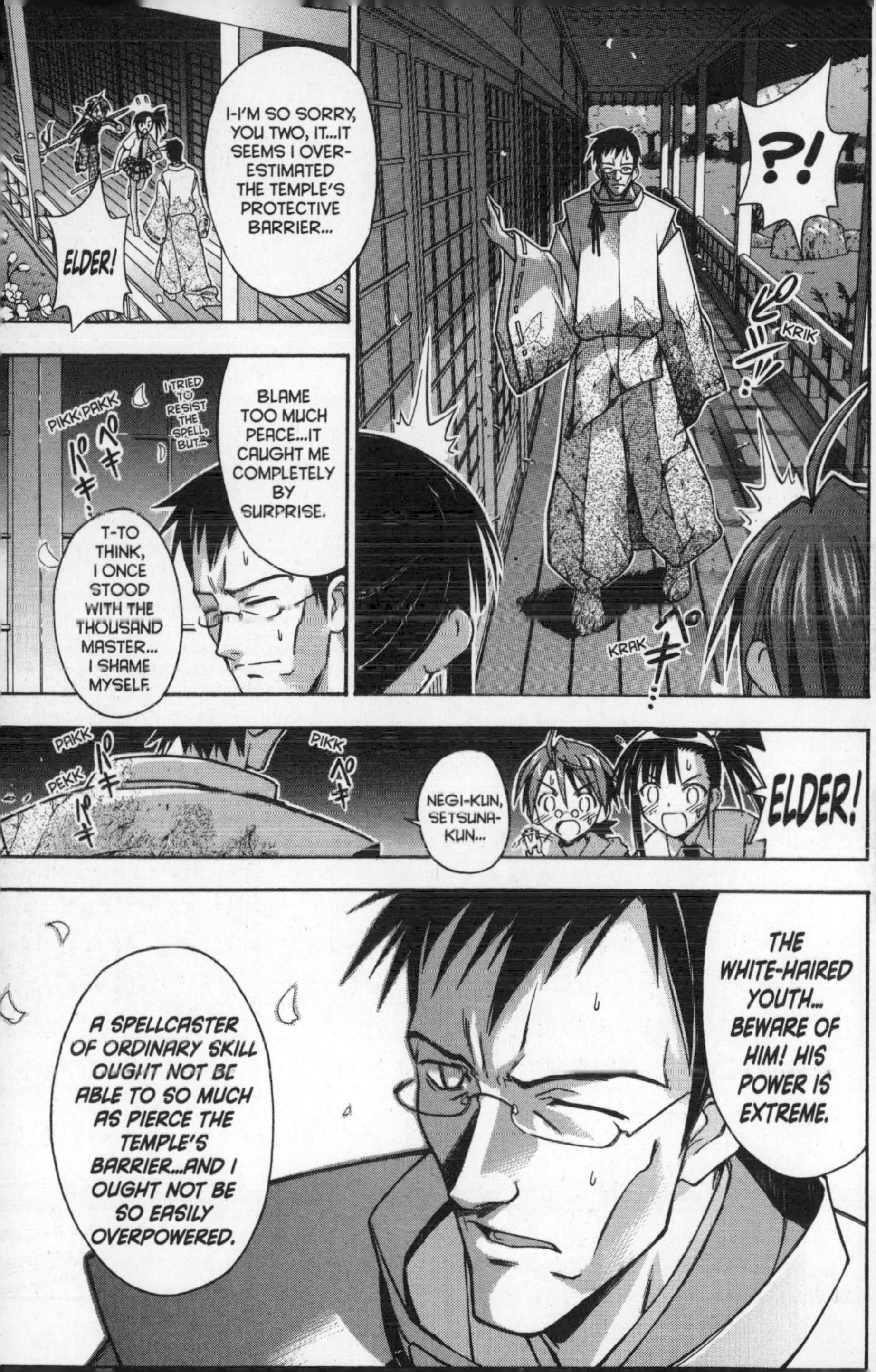
?!
KRIK
KRAK
I-I'M SO SORRY, YOU TWO, IT...IT SEEMS I OVER-ESTIMATED THE TEMPLE'S PROTECTIVE BARRIER...
ELDER!
BLAME TOO MUCH PEACE...IT CAUGHT ME COMPLETELY BY SURPRISE.
I TRIED TO RESIST THE SPELL, BUT...
PIKK PAKK
T-TO THINK, I ONCE STOOD WITH THE THOUSAND MASTER... I SHAME MYSELF.
ELDER!
NEGI-KUN, SETSUNA-KUN...
PIKK
PAKK
PEKK
THE WHITE-HAIRED YOUTH... BEWARE OF HIM! HIS POWER IS EXTREME.
A SPELLCASTER OF ORDINARY SKILL OUGHT NOT BE ABLE TO SO MUCH AS PIERCE THE TEMPLE'S BARRIER...AND I OUGHT NOT BE SO EASILY OVERPOWERED.

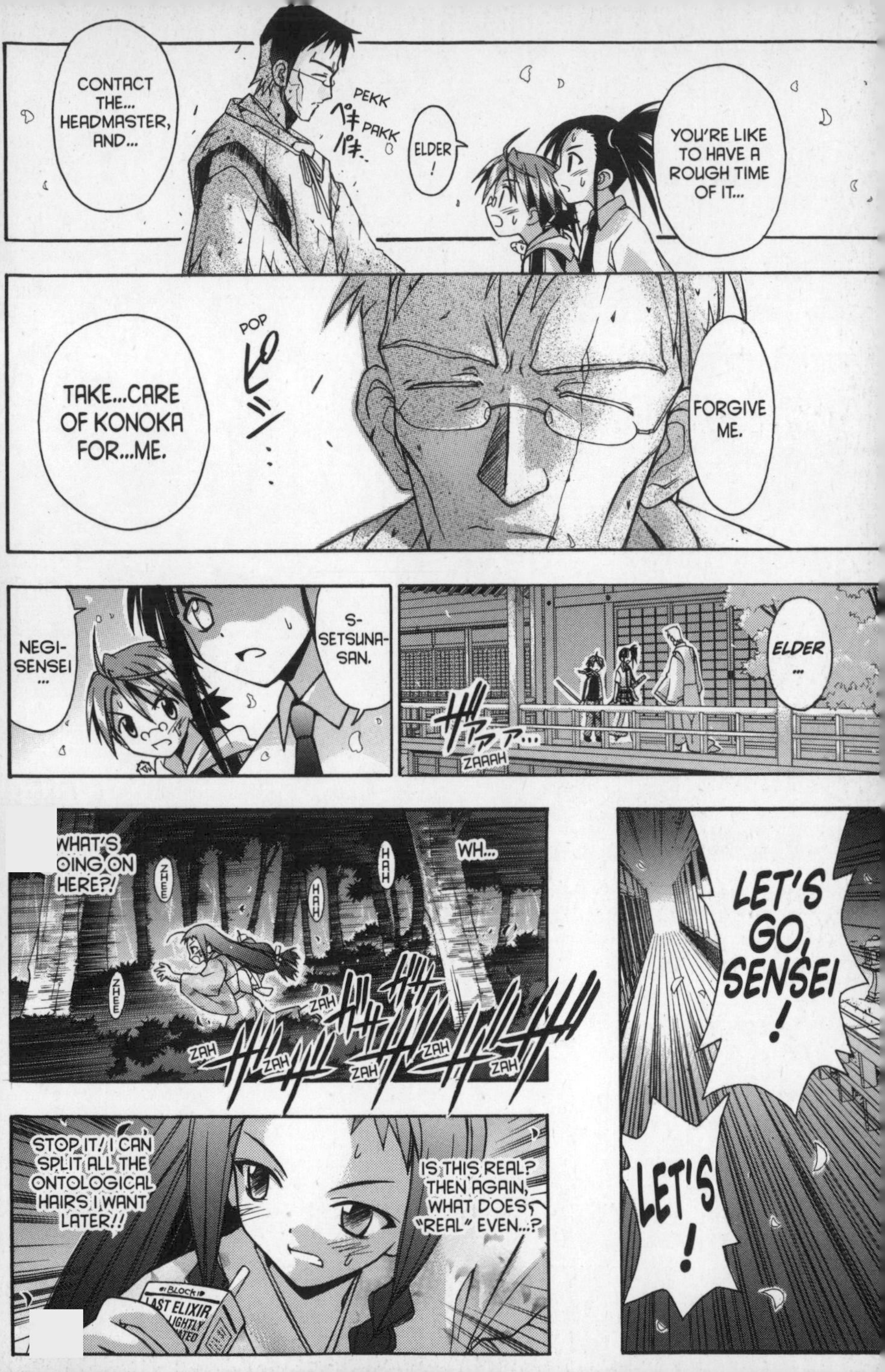
YOU'RE LIKE TO HAVE A ROUGH TIME OF IT...
ELDER!
PEKK PAKK
CONTACT THE... HEADMASTER, AND...
FORGIVE ME.
POP
TAKE...CARE OF KONOKA FOR...ME.
ELDER...
ZAAAH
S-SETSUNA-SAN.
NEGI-SENSEI...
LET'S GO, SENSEI!
LET'S!
WH...
HAH
HAH
WHAT'S
OING ON HERE?!
ZHEE
ZHEE
ZAH ZAH ZAH ZAH ZAH ZAH
IS THIS REAL? THEN AGAIN, WHAT DOES "REAL" EVEN...?
STOP IT! I CAN SPLIT ALL THE ONTOLOGICAL HAIRS I WANT LATER!!
BLOCK
LAST ELIXIR
LIGHTLY

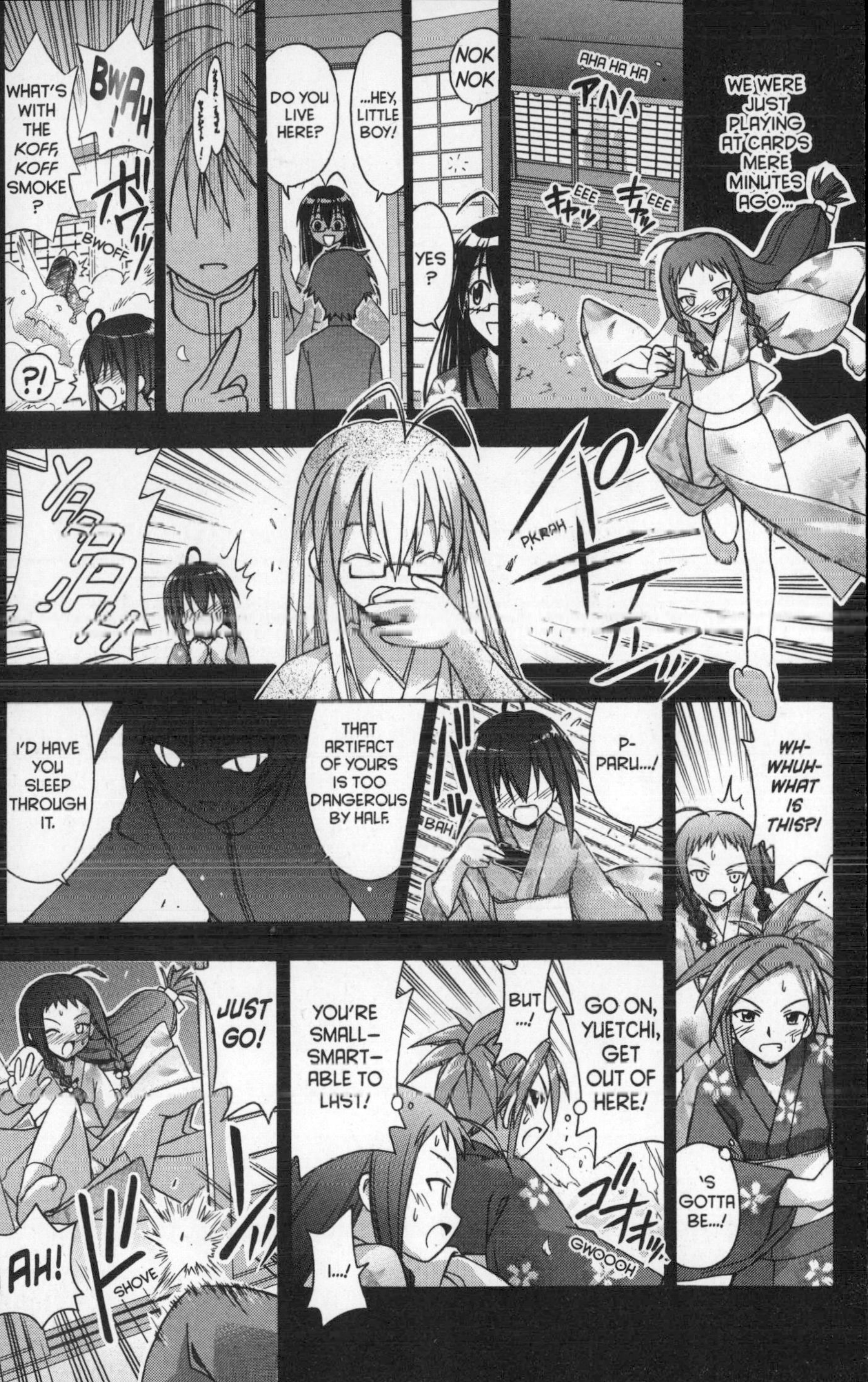
WE WERE JUST PLAYING AT CARDS MERE MINUTES AGO...
AHA HA HA
EEE
EEE
NOK NOK
YES?
...HEY, LITTLE BOY!
DO YOU LIVE HERE?
BWAH!
WHAT'S WITH THE KOFF, KOFF SMOKE?
BWOFF
?!
PKRAH
WH-WHUH-WHAT IS THIS?!
P-PARU...!
BAH
THAT ARTIFACT OF YOURS IS TOO DANGEROUS BY HALF.
I'D HAVE YOU SLEEP THROUGH IT.
'S GOTTA BE...!
GO ON, YUETCHI, GET OUT OF HERE!
GWOOOH
BUT ...!
YOU'RE SMALL-SMART-ABLE TO LAST!
I...!
JUST GO!
AH!
SHOVE

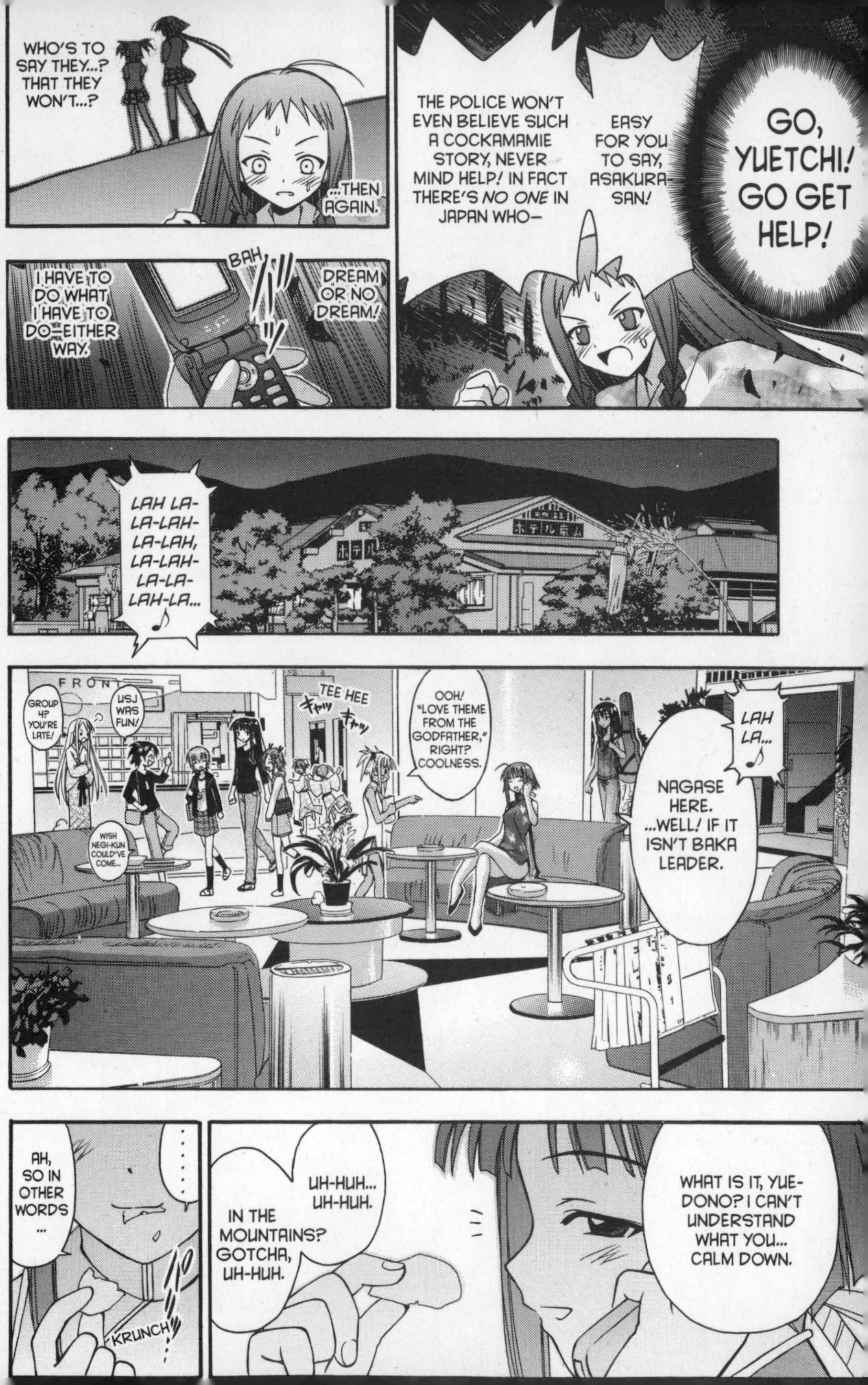
GO, YUETCHI! GO GET HELP!
EASY FOR YOU TO SAY, ASAKURA-SAN!
THE POLICE WON'T EVEN BELIEVE SUCH A COCKAMAMIE STORY, NEVER MIND HELP! IN FACT THERE'S *NO ONE* IN JAPAN WHO—
WHO'S TO SAY THEY...? THAT THEY WON'T...?
...THEN AGAIN.
DREAM OR NO DREAM!
BAH
I HAVE TO DO WHAT I HAVE TO DO—EITHER WAY.
LAH LA-LA-LAH-LA-LAH, LA-LAH-LA-LA-LAH-LA... ♪
LAH LA... ♪
NAGASE HERE. ...WELL! IF IT ISN'T BAKA LEADER.
OOH! "LOVE THEME FROM THE GODFATHER," RIGHT? COOLNESS.
TEE HEE
USJ WAS FUN!
GROUP 4? YOU'RE LATE!
WISH NEGI-KUN COULD'VE COME...
FRONT
WHAT IS IT, YUE-DONO? I CAN'T UNDERSTAND WHAT YOU... CALM DOWN.
UH-HUH... UH-HUH.
IN THE MOUNTAINS? GOTCHA, UH-HUH.
......
AH, SO IN OTHER WORDS...
KRUNCH

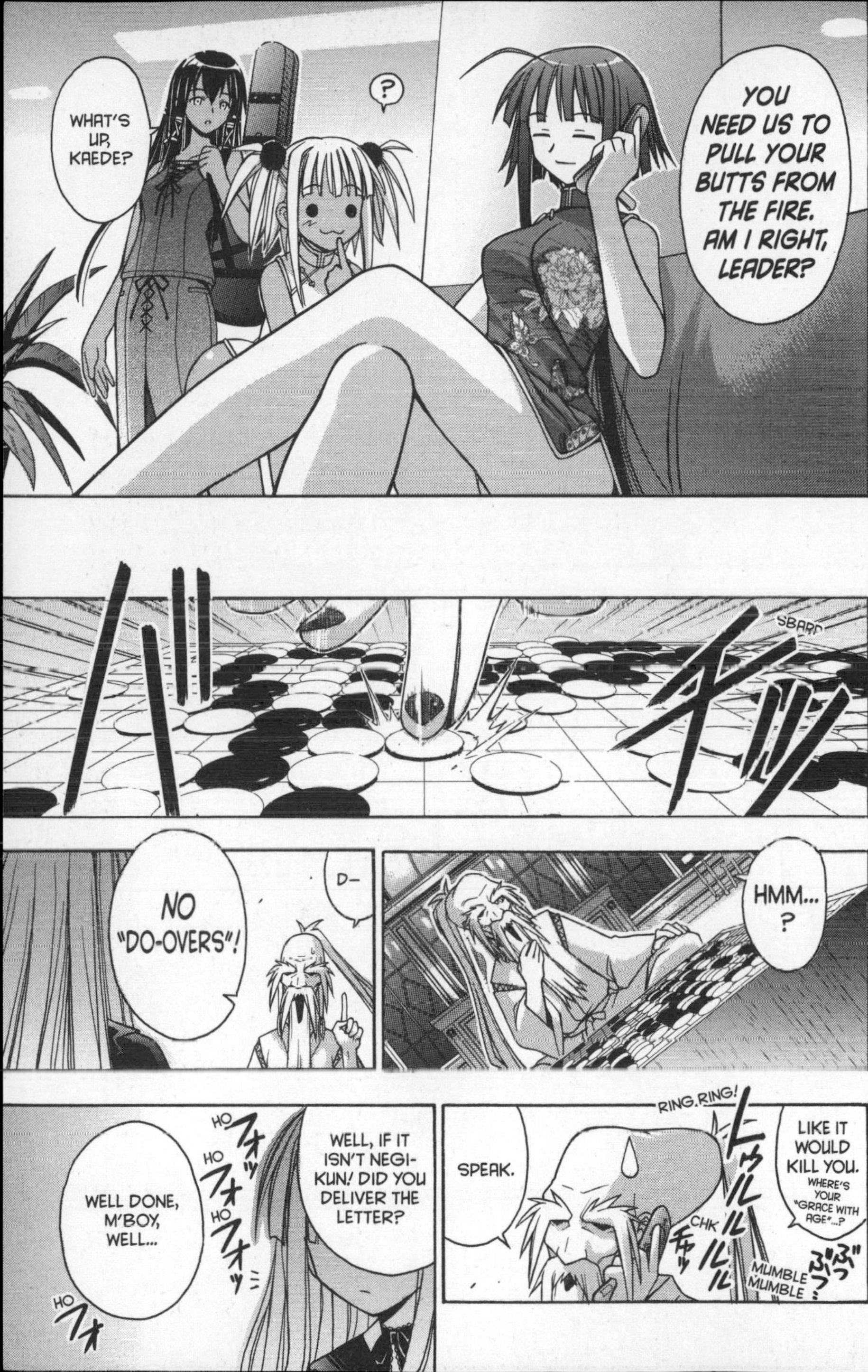
YOU NEED US TO PULL YOUR BUTTS FROM THE FIRE. AM I RIGHT, LEADER?
?
WHAT'S UP, KAEDE?
SBARP
HMM...?
D–
NO "DO-OVERS"!
RING, RING!
LIKE IT WOULD KILL YOU.
WHERE'S YOUR "GRACE WITH AGE"...?
CHK
MUMBLE MUMBLE
SPEAK.
WELL, IF IT ISN'T NEGI-KUN! DID YOU DELIVER THE LETTER?
HO HO HO HO
WELL DONE, M'BOY, WELL...

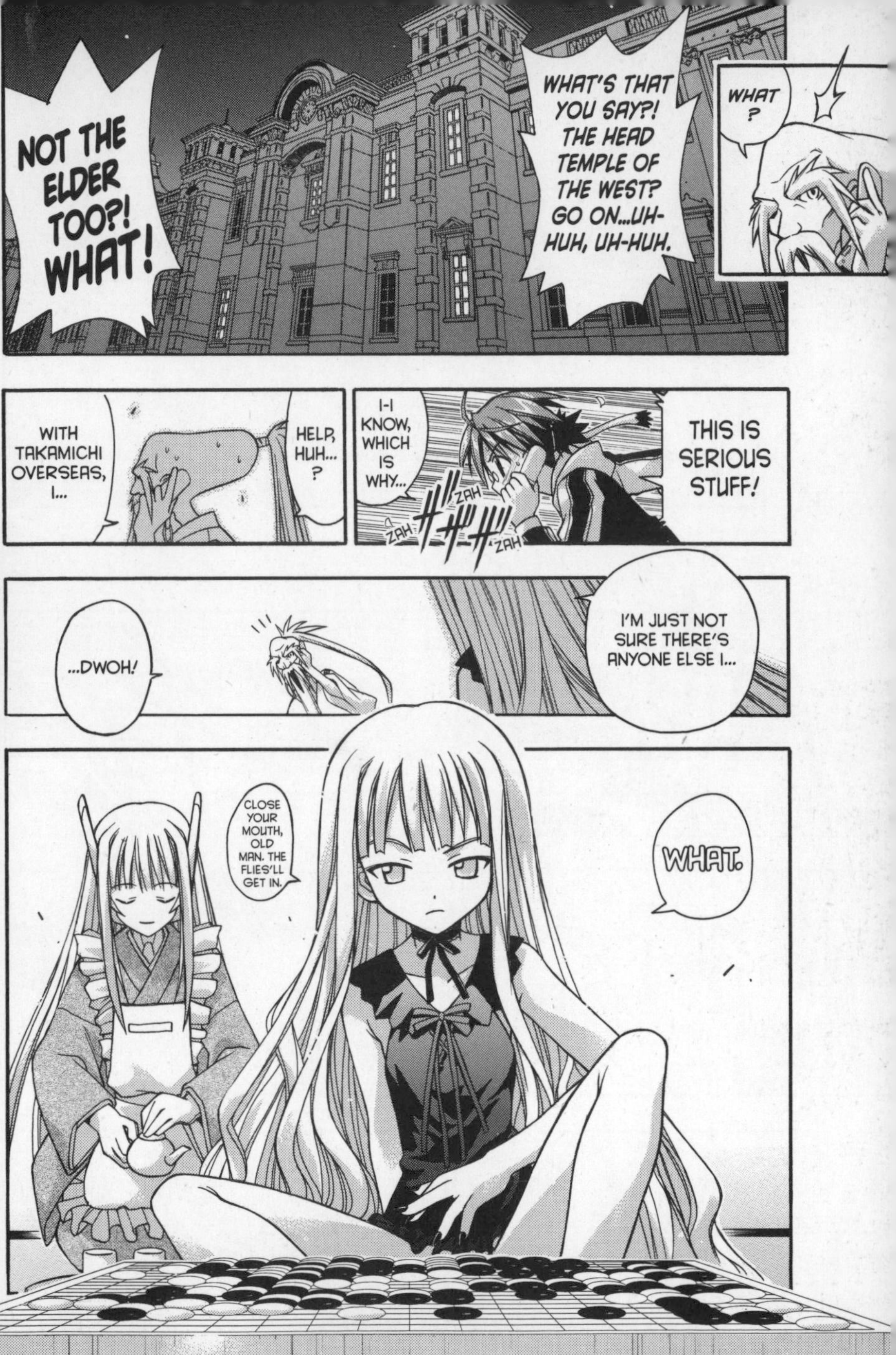
WHAT ?
WHAT'S THAT YOU SAY?! THE HEAD TEMPLE OF THE WEST? GO ON...UH-HUH, UH-HUH.
NOT THE ELDER TOO?! WHAT!
THIS IS SERIOUS STUFF!
I-I KNOW, WHICH IS WHY...
ZAH
ZAH
ZAH
HELP, HUH... ?
WITH TAKAMICHI OVERSEAS, I...
I'M JUST NOT SURE THERE'S ANYONE ELSE I...
...DWOH!
WHAT.
CLOSE YOUR MOUTH, OLD MAN. THE FLIES'LL GET IN.

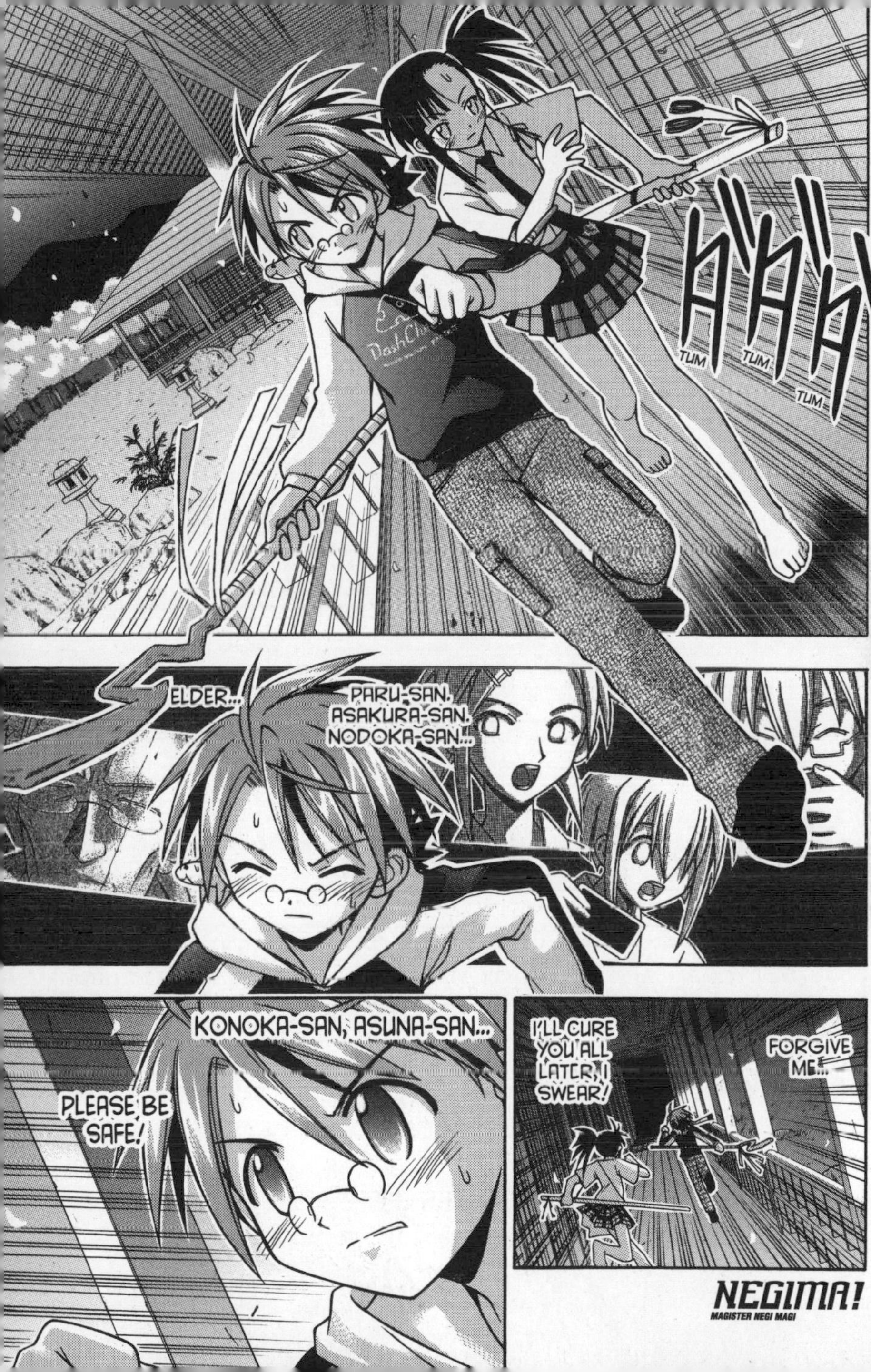
TUM
TUM
TUM
PARU-SAN, ASAKURA-SAN, NODOKA-SAN...
ELDER...
FORGIVE ME...
I'LL CURE YOU ALL LATER, I SWEAR!
KONOKA-SAN, ASUNA-SAN...
PLEASE BE SAFE!

NEGIMA!
MAGISTER NEGI MAGI

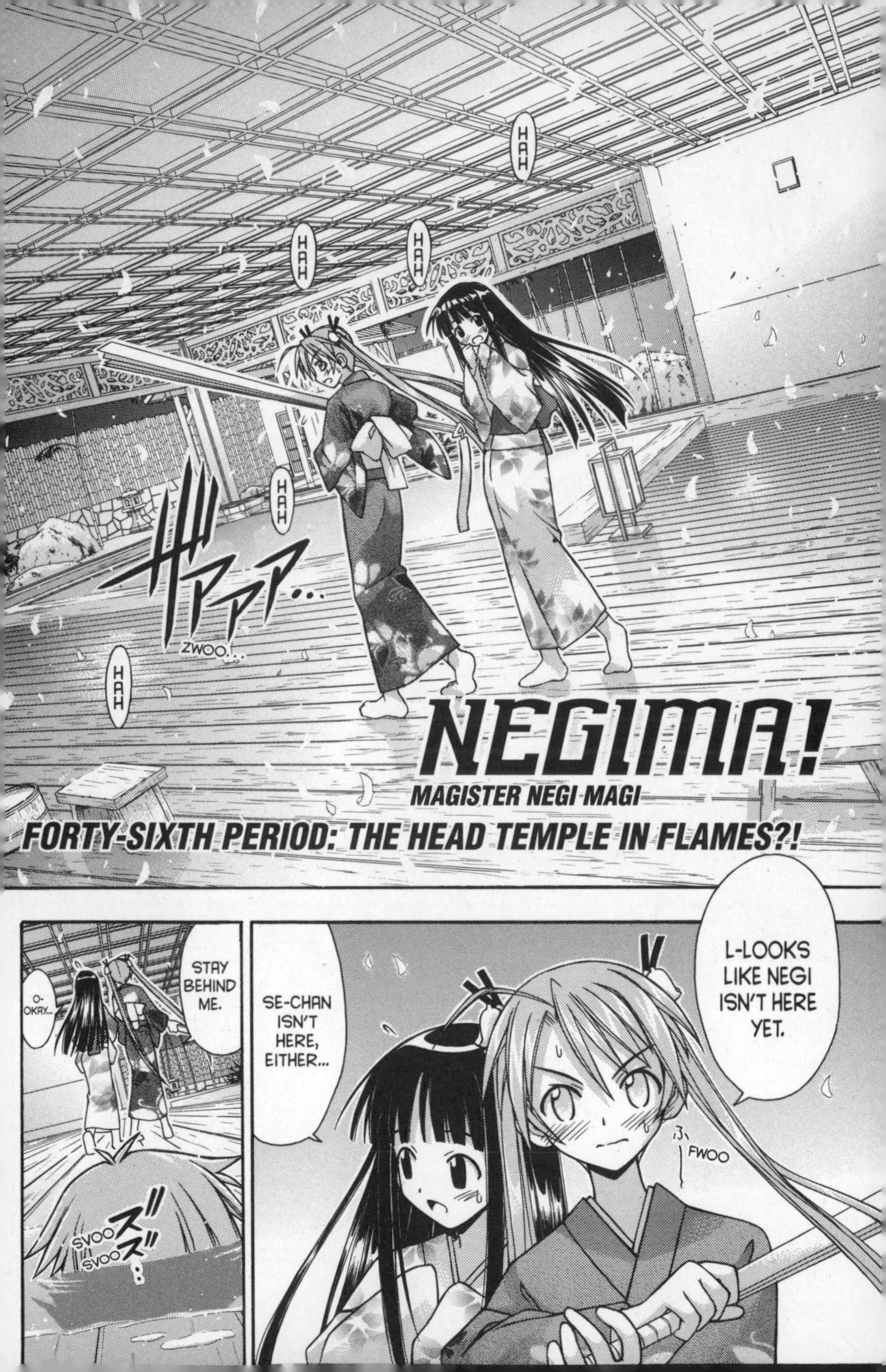
HAH
HAH
HAH
HAH
ZWOO...
HAH
NEGIMA!
MAGISTER NEGI-MAGI
FORTY-SIXTH PERIOD: THE HEAD TEMPLE IN FLAMES?!
L-LOOKS LIKE NEGI ISN'T HERE YET.
FWOO
SE-CHAN ISN'T HERE, EITHER...
STAY BEHIND ME.
O-OKAY...
SVOO SVOO

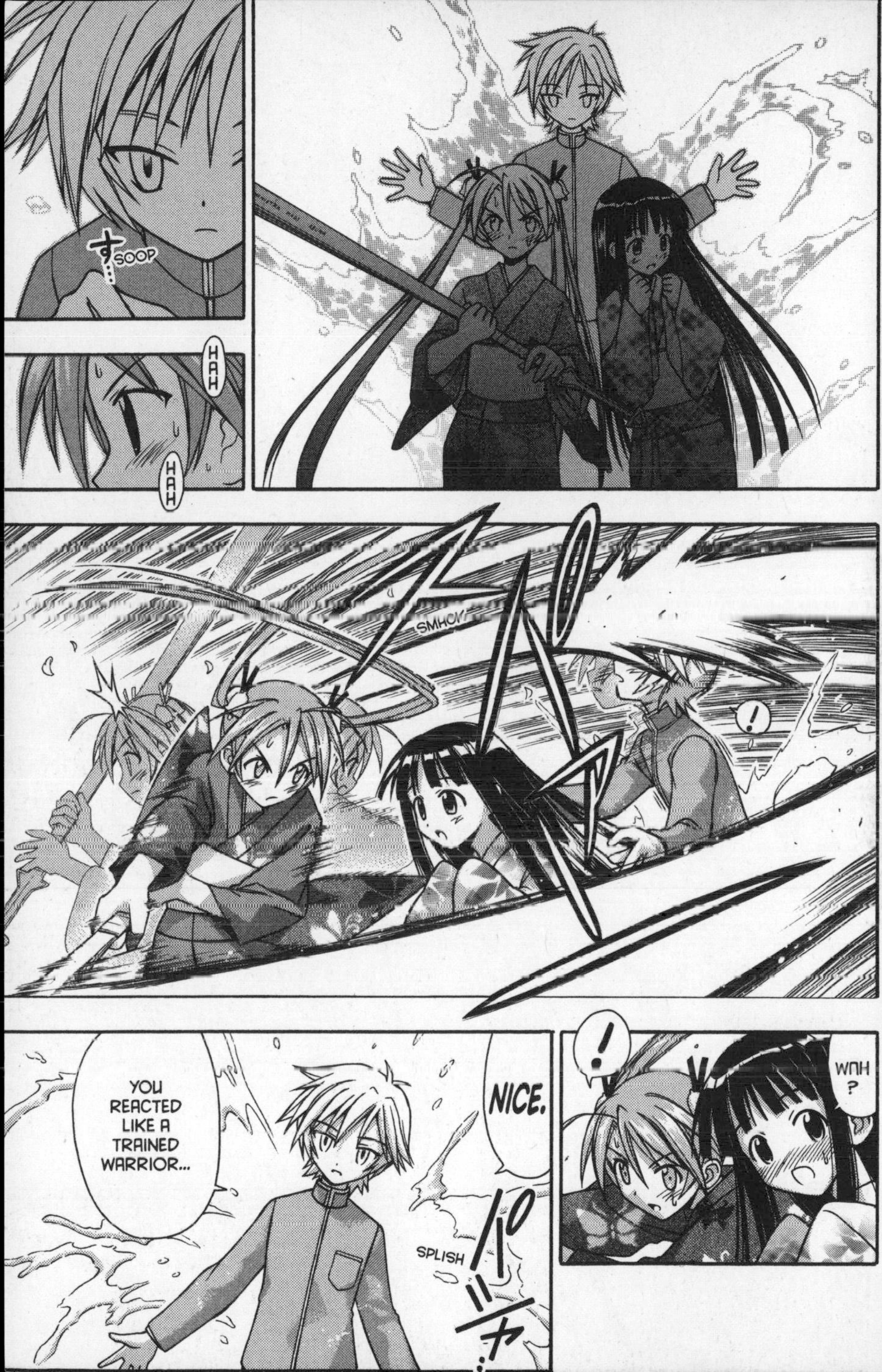

す SOOP
HAH
HAH
!
!
WAH?
NICE.
YOU REACTED LIKE A TRAINED WARRIOR...
SPLISH

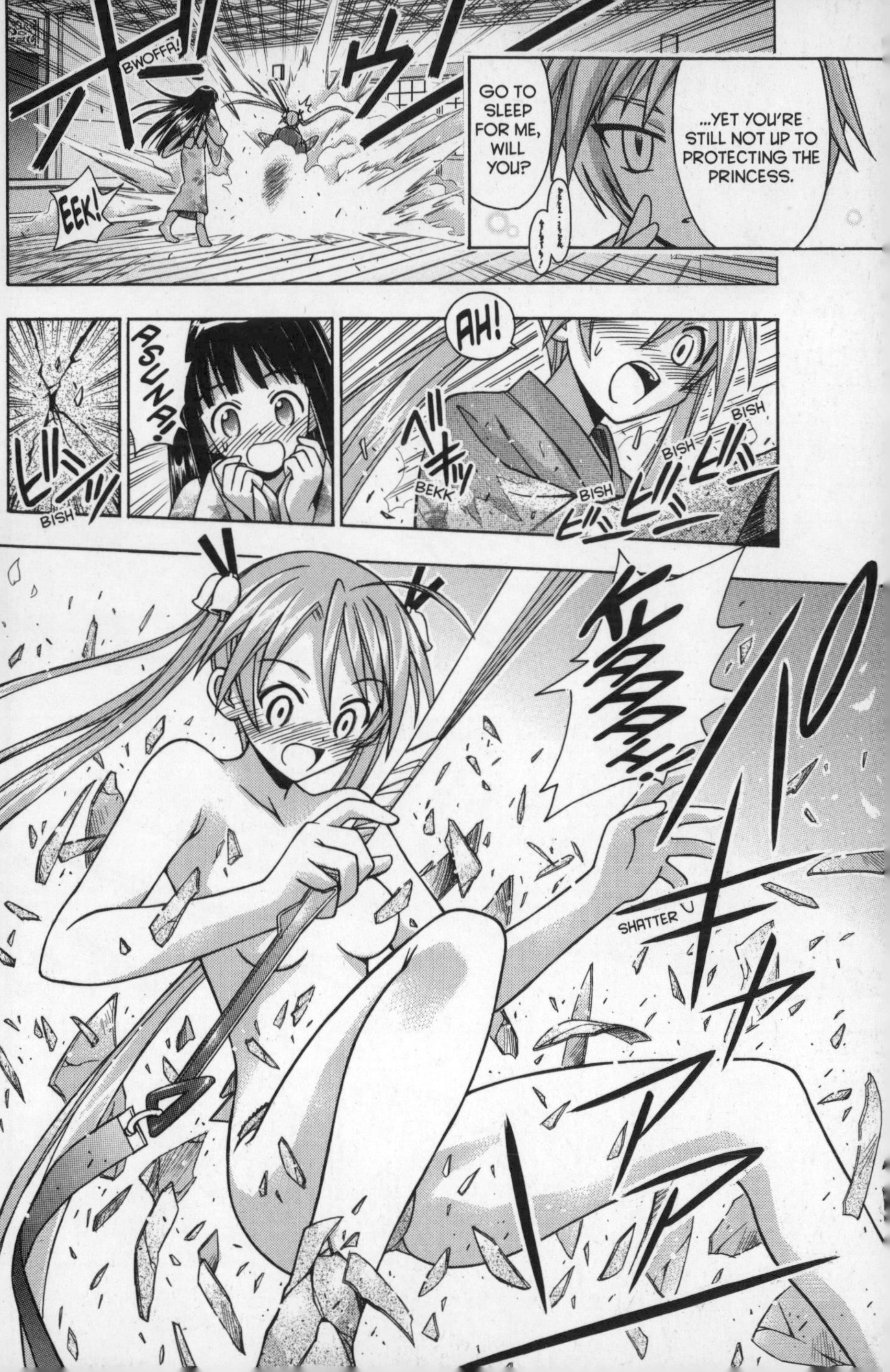
...YET YOU'RE STILL NOT UP TO PROTECTING THE PRINCESS.
GO TO SLEEP FOR ME, WILL YOU?
BWOFFA!
EEK!
AH!
BEKK
BISH
BISH
BISH
ASUNA!
BISH
KYAAAAH!!
SHATTER

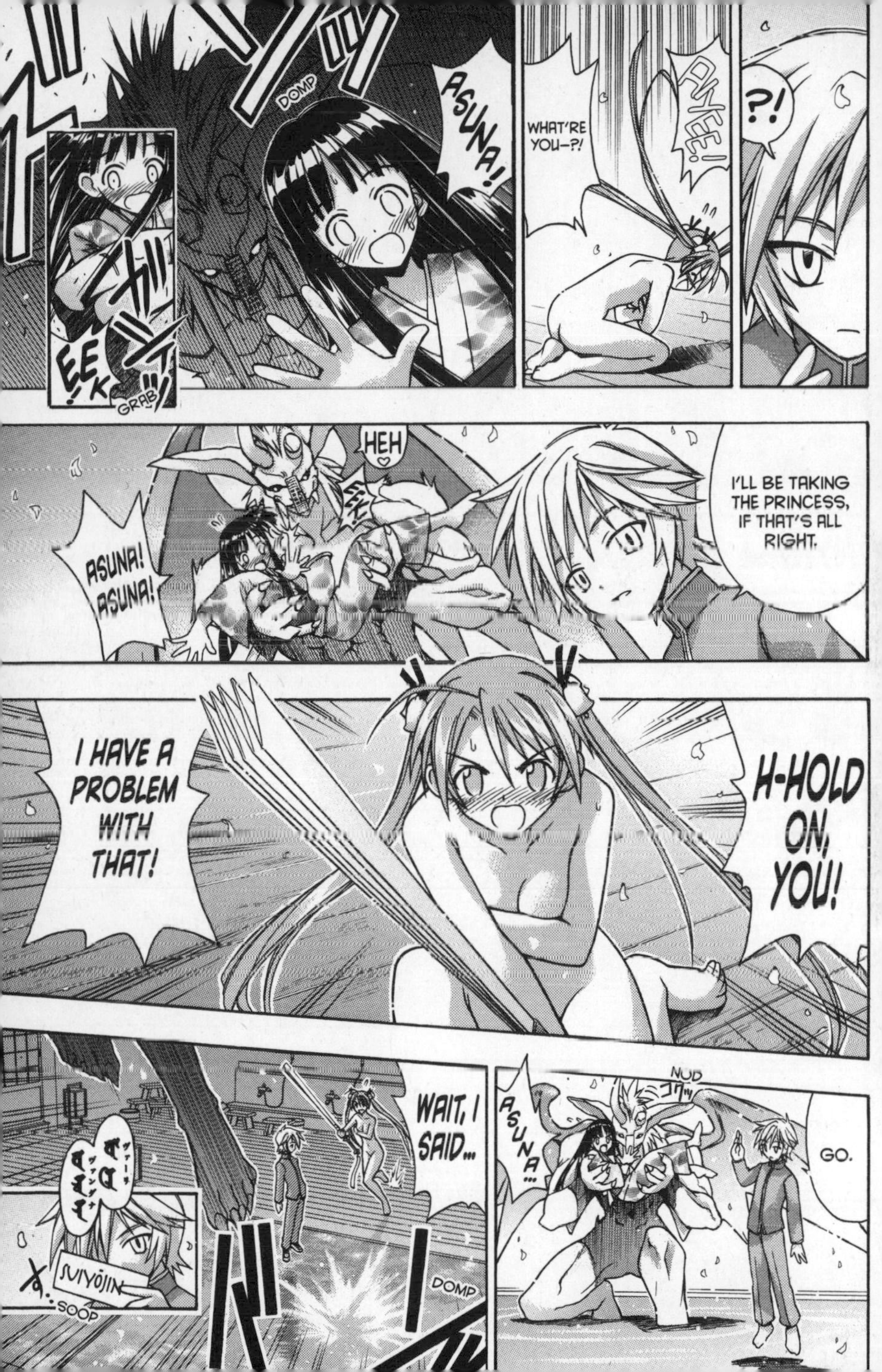
?!
AIYEEE!
WHAT'RE YOU—?!
ASUNA!
DOMP
EEK
GRAB
I'LL BE TAKING THE PRINCESS, IF THAT'S ALL RIGHT.
HEH ♡
EEK!
ASUNA! ASUNA!
H-HOLD ON, YOU!
I HAVE A PROBLEM WITH THAT!
GO.
NOD
ASUNA...
WAIT, I SAID...
DOMP
SUIYŌJIN
SOOP

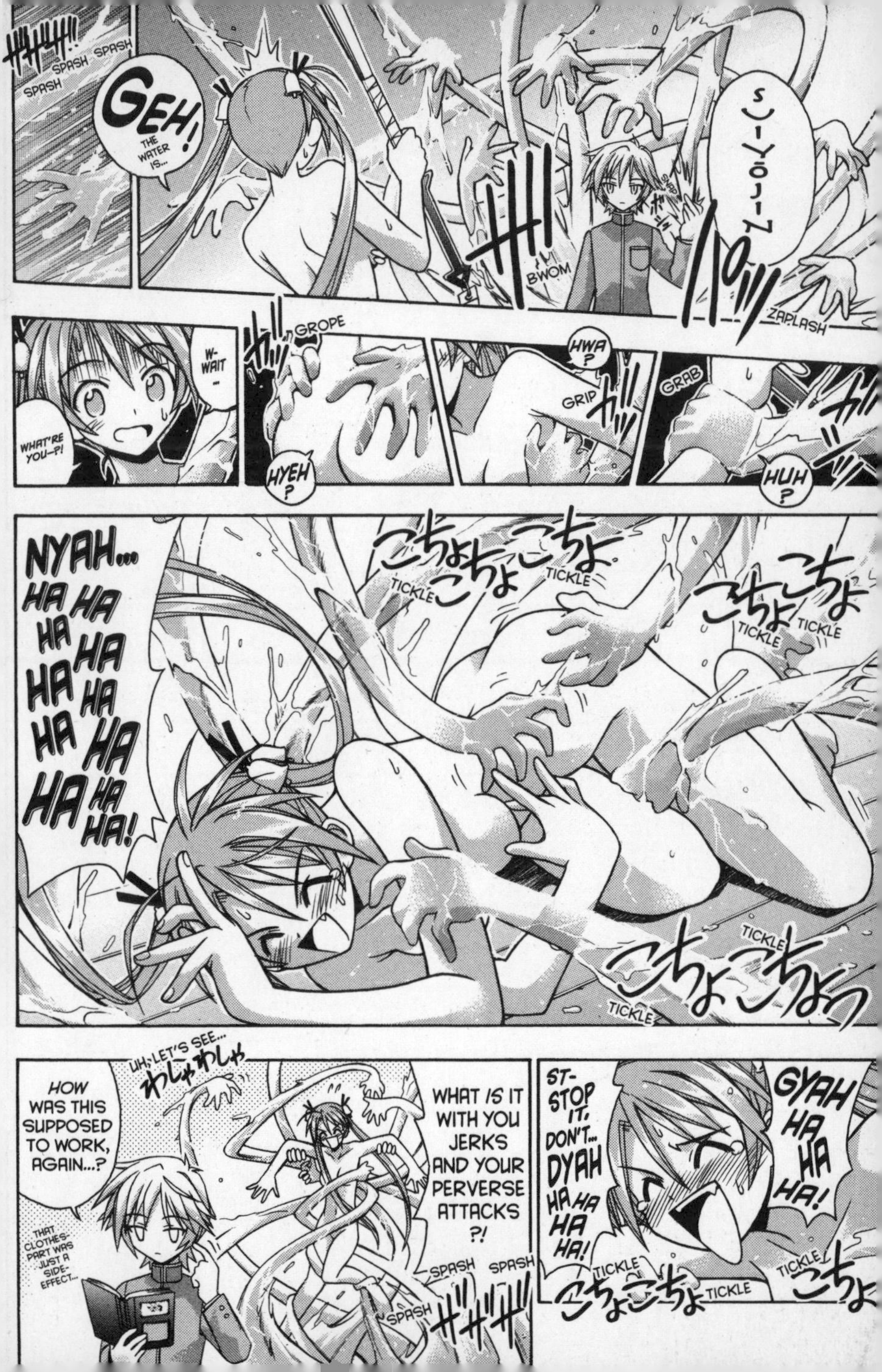
SUIYŌJIN
SNAP
BWOM
ZAPLASH
SPASH SPASH SPASH
GEH! THE WATER IS...
GRAB
HUH?
HWA?
GRIP
GROPE
HYEH?
W-WAIT...
WHAT'RE YOU--?!
NYAH... HA HA HA HA HA HA HA HA HA HA HA HA HA!
TICKLE TICKLE TICKLE TICKLE TICKLE TICKLE
GYAH HA HA HA!
ST-STOP IT, DON'T... DYAH HA HA HA HA HA!
TICKLE TICKLE TICKLE
WHAT *IS* IT WITH YOU JERKS AND YOUR PERVERSE ATTACKS?!
UH, LET'S SEE...
HOW WAS THIS SUPPOSED TO WORK, AGAIN...?
THAT CLOTHES-PART WAS JUST A SIDE-EFFECT...
SPASH SPASH SPASH

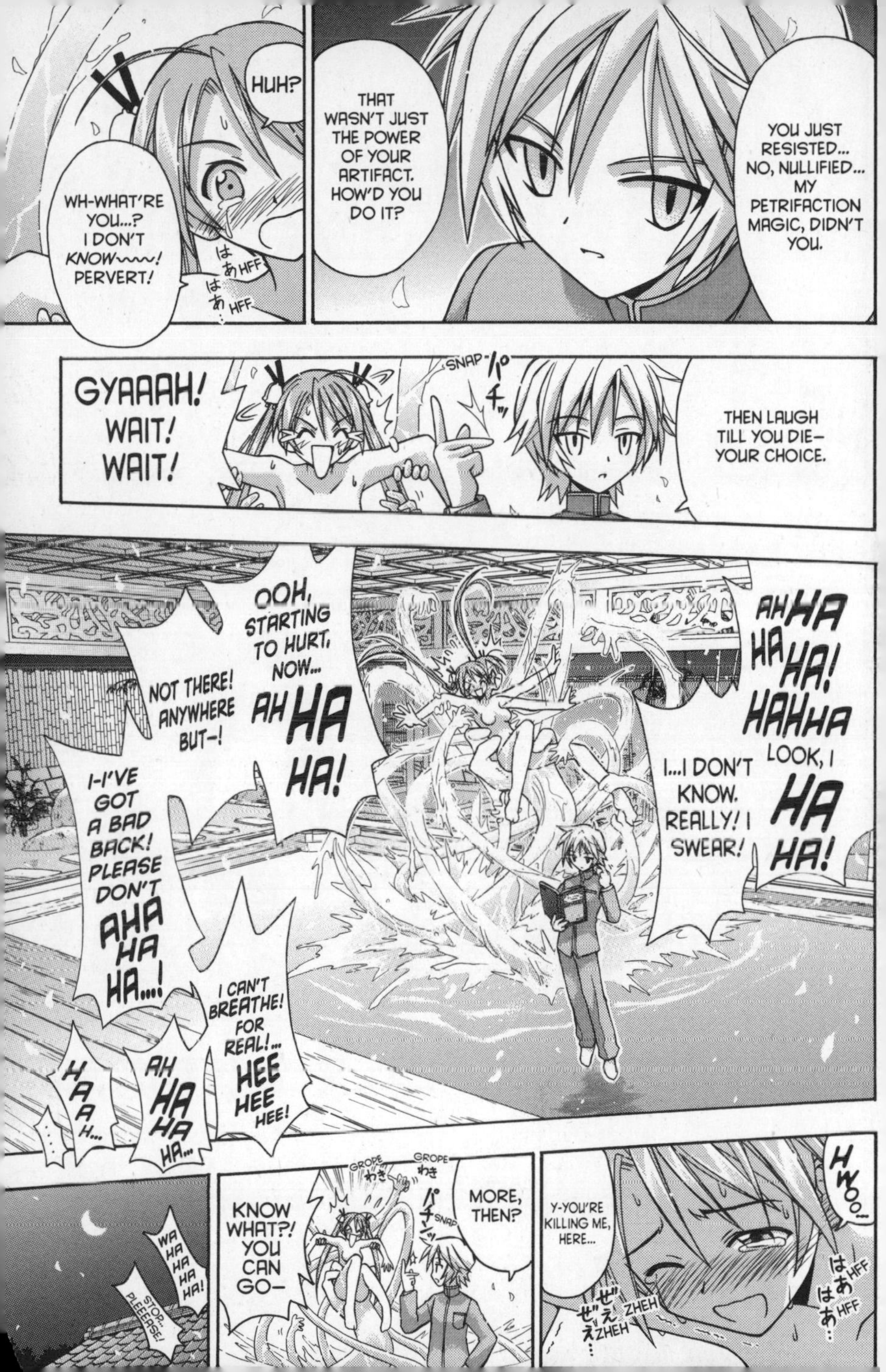
YOU JUST RESISTED... NO, NULLIFIED... MY PETRIFACTION MAGIC, DIDN'T YOU.
THAT WASN'T JUST THE POWER OF YOUR ARTIFACT. HOW'D YOU DO IT?
HUH?
WH-WHAT'RE YOU...? I DON'T KNOW~~~! PERVERT!
はあ HFF はあ… HFF
THEN LAUGH TILL YOU DIE— YOUR CHOICE.
パチッ SNAP
GYAAAH! WAIT! WAIT!
AH HA HA HA! HAHHA LOOK, I HA HA!
I...I DON'T KNOW. REALLY! I SWEAR!
OOH, STARTING TO HURT, NOW... AH HA HA!
NOT THERE! ANYWHERE BUT—!
I-I'VE GOT A BAD BACK! PLEASE DON'T AHA HA HA...!
I CAN'T BREATHE! FOR REAL!... HEE HEE HEE!
AH HA HA HA HA...
HA A A H...
...
HWOO...
Y-YOU'RE KILLING ME, HERE...
はあ HFF はあ… HFF
ぜぇ ZHEH ぜぇ… ZHEH
MORE, THEN?
パチンッ SNAP
GROPE わき GROPE わき
KNOW WHAT?! YOU CAN GO—
WA HA HA HA HA!
STOP... PLEEEASE!

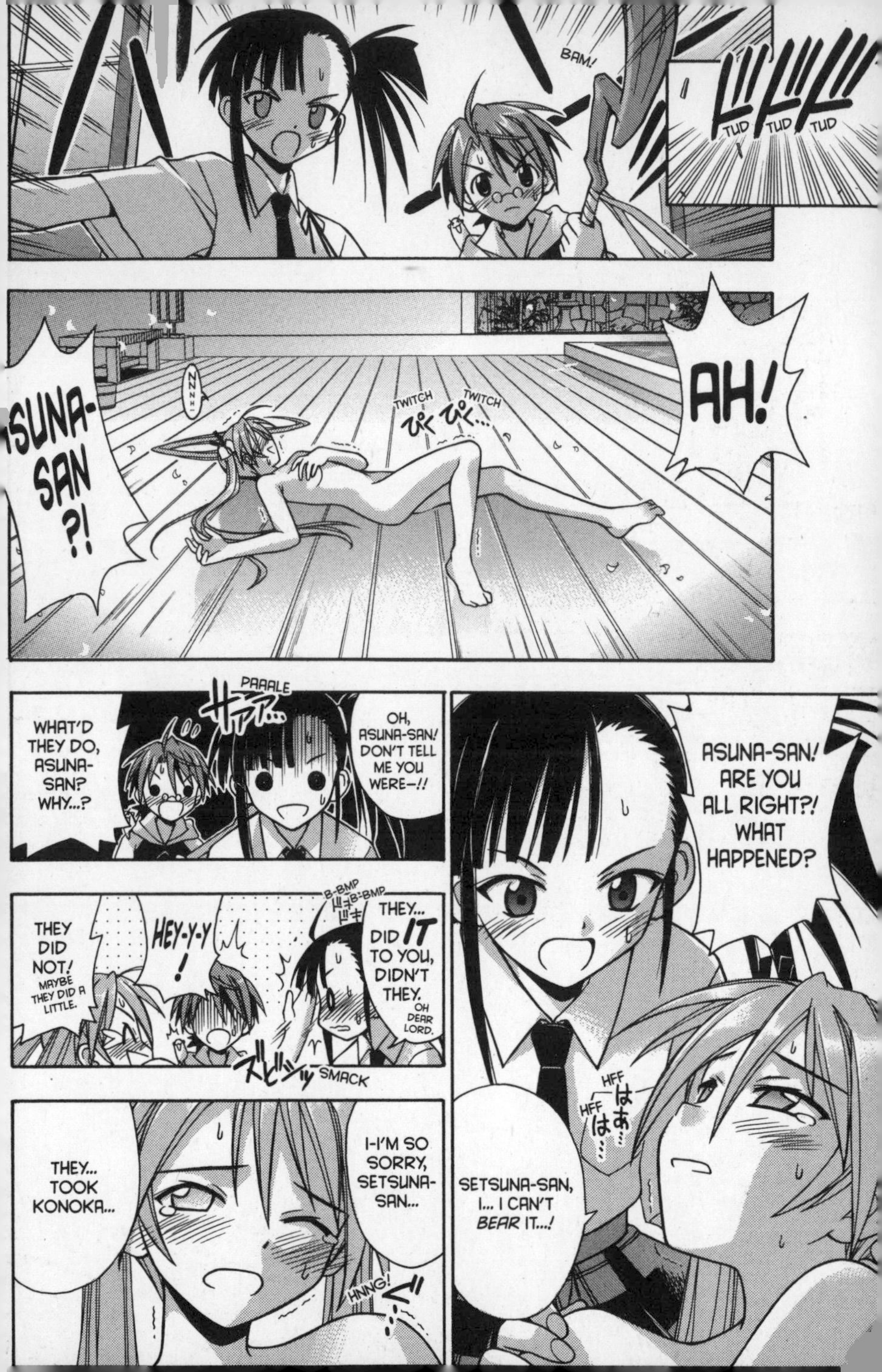
ドドドド!!
TUD TUD TUD
BAM!
AH!
TWITCH ぴく TWITCH ぴく...
NNNH
ASUNA-SAN?!
ASUNA-SAN! ARE YOU ALL RIGHT?! WHAT HAPPENED?
HFF はぁ HFF はぁ...
SETSUNA-SAN, I... I CAN'T *BEAR* IT...!
PAAALE サァア...
OH, ASUNA-SAN! DON'T TELL ME YOU WERE—!!
WHAT'D THEY DO, ASUNA-SAN? WHY...?
B-BMP B-BMP ドキ ドキ
THEY... DID *IT* TO YOU, DIDN'T THEY.
OH DEAR LORD.
HEY-Y-Y!
THEY DID NOT!
MAYBE THEY DID A LITTLE.
ズビシッ SMACK
I-I'M SO SORRY, SETSUNA-SAN...
THEY... TOOK KONOKA...
HNNG! ぐ

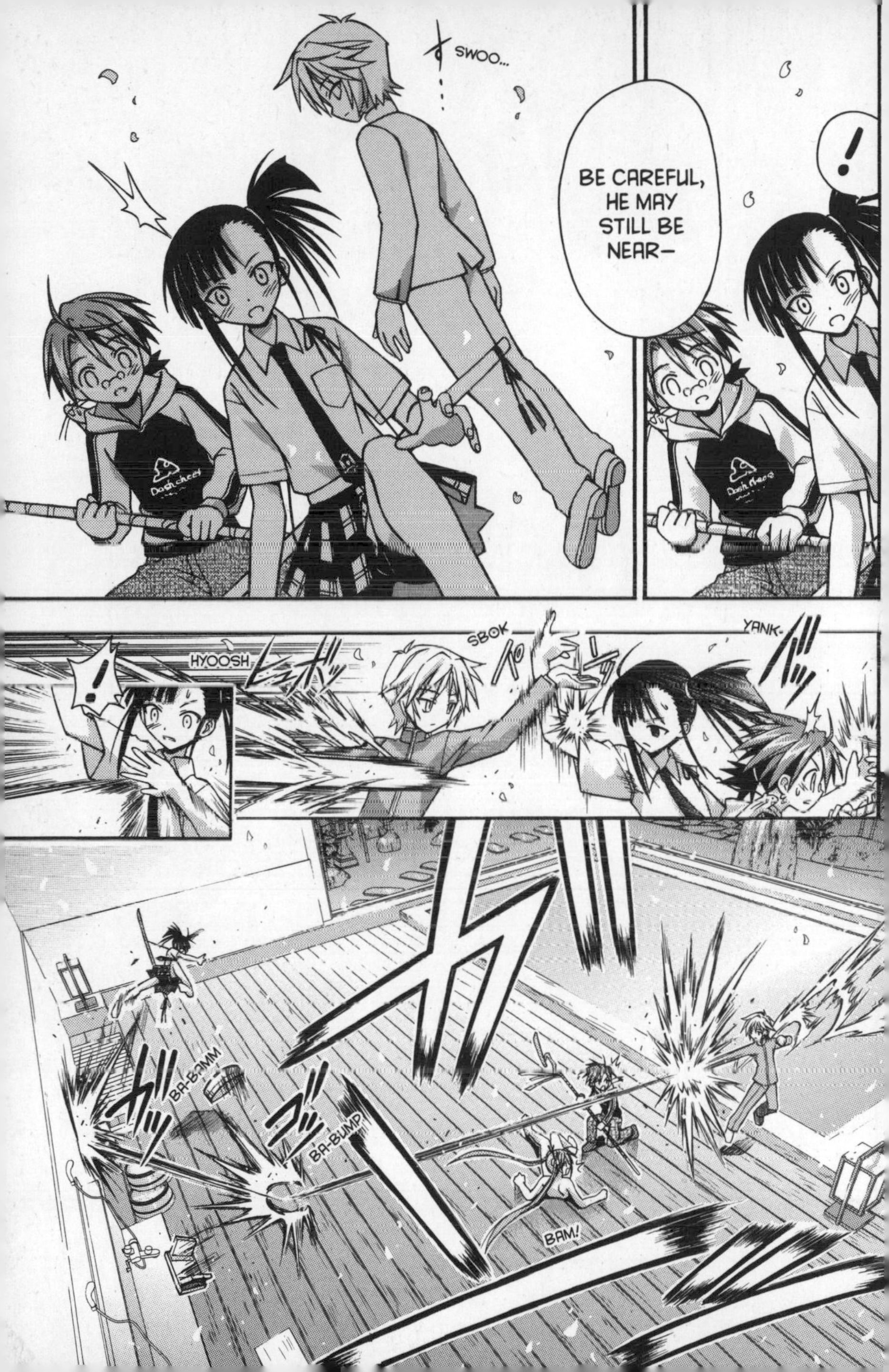
!
BE CAREFUL, HE MAY STILL BE NEAR—
SWOO...
YANK-
SBOK
HYOOSH
!
BA-BAMM
BA-BUMP
BAM!

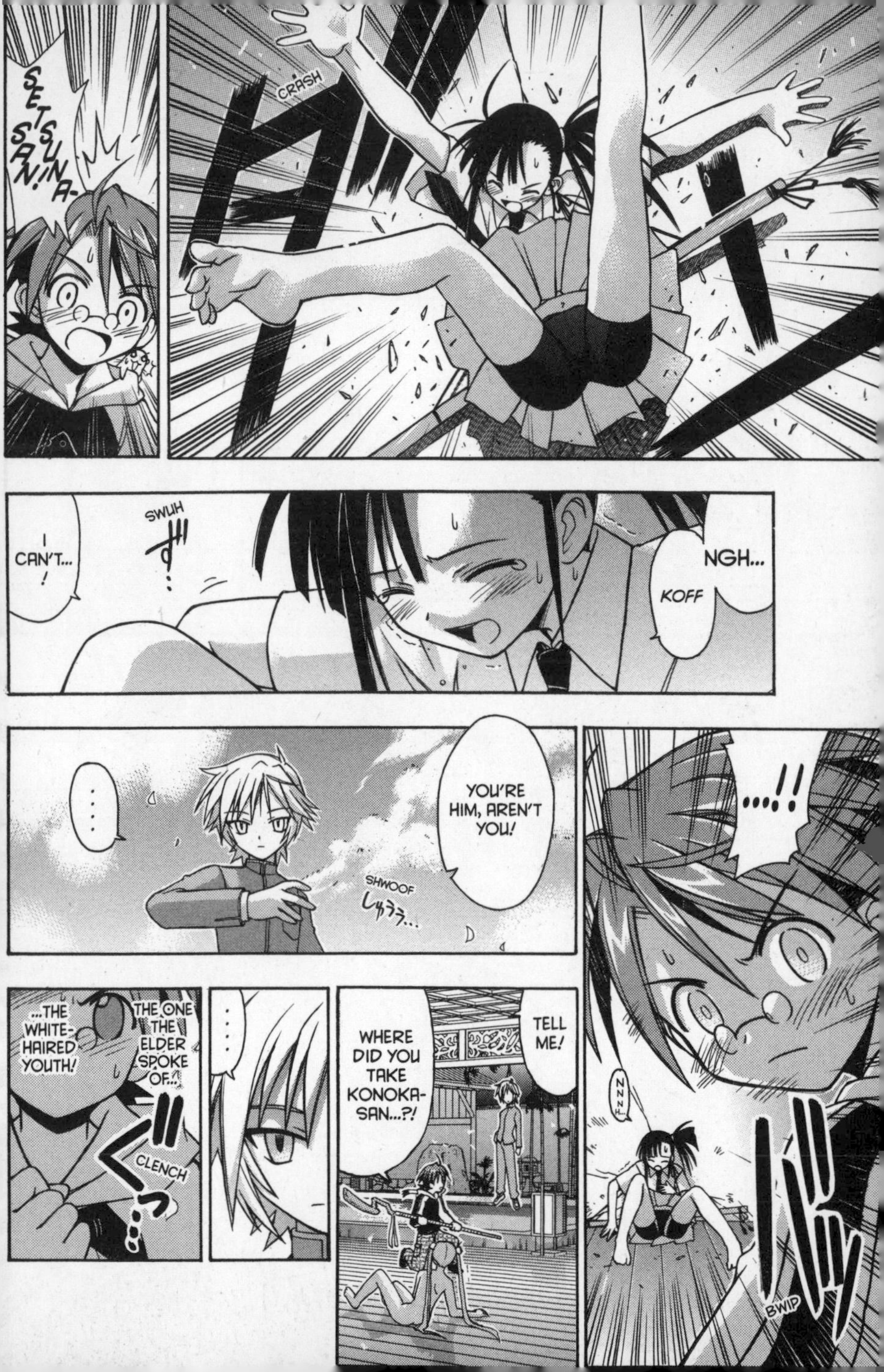
CRASH
SETSUNA-SAN!!
NGH...
KOFF
SWUH
I CAN'T...!
...!!
NNN...
BWIP
YOU'RE HIM, AREN'T YOU!
SHWOOF
....
TELL ME!
WHERE DID YOU TAKE KONOKA-SAN...?!
....
THE ONE THE ELDER SPOKE OF...!
...THE WHITE-HAIRED YOUTH!
CLENCH

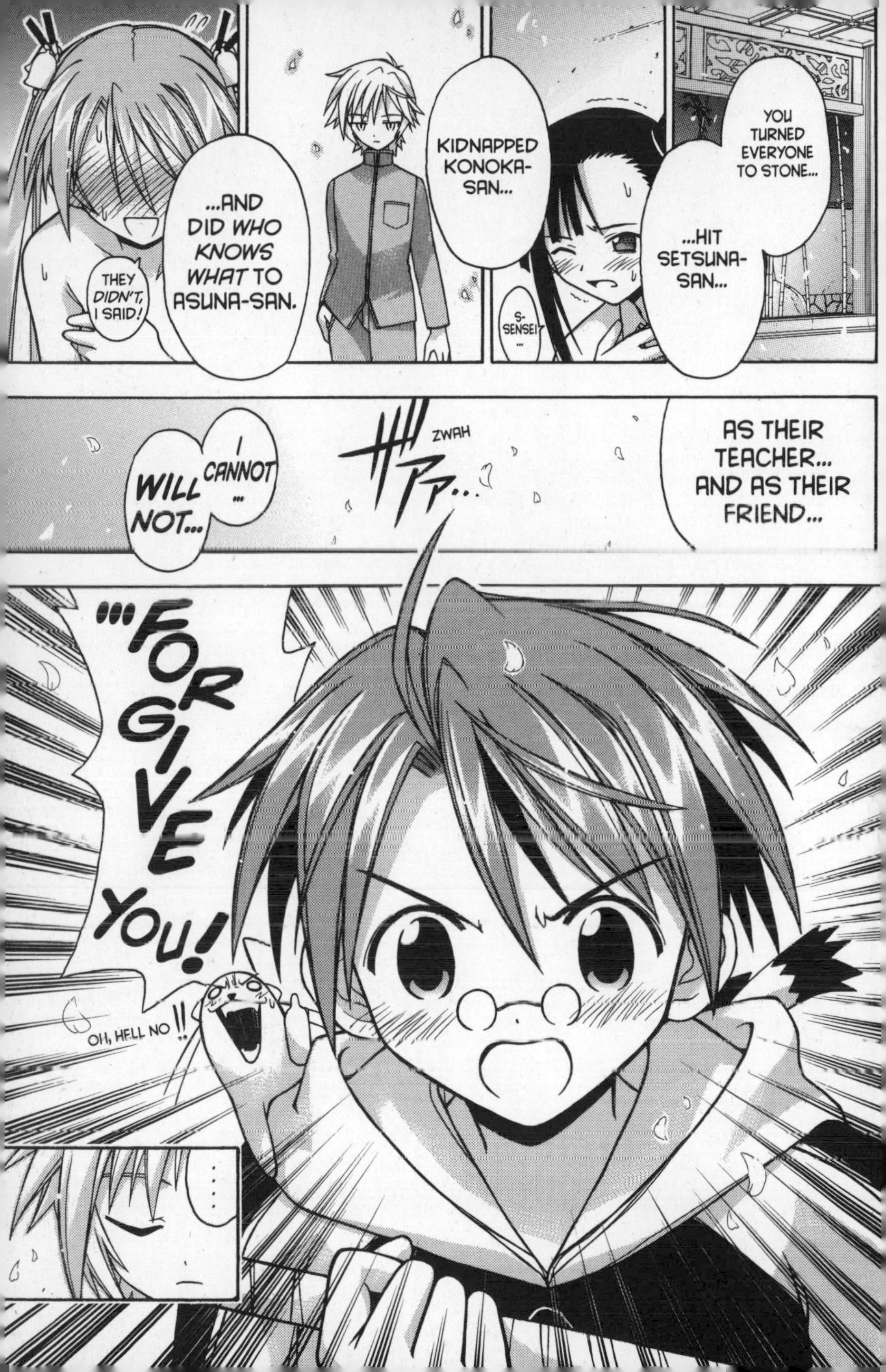
YOU TURNED EVERYONE TO STONE...
...HIT SETSUNA-SAN...
S-SENSEI...
KIDNAPPED KONOKA-SAN...
...AND DID WHO KNOWS WHAT TO ASUNA-SAN.
THEY DIDN'T, I SAID!
AS THEIR TEACHER... AND AS THEIR FRIEND...
ZWAH
I CANNOT...
WILL NOT...
..."FORGIVE YOU!
OH, HELL NO!!
.....

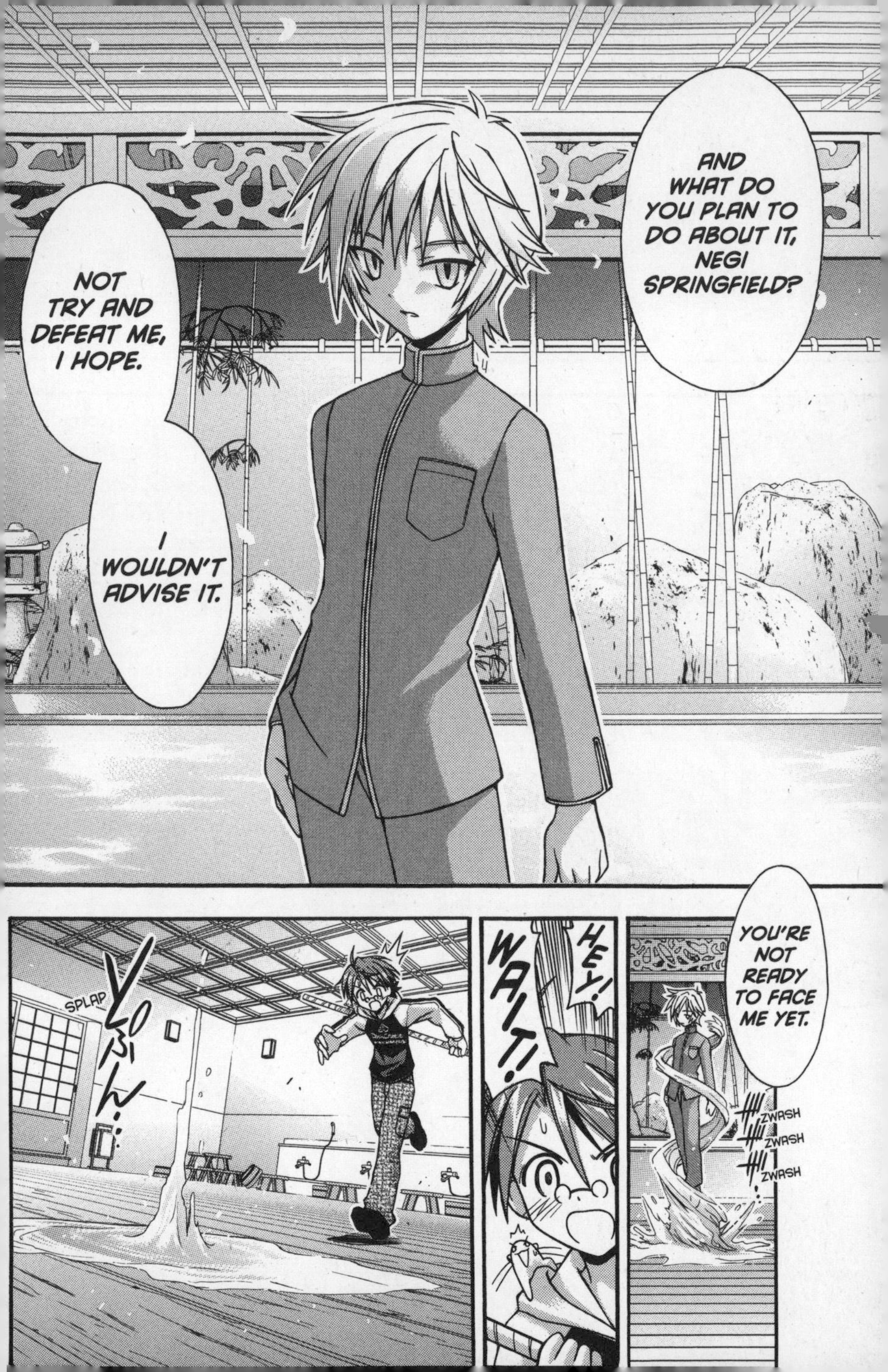
AND WHAT DO YOU PLAN TO DO ABOUT IT, NEGI SPRINGFIELD?
NOT TRY AND DEFEAT ME, I HOPE.
I WOULDN'T ADVISE IT.
YOU'RE NOT READY TO FACE ME YET.
ZWASH
ZWASH
ZWASH
HEY!
WAIT!
SPLAP

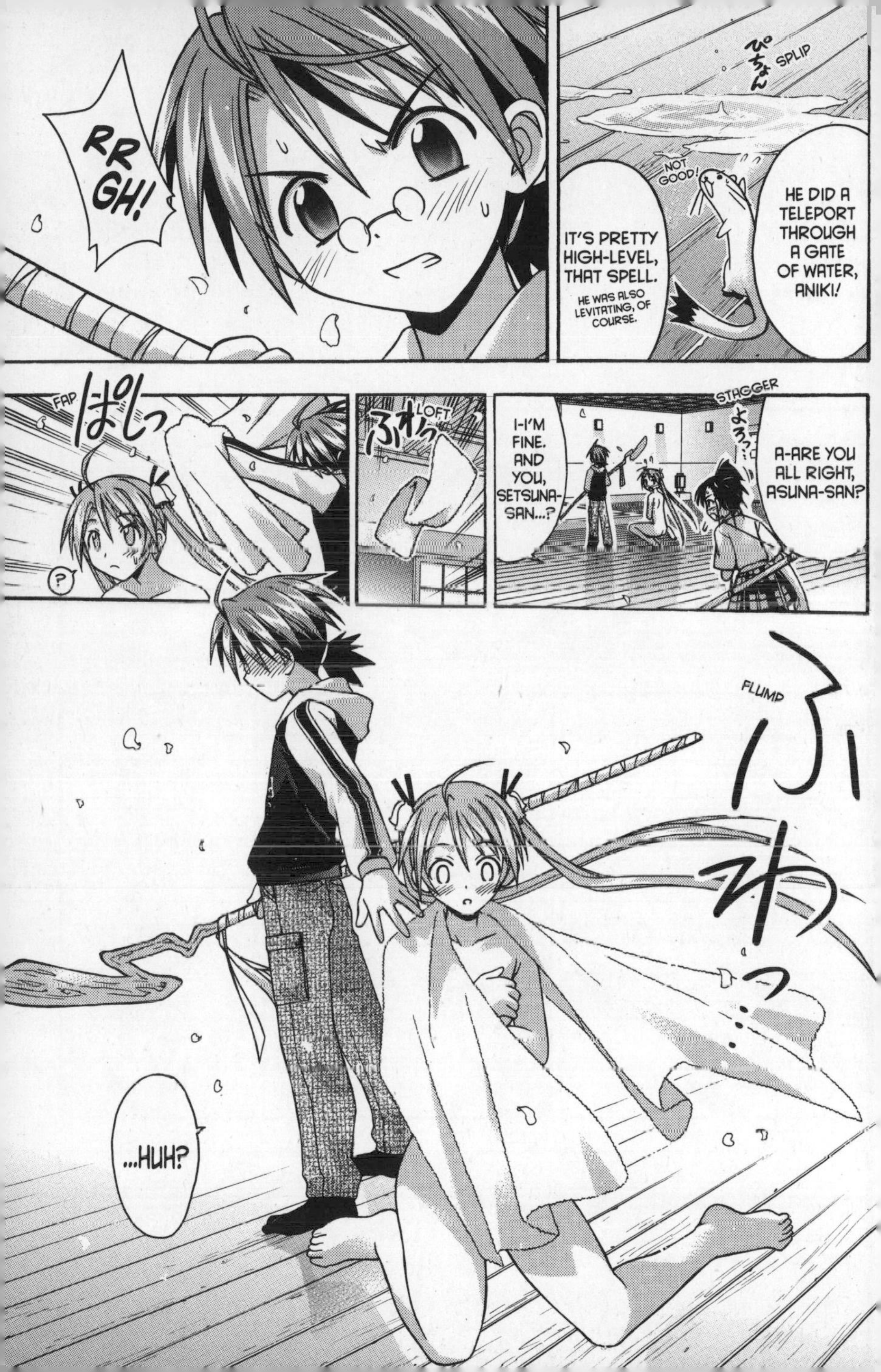

ぴちょん
SPLIP
NOT GOOD!
HE DID A TELEPORT THROUGH A GATE OF WATER, ANIKI!
IT'S PRETTY HIGH-LEVEL, THAT SPELL.
HE WAS ALSO LEVITATING, OF COURSE.
RRGH!
よろっ
STAGGER
A-ARE YOU ALL RIGHT, ASUNA-SAN?
I-I'M FINE. AND YOU, SETSUNA-SAN...?
ふわっ
LOFT
ぱしっ
FAP
?
ふわっ…
FLUMP
...HUH?

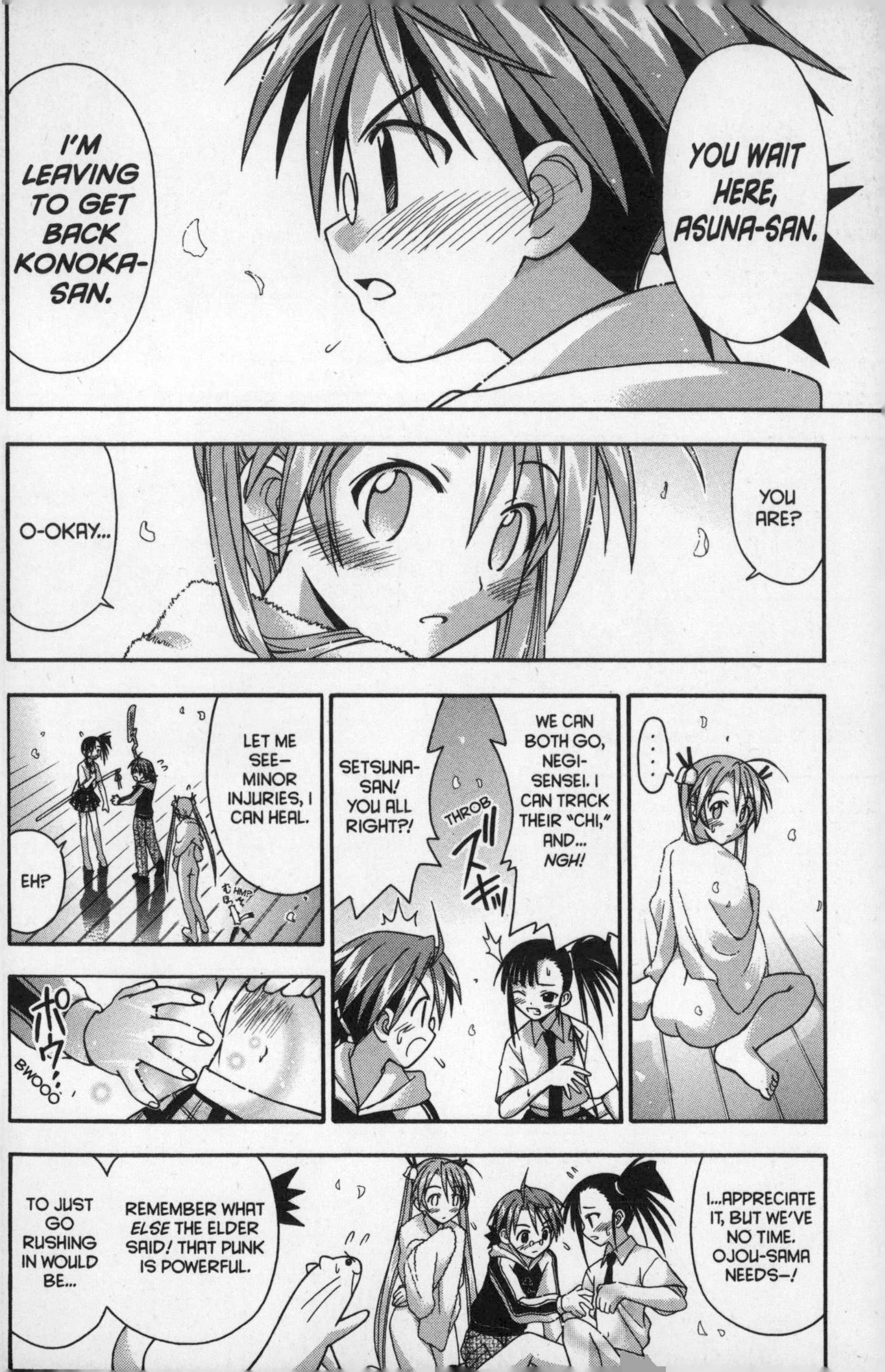
YOU WAIT HERE, ASUNA-SAN.
I'M LEAVING TO GET BACK KONOKA-SAN.
YOU ARE?
O-OKAY...
....
WE CAN BOTH GO, NEGI-SENSEI. I CAN TRACK THEIR "CHI," AND... *NGH!*
THROB
SETSUNA-SAN! YOU ALL RIGHT?!
LET ME SEE— MINOR INJURIES, I CAN HEAL.
EH?
HM?
BWOOO
I...APPRECIATE IT, BUT WE'VE NO TIME. OJOU-SAMA NEEDS—!
REMEMBER WHAT *ELSE* THE ELDER SAID! THAT PUNK IS POWERFUL.
TO JUST GO RUSHING IN WOULD BE...

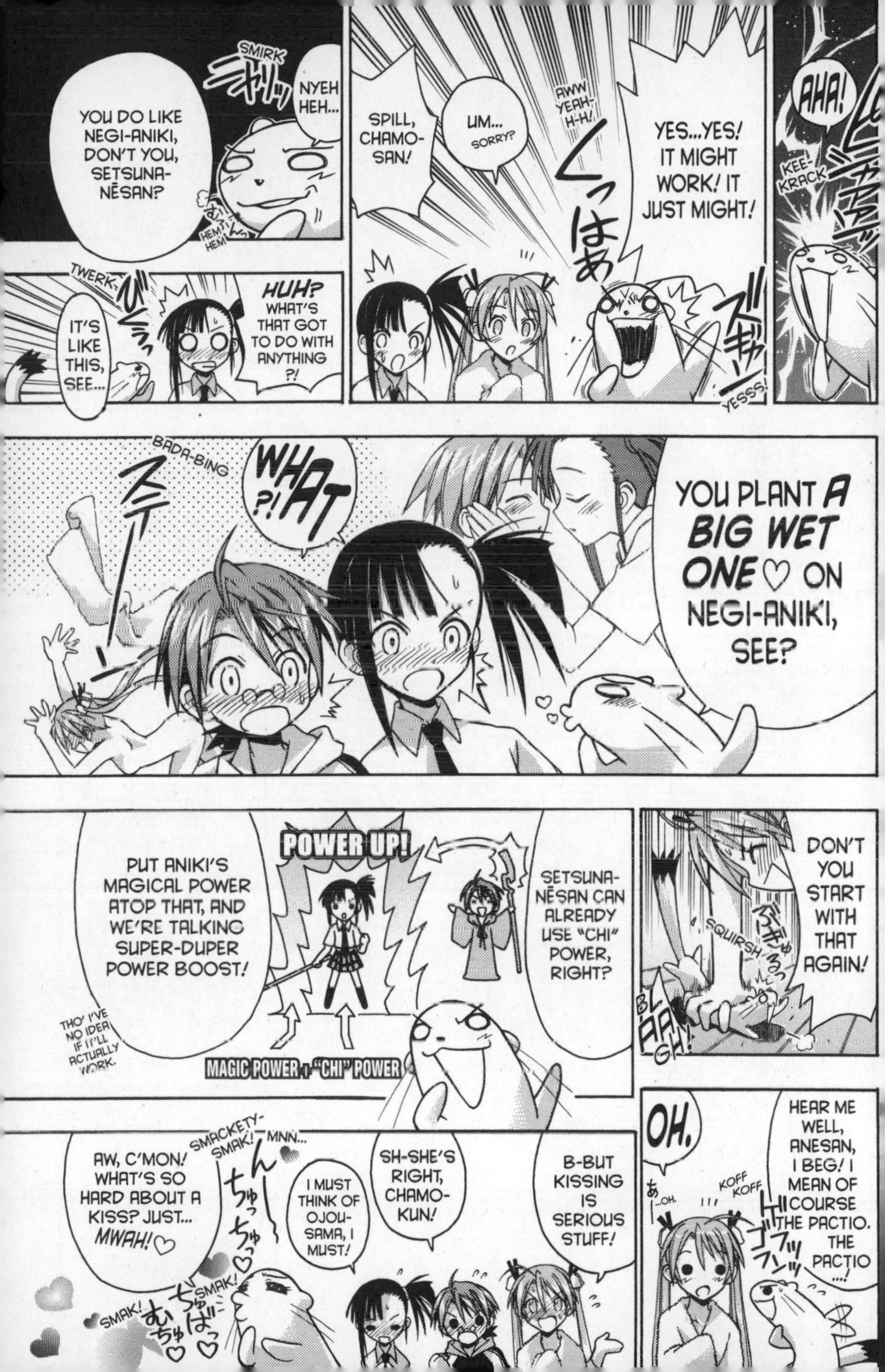
AHA!
KEE-KRACK
YESSS!
YES...YES! IT MIGHT WORK! IT JUST MIGHT!
AWW YEAH-H-H!
UM... SORRY?
SPILL, CHAMO-SAN!
SMIRK
NYEH HEH...
YOU DO LIKE NEGI-ANIKI, DON'T YOU, SETSUNA-NĒSAN?
HEM HEM
HUH? WHAT'S THAT GOT TO DO WITH ANYTHING ?!
TWERK
IT'S LIKE THIS, SEE...
YOU PLANT A BIG WET ONE ♡ ON NEGI-ANIKI, SEE?
WHAT ?!
BADA-BING
DON'T YOU START WITH THAT AGAIN!
SQUIRSH
BLAAGH!
SETSUNA-NĒSAN CAN ALREADY USE "CHI" POWER, RIGHT?
POWER UP!
PUT ANIKI'S MAGICAL POWER ATOP THAT, AND WE'RE TALKING SUPER-DUPER POWER BOOST!
THO' I'VE NO IDEA IF IT'LL ACTUALLY WORK.
MAGIC POWER + "CHI" POWER
HEAR ME WELL, ANESAN, I BEG! I MEAN OF COURSE THE PACTIO. THE PACTIO ...!
KOFF KOFF
OH.
...OH.
B-BUT KISSING IS SERIOUS STUFF!
SH-SHE'S RIGHT, CHAMO-KUN!
I MUST THINK OF OJOU-SAMA, I MUST!
SMACKETY-SMAK!
MNN...
AW, C'MON! WHAT'S SO HARD ABOUT A KISS? JUST... MWAH! ♡
SMAK!
SMAK!

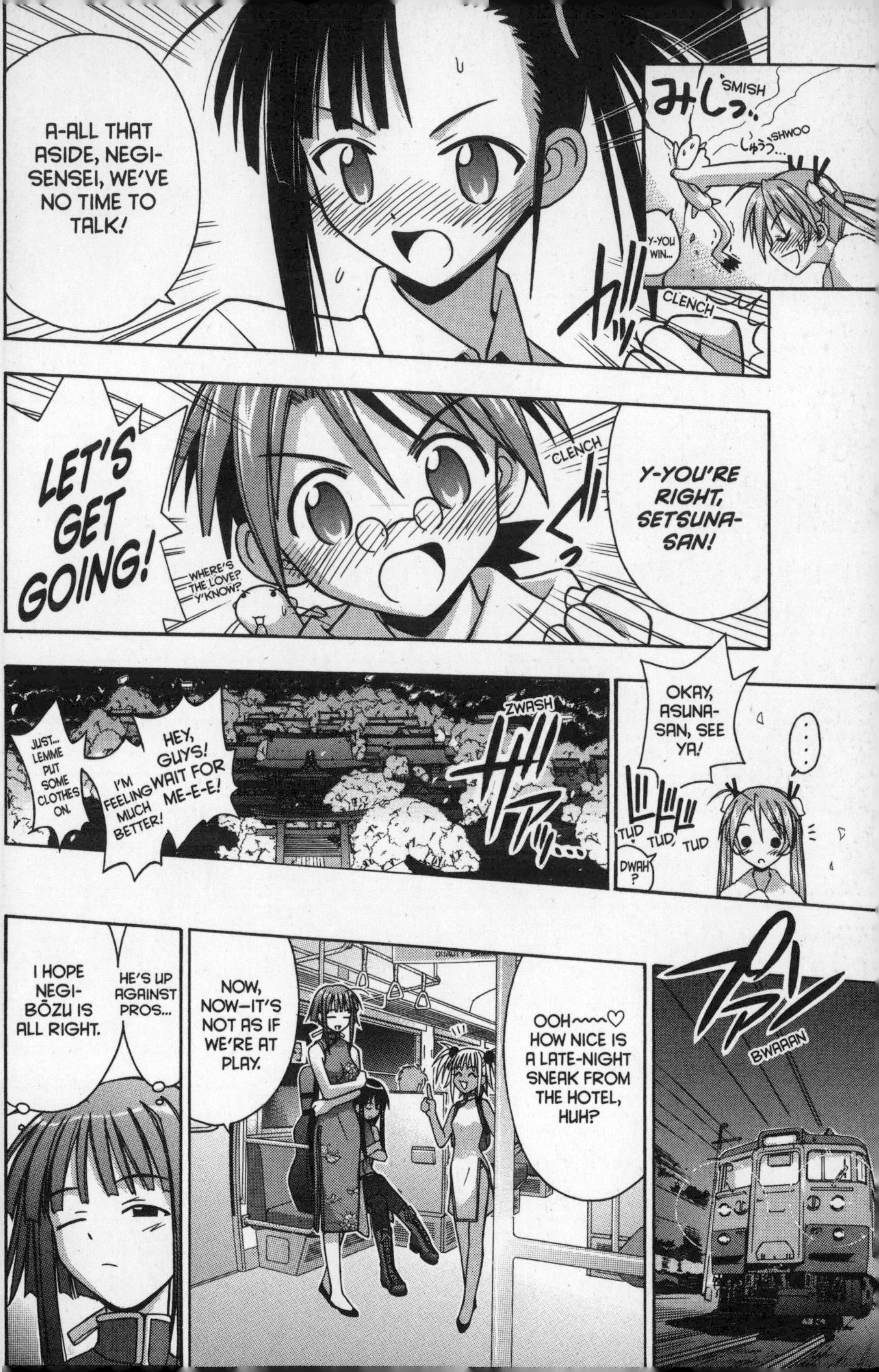
みしっ..
SMISH
しゅううー...
SHWOO
Y-YOU WIN...
A-ALL THAT ASIDE, NEGI-SENSEI, WE'VE NO TIME TO TALK!
CLENCH
Y-YOU'RE RIGHT, SETSUNA-SAN!
CLENCH
LET'S GET GOING!
WHERE'S THE LOVE? Y'KNOW?
OKAY, ASUNA-SAN, SEE YA!
...
TUD TUD TUD
DWAH?
ZWASH
HEY, GUYS! WAIT FOR ME-E-E!
I'M FEELING MUCH BETTER!
JUST... LEMME PUT SOME CLOTHES ON.
BWAAAN
OOH~~♡ HOW NICE IS A LATE-NIGHT SNEAK FROM THE HOTEL, HUH?
NOW, NOW—IT'S NOT AS IF WE'RE AT PLAY.
HE'S UP AGAINST PROS...
I HOPE NEGI-BŌZU IS ALL RIGHT.

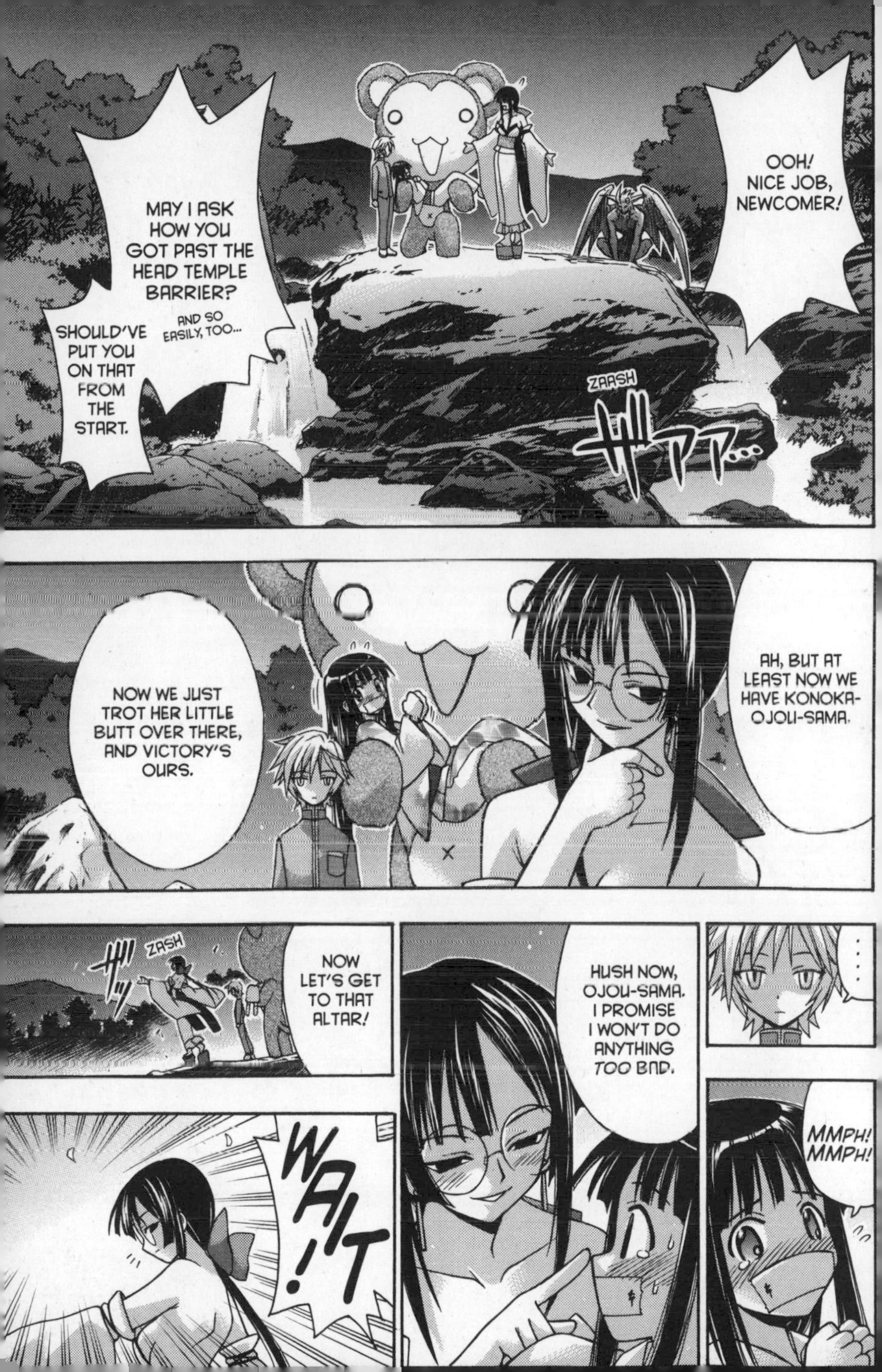
OOH! NICE JOB, NEWCOMER!
MAY I ASK HOW YOU GOT PAST THE HEAD TEMPLE BARRIER?
AND SO EASILY, TOO...
SHOULD'VE PUT YOU ON THAT FROM THE START.
ZAASH
AH, BUT AT LEAST NOW WE HAVE KONOKA-OJOU-SAMA.
NOW WE JUST TROT HER LITTLE BUTT OVER THERE, AND VICTORY'S OURS.
....
MMPH! MMPH!
HUSH NOW, OJOU-SAMA. I PROMISE I WON'T DO ANYTHING *TOO* BAD.
NOW LET'S GET TO THAT ALTAR!
ZASH
WAIT!!

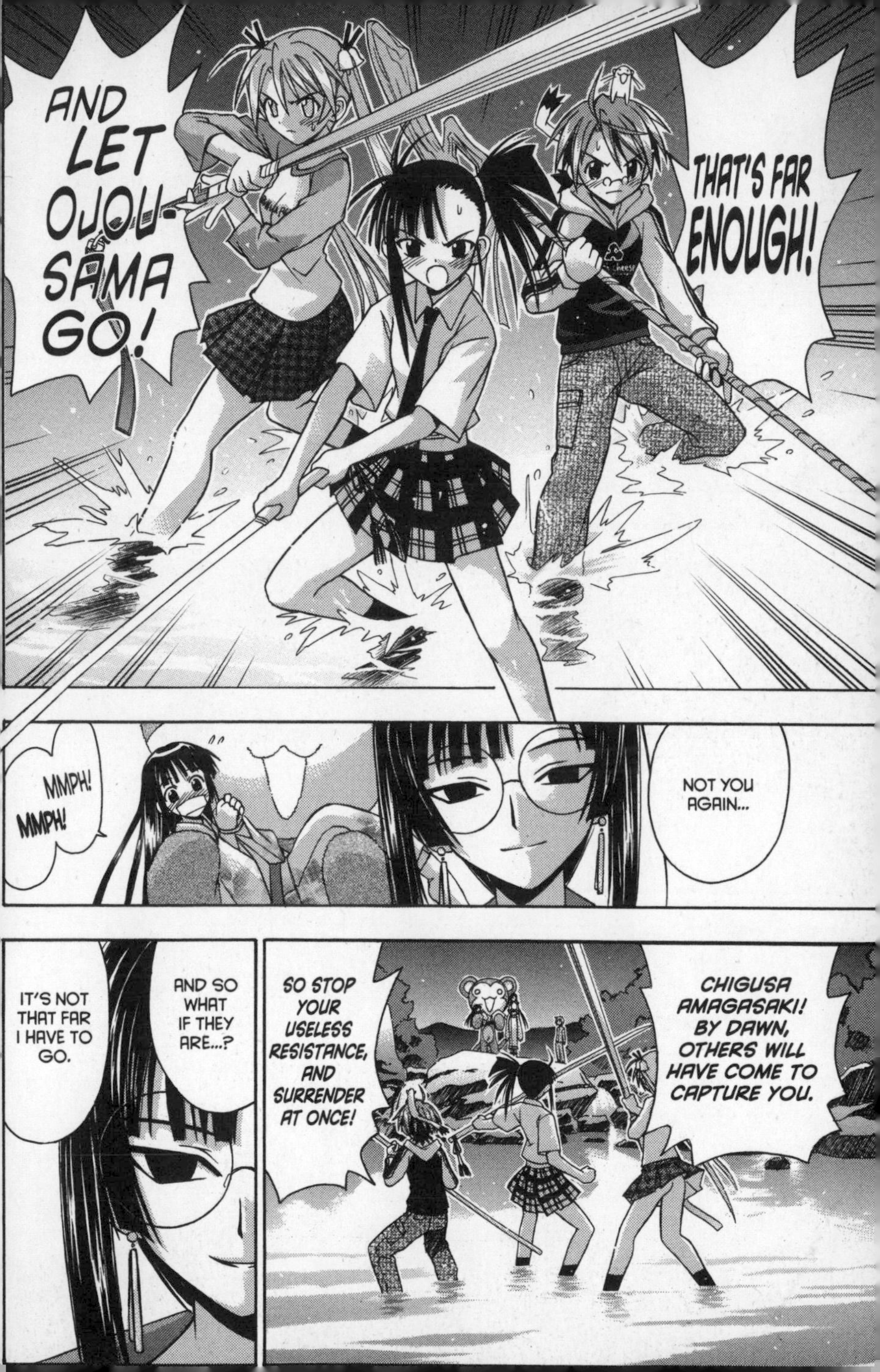
THAT'S FAR ENOUGH!
AND LET OJOU-SAMA GO!
NOT YOU AGAIN...
MMPH! MMPH!
CHIGUSA AMAGASAKI! BY DAWN, OTHERS WILL HAVE COME TO CAPTURE YOU.
SO STOP YOUR USELESS RESISTANCE, AND SURRENDER AT ONCE!
AND SO WHAT IF THEY ARE...?
IT'S NOT THAT FAR I HAVE TO GO.

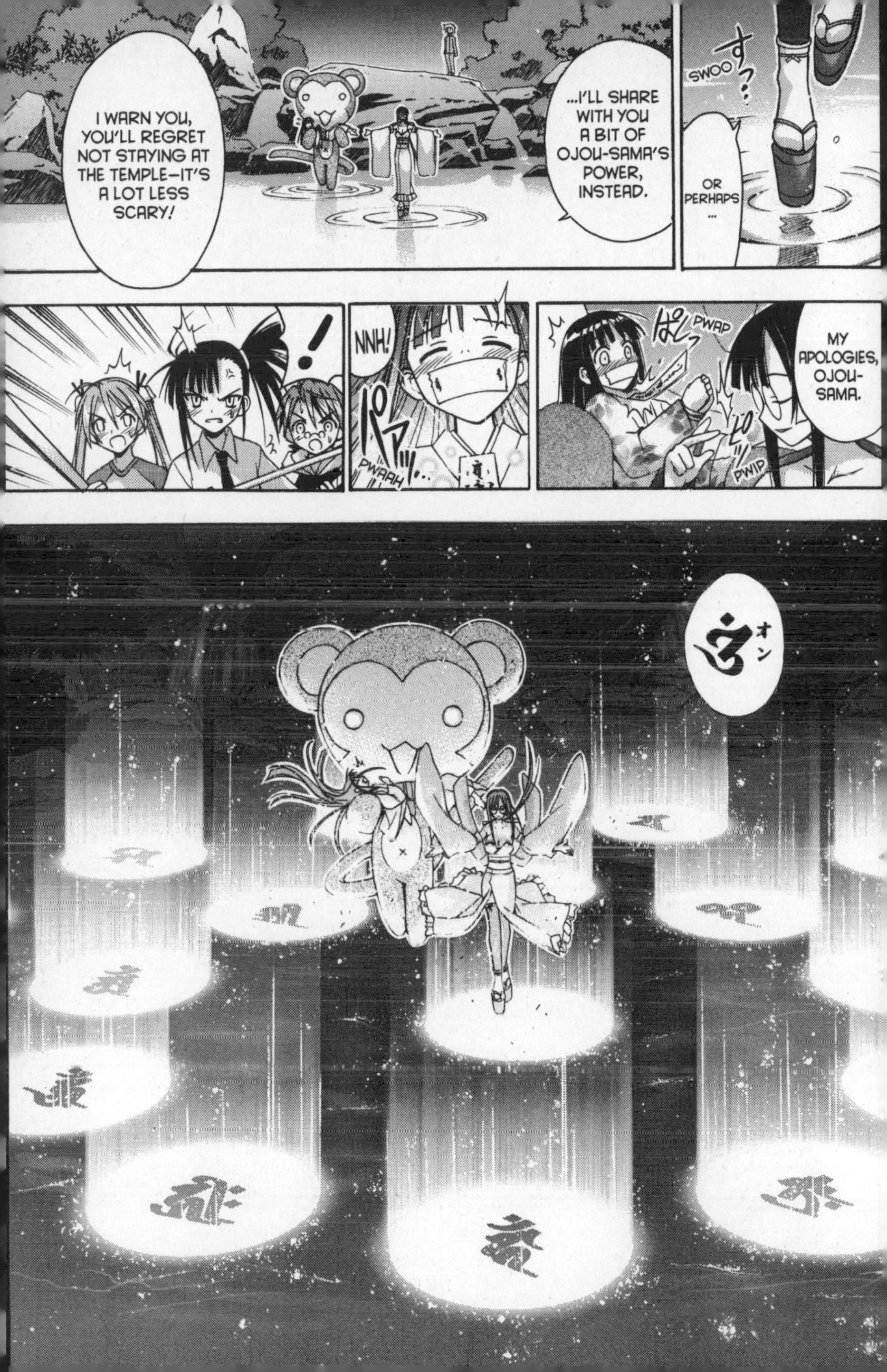
SWOO
OR PERHAPS ...
...I'LL SHARE WITH YOU A BIT OF OJOU-SAMA'S POWER, INSTEAD.
I WARN YOU, YOU'LL REGRET NOT STAYING AT THE TEMPLE—IT'S A LOT LESS SCARY!
PWAP
MY APOLOGIES, OJOU-SAMA.
PWIP
NNH!
PWAAH
!
オン

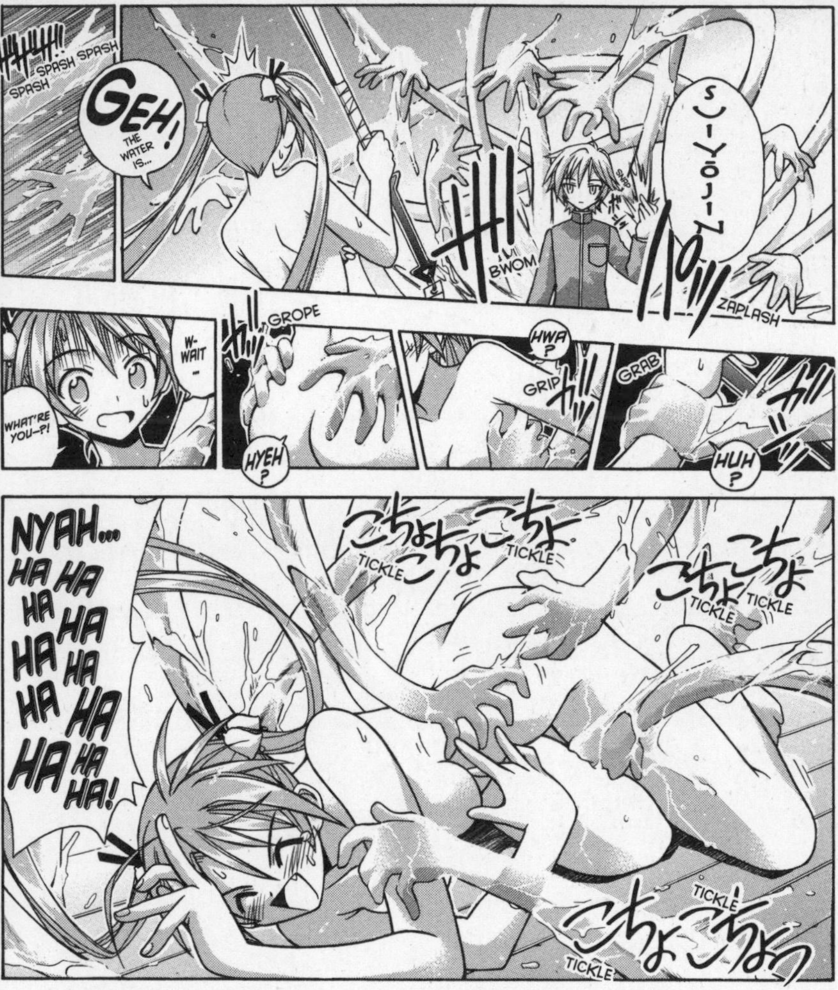
ZAPLASH
SUIYŌJIN
SNAP
BWOM
GEH!
THE WATER IS...
SPASH SPASH
SPASH
GRAB
HUH?
HWA?
GRIP
GROPE
HYEH?
W-WAIT...
WHAT'RE YOU—?!
TICKLE TICKLE
TICKLE TICKLE
NYAH... HA HA HA HA HA HA HA HA HA HA HA HA HA HA!
TICKLE
TICKLE

NEGIMA! FORTY-SIXTH PERIOD: LEXICON NEGIMARIUM

■वरि वन्दन

VARI VANDANA

In the 27th chapter of *Konjaku Monogatari-shû* (a Heian Period [twelfth-century] story collection), a watersprite inhabiting a lake near Yôsei-in (near the present-day Kyoto capitol building) teases and plays pranks on the face of a sleeping man before disappearing into a full bucket of water. The spell—which in Sanskrit means "water is the spell of binding"—uses the spirits of water to bind its target. In Asuna's case, however, the spell seems to come off not *quite* the way it may have been intended....

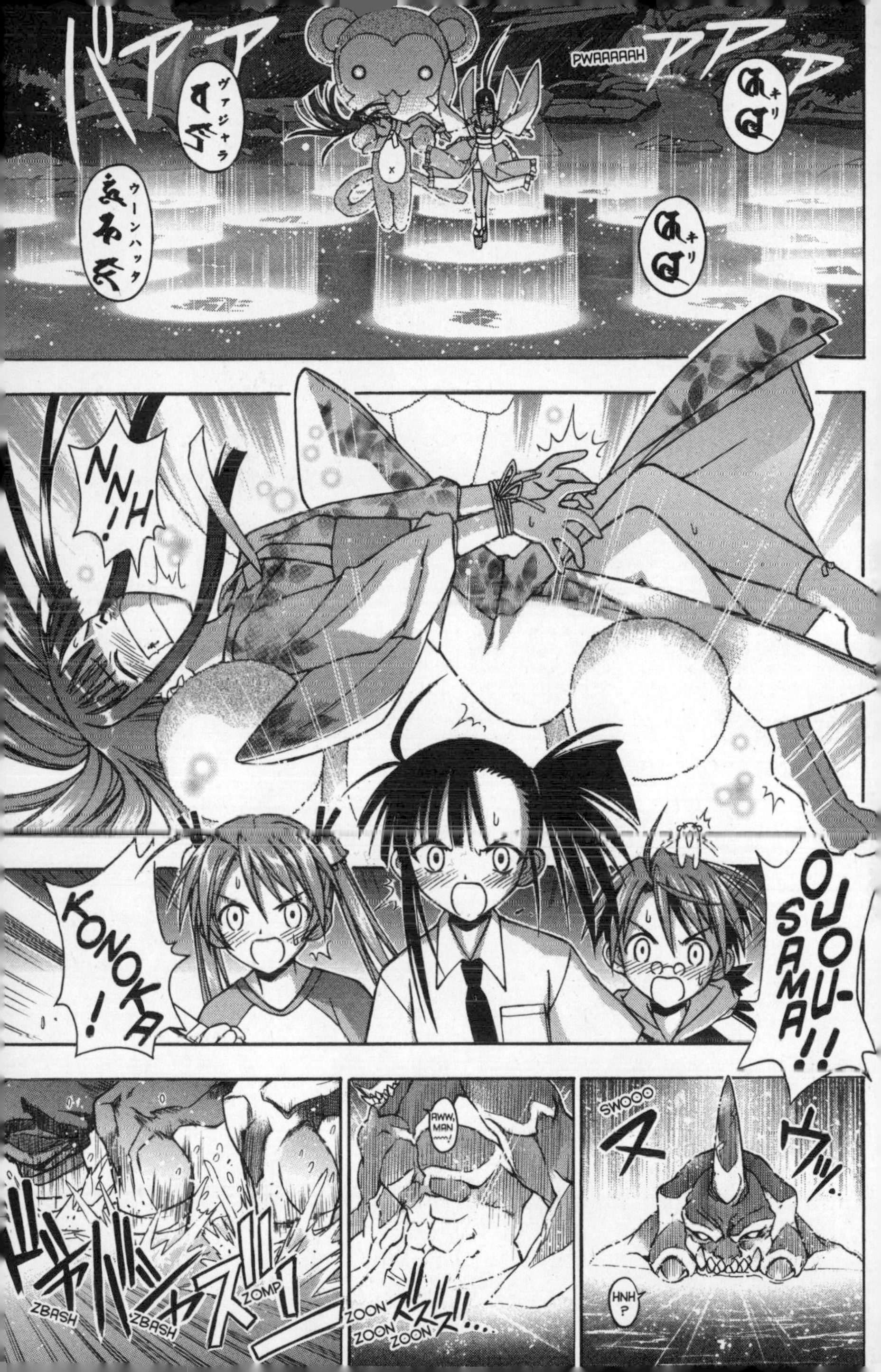
PWAAAAAH
キリ
キリ
ヴァジャラ
ウーンハッタ
NNH!
OJOU-SAMA!!
KONOKA!
SWOOO
HNH?
AWW, MAN~!
ZOON ZOON ZOON
ZBASH ZBASH ZOMP

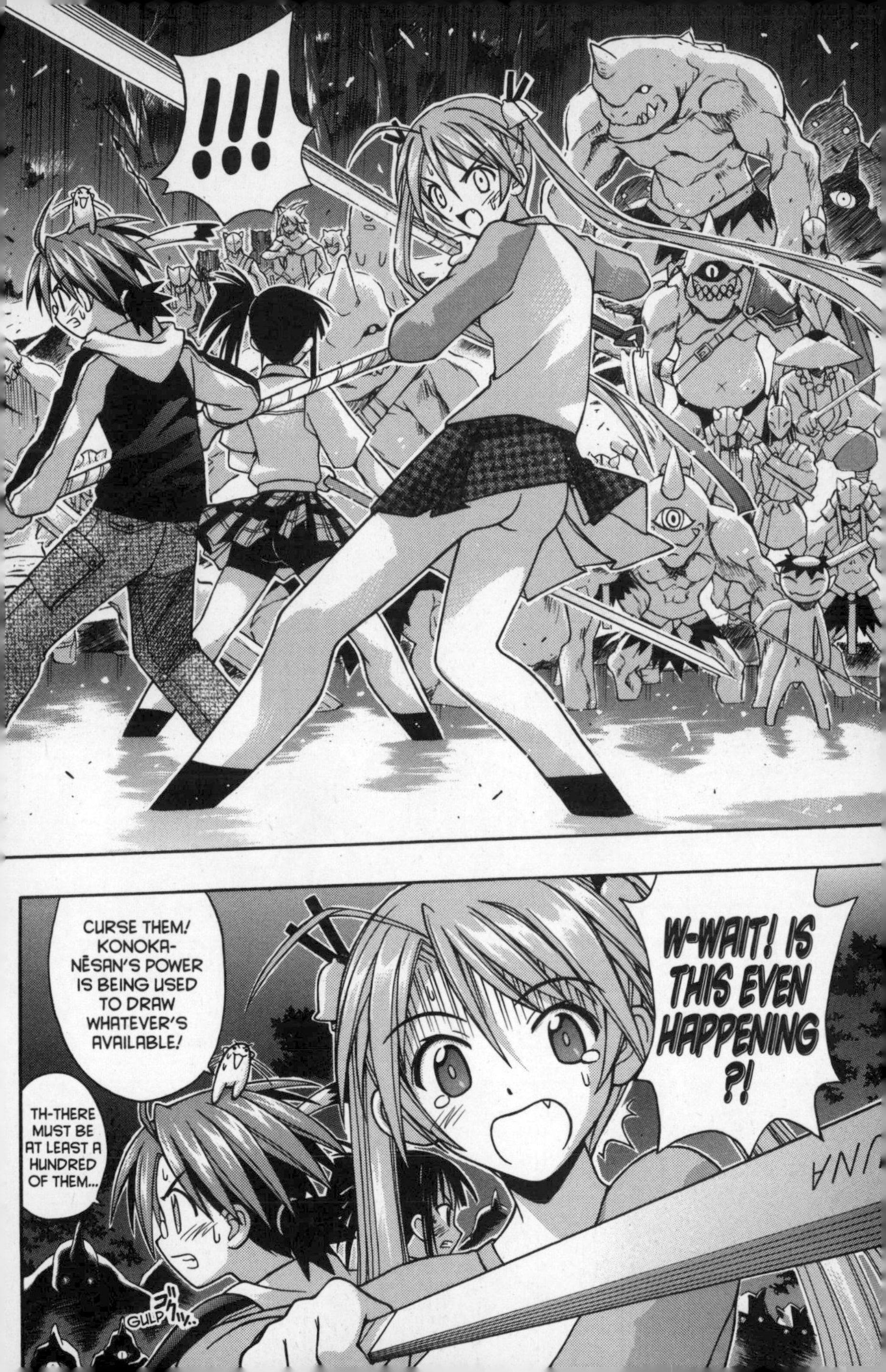
!!!
W-WAIT! IS THIS EVEN HAPPENING ?!
CURSE THEM! KONOKA-NĒSAN'S POWER IS BEING USED TO DRAW WHATEVER'S AVAILABLE!
TH-THERE MUST BE AT LEAST A HUNDRED OF THEM...
GULP

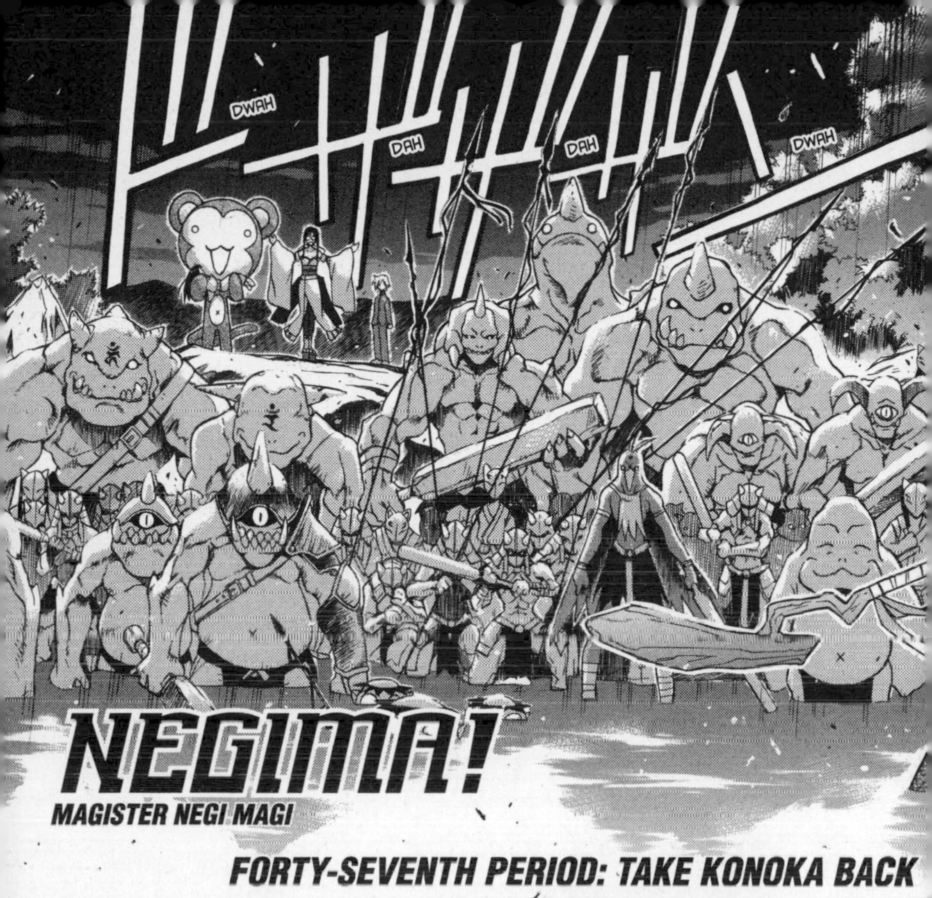
DWAH
DAH
DAH
DWAH
NEGIMA!
MAGISTER NEGI MAGI
FORTY-SEVENTH PERIOD: TAKE KONOKA BACK

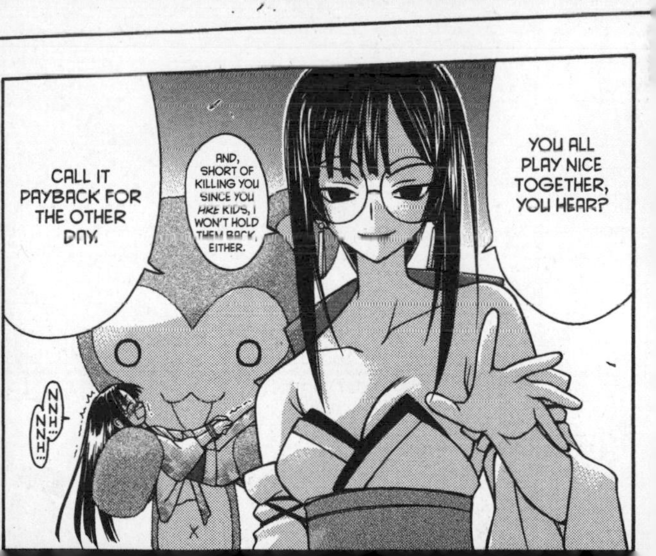
YOU ALL PLAY NICE TOGETHER, YOU HEAR?
AND, SHORT OF KILLING YOU SINCE YOU ARE KIDS, I WON'T HOLD THEM BACK, EITHER.
CALL IT PAYBACK FOR THE OTHER DAY.
NNH... NNH...

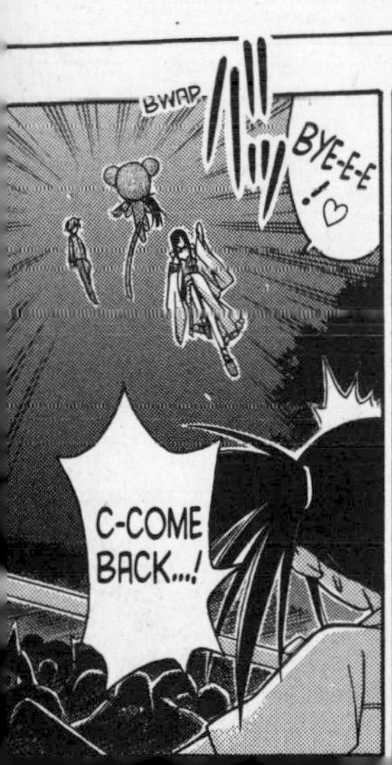
BWAP
BYE-E-E-E!♡
C-COME BACK...!

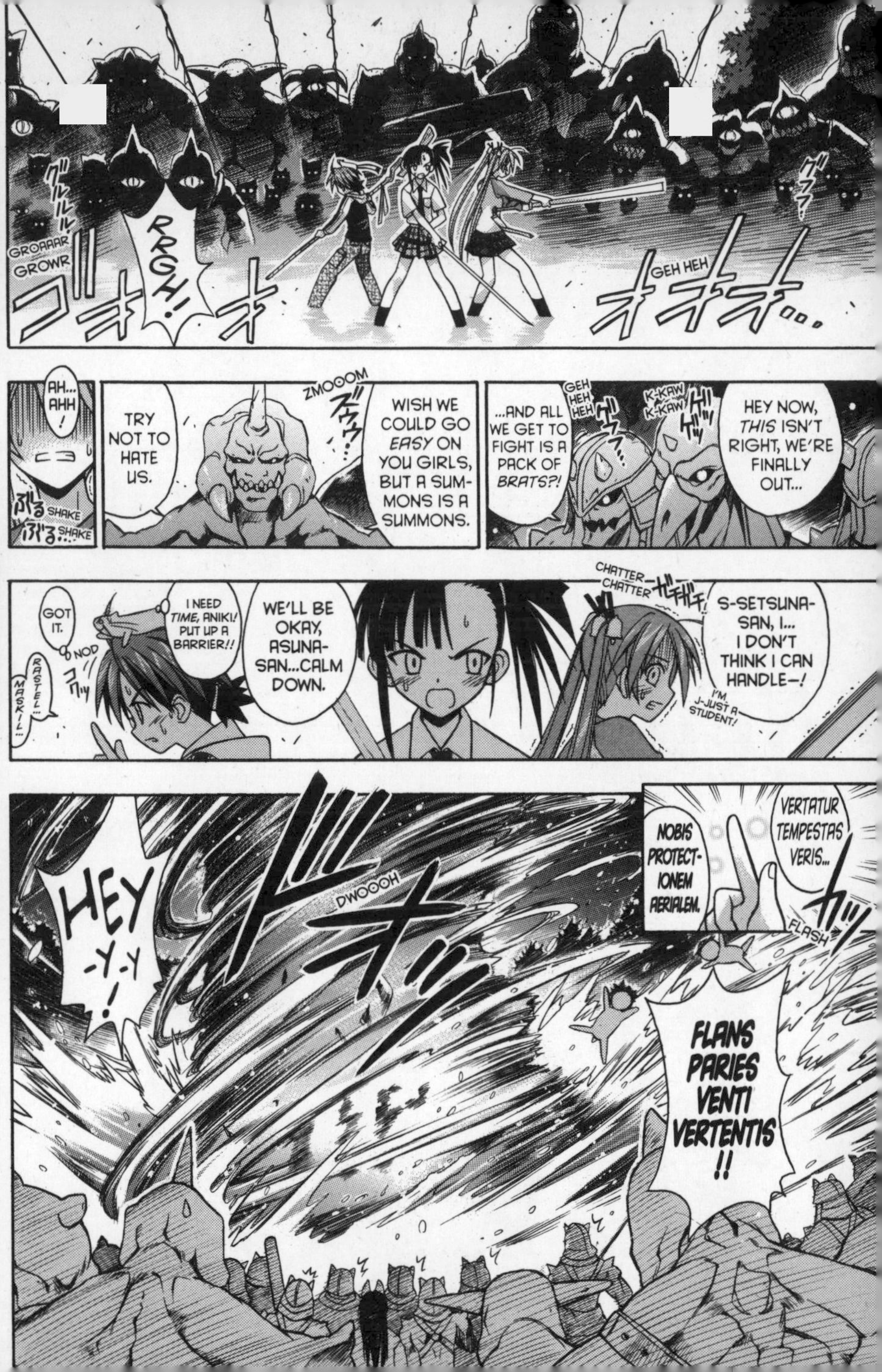
GEH HEH
GROAAAR GROWR
RRGH!!
HEY NOW, THIS ISN'T RIGHT, WE'RE FINALLY OUT...
K-KAW K-KAW
GEH HEH HEH
...AND ALL WE GET TO FIGHT IS A PACK OF BRATS?!
ZMOOOM
WISH WE COULD GO EASY ON YOU GIRLS, BUT A SUMMONS IS A SUMMONS.
TRY NOT TO HATE US.
AH... AHH!
SHAKE SHAKE
CHATTER CHATTER
S-SETSUNA-SAN, I... I DON'T THINK I CAN HANDLE—!
I'M J-JUST A STUDENT!
WE'LL BE OKAY, ASUNA-SAN...CALM DOWN.
I NEED TIME, ANIKI! PUT UP A BARRIER!!
GOT IT.
NOD
RASTEL... MASKIL...
VERTATUR TEMPESTAS VERIS...
NOBIS PROTECTIONEM AERIALEM.
FLASH
FLANS PARIES VENTI VERTENTIS!!
DWOOOH
HEY-Y-Y!

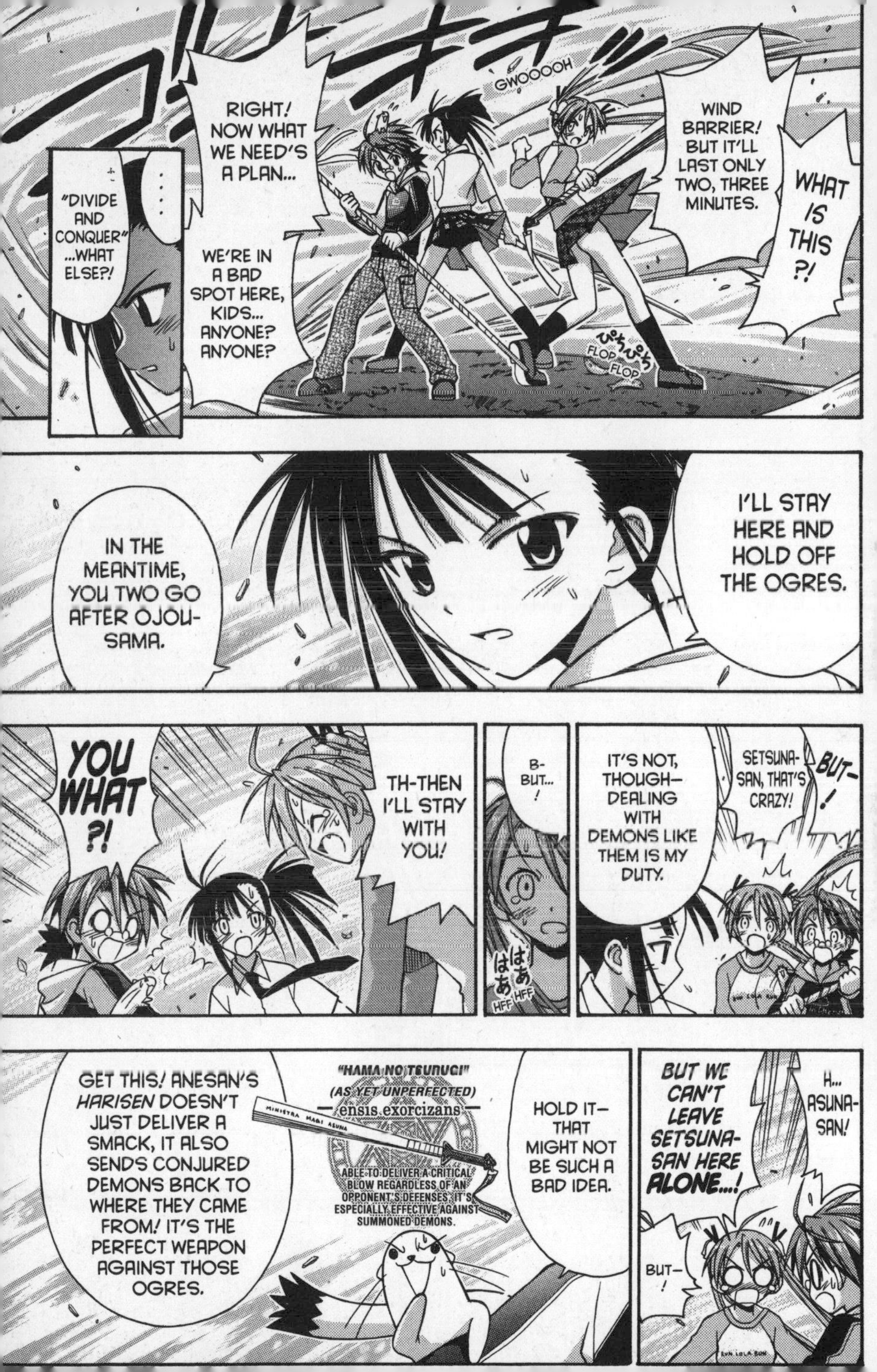
WHAT IS THIS?!
WIND BARRIER! BUT IT'LL LAST ONLY TWO, THREE MINUTES.
GWOOOOH
RIGHT! NOW WHAT WE NEED'S A PLAN...
WE'RE IN A BAD SPOT HERE, KIDS... ANYONE? ANYONE?
FLOP FLOP
....
"DIVIDE AND CONQUER" ...WHAT ELSE?!
I'LL STAY HERE AND HOLD OFF THE OGRES.
IN THE MEANTIME, YOU TWO GO AFTER OJOU-SAMA.
BUT—!
SETSUNA-SAN, THAT'S CRAZY!
IT'S NOT, THOUGH—DEALING WITH DEMONS LIKE THEM IS MY DUTY.
B-BUT...!
HFF HFF
TH-THEN I'LL STAY WITH YOU!
YOU WHAT?!
H... ASUNA-SAN!
BUT WE CAN'T LEAVE SETSUNA-SAN HERE ALONE...!
BUT—!
HOLD IT—THAT MIGHT NOT BE SUCH A BAD IDEA.
"HAMA NO TSURUGI" (AS YET UNPERFECTED)
ensis exorcizans
ABLE TO DELIVER A CRITICAL BLOW REGARDLESS OF AN OPPONENT'S DEFENSES. IT'S ESPECIALLY EFFECTIVE AGAINST SUMMONED DEMONS.
GET THIS! ANESAN'S HARISEN DOESN'T JUST DELIVER A SMACK, IT ALSO SENDS CONJURED DEMONS BACK TO WHERE THEY CAME FROM! IT'S THE PERFECT WEAPON AGAINST THOSE OGRES.

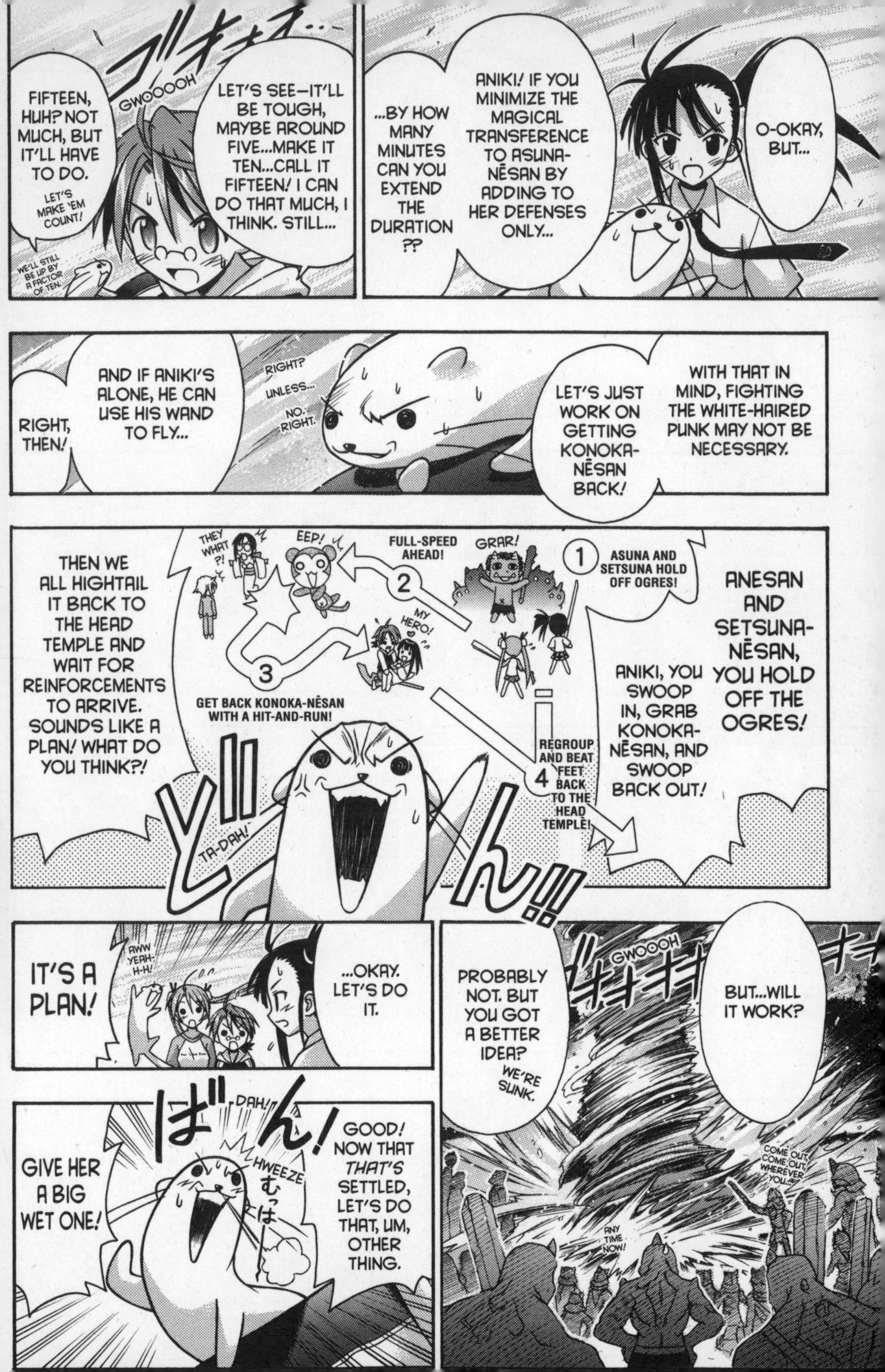

O-OKAY, BUT...
ANIKI! IF YOU MINIMIZE THE MAGICAL TRANSFERENCE TO ASUNA-NĒSAN BY ADDING TO HER DEFENSES ONLY...
...BY HOW MANY MINUTES CAN YOU EXTEND THE DURATION ??
LET'S SEE—IT'LL BE TOUGH, MAYBE AROUND FIVE...MAKE IT TEN...CALL IT FIFTEEN! I CAN DO THAT MUCH, I THINK. STILL...
GWOOOOH
FIFTEEN, HUH? NOT MUCH, BUT IT'LL HAVE TO DO.
LET'S MAKE 'EM COUNT!
WE'LL STILL BE UP BY A FACTOR OF TEN.
WITH THAT IN MIND, FIGHTING THE WHITE-HAIRED PUNK MAY NOT BE NECESSARY.
LET'S JUST WORK ON GETTING KONOKA-NĒSAN BACK!
RIGHT?
UNLESS...
NO. RIGHT.
AND IF ANIKI'S ALONE, HE CAN USE HIS WAND TO FLY...
RIGHT, THEN!
ANESAN AND SETSUNA-NĒSAN, YOU HOLD OFF THE OGRES!
ANIKI, YOU SWOOP IN, GRAB KONOKA-NĒSAN, AND SWOOP BACK OUT!
1 ASUNA AND SETSUNA HOLD OFF OGRES!
GRAR!
2 FULL-SPEED AHEAD!
EEP!
THEY WHAT ?!
3 GET BACK KONOKA-NĒSAN WITH A HIT-AND-RUN!
MY HERO!
4 REGROUP AND BEAT FEET BACK TO THE HEAD TEMPLE!
THEN WE ALL HIGHTAIL IT BACK TO THE HEAD TEMPLE AND WAIT FOR REINFORCEMENTS TO ARRIVE. SOUNDS LIKE A PLAN! WHAT DO YOU THINK?!
TA-DAH!
BUT...WILL IT WORK?
GWOOOH
PROBABLY NOT. BUT YOU GOT A BETTER IDEA?
WE'RE SUNK.
COME OUT, COME OUT, WHEREVER YOU...
ANY TIME NOW!
...OKAY. LET'S DO IT.
AWW YEAH-H-H!
IT'S A PLAN!
GOOD! NOW THAT THAT'S SETTLED, LET'S DO THAT, UM, OTHER THING.
HWEEZE
DAH!
GIVE HER A BIG WET ONE!

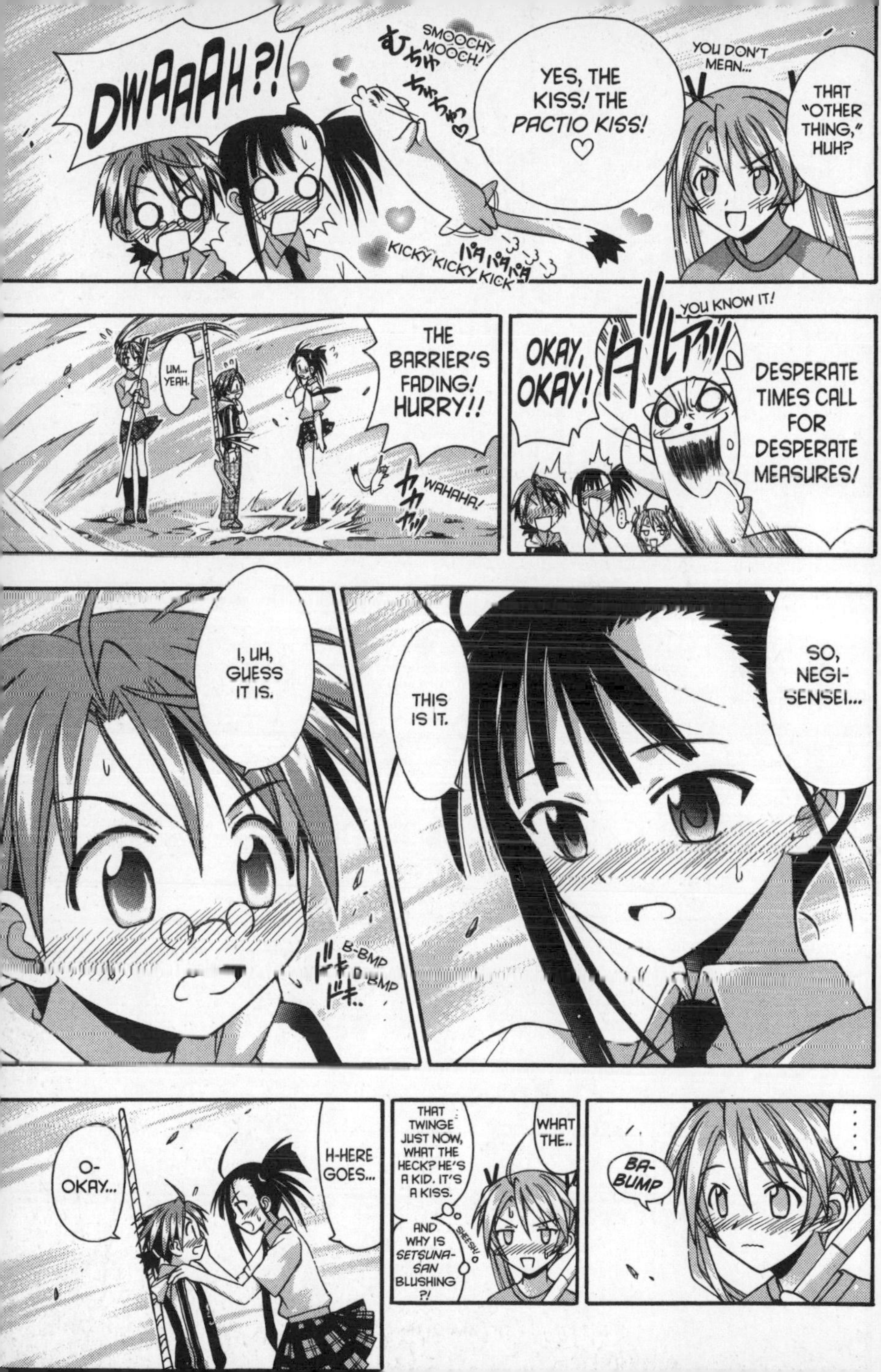

YOU DON'T MEAN...
THAT "OTHER THING," HUH?
YES, THE KISS! THE PACTIO KISS! ♡
SMOOCHY MOOCH!
DWAAAH?!
KICKY KICKY KICK
YOU KNOW IT!
DESPERATE TIMES CALL FOR DESPERATE MEASURES!
OKAY, OKAY!
THE BARRIER'S FADING! HURRY!!
WAHAHA!
UM... YEAH.
SO, NEGI-SENSEI...
THIS IS IT.
I, UH, GUESS IT IS.
B-BMP B-BMP
...
BA-BUMP
WHAT THE..
THAT TWINGE JUST NOW, WHAT THE HECK? HE'S A KID. IT'S A KISS.
AND WHY IS SETSUNA-SAN BLUSHING?!
SHEESH!
H-HERE GOES...
O-OKAY...

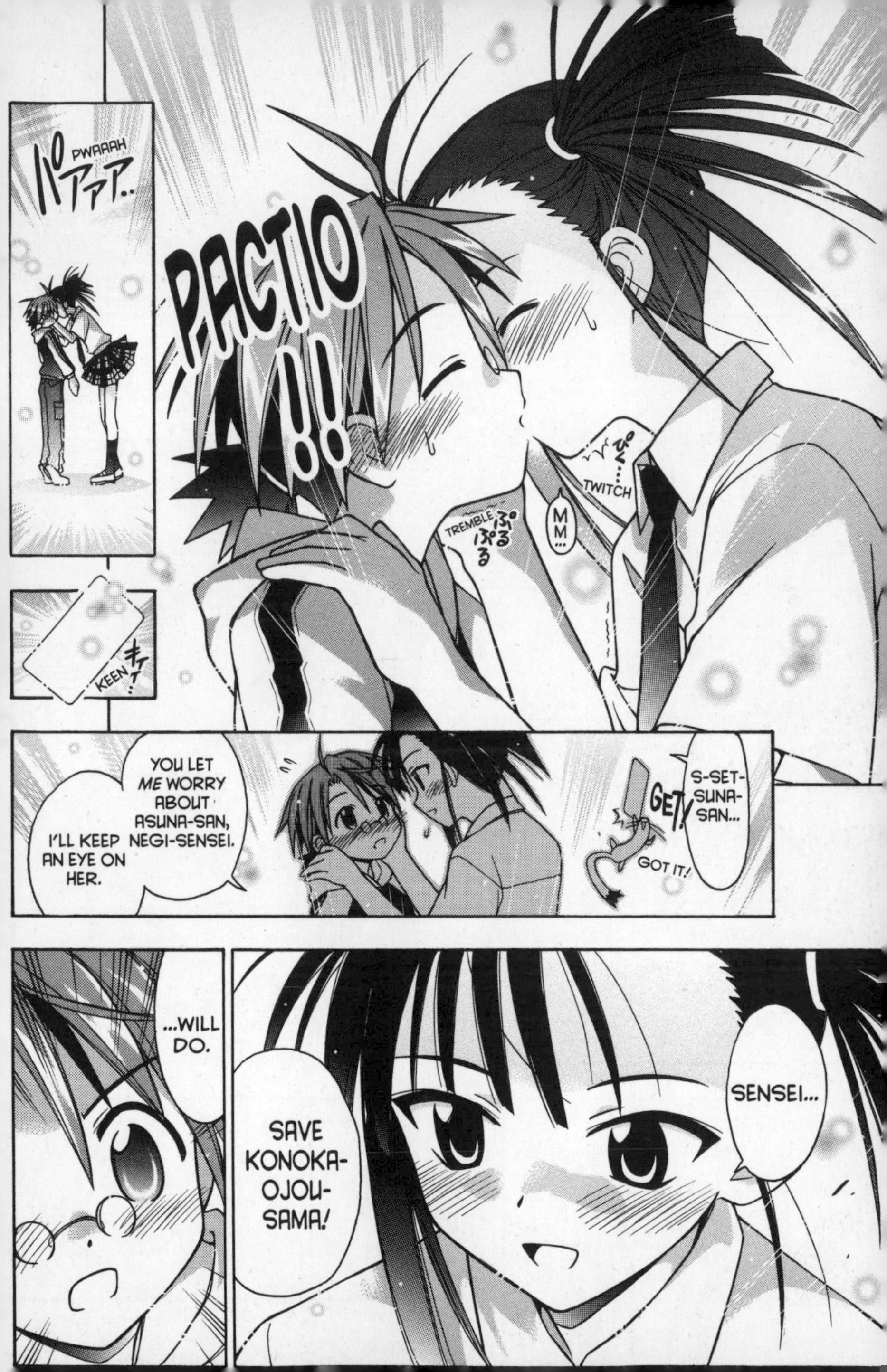
ぴく…
TWITCH
MM...
TREMBLE
ぷるぷる
PACTIO!!
パァァア..
PWAAAH
KEEN
S-SET-SUNA-SAN...
GET!
GOT IT!
YOU LET ME WORRY ABOUT ASUNA-SAN, NEGI-SENSEI.
I'LL KEEP AN EYE ON HER.
SENSEI...
SAVE KONOKA-OJOU-SAMA!
...WILL DO.

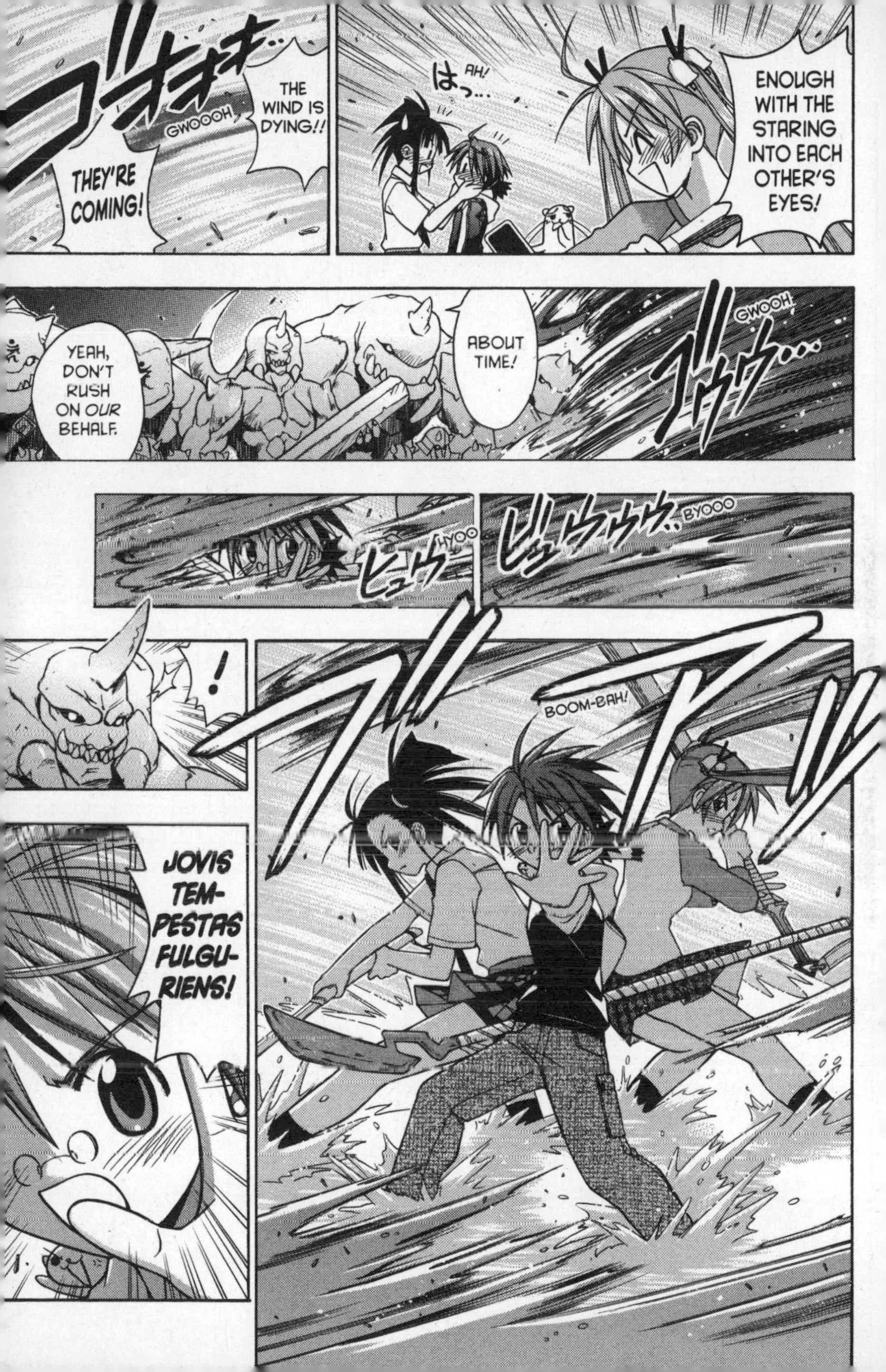
ENOUGH WITH THE STARING INTO EACH OTHER'S EYES!
はっ…
AH!
THE WIND IS DYING!!
GWOOOH
THEY'RE COMING!
GWOOOH
ABOUT TIME!
YEAH, DON'T RUSH ON *OUR* BEHALF.
BYOOO
HYOO
BOOM-BAH!
!
JOVIS TEMPESTAS FULGURIENS!

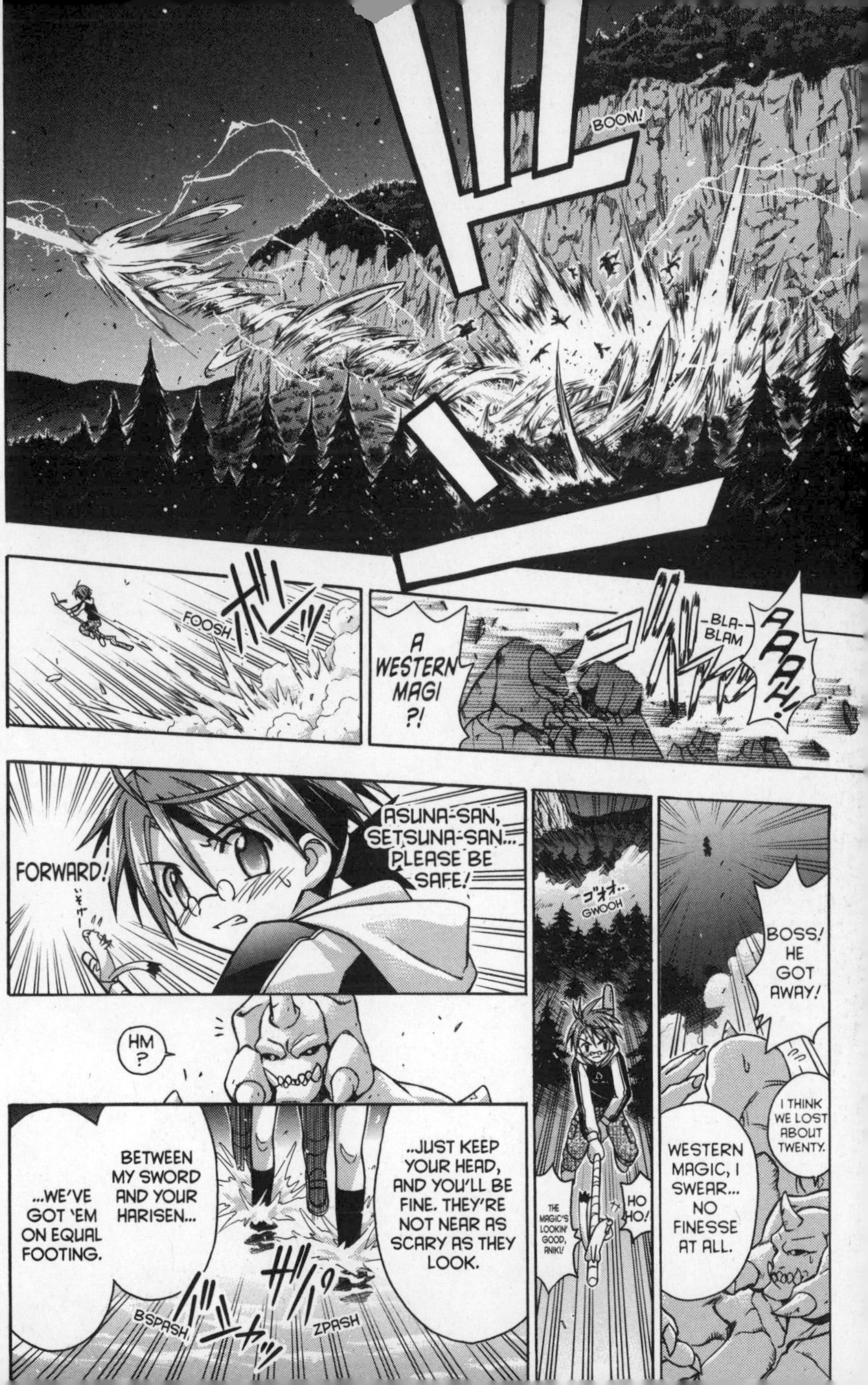
BOOM!
AAAH!
BLA-BLAM
A WESTERN MAGI?!
FOOSH
BOSS! HE GOT AWAY!
I THINK WE LOST ABOUT TWENTY.
WESTERN MAGIC, I SWEAR... NO FINESSE AT ALL.
GWOOH
HO HO!
THE MAGIC'S LOOKIN' GOOD, ANIKI!
ASUNA-SAN, SETSUNA-SAN... PLEASE BE SAFE!
FORWARD!
HM?
...JUST KEEP YOUR HEAD, AND YOU'LL BE FINE. THEY'RE NOT NEAR AS SCARY AS THEY LOOK.
BETWEEN MY SWORD AND YOUR HARISEN...
...WE'VE GOT 'EM ON EQUAL FOOTING.
ZPASH
BSPASH

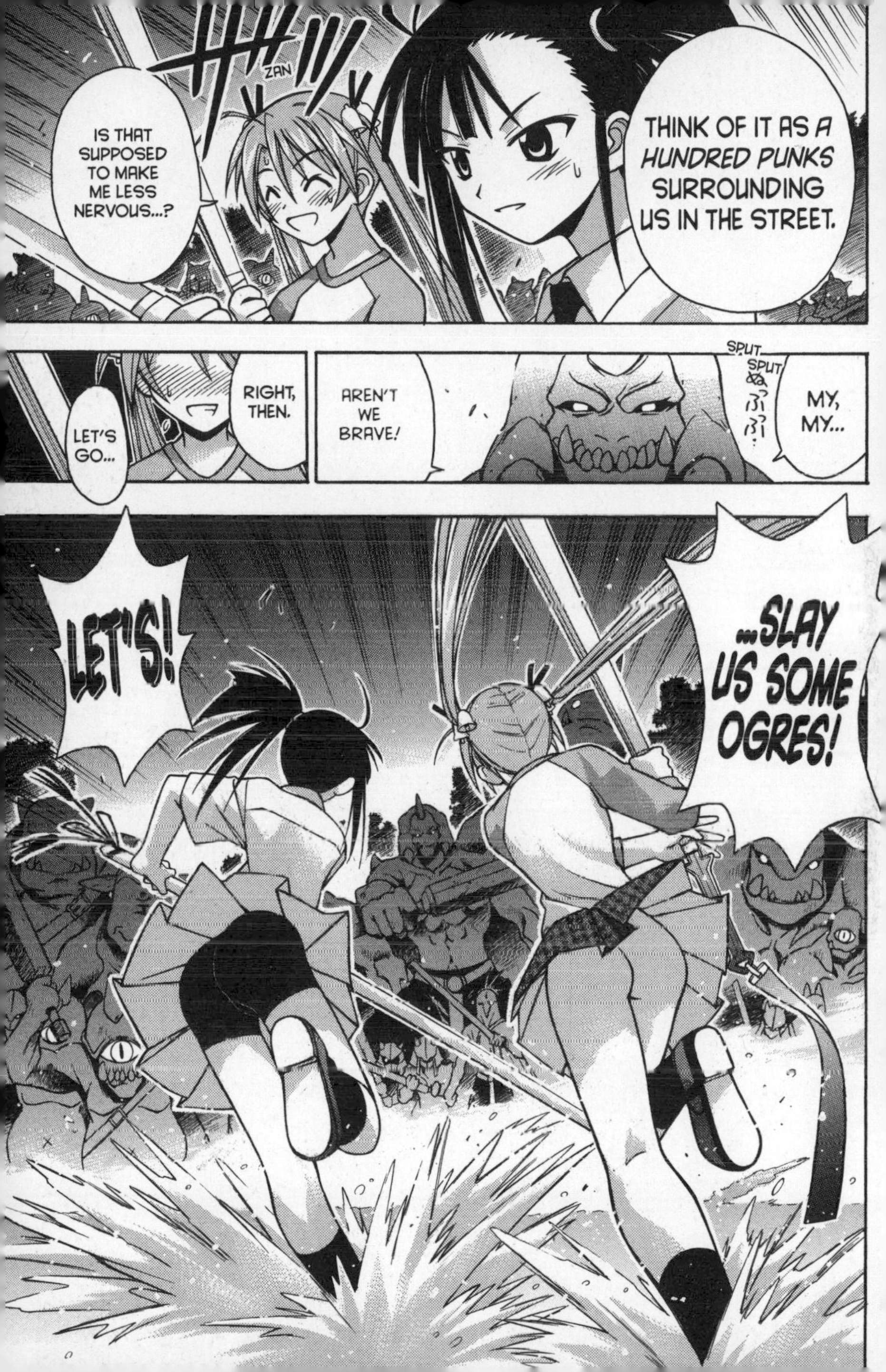
ZAN
THINK OF IT AS A HUNDRED PUNKS SURROUNDING US IN THE STREET.
IS THAT SUPPOSED TO MAKE ME LESS NERVOUS...?
SPUT SPUT
MY, MY...
AREN'T WE BRAVE!
RIGHT, THEN.
LET'S GO...
LET'S!
...SLAY US SOME OGRES!

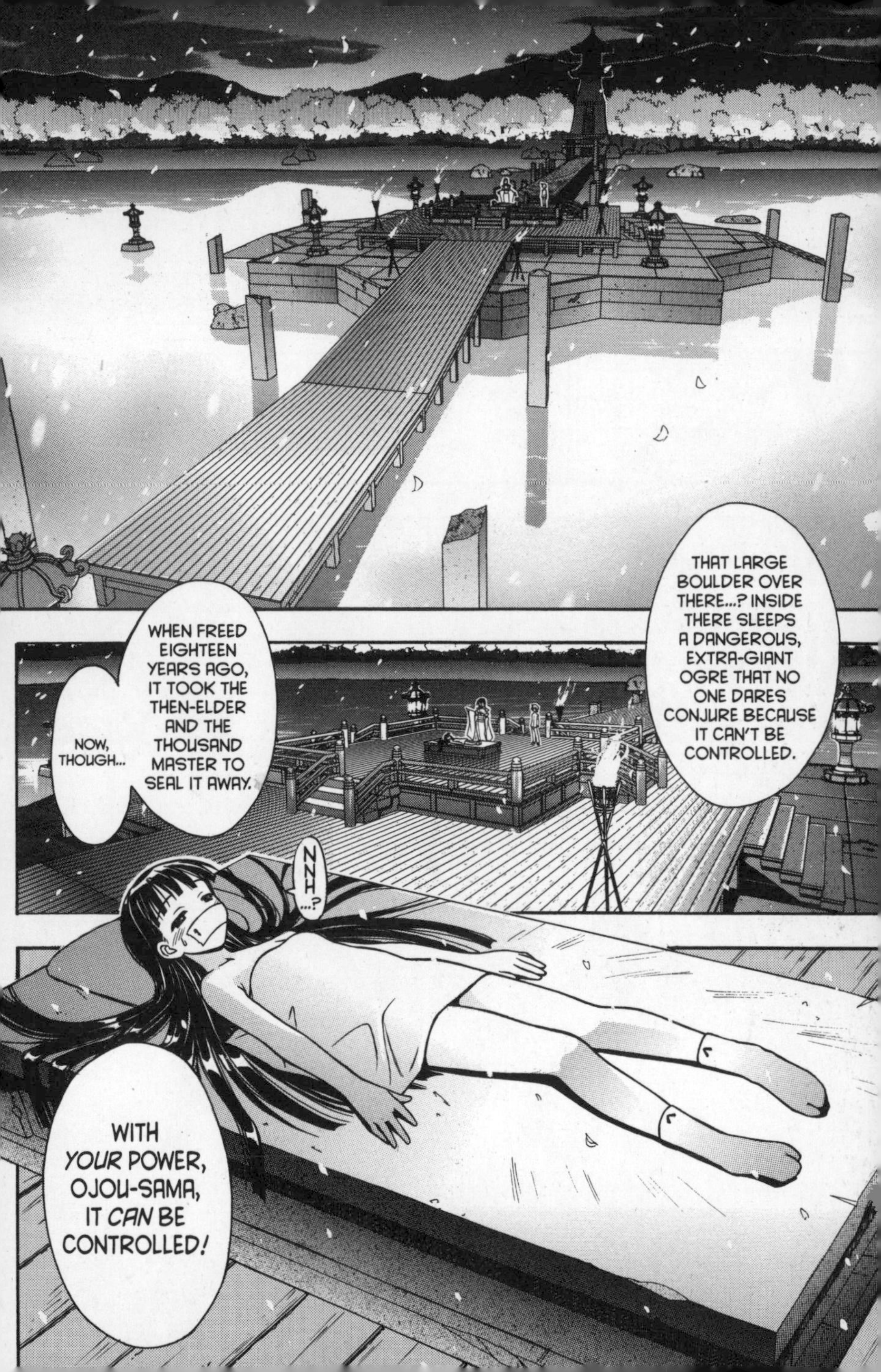
THAT LARGE BOULDER OVER THERE...? INSIDE THERE SLEEPS A DANGEROUS, EXTRA-GIANT OGRE THAT NO ONE DARES CONJURE BECAUSE IT CAN'T BE CONTROLLED.
WHEN FREED EIGHTEEN YEARS AGO, IT TOOK THE THEN-ELDER AND THE THOUSAND MASTER TO SEAL IT AWAY.
NOW, THOUGH...
NNH...?
WITH *YOUR* POWER, OJOU-SAMA, IT *CAN* BE CONTROLLED!

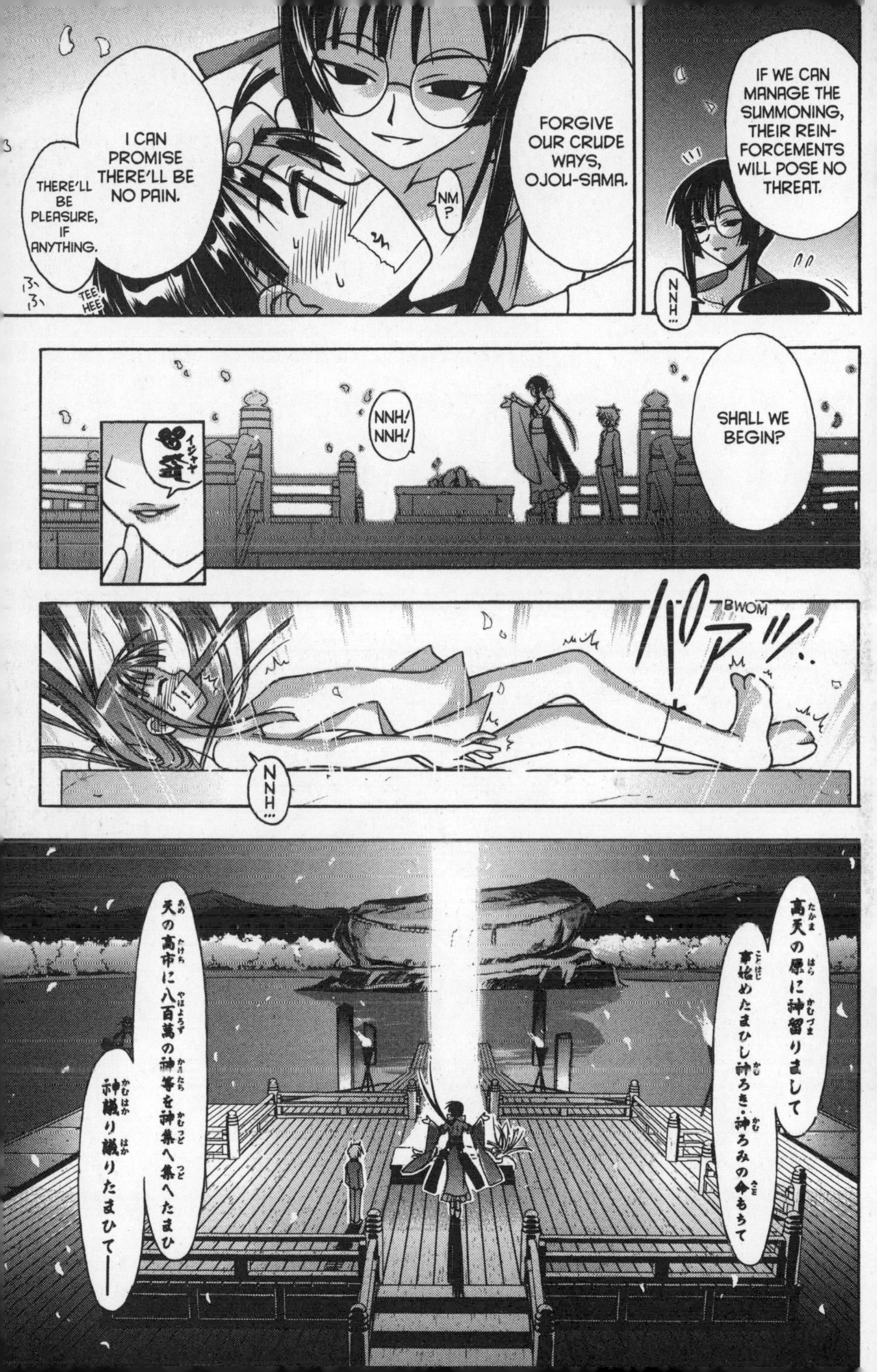
IF WE CAN MANAGE THE SUMMONING, THEIR REINFORCEMENTS WILL POSE NO THREAT.
NNH...
FORGIVE OUR CRUDE WAYS, OJOU-SAMA.
NM?
I CAN PROMISE THERE'LL BE NO PAIN.
THERE'LL BE PLEASURE, IF ANYTHING.
ふふ
TEE HEE
SHALL WE BEGIN?
NNH! NNH!
BWOM
パァッ
NNH...
高天の原に神留りまして
事始めたまひし神ろき・神ろみの命もちて
天の高市に八百萬の神等を神集へ集へたまひ
神議り議りたまひて——

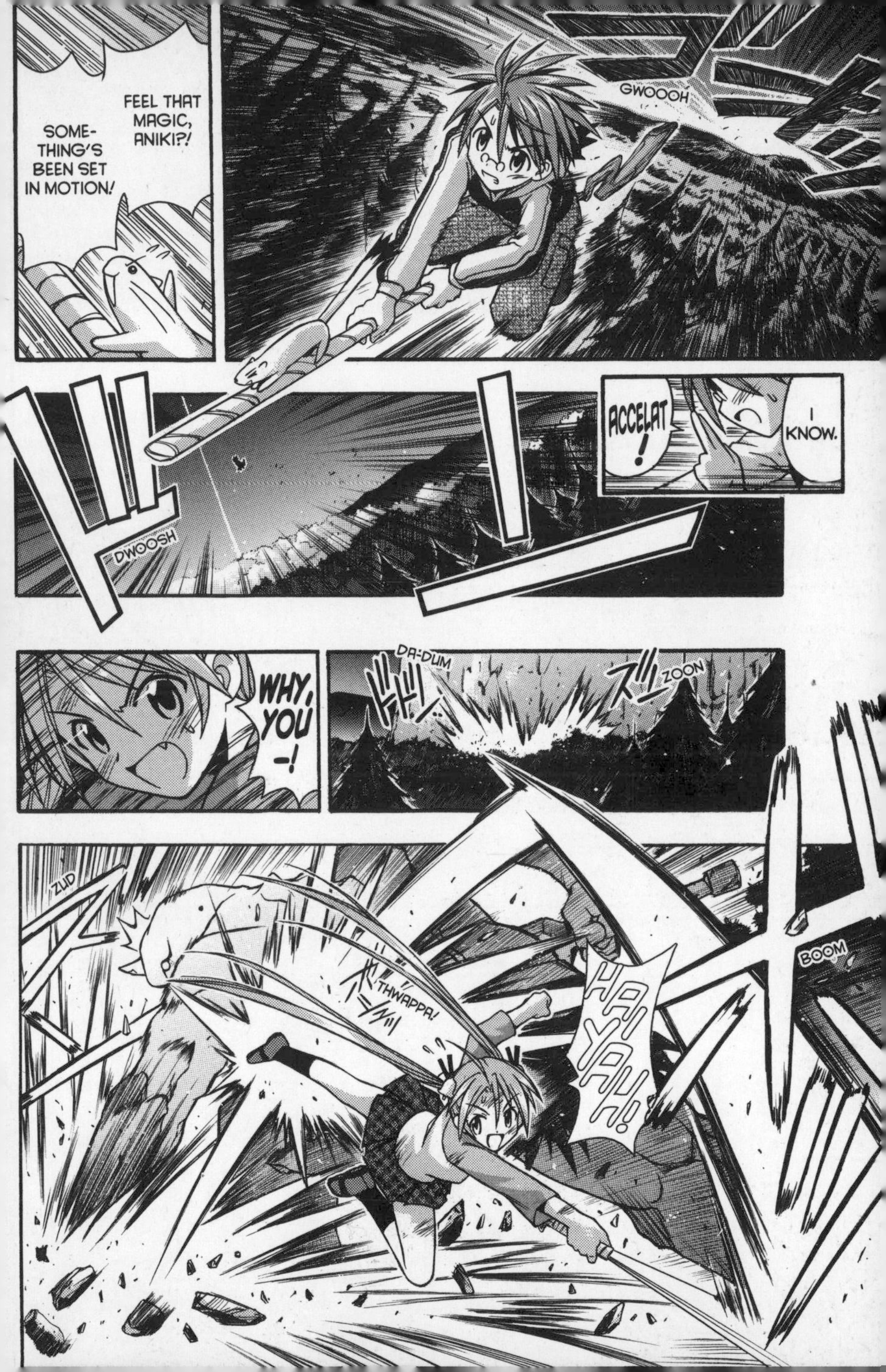
GWOOOH
FEEL THAT MAGIC, ANIKI?!
SOME-THING'S BEEN SET IN MOTION!
I KNOW.
ACCELAT!
DWOOSH
DA-DUM
ZOON
WHY, YOU-!
BOOM
HAI-YAH!
THWAPPA!
ZUD

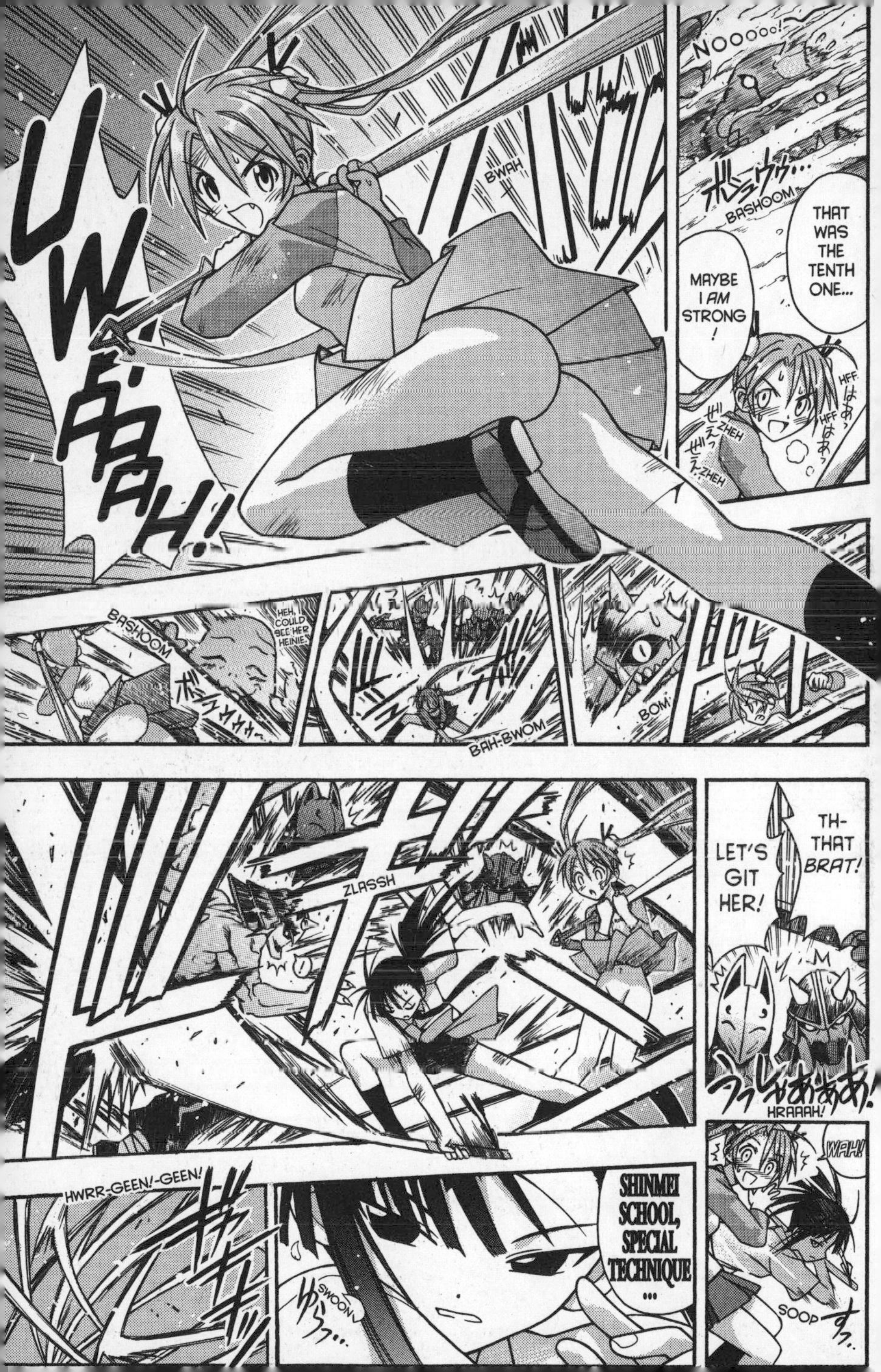
NOOOOO!
BASHOOM
THAT WAS THE TENTH ONE...
MAYBE I AM STRONG!
HFF
HFF
ZHEH
ZHEH
BWAH
UWAAAH!
BOM
BAH-BWOM
HEH, COULD SEE HER HEINIE.
BASHOOM
TH-THAT BRAT!
LET'S GIT HER!
HRAAAH!
ZLASSH
WAH!
SOOP
SHINMEI SCHOOL, SPECIAL TECHNIQUE...
SWOON
HWRR-GEEN!-GEEN!

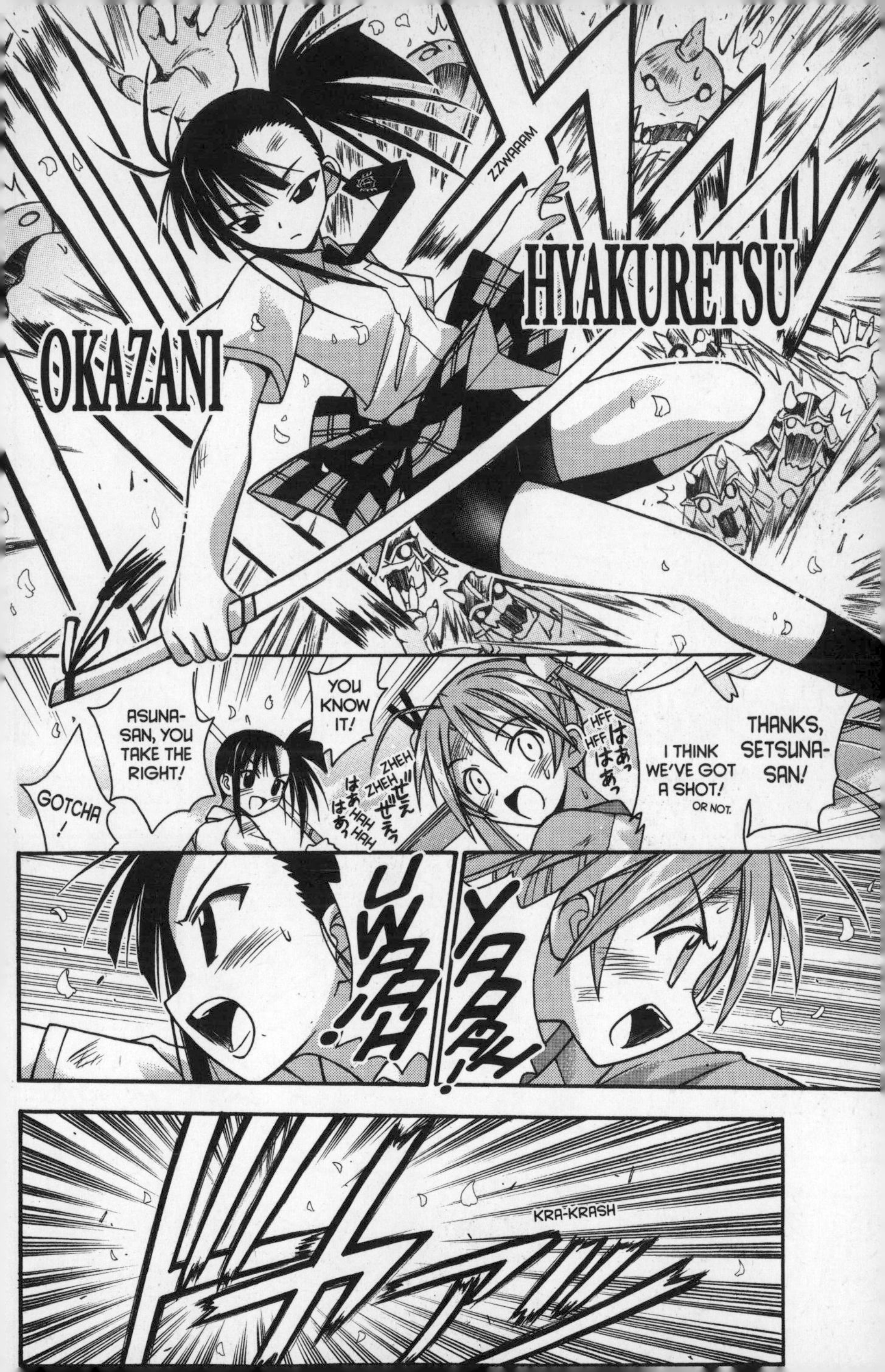
ZZWAAAM
HYAKURETSU
OKAZANI
THANKS, SETSUNA-SAN!
I THINK WE'VE GOT A SHOT!
OR NOT.
HFF HFF はあっ はあっ
YOU KNOW IT!
ZHEH ZHEH ぜぇ ぜぇっ
HAH HAH はあ はあっ
ASUNA-SAN, YOU TAKE THE RIGHT!
GOTCHA!
YAAAH!
UWAAH!
KRA-KRASH

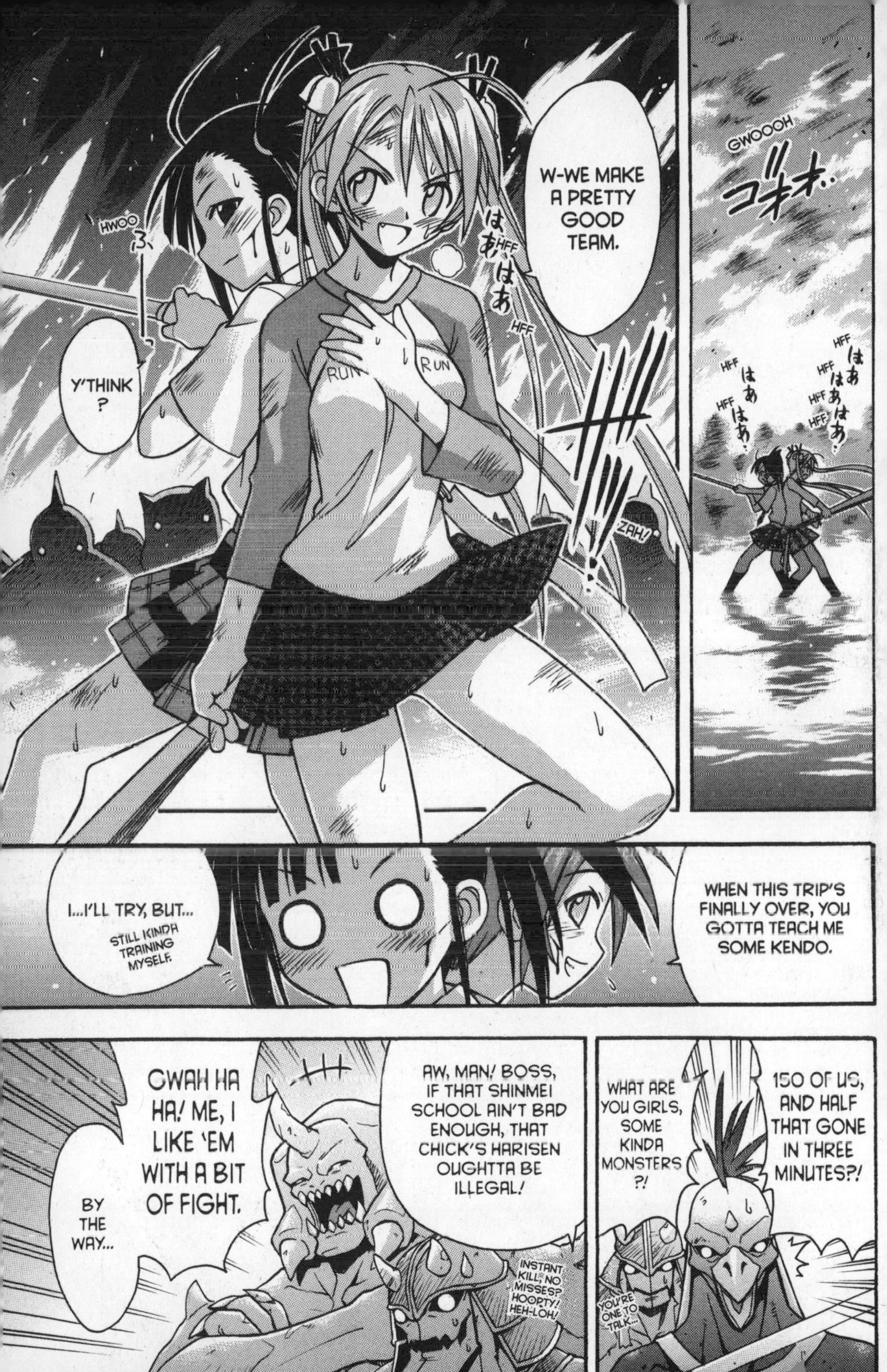
GWOOOH
ゴオオ…
HFF はあ
HFF はあ
HFF はあ
HFF はあ
HFF はあ
HFF はあ。
W-WE MAKE A PRETTY GOOD TEAM.
HFF はあ
HFF はあ
HWOO ふ
Y'THINK?
ZAH!
RUN
RUN
WHEN THIS TRIP'S FINALLY OVER, YOU GOTTA TEACH ME SOME KENDO.
I...I'LL TRY, BUT...
STILL KINDA TRAINING MYSELF.
150 OF US, AND HALF THAT GONE IN THREE MINUTES?!
WHAT ARE YOU GIRLS, SOME KINDA MONSTERS?!
YOU'RE ONE TO TALK...
AW, MAN! BOSS, IF THAT SHINMEI SCHOOL AIN'T BAD ENOUGH, THAT CHICK'S HARISEN OUGHTTA BE ILLEGAL!
INSTANT KILL, NO MISSES? HOORTY! HEH-LOH!
GWAH HA HA! ME, I LIKE 'EM WITH A BIT OF FIGHT.
BY THE WAY...

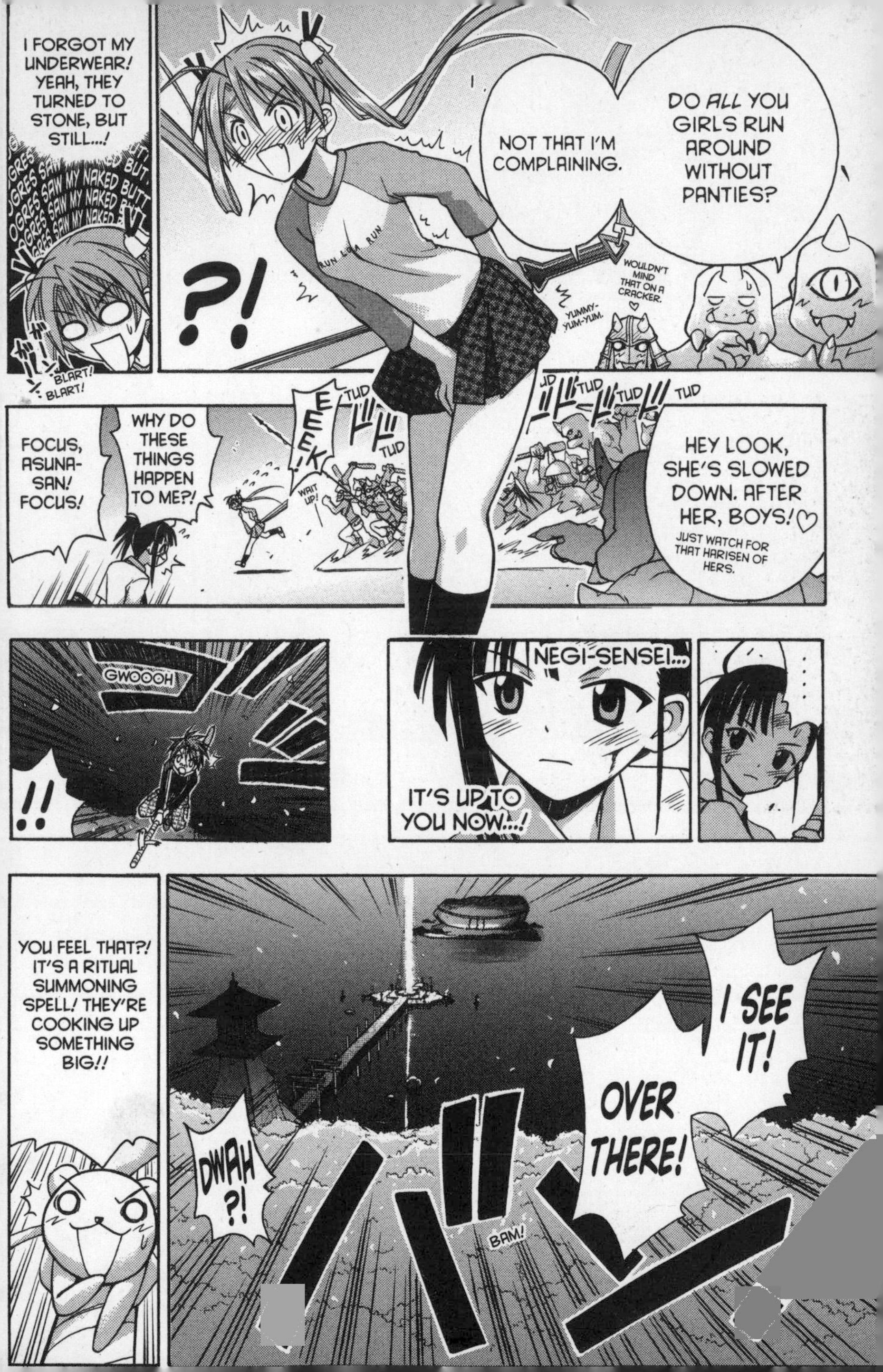

DO *ALL* YOU GIRLS RUN AROUND WITHOUT PANTIES?
NOT THAT I'M COMPLAINING.
?!
RUN LOLA RUN
WOULDN'T MIND THAT ON A CRACKER. ♡
YUMMY-YUM-YUM.
I FORGOT MY UNDERWEAR! YEAH, THEY TURNED TO STONE, BUT STILL...!
OGRES SAW MY NAKED BUTT. OGRES SAW MY NAKED BUTT.
BLART! BLART!
TUD TUD TUD TUD
HEY LOOK, SHE'S SLOWED DOWN. AFTER HER, BOYS! ♡
JUST WATCH FOR THAT HARISEN OF HERS.
TUD TUD
EEEEK!
WAIT UP!
WHY DO THESE THINGS HAPPEN TO ME?!
FOCUS, ASUNA-SAN! FOCUS!
...
NEGI-SENSEI...
IT'S UP TO YOU NOW...!
GWOOOH
!!
I SEE IT!
OVER THERE!
BAM!
DWAH ?!
YOU FEEL THAT?! IT'S A RITUAL SUMMONING SPELL! THEY'RE COOKING UP SOMETHING BIG!!

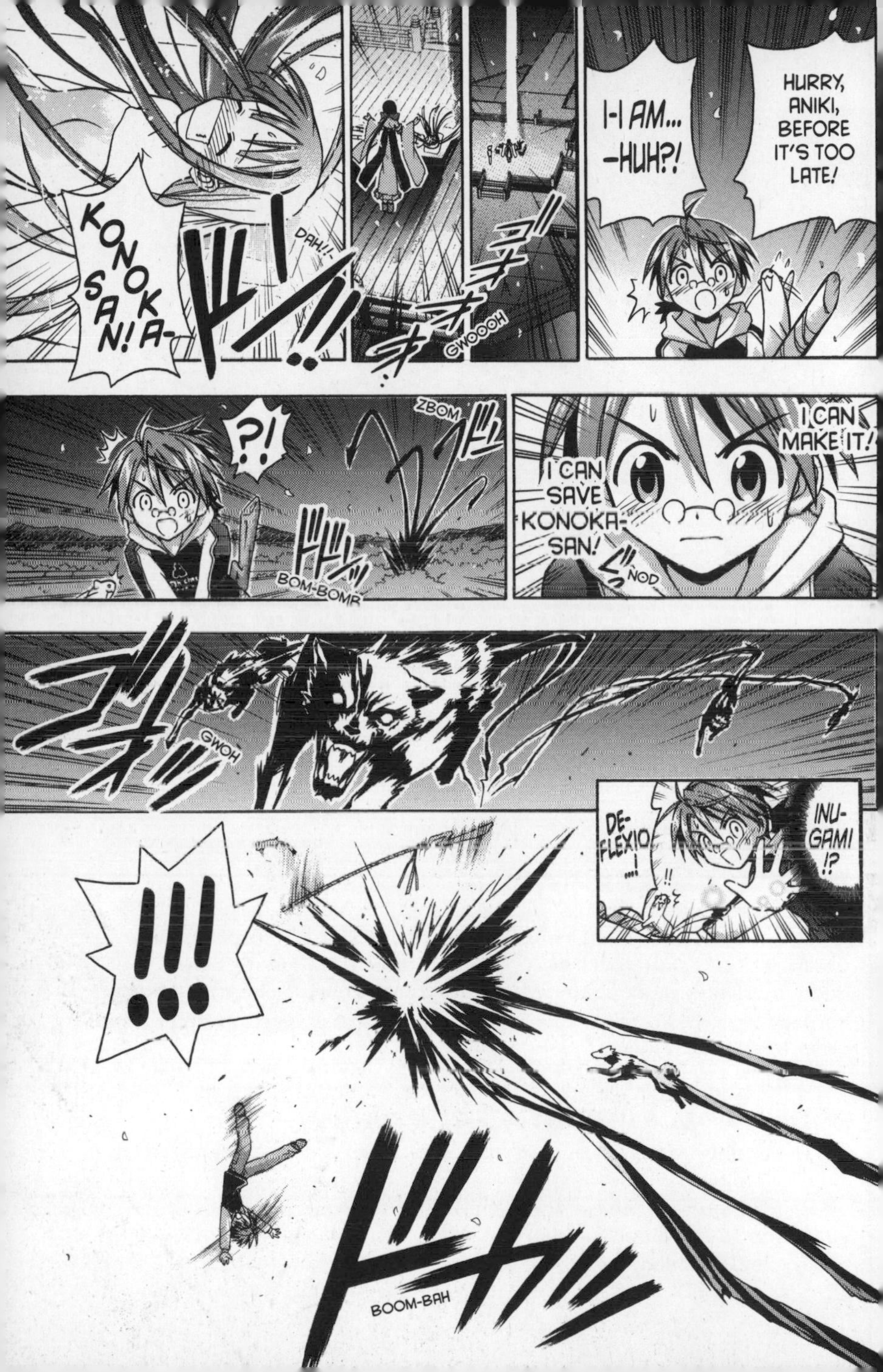
HURRY, ANIKI, BEFORE IT'S TOO LATE!
I-I AM... —HUH?!
GWOOOH
DAH!!
KONOKA-SAN! A-
I CAN MAKE IT!
I CAN SAVE KONOKA-SAN!
NOD
ZBOM
?!
BOM-BOMB
GWOH
INU-GAMI!?
DE-FLEXIO...!
!!
!!!...
BOOM-BAH

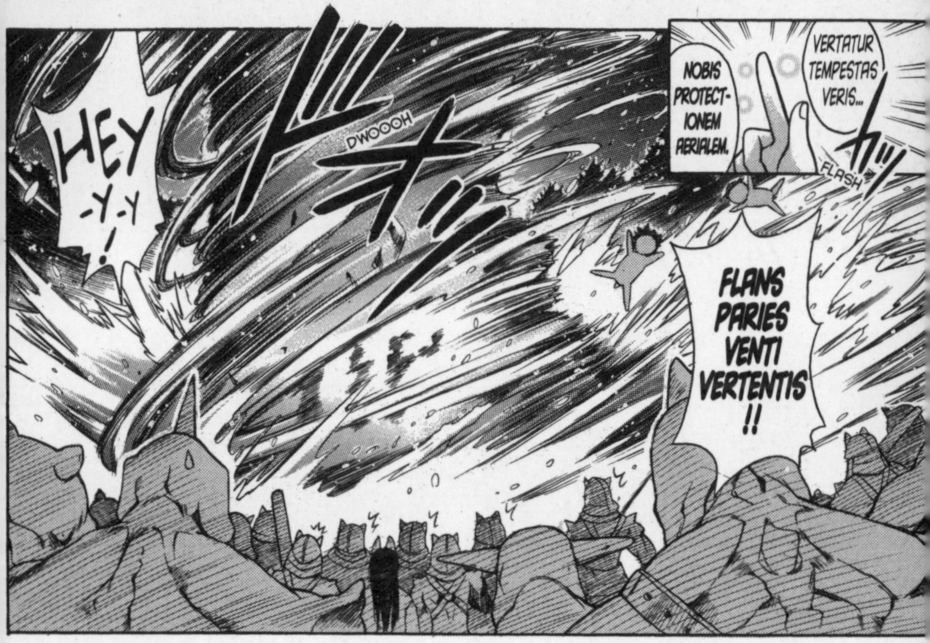
VERTATUR TEMPESTAS VERIS...
NOBIS PROTECTIONEM AERIALEM.
FLASH
FLANS PARIES VENTI VERTENTIS!!
DWOOOH
HEY-Y-Y!

NEGIMA! FORTY-SEVENTH PERIOD: LEXICON NEGIMARIUM

■

OM KIRI KIRI VAJRA UN HATTA

Used by members of an esoteric branch of Buddhism as part of a consecration ritual—specifically, to purify offerings to deities (be it Buddha, a saint, or a demon-god). In *Negima!*'s Forty-seventh Period, it's used to offer Konoka's *chi* or "spiritual power" to various demons in order to summon them.

■「逆巻け、春の嵐。我らに風の加護を。「風花旋風風障壁」」

VERTATUR TEMPEPSTAS VERIS. NOBIS PROTECTIONEM AERIALEM. FLANS PARIES VENTI VERTENTIS.

Conjures up a whirlwind of several minutes' duration, protecting the caster from outside attack. Although the area around the edges of the whirlwind is turbulent and therefore dangerous, the area inside is calm, much like the fabled "eye of the storm."

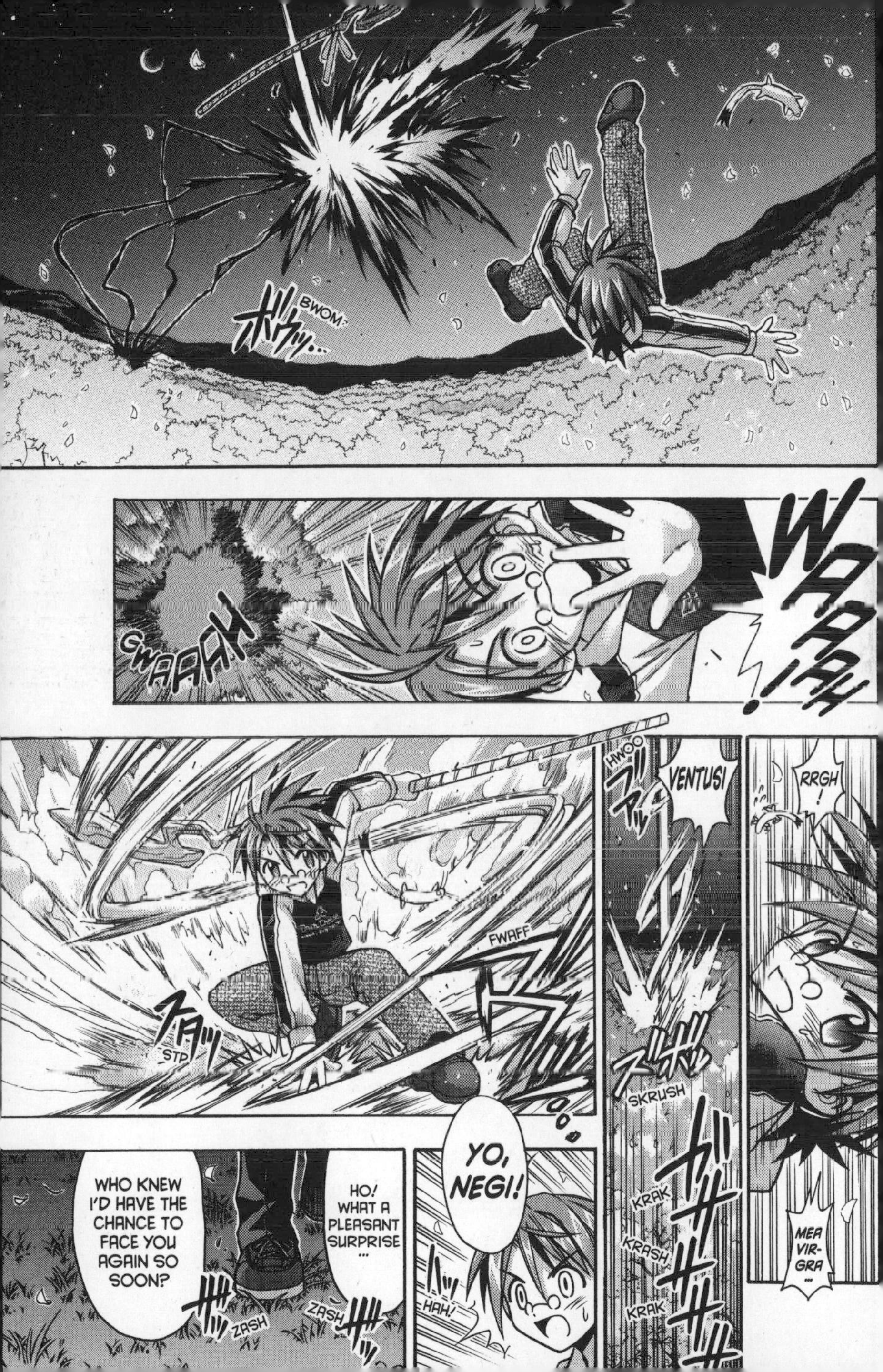
BWOM
WAAAH!!
GWAAAH
RRGH!
MEA VIR-GRA...
HWOO
VENTUS!
SKRUSH
KRAK
KRASH
KRAK
FWAFF
STP
YO, NEGI!
HAH!
HO! WHAT A PLEASANT SURPRISE...
WHO KNEW I'D HAVE THE CHANCE TO FACE YOU AGAIN SO SOON?
ZASH
ZASH

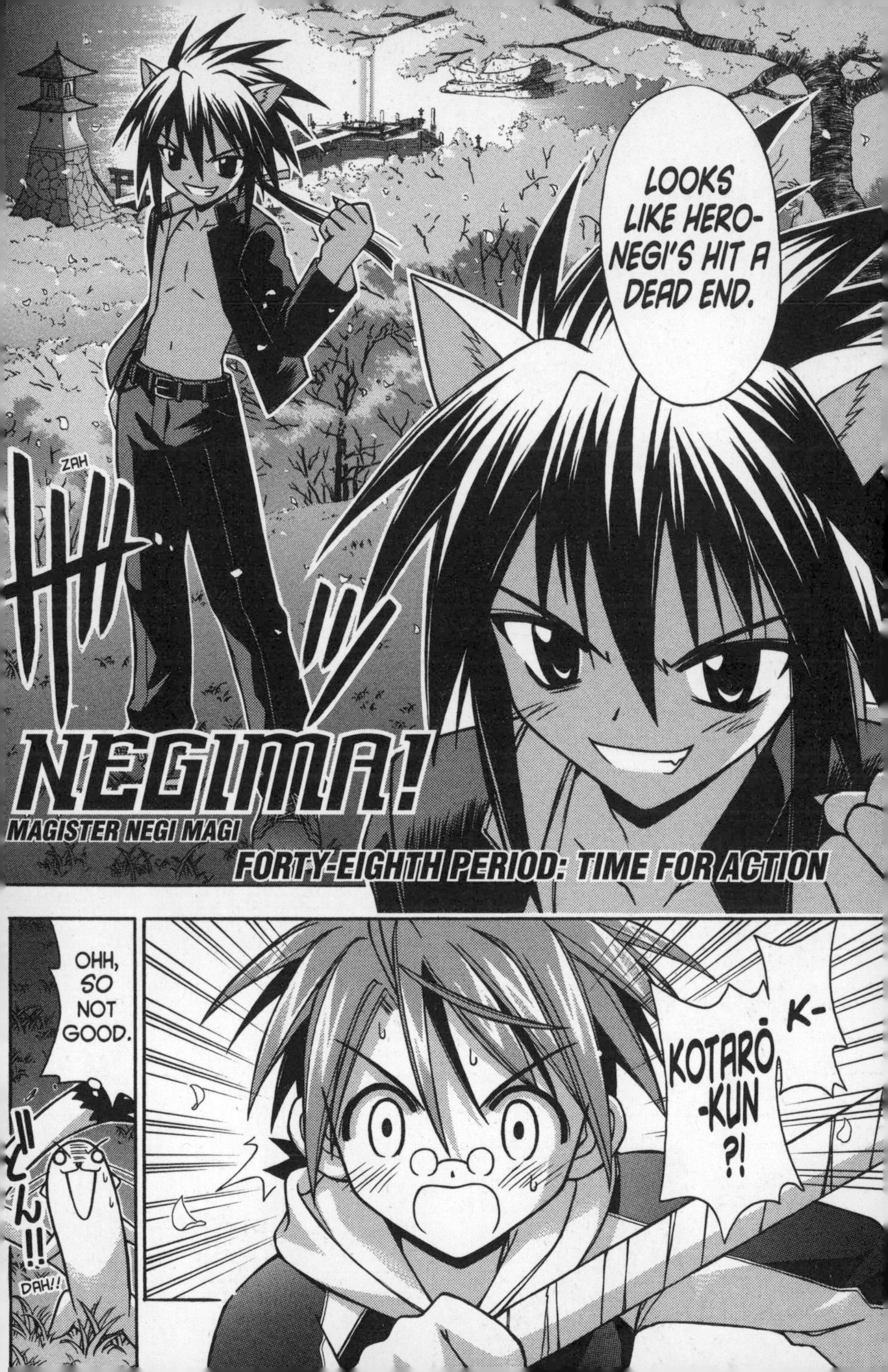
LOOKS LIKE HERO-NEGI'S HIT A DEAD END.
ZAH
NEGIMA!
MAGISTER NEGI MAGI
FORTY-EIGHTH PERIOD: TIME FOR ACTION
K- KOTARŌ-KUN ?!
OHH, SO NOT GOOD.
DAH!!

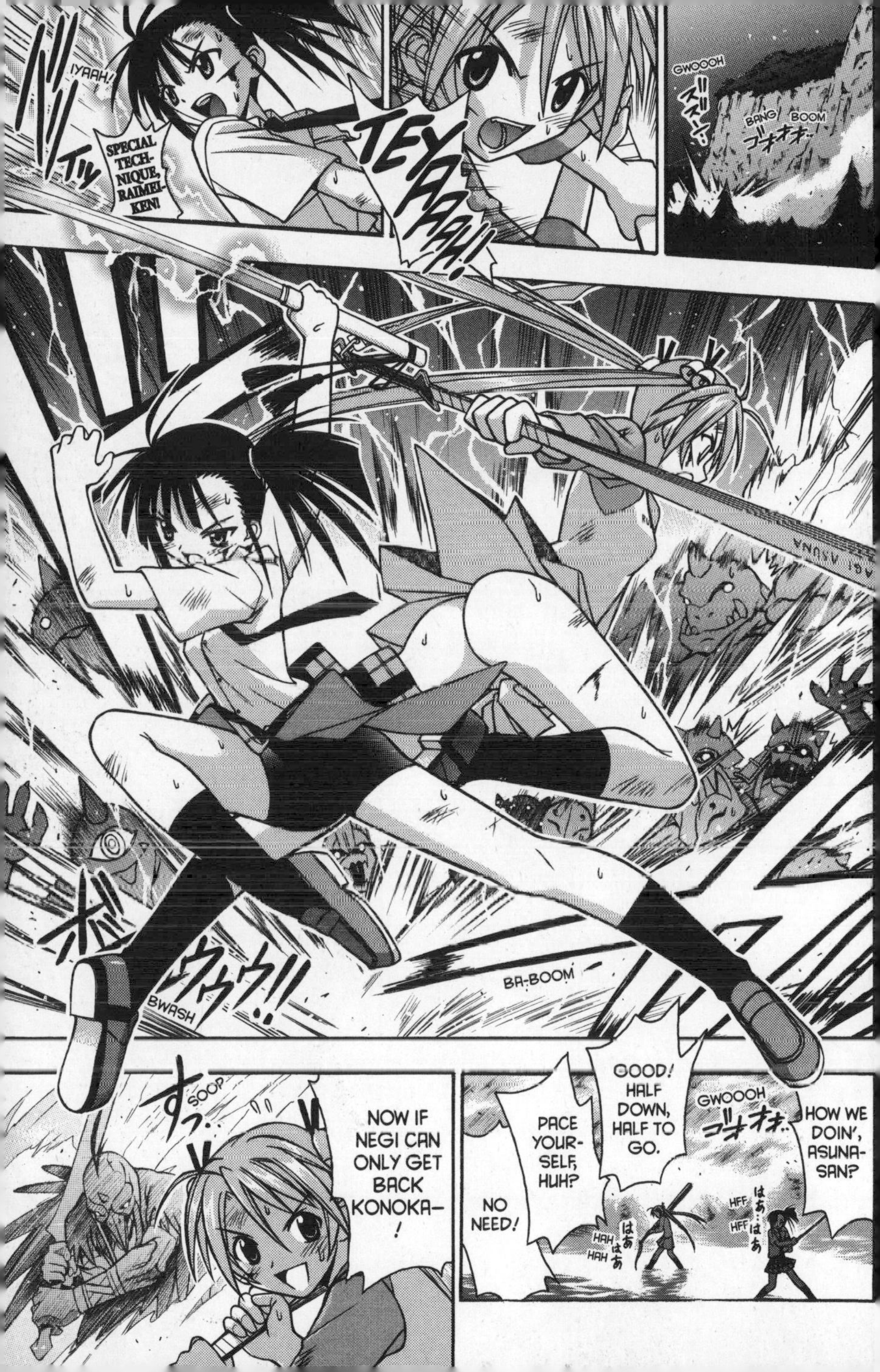
GWOOOH
ズズー
BANG BOOM
ゴオオオ
TEYAAAH!
IYAAH!
SPECIAL TECHNIQUE, RAIMEI-KEN!
BWASH
ボシュウウ!!
BA-BOOM
GWOOOH
ゴオオオ
HOW WE DOIN', ASUNA-SAN?
HFF HFF
はあ…はあ
GOOD! HALF DOWN, HALF TO GO.
PACE YOURSELF, HUH?
NO NEED!
HAH HAH
はあ はあ
SOOP
すっ
NOW IF NEGI CAN ONLY GET BACK KONOKA—!

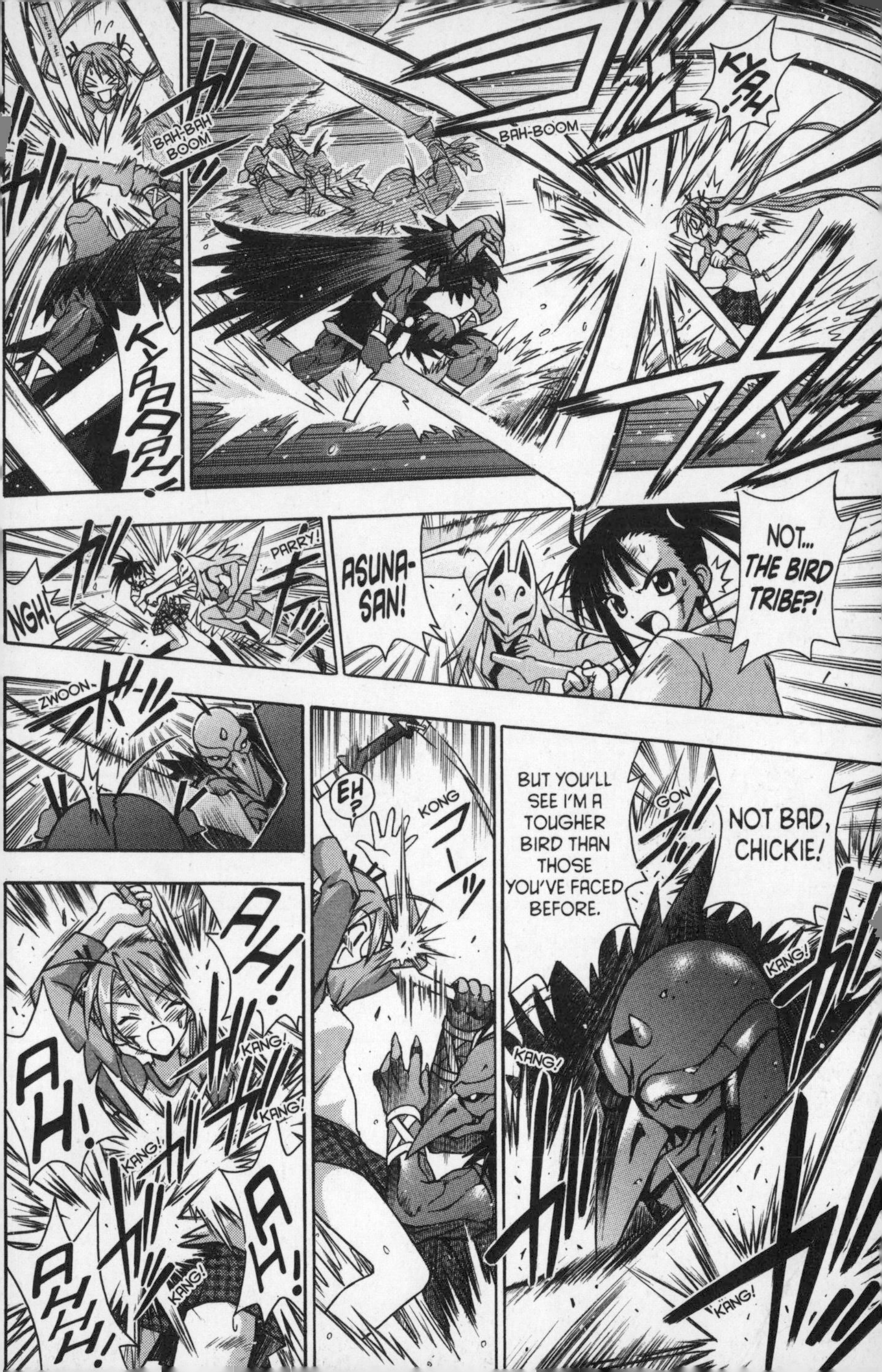
KYAH!
BAH-BOOM
BAH-BAH BOOM
KYAAAAH!
NOT... THE BIRD TRIBE?!
ASUNA-SAN!
PARRY!
NGH!
NOT BAD, CHICKIE!
BUT YOU'LL SEE I'M A TOUGHER BIRD THAN THOSE YOU'VE FACED BEFORE.
GON
KANG!
KANG!
KANG!
EH?
KONG
ZWOON-
AH!
KANG!
KANG!
AH!
KANG!
AH!
KANG!
AAHHH!

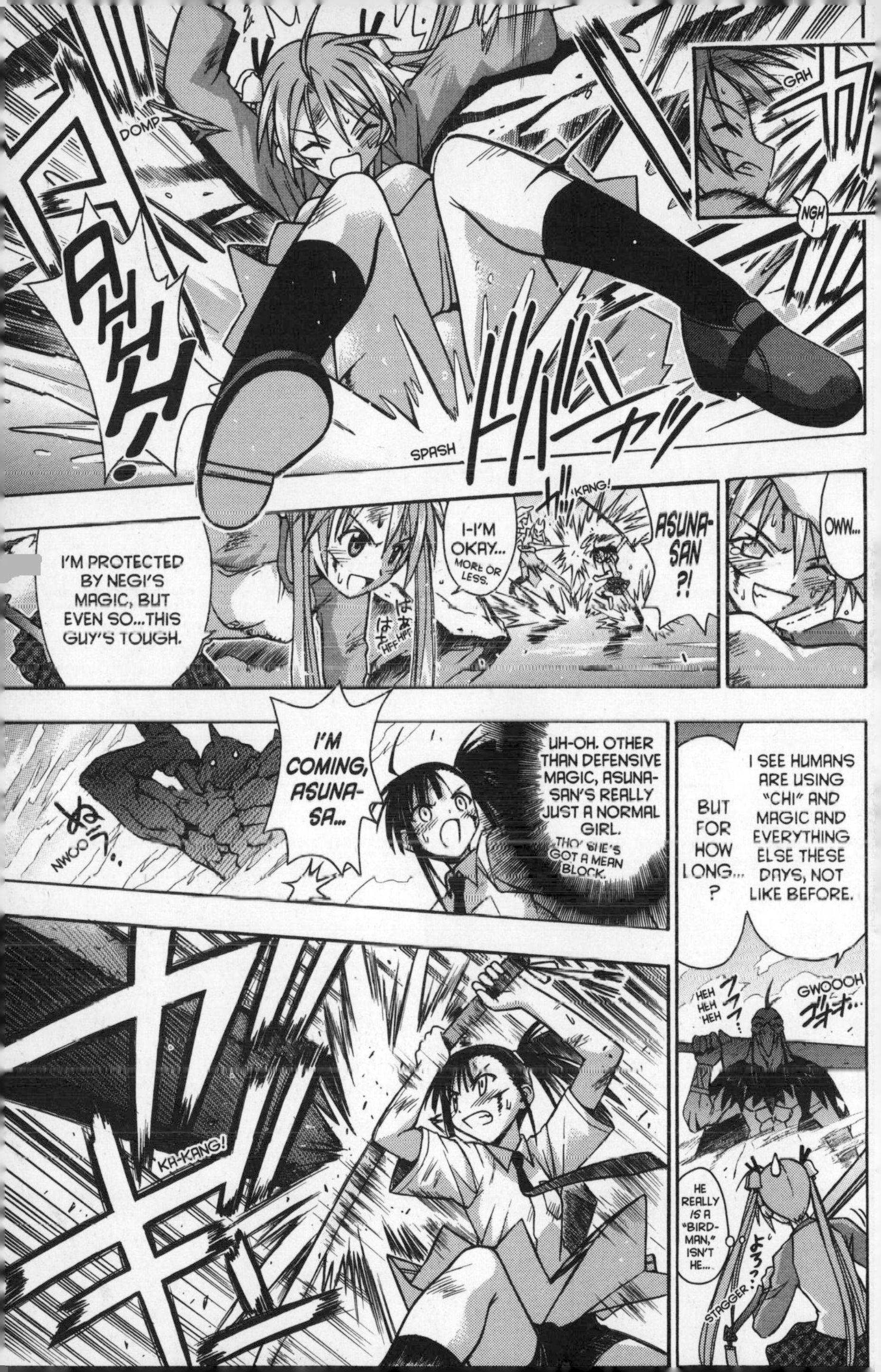
GAH
NGH!
DOMP
SPASH
OWW...
ASUNA-SAN?!
KANG!
I-I'M OKAY... MORE OR LESS.
HFF HFF
I'M PROTECTED BY NEGI'S MAGIC, BUT EVEN SO...THIS GUY'S TOUGH.
I SEE HUMANS ARE USING "CHI" AND MAGIC AND EVERYTHING ELSE THESE DAYS, NOT LIKE BEFORE.
BUT FOR HOW LONG...?
GWOOOH
HEH HEH HEH
HE REALLY IS A "BIRD-MAN," ISN'T HE...
STAGGER
UH-OH. OTHER THAN DEFENSIVE MAGIC, ASUNA-SAN'S REALLY JUST A NORMAL GIRL.
THO' SHE'S GOT A MEAN BLOCK.
I'M COMING, ASUNA-SA...
NWOO
KA-KANG!

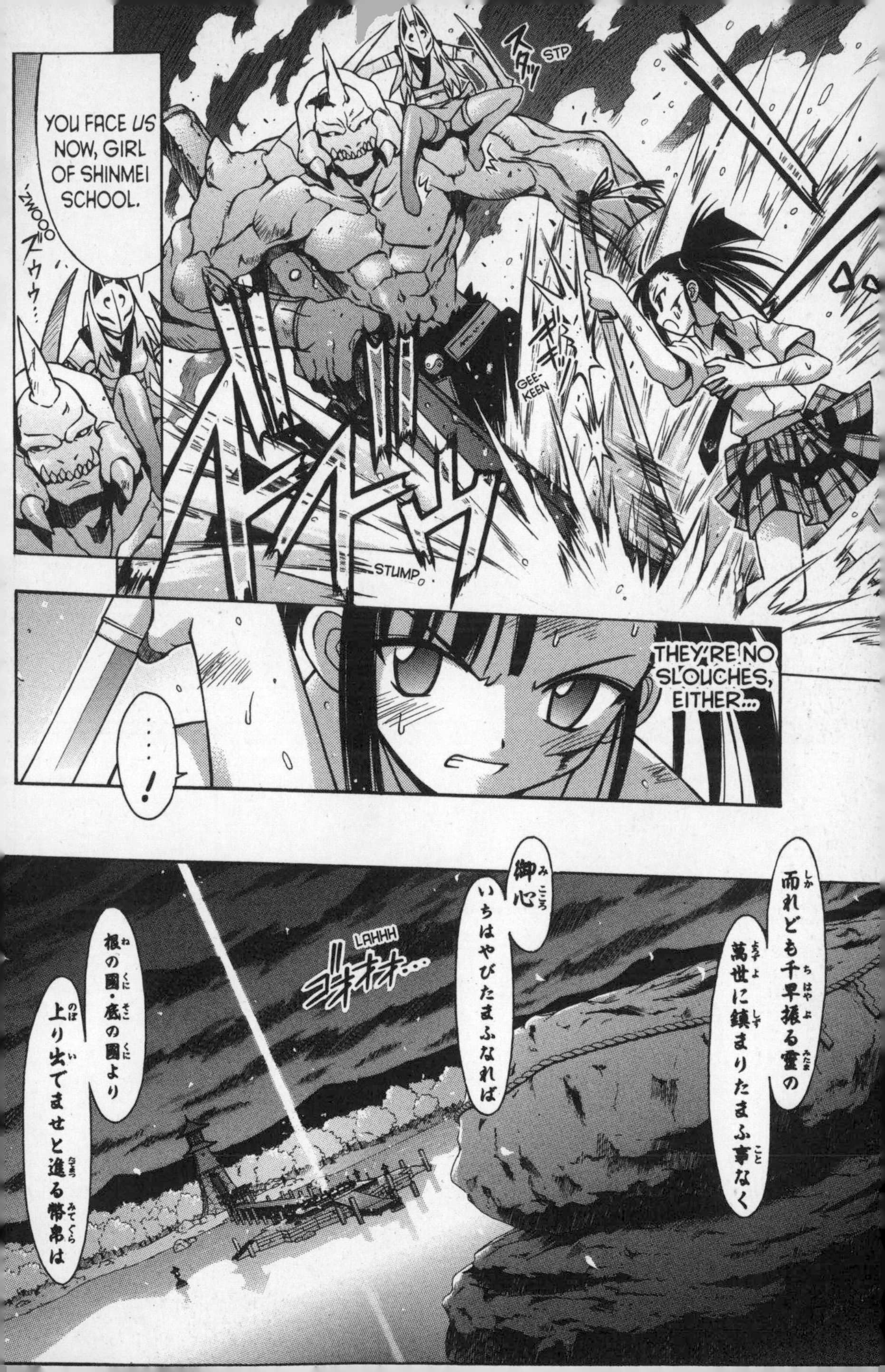
スタッ STP
GEE-KEEN
YOU FACE US NOW, GIRL OF SHINMEI SCHOOL.
ZWOOO ズゥウ…
STUMP
THEY'RE NO SLOUCHES, EITHER...
……!
而れども千早振る霊の
萬世に鎮まりたまふ事なく
御心いちはやびたまふなれば
LAHHH ゴォオオ…
根の國・底の國より
上り出でませと進る幣帛は

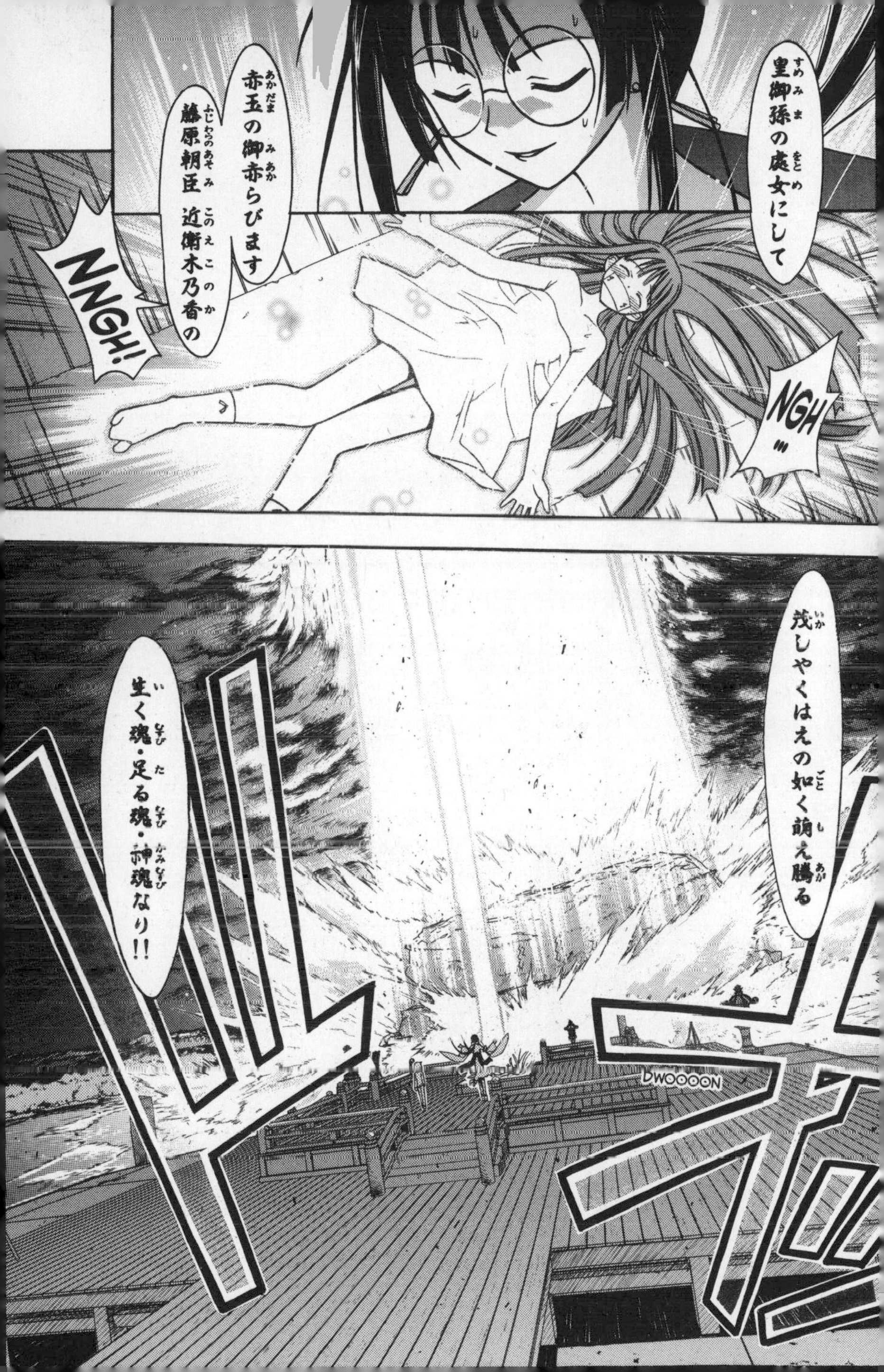
皇御孫の處女にして
赤玉の御赤らびます 藤原朝臣 近衛木乃香の
NGH...
NNGH!
茂しやくはえの如く萌え騰る
生く魂・足る魂・神魂なり!!
DWOOOON

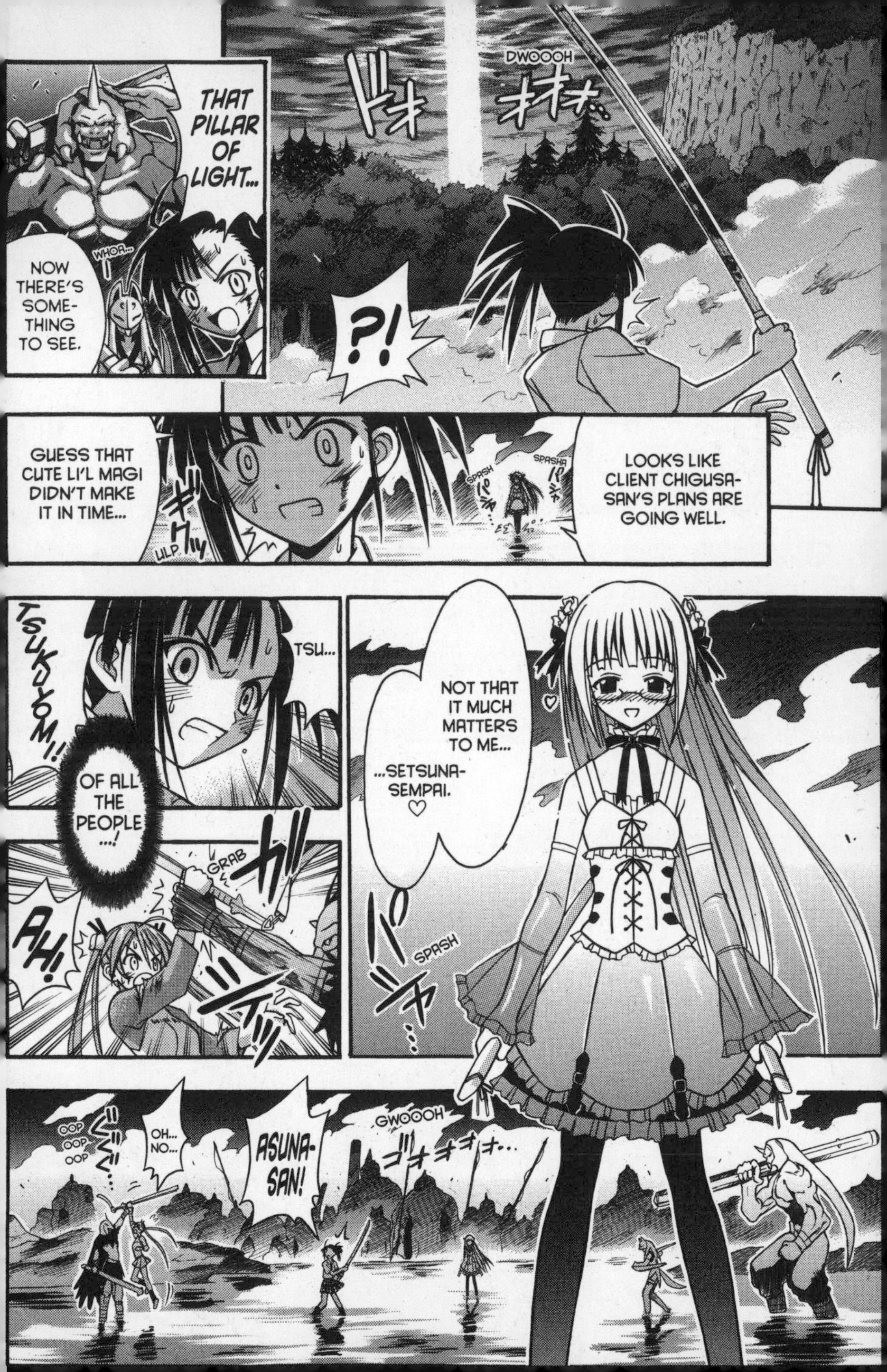
DWOOOH
?!
THAT PILLAR OF LIGHT...
WHOA...
NOW THERE'S SOME-THING TO SEE.
LOOKS LIKE CLIENT CHIGUSA-SAN'S PLANS ARE GOING WELL.
SPASHA
SPASH
GUESS THAT CUTE LI'L MAGI DIDN'T MAKE IT IN TIME...
ULP
NOT THAT IT MUCH MATTERS TO ME...
...SETSUNA-SEMPAI. ♡
SPASH
TSU...
TSUKUYOMI!!
OF ALL THE PEOPLE...!
GRAB
AH!!
GWOOOH
ASUNA-SAN!
OH... NO...
OOP OOP OOP

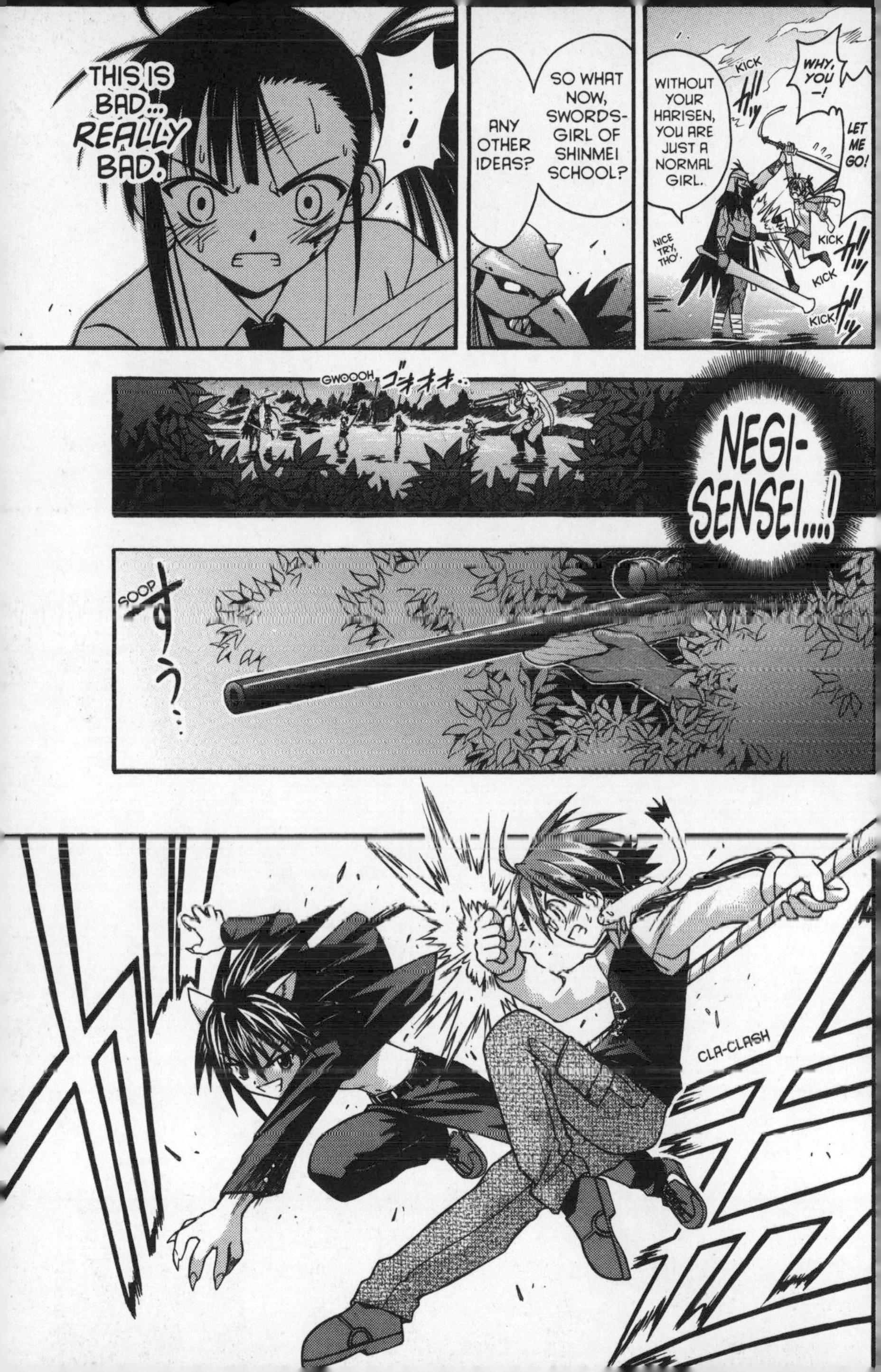
WHY, YOU—!
LET ME GO!
KICK
WITHOUT YOUR HARISEN, YOU ARE JUST A NORMAL GIRL.
NICE TRY, THO'.
KICK
KICK
KICK
SO WHAT NOW, SWORDS-GIRL OF SHINMEI SCHOOL?
ANY OTHER IDEAS?
...!
THIS IS BAD... REALLY BAD.
NEGI-SENSEI...!
GWOOOH ゴォォォ..
SOOP すぅ...
CLA-CLASH

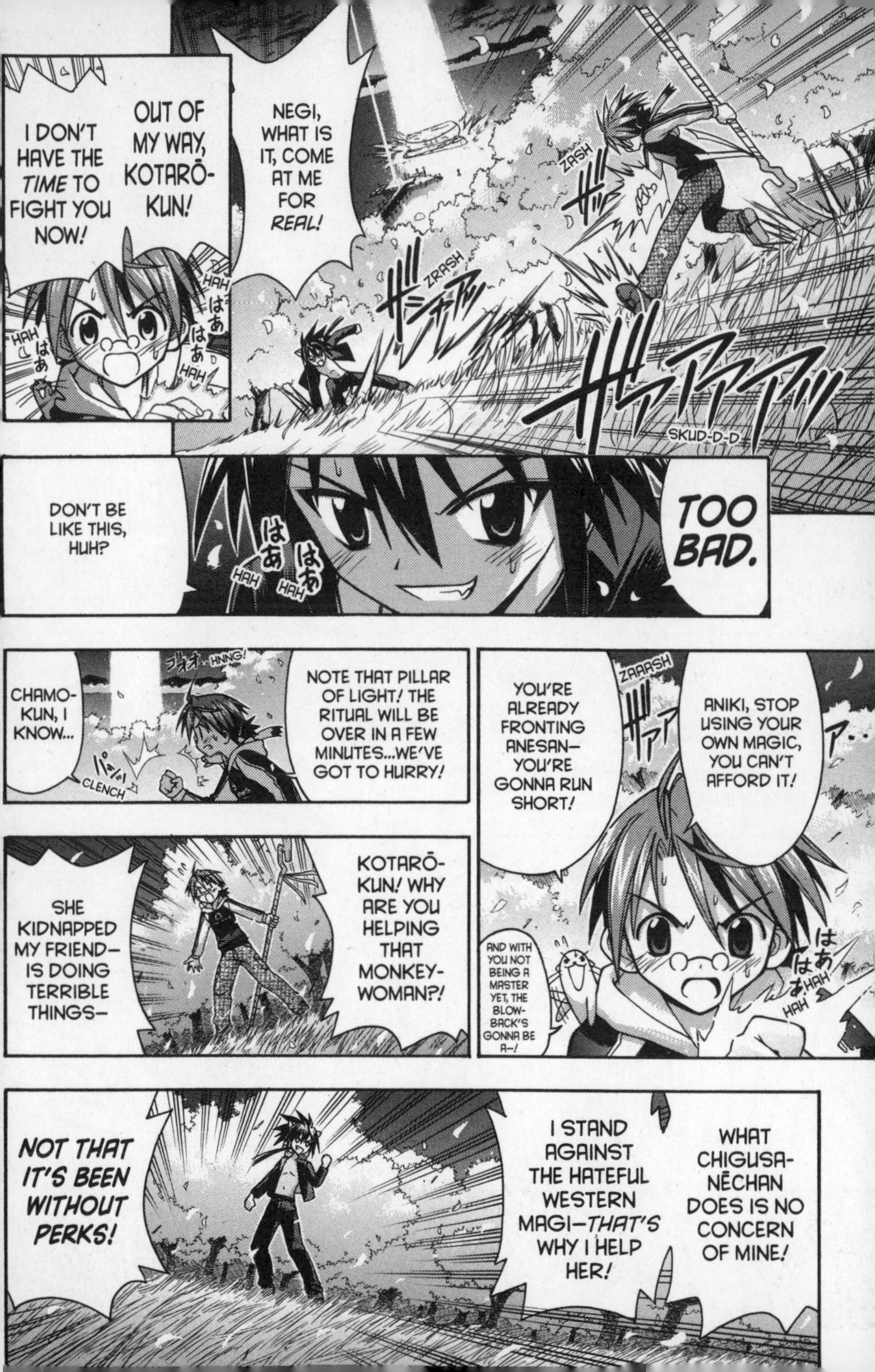
NEGI, WHAT IS IT, COME AT ME FOR *REAL*!
ZASH
ZRASH
SKUD-D-D
OUT OF MY WAY, KOTARŌ-KUN!
I DON'T HAVE THE *TIME* TO FIGHT YOU NOW!
HAH HAH HAH HAH
TOO BAD.
DON'T BE LIKE THIS, HUH?
HAH HAH
ZAAASH
ANIKI, STOP USING YOUR OWN MAGIC, YOU CAN'T AFFORD IT!
YOU'RE ALREADY FRONTING ANESAN— YOU'RE GONNA RUN SHORT!
AND WITH YOU NOT BEING A MASTER YET, THE BLOW-BACK'S GONNA BE A—!
HAH HAH
HNNG!
NOTE THAT PILLAR OF LIGHT! THE RITUAL WILL BE OVER IN A FEW MINUTES...WE'VE GOT TO HURRY!
CHAMO-KUN, I KNOW...
CLENCH
KOTARŌ-KUN! WHY ARE YOU HELPING THAT MONKEY-WOMAN?!
SHE KIDNAPPED MY FRIEND— IS DOING TERRIBLE THINGS—
WHAT CHIGUSA-NĒCHAN DOES IS NO CONCERN OF MINE!
I STAND AGAINST THE HATEFUL WESTERN MAGI—*THAT'S* WHY I HELP HER!
NOT THAT IT'S BEEN WITHOUT PERKS!

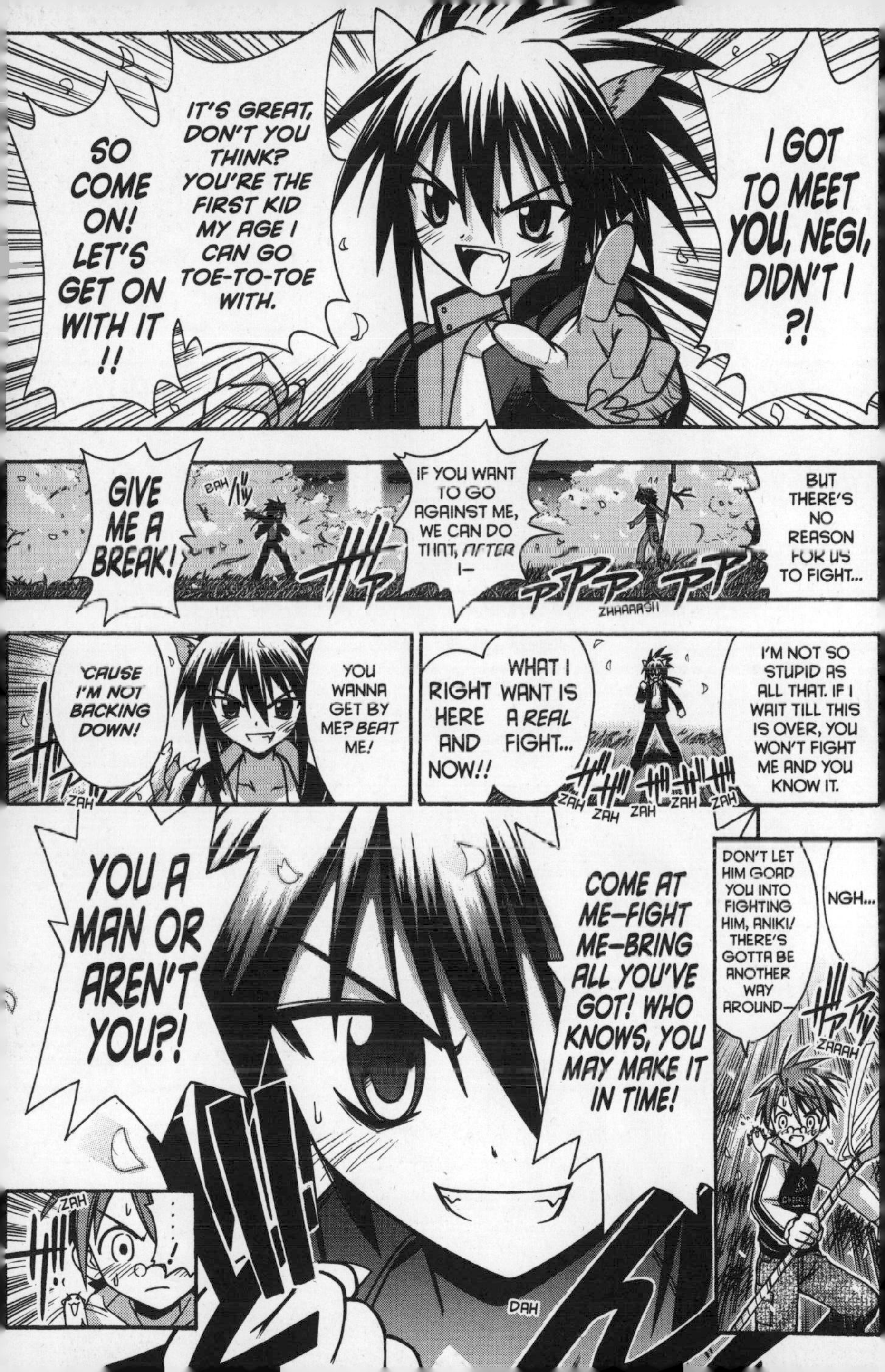
I GOT TO MEET YOU, NEGI, DIDN'T I ?!
IT'S GREAT, DON'T YOU THINK? YOU'RE THE FIRST KID MY AGE I CAN GO TOE-TO-TOE WITH.
SO COME ON! LET'S GET ON WITH IT !!
BUT THERE'S NO REASON FOR US TO FIGHT...
ZHHAAAASH
IF YOU WANT TO GO AGAINST ME, WE CAN DO THAT, AFTER I—
BAH
GIVE ME A BREAK!
I'M NOT SO STUPID AS ALL THAT. IF I WAIT TILL THIS IS OVER, YOU WON'T FIGHT ME AND YOU KNOW IT.
WHAT I WANT IS A REAL FIGHT...
RIGHT HERE AND NOW!!
ZAH ZAH ZAH ZAH ZAH
YOU WANNA GET BY ME? BEAT ME!
'CAUSE I'M NOT BACKING DOWN!
ZAH
NGH...
DON'T LET HIM GOAD YOU INTO FIGHTING HIM, ANIKI! THERE'S GOTTA BE ANOTHER WAY AROUND—
ZAAAH
COME AT ME—FIGHT ME—BRING ALL YOU'VE GOT! WHO KNOWS, YOU MAY MAKE IT IN TIME!
YOU A MAN OR AREN'T YOU?!
DAH
ZAH
...!

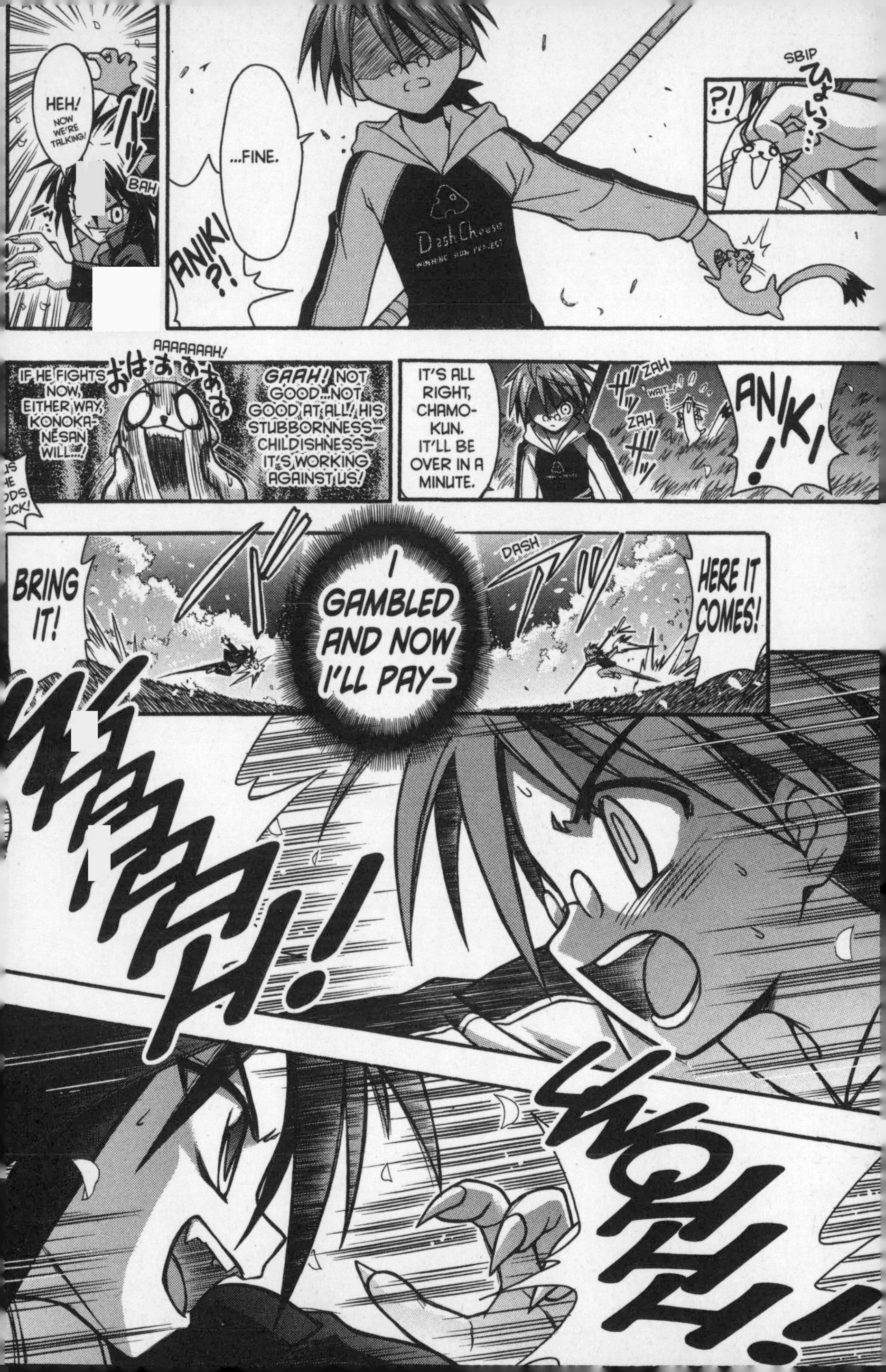
SBIP
ひょいっ
?!
...FINE.
ANIKI?!
HEH! NOW WE'RE TALKING!
BAH
ANIKI!
ZAH
WAIT...!
ZAH
IT'S ALL RIGHT, CHAMO-KUN. IT'LL BE OVER IN A MINUTE.
AAAAAAAAH!
おはあああ
GAAH! NOT GOOD...NOT GOOD AT ALL! HIS STUBBORNNESS—CHILDISHNESS—IT'S WORKING AGAINST US!
IF HE FIGHTS NOW, EITHER WAY, KONOKA-NESAN WILL...!
HERE IT COMES!
DASH
I GAMBLED AND NOW I'LL PAY—
BRING IT!
WOAH!!

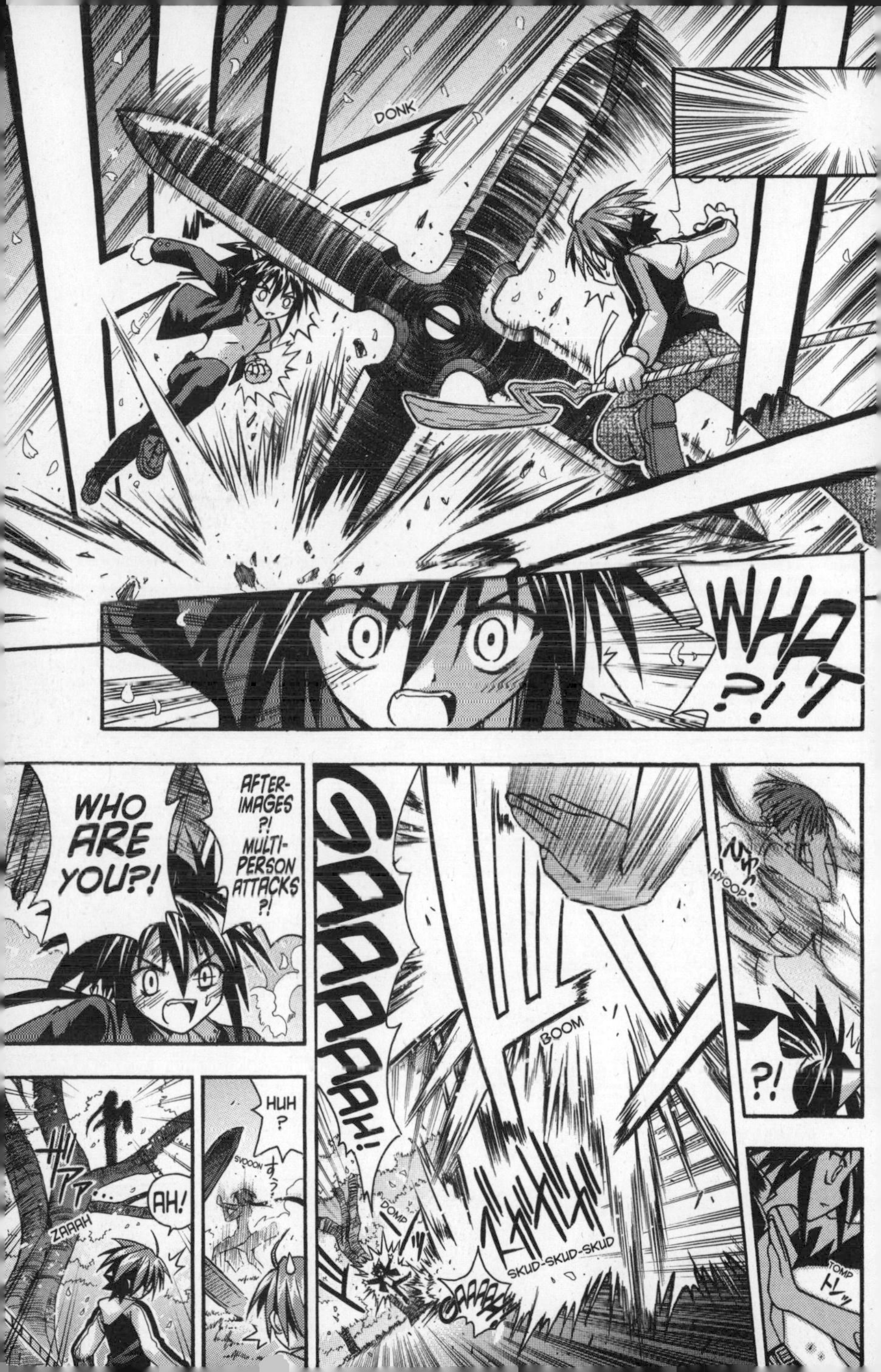
DONK
WHAT?!
HYOOP
?!
SAAAAAAAH!
BOOM
AFTER-IMAGES?! MULTI-PERSON ATTACKS?!
WHO ARE YOU?!
TOMP
SKUD-SKUD-SKUD
DOMP
HUH?
SVOOON
AH!
ZAAAH

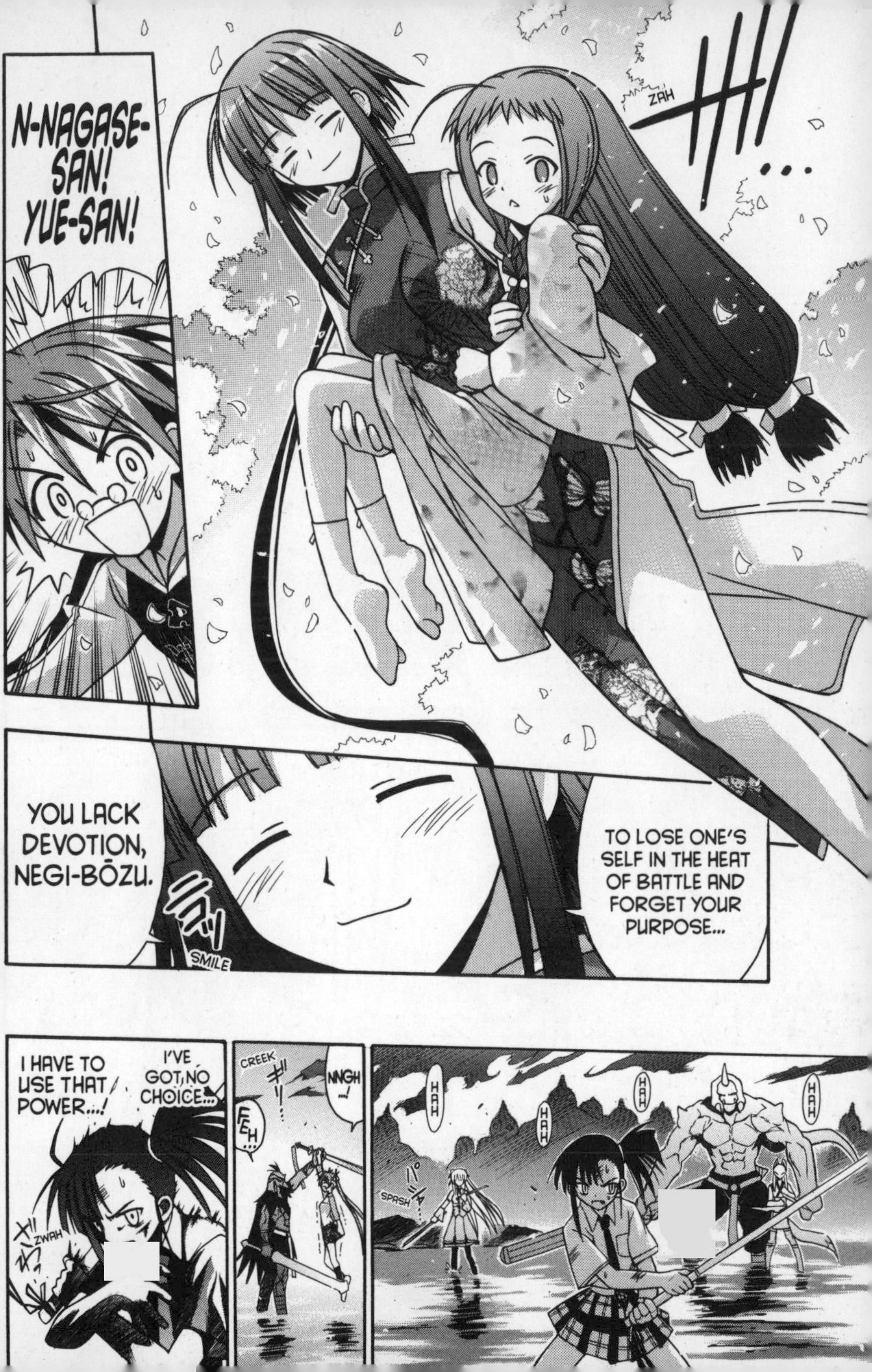
ZAH
...
N-NAGASE-SAN! YUE-SAN!
TO LOSE ONE'S SELF IN THE HEAT OF BATTLE AND FORGET YOUR PURPOSE...
YOU LACK DEVOTION, NEGI-BŌZU.
SMILE
HAH
HAH
HAH
HAH
SPASH
NNGH ...!
CREEK
FEH ...
I'VE GOT NO CHOICE...
I HAVE TO USE THAT POWER...!
ZWAH

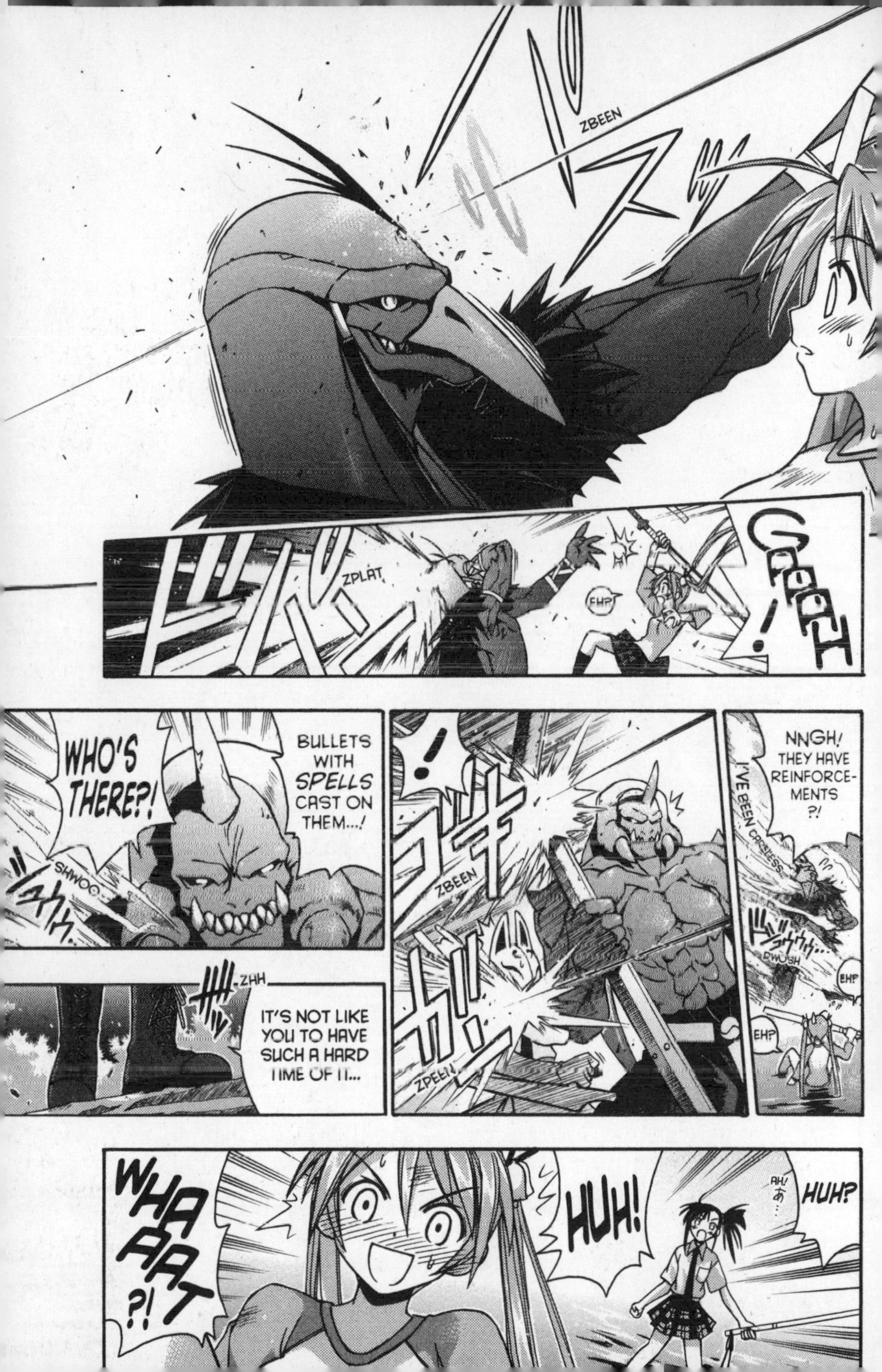
ZBEEN
GOOOH!
EH?
ZPLAT
NNGH! THEY HAVE REINFORCEMENTS?!
I'VE BEEN CARELESS...
RWUSH
EH?
EH?
ZBEEN
ZPEEN
BULLETS WITH SPELLS CAST ON THEM...!
WHO'S THERE?!
SHWOO...
ZHH
IT'S NOT LIKE YOU TO HAVE SUCH A HARD TIME OF IT...
HUH?
AH!
HUH!
WHAAAT?!

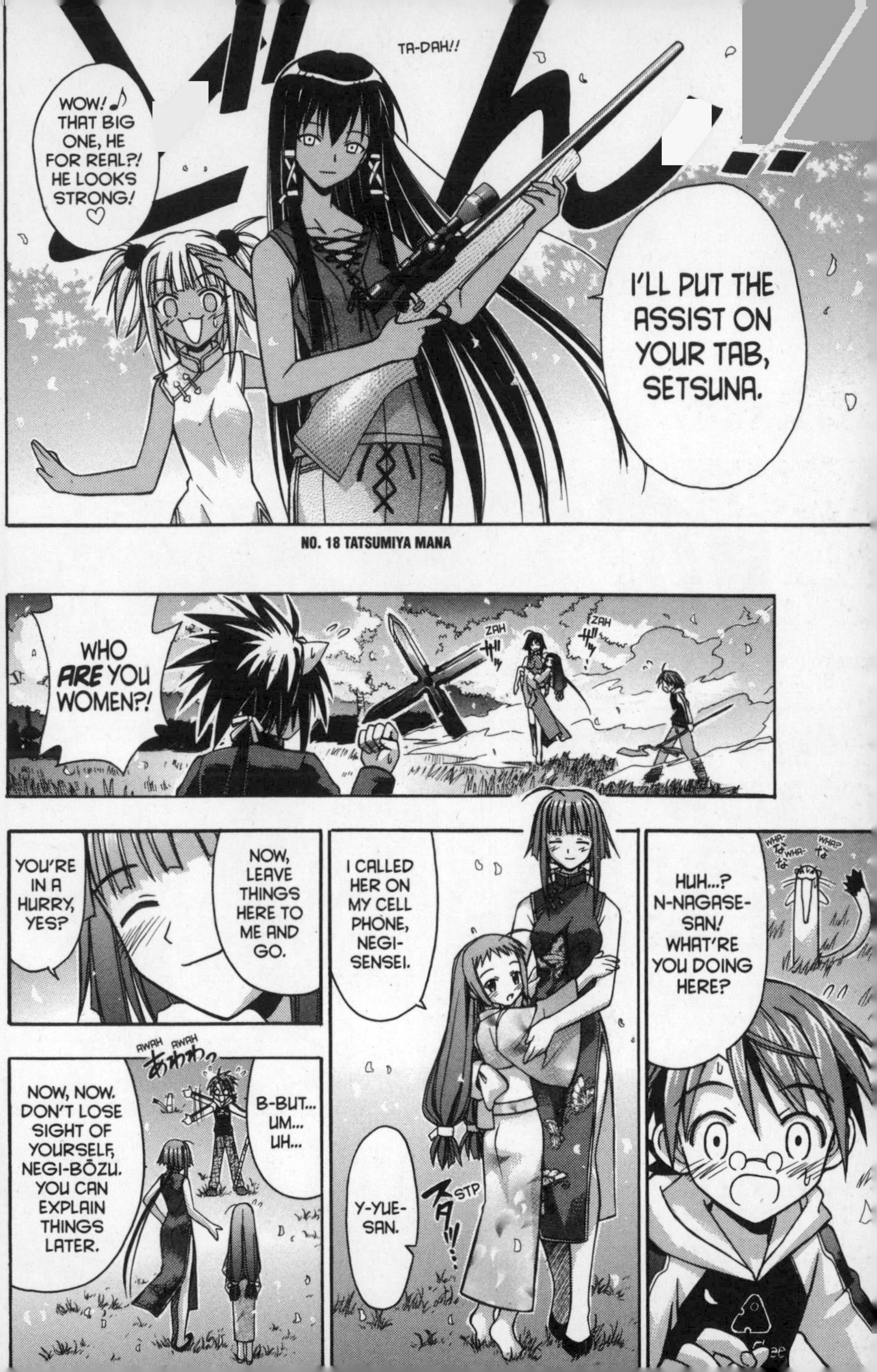
I'LL PUT THE ASSIST ON YOUR TAB, SETSUNA.
TA-DAH!!
WOW! ♪ THAT BIG ONE, HE FOR REAL?! HE LOOKS STRONG! ♡
NO. 18 TATSUMIYA MANA
ZAH
ZAH
WHO ARE YOU WOMEN?!
WHA- WHA- WHAP
HUH...? N-NAGASE-SAN! WHAT'RE YOU DOING HERE?
I CALLED HER ON MY CELL PHONE, NEGI-SENSEI.
Y-YUE-SAN.
STP
NOW, LEAVE THINGS HERE TO ME AND GO.
YOU'RE IN A HURRY, YES?
AWAH AWAH
B-BUT... UM... UH...
NOW, NOW. DON'T LOSE SIGHT OF YOURSELF, NEGI-BŌZU. YOU CAN EXPLAIN THINGS LATER.

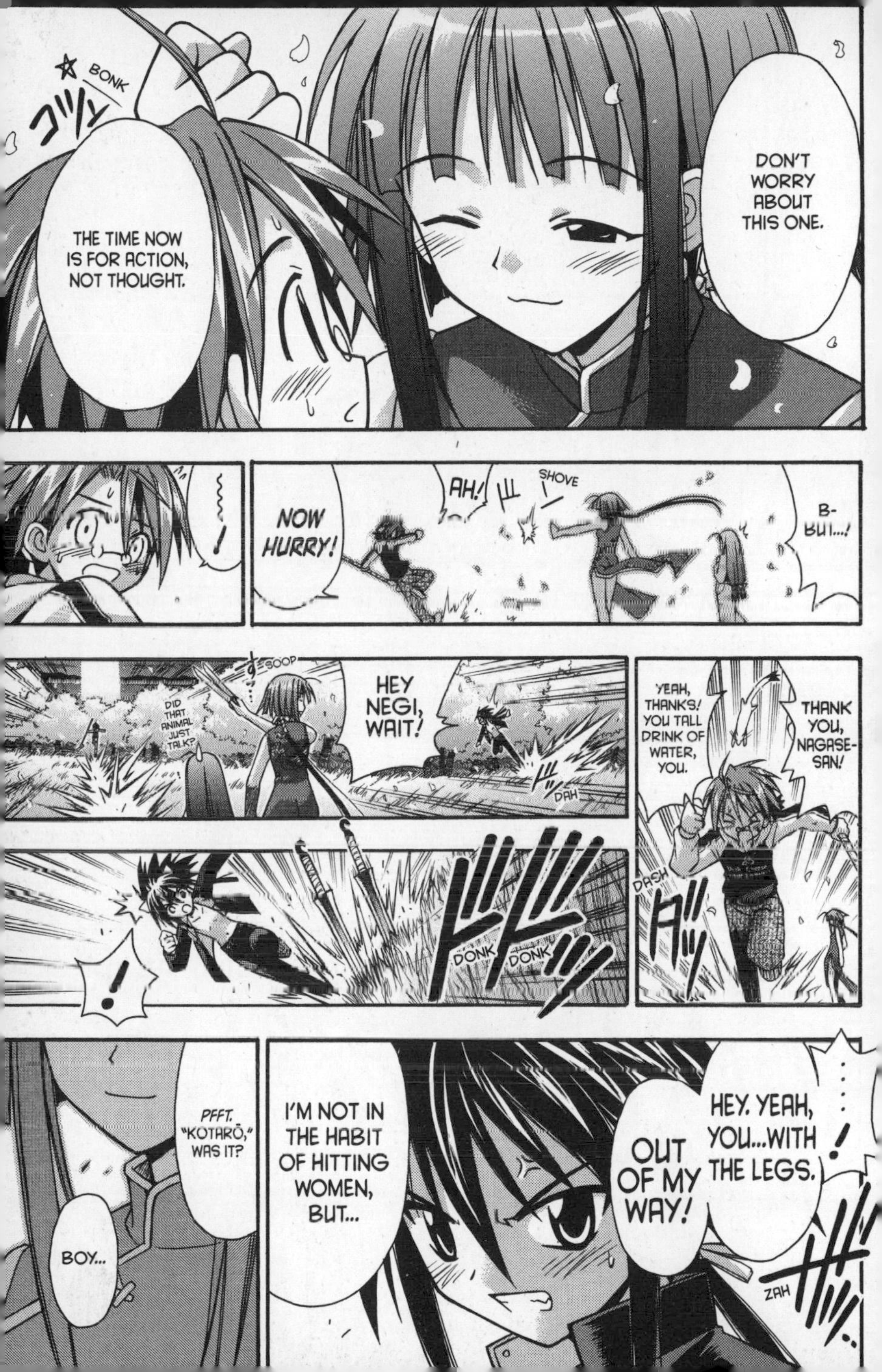

DON'T WORRY ABOUT THIS ONE.
BONK
THE TIME NOW IS FOR ACTION, NOT THOUGHT.
B- BUT...!
SHOVE
AH!
NOW HURRY!
...!
THANK YOU, NAGASE-SAN!
YEAH, THANKS! YOU TALL DRINK OF WATER, YOU.
DASH
HEY NEGI, WAIT!
DAH
SOOP
DID THAT ANIMAL JUST TALK?
DONK
DONK
!
...!
HEY. YEAH, YOU...WITH THE LEGS.
OUT OF MY WAY!
I'M NOT IN THE HABIT OF HITTING WOMEN, BUT...
ZAH
PFFT. "KOTARŌ," WAS IT?
BOY...

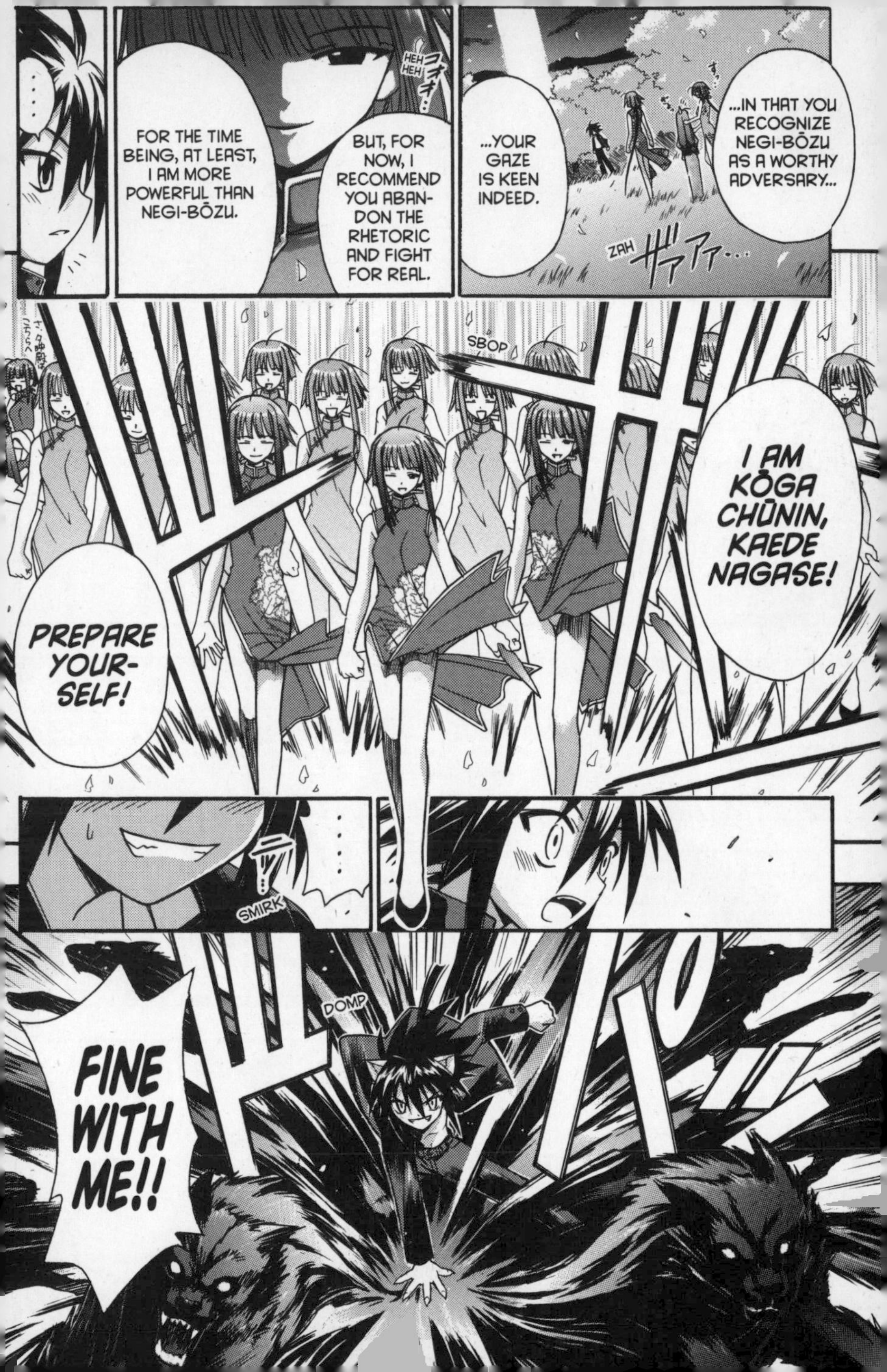
...IN THAT YOU RECOGNIZE NEGI-BŌZU AS A WORTHY ADVERSARY...
ZAH
...YOUR GAZE IS KEEN INDEED.
HEH HEH
BUT, FOR NOW, I RECOMMEND YOU ABAN-DON THE RHETORIC AND FIGHT FOR REAL.
FOR THE TIME BEING, AT LEAST, I AM MORE POWERFUL THAN NEGI-BŌZU.
...
SBOP
I AM KŌGA CHŪNIN, KAEDE NAGASE!
PREPARE YOUR-SELF!
...
SMIRK
DOMP
FINE WITH ME!!

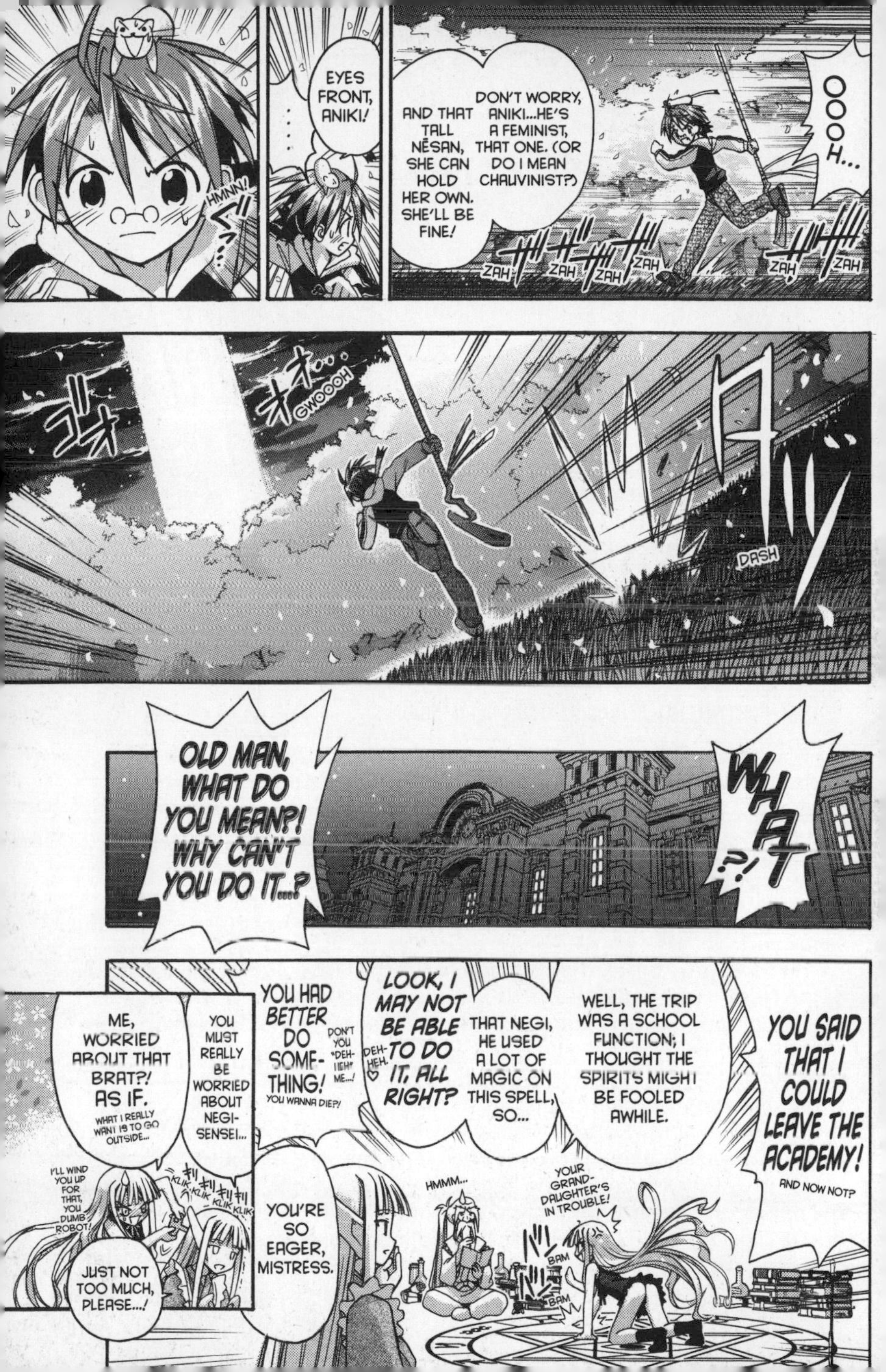
OOOOH...
ZAH ZAH
ZAH ZAH ZAH ZAH
DON'T WORRY, ANIKI...HE'S A FEMINIST, THAT ONE. (OR DO I MEAN CHAUVINIST?)
AND THAT TALL NĒSAN, SHE CAN HOLD HER OWN. SHE'LL BE FINE!
EYES FRONT, ANIKI!
...
HMNN!
DASH
GWOOOH
WHAT ?!
OLD MAN, WHAT DO YOU MEAN?! WHY CAN'T YOU DO IT...?
YOU SAID THAT I COULD LEAVE THE ACADEMY!
AND NOW NOT?
WELL, THE TRIP WAS A SCHOOL FUNCTION; I THOUGHT THE SPIRITS MIGHT BE FOOLED AWHILE.
THAT NEGI, HE USED A LOT OF MAGIC ON THIS SPELL, SO...
YOUR GRAND-DAUGHTER'S IN TROUBLE!
BAM
BAM
HMMM...
LOOK, I MAY NOT BE ABLE TO DO IT, ALL RIGHT?
DEH-HEH.♡
DON'T YOU "DEH-HEH" ME...!
YOU HAD BETTER DO SOME-THING!
YOU WANNA DIE?!
YOU'RE SO EAGER, MISTRESS.
YOU MUST REALLY BE WORRIED ABOUT NEGI-SENSEI...
ME, WORRIED ABOUT THAT BRAT?! AS IF.
WHAT I REALLY WANT IS TO GO OUTSIDE...
KLIK KLIK KLIK KLIK
I'LL WIND YOU UP FOR THAT, YOU DUMB ROBOT!
JUST NOT TOO MUCH, PLEASE...!

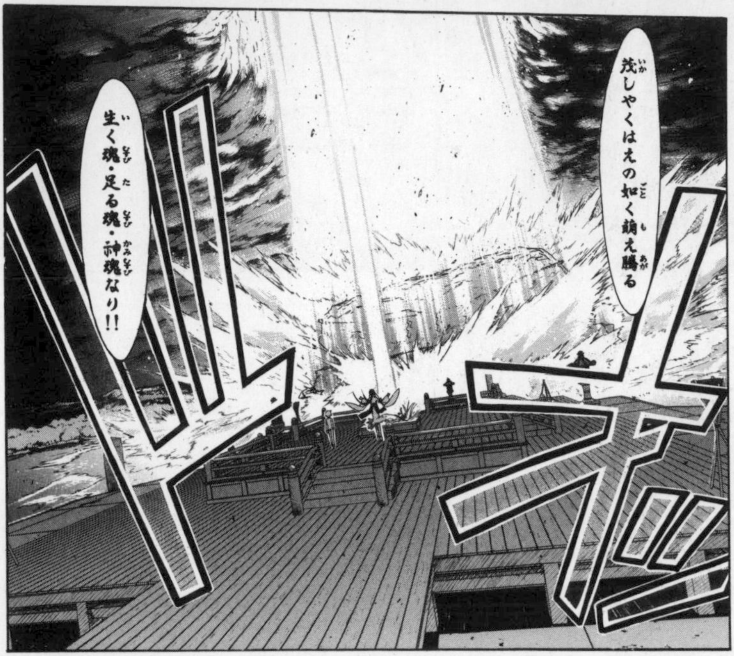
茂しやくはえの如く萌え騰る
生く魂・足る魂・神魂なり!!

NEGIMA! FORTY-EIGHTH PERIOD: LEXICON NEGIMARIUM

■「高天之原尓神留坐氐事始給志神漏伎神漏美能命以氐天之高市尓八百萬神等乎神集集給比神議議給氐〔…〕然毛千早振留靈能萬世爾鎮給事無久御心一速比給波根國底之國爾里上出坐世止進幣帛者皇御孫之處女赤玉能御阿加良毘坐藤原朝臣近衛木乃香乃伊賀志夜具波江能如久萌騰留生魂足魂神魂也〔…〕」

たかまのはらにかむづまりまして、ことはじめたまひしかむろき、かむろみのみことをもちて、あめのたけちに、やおよろずのかみたちを、かむつどへつどへたまひ、かむはかりはかりたまひて〔…〕しかれども、ちはやぶるみたまのよろずよにしずまりたまふことなく、みこころいちはやびたまふなれば、ねのくに、そこのくによりのぼりいでませ、とたてまつるみてぐらは、すめみまのをとめにして、あかだまのみあからびます、ふじわらのあそみ、このえこのかの、いかしやくはえのごとくもえあがる、いくむずびたるむすび、かむむすびなり〔…〕

The above text is in ancient Japanese. In the first passage, the roots of the ceremony are discussed vis-à-vis a recitation of the origins of the deities, and an invocation for their blessings is made. Following is a lesser-known Japanese mythological passage unlisted in the more common texts (in this case, the musubi or musuhi refers to Konoka's spirit). Musuhi—which, incidentally, is taken from the names of deities in the beginning of the Kojiki ("Takami Mushi no Kami" and "Kami Musuhi no Kami")—refers to the power of objective creation. The "musu" from kokemusu relates to the divine generative power, while the "hi" refers to the power of the spirit. Taken as compounds, iku musubi means "power of life," taru musubi "overflowing power," and kamu musubi the "power of a demon-god." It's interesting to note that although "Fujisawa no Asomi, Konoe Konoka" is recited, the direct line of descent of the Konoka family was broken in the 19th year of Keichô (A.D. 1615).

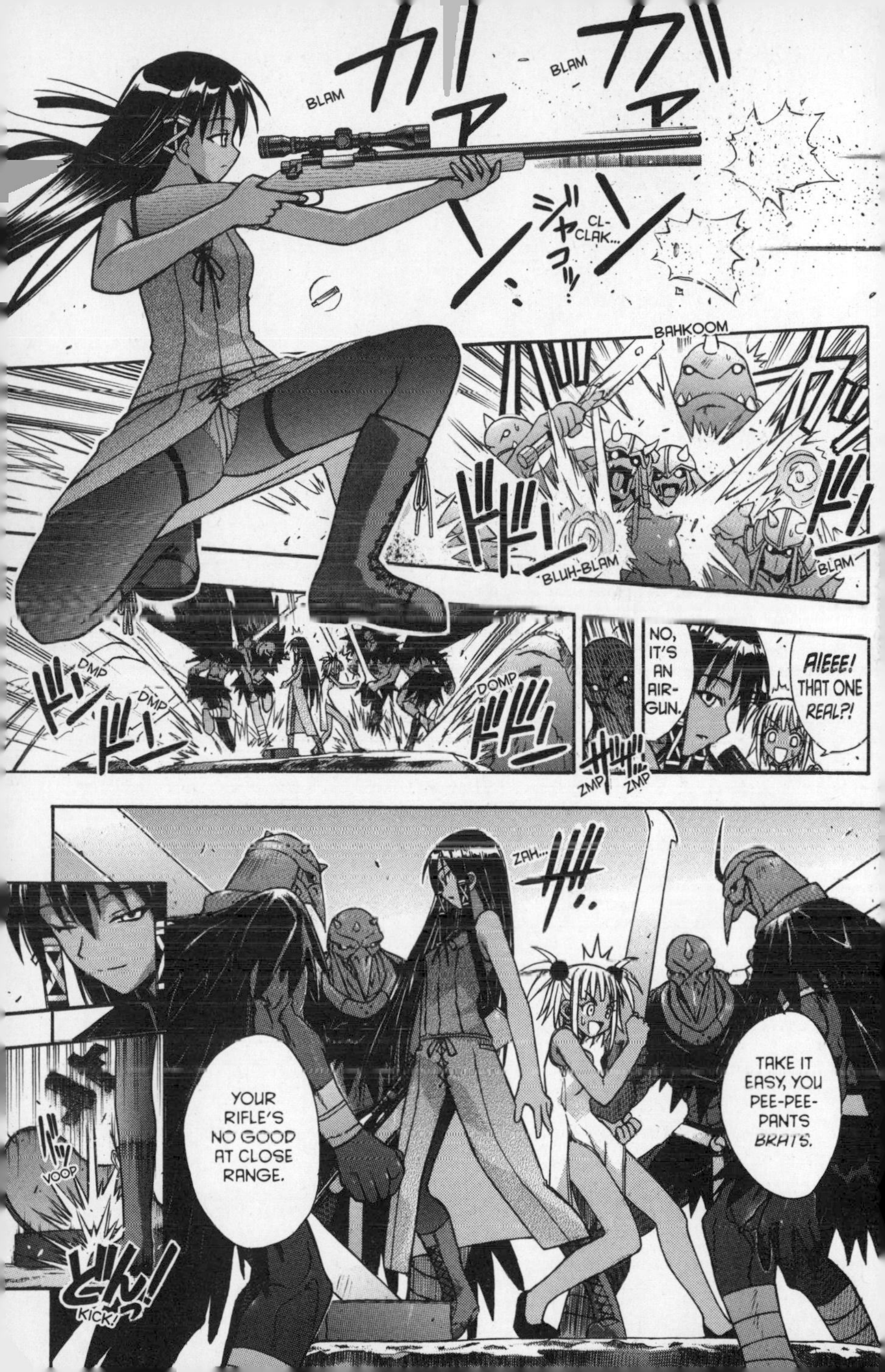
BLAM
BLAM
CL-CLAK...
BAHKOOM
BLAM
BLUH-BLAM
AIEEE! THAT ONE REAL?!
NO, IT'S AN AIR-GUN.
ZMP
ZMP
DOMP
DMP
DMP
ZAH...
TAKE IT EASY, YOU PEE-PEE-PANTS BRATS.
YOUR RIFLE'S NO GOOD AT CLOSE RANGE.
VOOP
KICK!

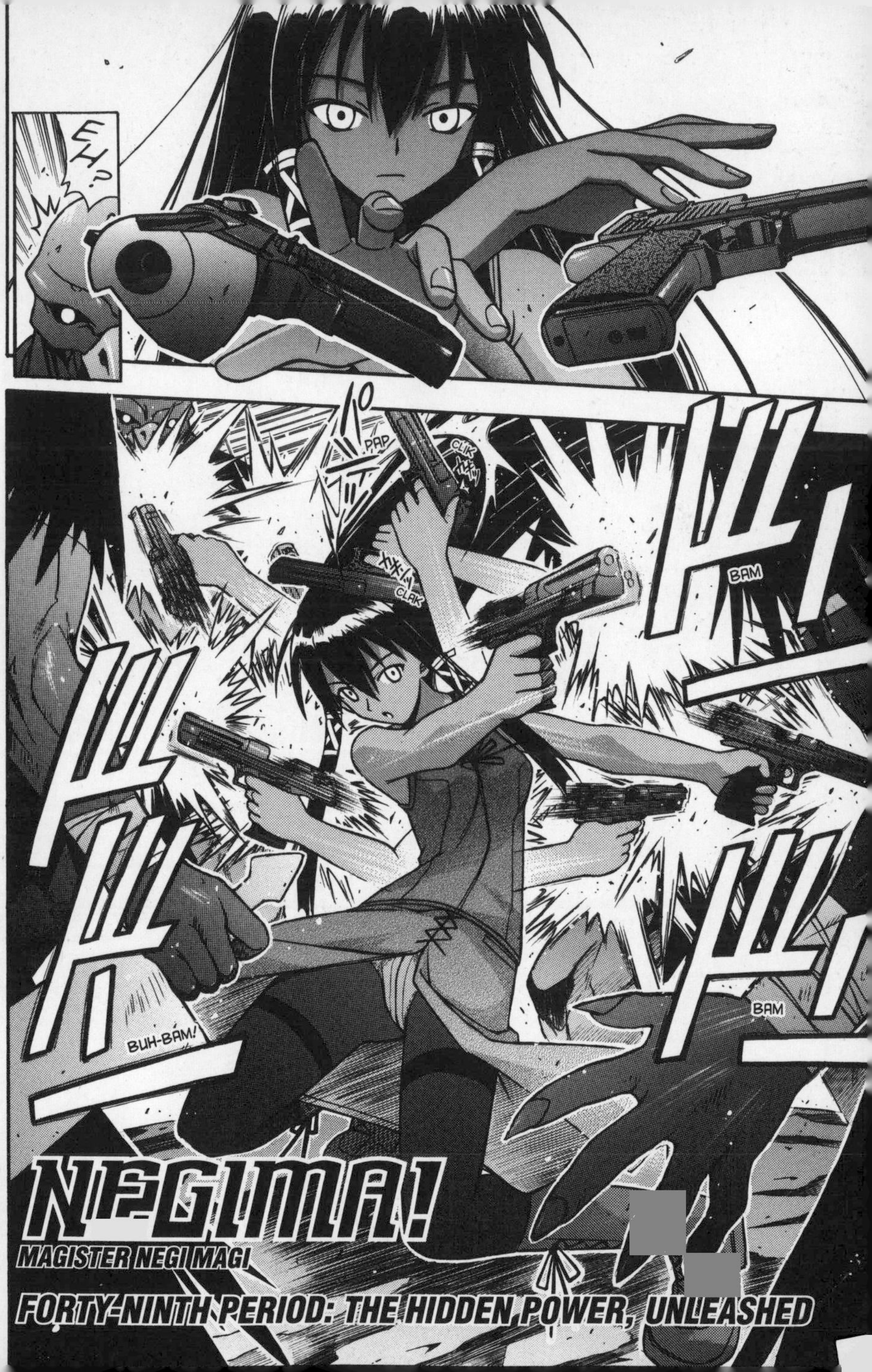
EH?
BAM
CLIK
PAP
CLAK
BAM
BUH-BAM!
NEGIMA!
MAGISTER NEGI MAGI
FORTY-NINTH PERIOD: THE HIDDEN POWER, UNLEASHED

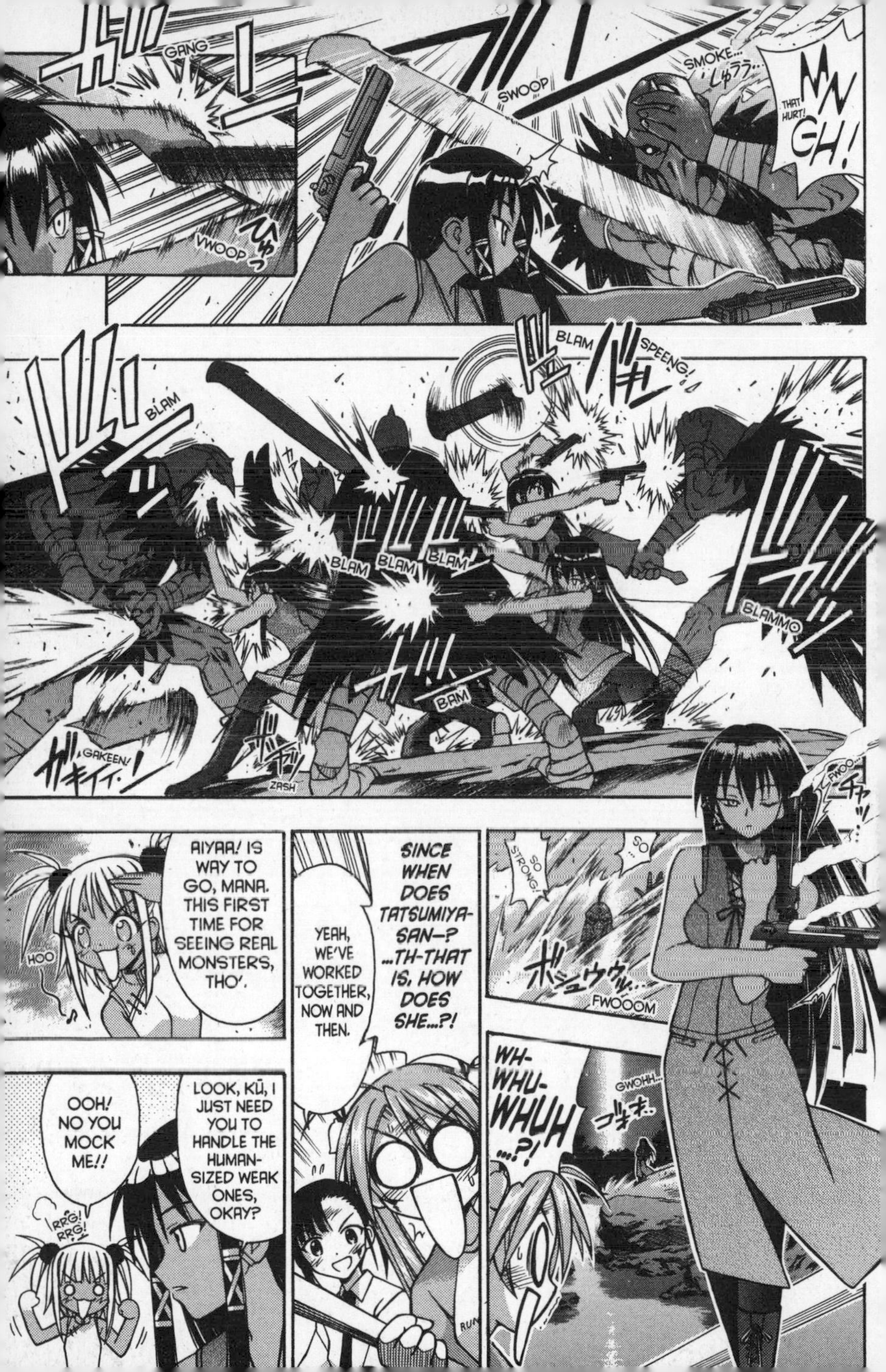
SMOKE... しゅララ...
MNNGH!
THAT HURT!
SWOOP
GANG
VWOOP
SPEENG!
BLAM
BLAMMO
BLAM
BLAM
BLAM
BAM
BLAM
ZASH
GAKEEN!
FWOO...
SO...
SO STRONG!
FWOOOM
SINCE WHEN DOES TATSUMIYA-SAN—? ...TH-THAT IS, HOW DOES SHE...?!
YEAH, WE'VE WORKED TOGETHER, NOW AND THEN.
AIYAA! IS WAY TO GO, MANA. THIS FIRST TIME FOR SEEING REAL MONSTERS, THO'.
HOO
WH-WHU-WHUH...?!
GWOHH...
RUN
LOOK, KŪ, I JUST NEED YOU TO HANDLE THE HUMAN-SIZED WEAK ONES, OKAY?
OOH! NO YOU MOCK ME!!
RRG! RRG!

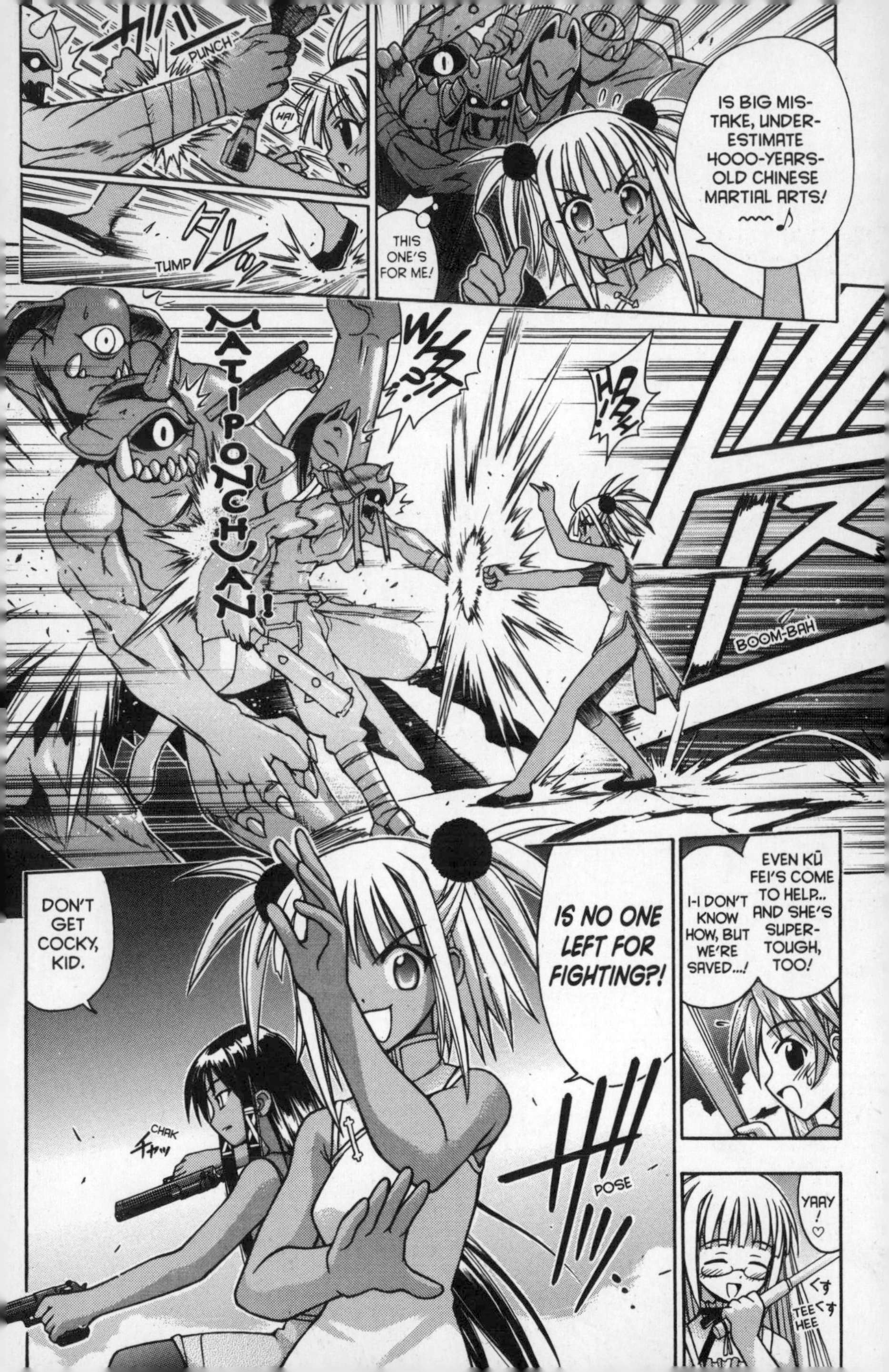
IS BIG MIS-TAKE, UNDER-ESTIMATE 4000-YEARS-OLD CHINESE MARTIAL ARTS! ~~~♪
THIS ONE'S FOR ME!
PUNCH
HA!
TUMP
HAAH!
WHAT?!
MATIPONCHUAN!
BOOM-BAH
EVEN KŪ FEI'S COME TO HELP... AND SHE'S SUPER-TOUGH, TOO!
I-I DON'T KNOW HOW, BUT WE'RE SAVED...!
YAAY! ♡
TEE HEE
IS NO ONE LEFT FOR FIGHTING?!
DON'T GET COCKY, KID.
CHAK
POSE

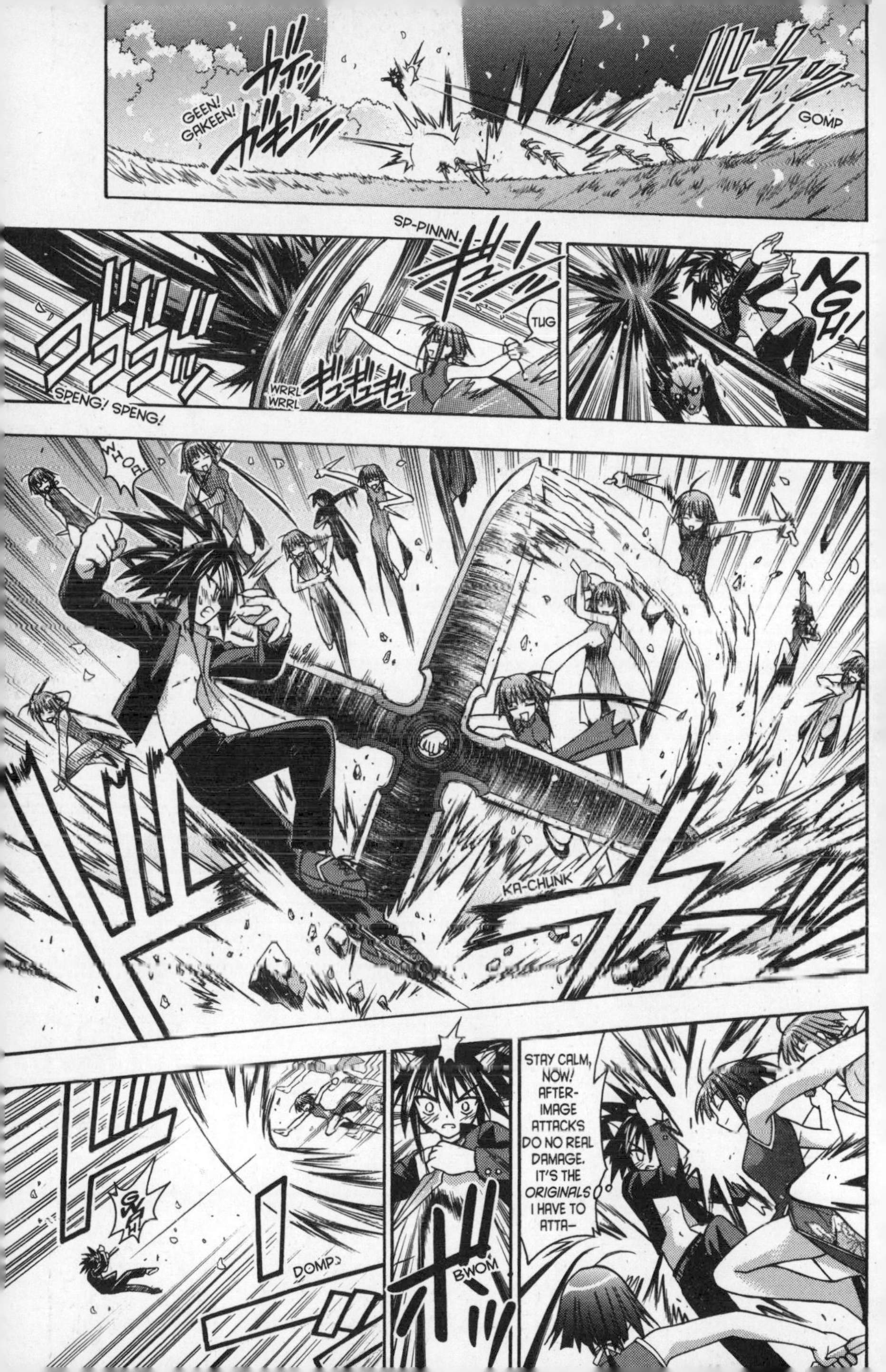
GOMP
GEEN! GAKEEN!
NGH!
SP-PINNN.
TUG
WRRL WRRL
SPENG! SPENG!
KA-CHUNK
STAY CALM, NOW! AFTER-IMAGE ATTACKS DO NO REAL DAMAGE. IT'S THE *ORIGINALS* I HAVE TO ATTA—
BWOM
DOMP

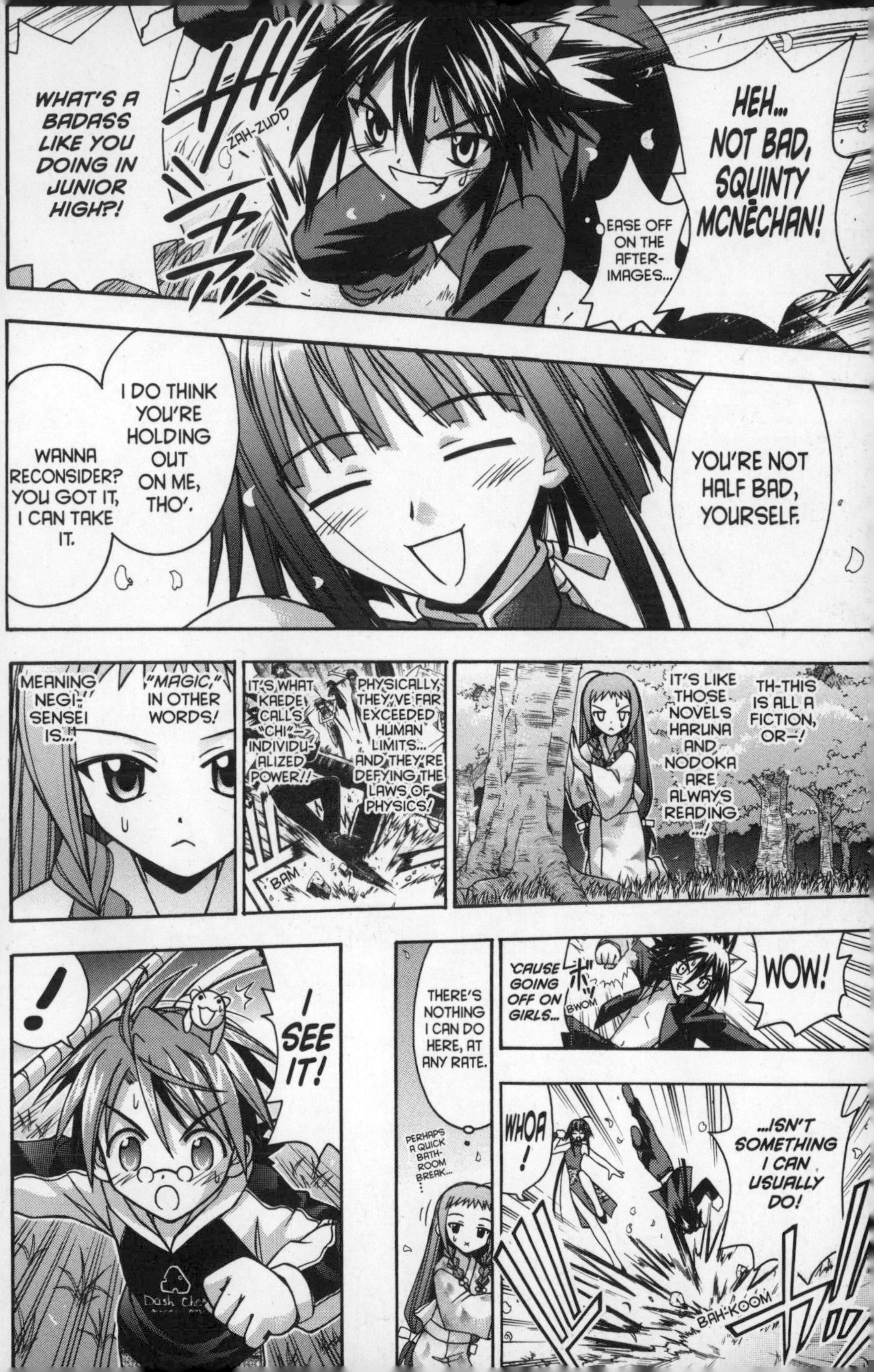
HEH... NOT BAD, SQUINTY MCNÉCHAN!
EASE OFF ON THE AFTER-IMAGES...
ZAH-ZUDD
WHAT'S A BADASS LIKE YOU DOING IN JUNIOR HIGH?!
YOU'RE NOT HALF BAD, YOURSELF.
I DO THINK YOU'RE HOLDING OUT ON ME, THO'.
WANNA RECONSIDER? YOU GOT IT, I CAN TAKE IT.
TH-THIS IS ALL A FICTION, OR—!
IT'S LIKE THOSE NOVELS HARUNA AND NODOKA ARE ALWAYS READING...!
PHYSICALLY, THEY'VE FAR EXCEEDED HUMAN LIMITS... AND THEY'RE DEFYING THE LAWS OF PHYSICS!
IT'S WHAT KAEDE CALLS "CHI"— INDIVIDUALIZED POWER!!
BAM
"MAGIC," IN OTHER WORDS!
MEANING NEGI-SENSEI IS...!
WOW!
'CAUSE GOING OFF ON GIRLS...
BWOM
...ISN'T SOMETHING I CAN USUALLY DO!
WHOA!
BAH-KOOM
THERE'S NOTHING I CAN DO HERE, AT ANY RATE.
PERHAPS A QUICK BATH-ROOM BREAK...
!
I SEE IT!

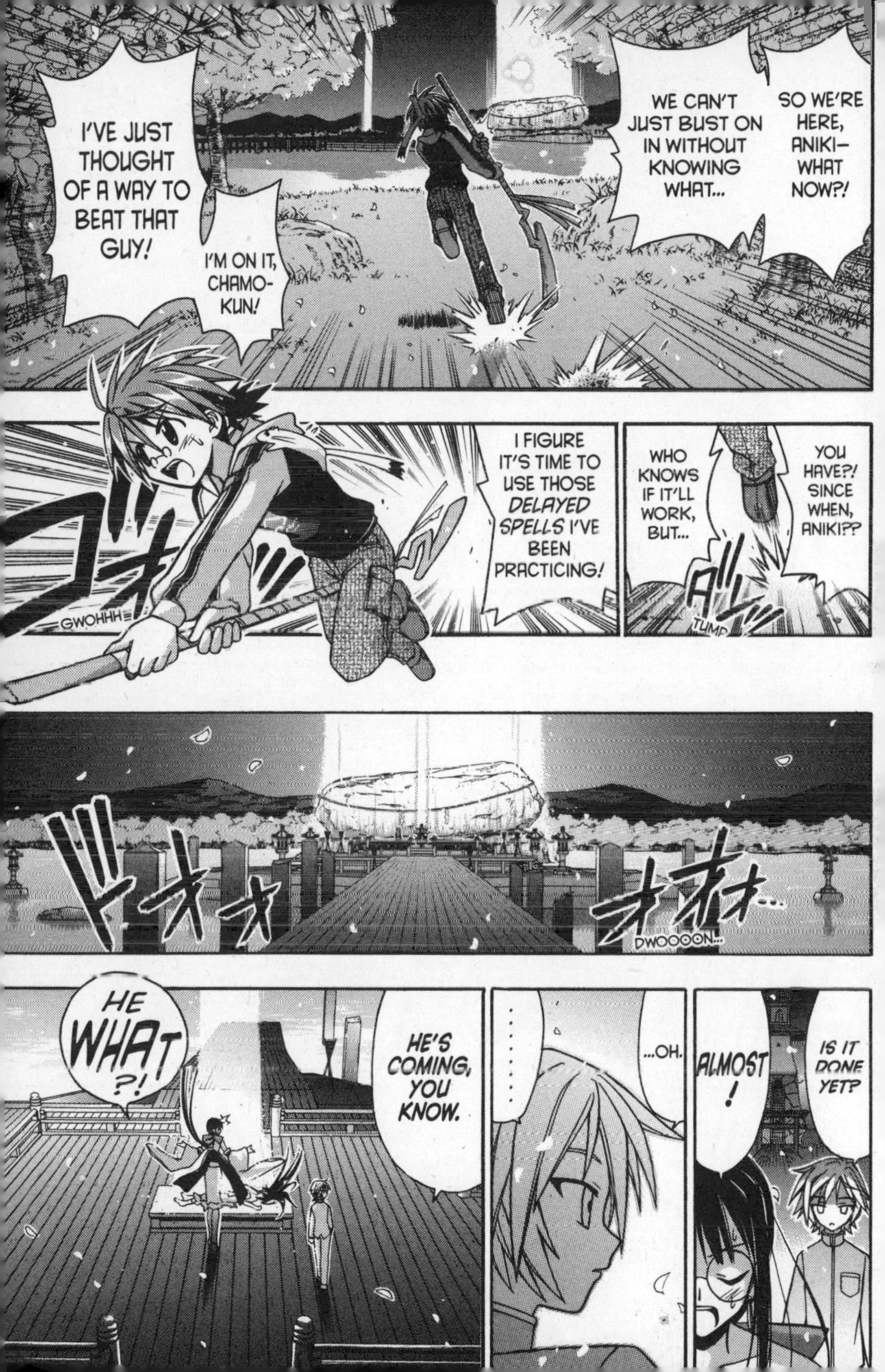
SO WE'RE HERE, ANIKI— WHAT NOW?!
WE CAN'T JUST BUST ON IN WITHOUT KNOWING WHAT...
I'VE JUST THOUGHT OF A WAY TO BEAT THAT GUY!
I'M ON IT, CHAMO-KUN!
YOU HAVE?! SINCE WHEN, ANIKI??
WHO KNOWS IF IT'LL WORK, BUT...
TUMP
I FIGURE IT'S TIME TO USE THOSE *DELAYED SPELLS* I'VE BEEN PRACTICING!
GWOHHH
DWOOOON...
IS IT DONE YET?
ALMOST!
...OH.
......
HE'S COMING, YOU KNOW.
HE WHAT?!

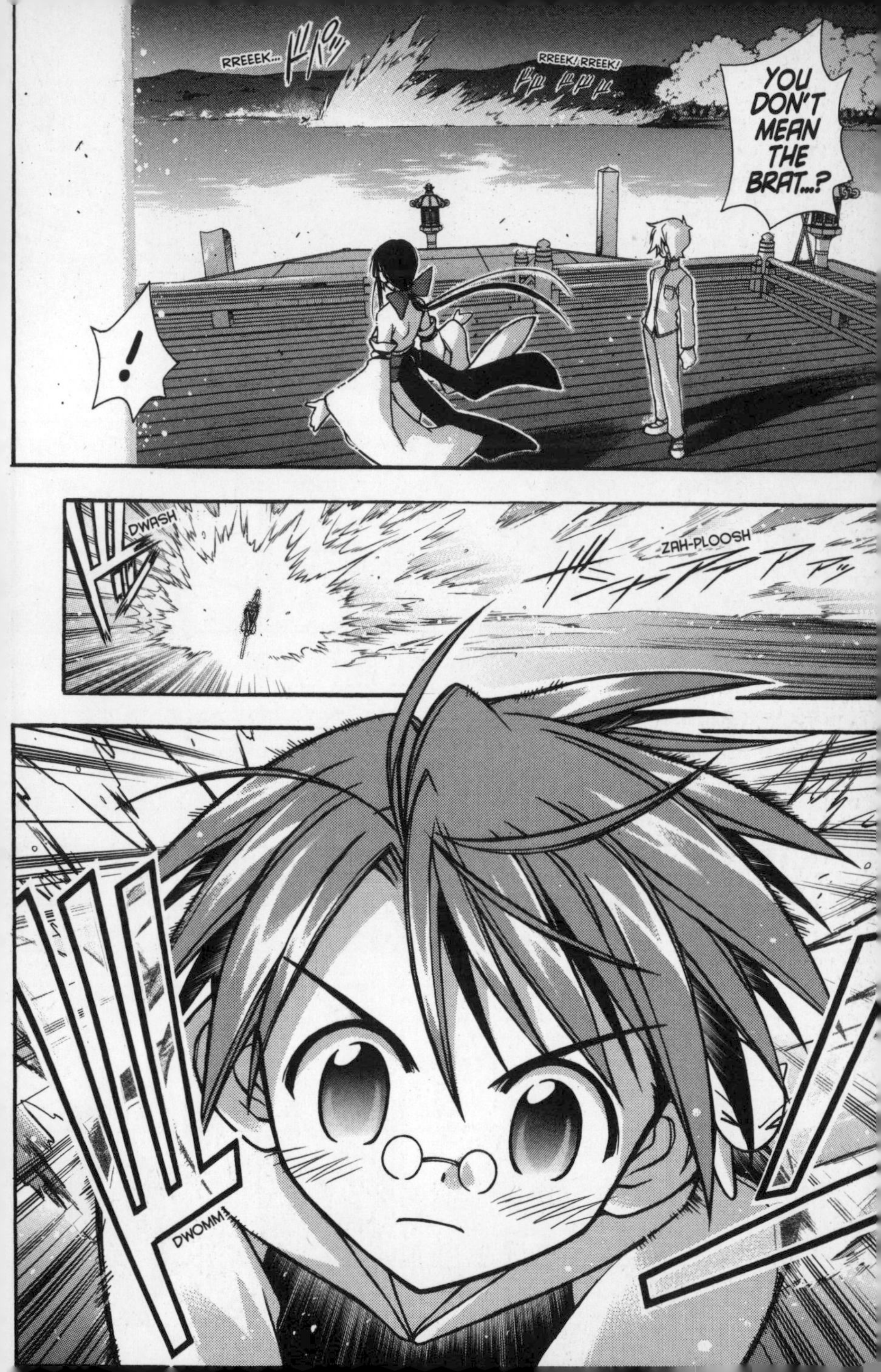
YOU DON'T MEAN THE BRAT...?
RREEK! RREEK!
RREEEK...
!
ZAH-PLOOSH
DWASH
DWOMM

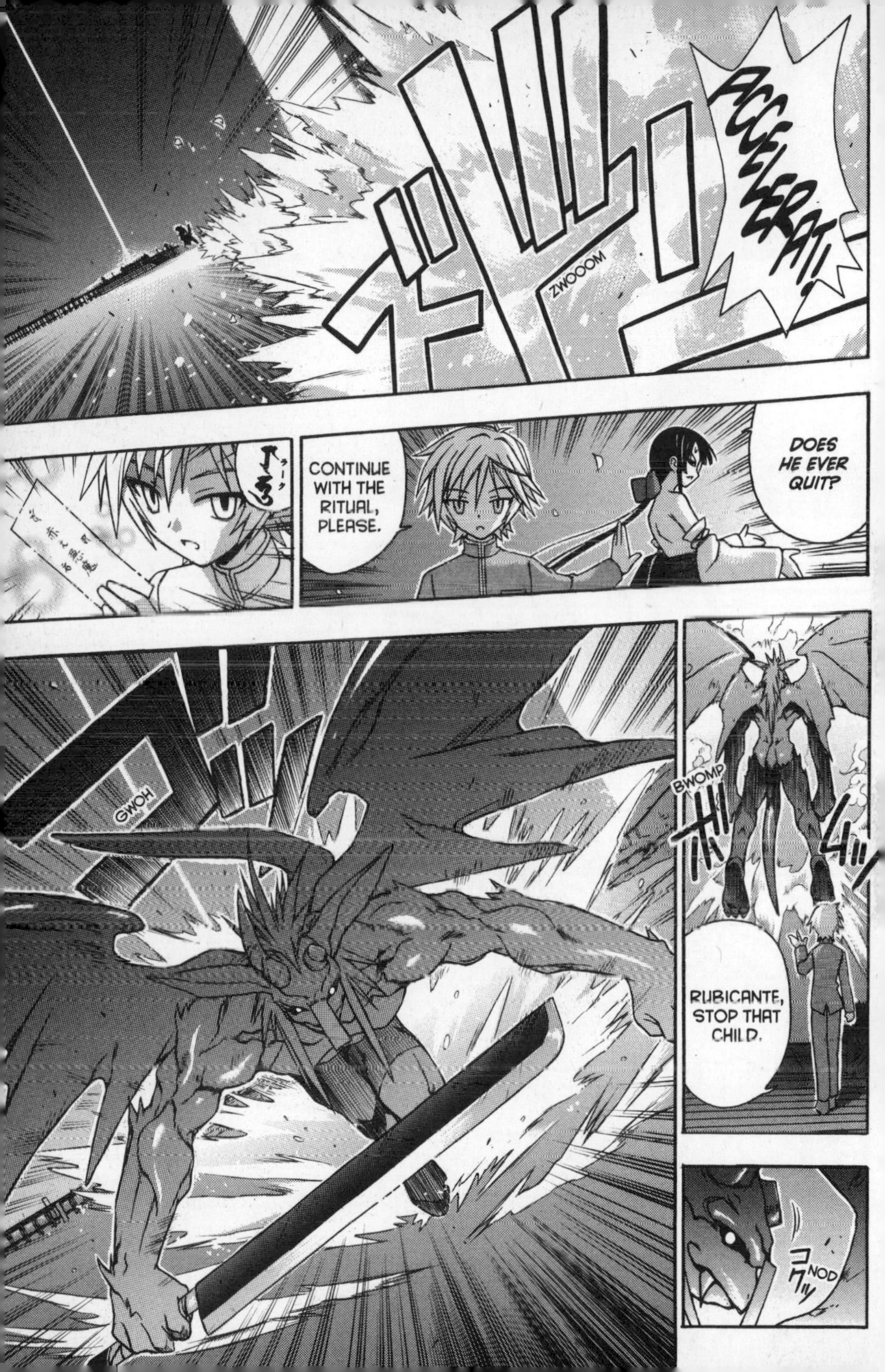
ACCELERAT!!
ZWOOOM
DOES HE EVER QUIT?
CONTINUE WITH THE RITUAL, PLEASE.
BWOMP
RUBICANTE, STOP THAT CHILD.
NOD
GWOH

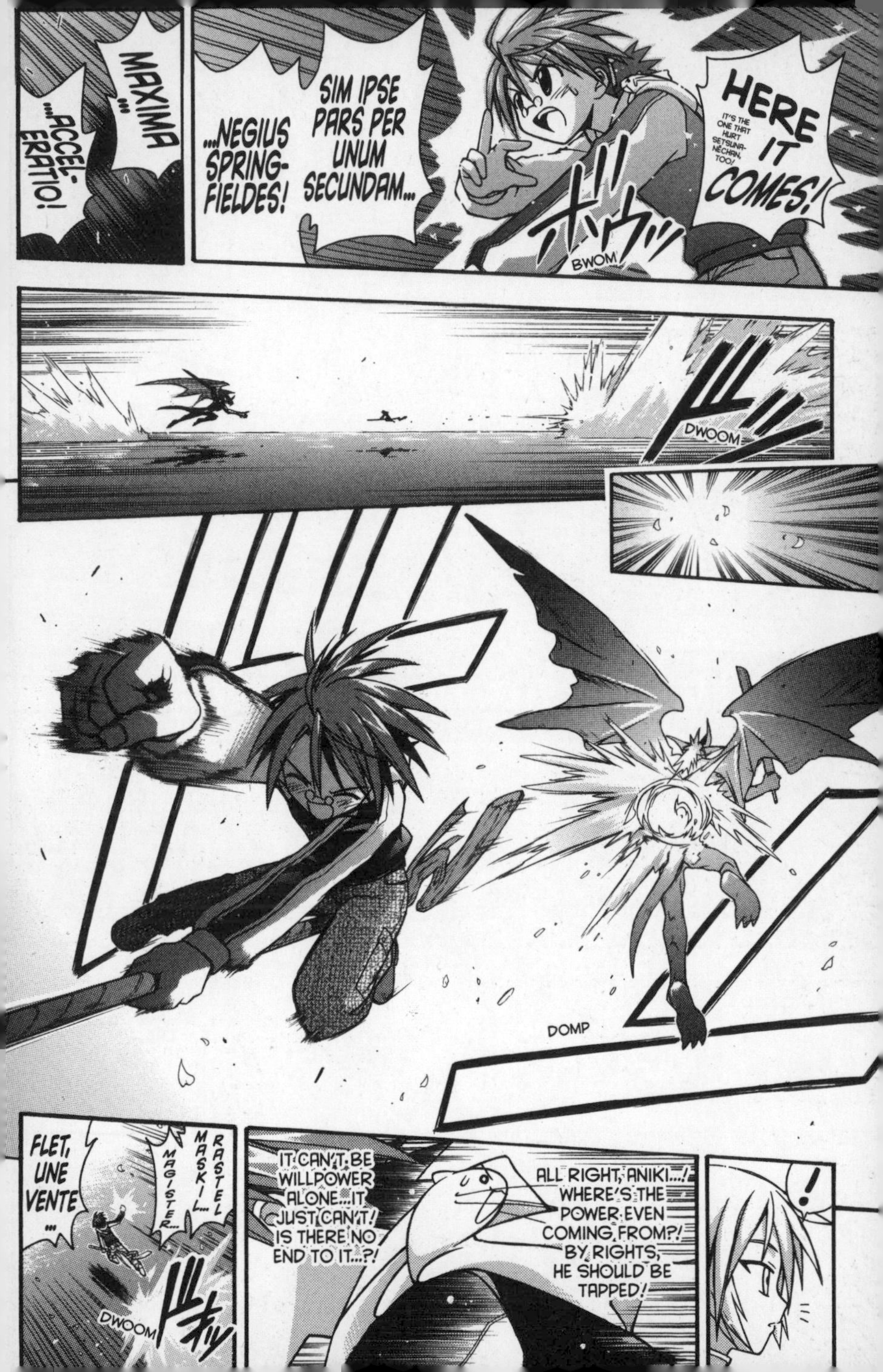
HERE IT COMES!
IT'S THE ONE THAT HURT SETSUNA-NÉCHAN, TOO!
BWOM
SIM IPSE PARS PER UNUM SECUNDAM...
...NEGIUS SPRINGFIELDES!
MAXIMA...
...ACCELERATIO!
DWOOM
DOMP
!
ALL RIGHT, ANIKI...! WHERE'S THE POWER EVEN COMING FROM?! BY RIGHTS, HE SHOULD BE TAPPED!
IT CAN'T BE WILLPOWER ALONE... IT JUST CAN'T! IS THERE NO END TO IT...?!
RASTEL MASKIL... MAGISTER...
FLET, UNE VENTE...
DWOOM

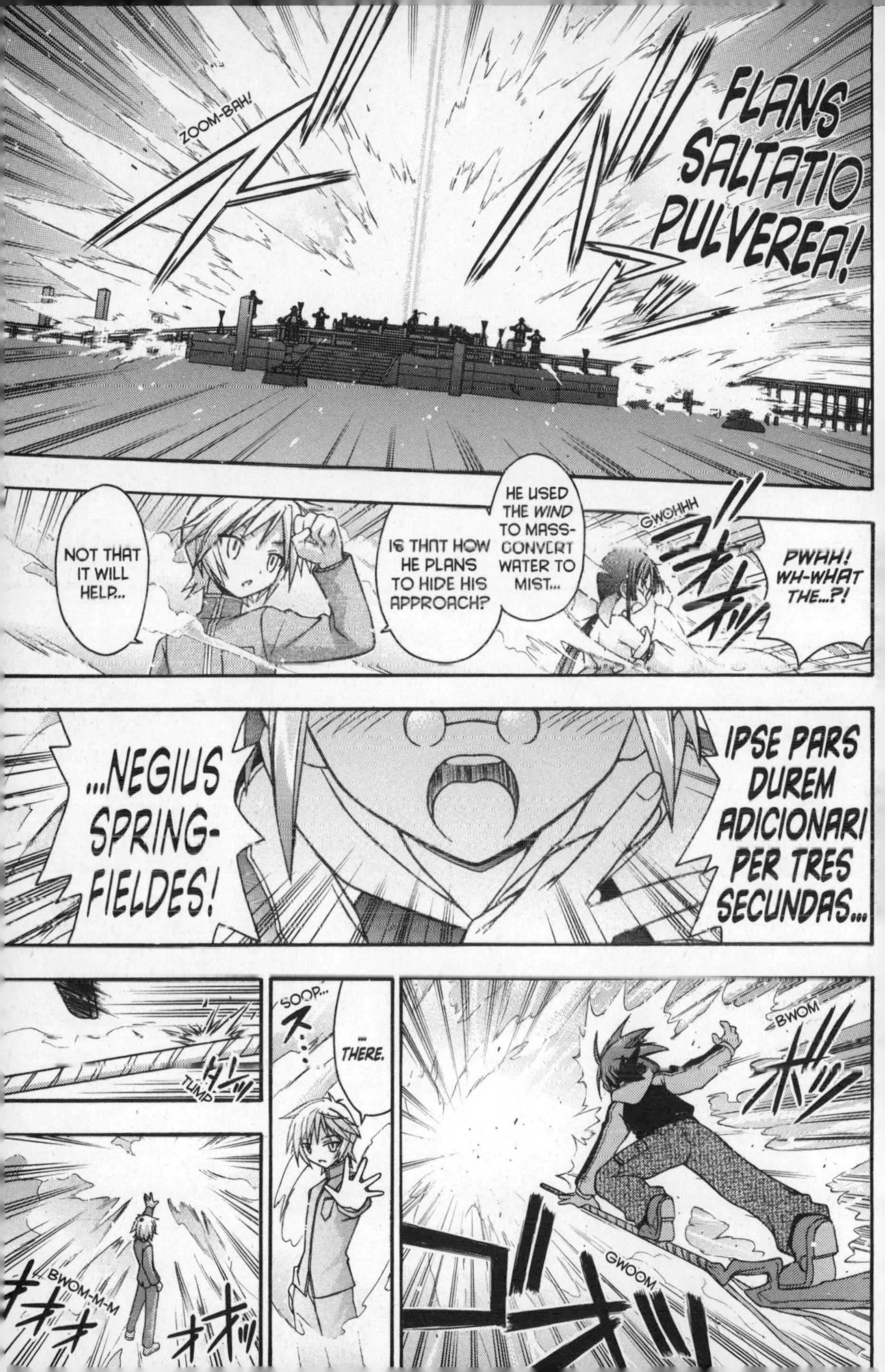
FLANS SALTATIO PULVEREA!
ZOOM-BAH!
PWAH! WH-WHAT THE...?!
GWOHHH
HE USED THE *WIND* TO MASS-CONVERT WATER TO MIST...
IS THAT HOW HE PLANS TO HIDE HIS APPROACH?
NOT THAT IT WILL HELP...
IPSE PARS DUREM ADICIONARI PER TRES SECUNDAS...
...NEGIUS SPRING-FIELDES!
BWOM
GWOOM
SOOP...
... THERE.
TUMP
BWOM-M-M

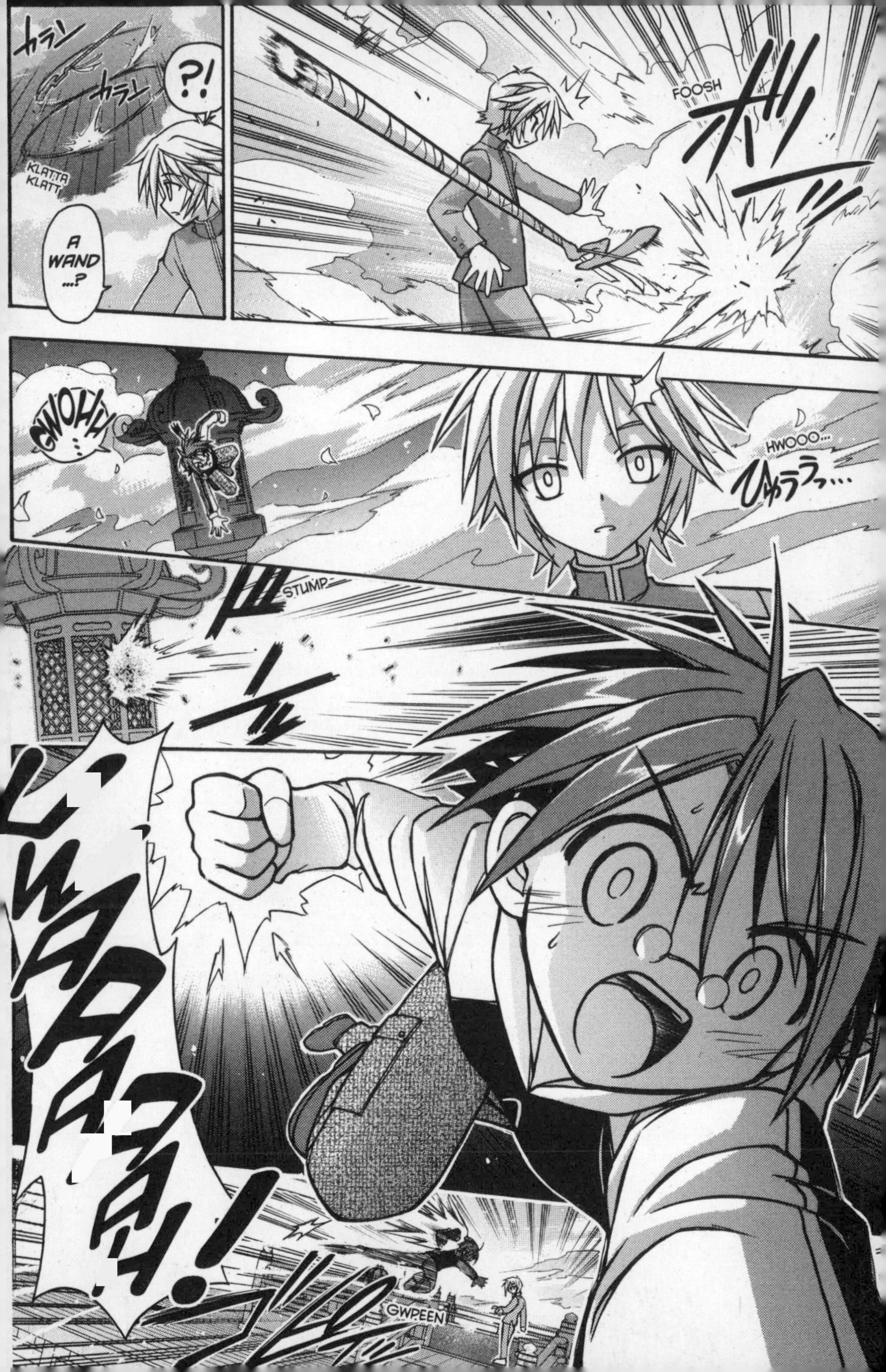
FOOSH
カラン
カラン
?!
KLATTA KLATT
A WAND ...?
GWOHH...
HWOOO...
ひゅららっ...
STUMP
GWPEEN

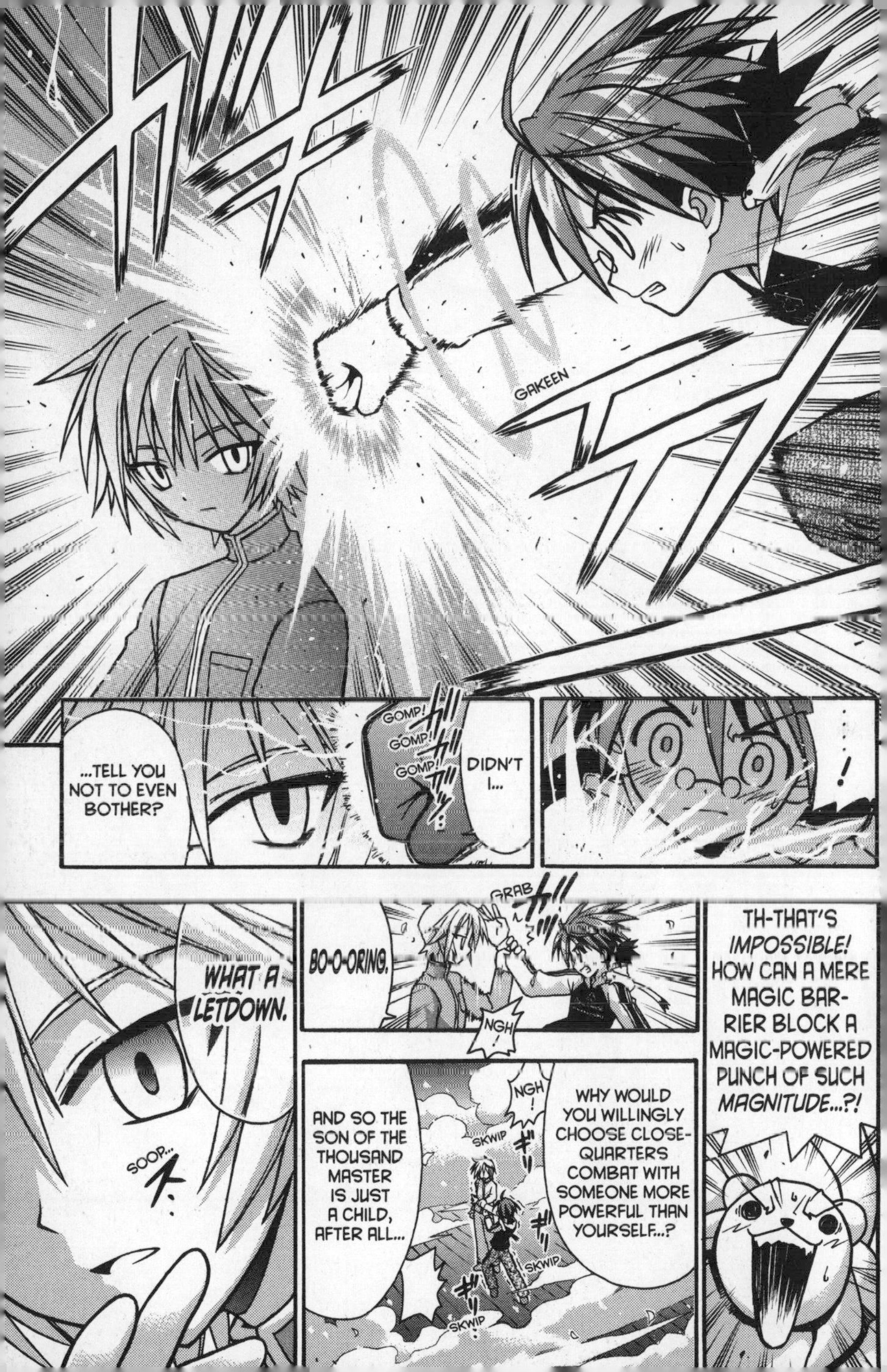
GAKEEN
!
DIDN'T I...
GOMP!
GOMP!
GOMP!
...TELL YOU NOT TO EVEN BOTHER?
TH-THAT'S *IMPOSSIBLE!* HOW CAN A MERE MAGIC BARRIER BLOCK A MAGIC-POWERED PUNCH OF SUCH *MAGNITUDE*...?!
GRAB
BO-O-ORING.
NGH!
NGH!
WHY WOULD YOU WILLINGLY CHOOSE CLOSE-QUARTERS COMBAT WITH SOMEONE MORE POWERFUL THAN YOURSELF...?
SKWIP
SKWIP
AND SO THE SON OF THE THOUSAND MASTER IS JUST A CHILD, AFTER ALL...
SKWIP
WHAT A LETDOWN.
SOOP...

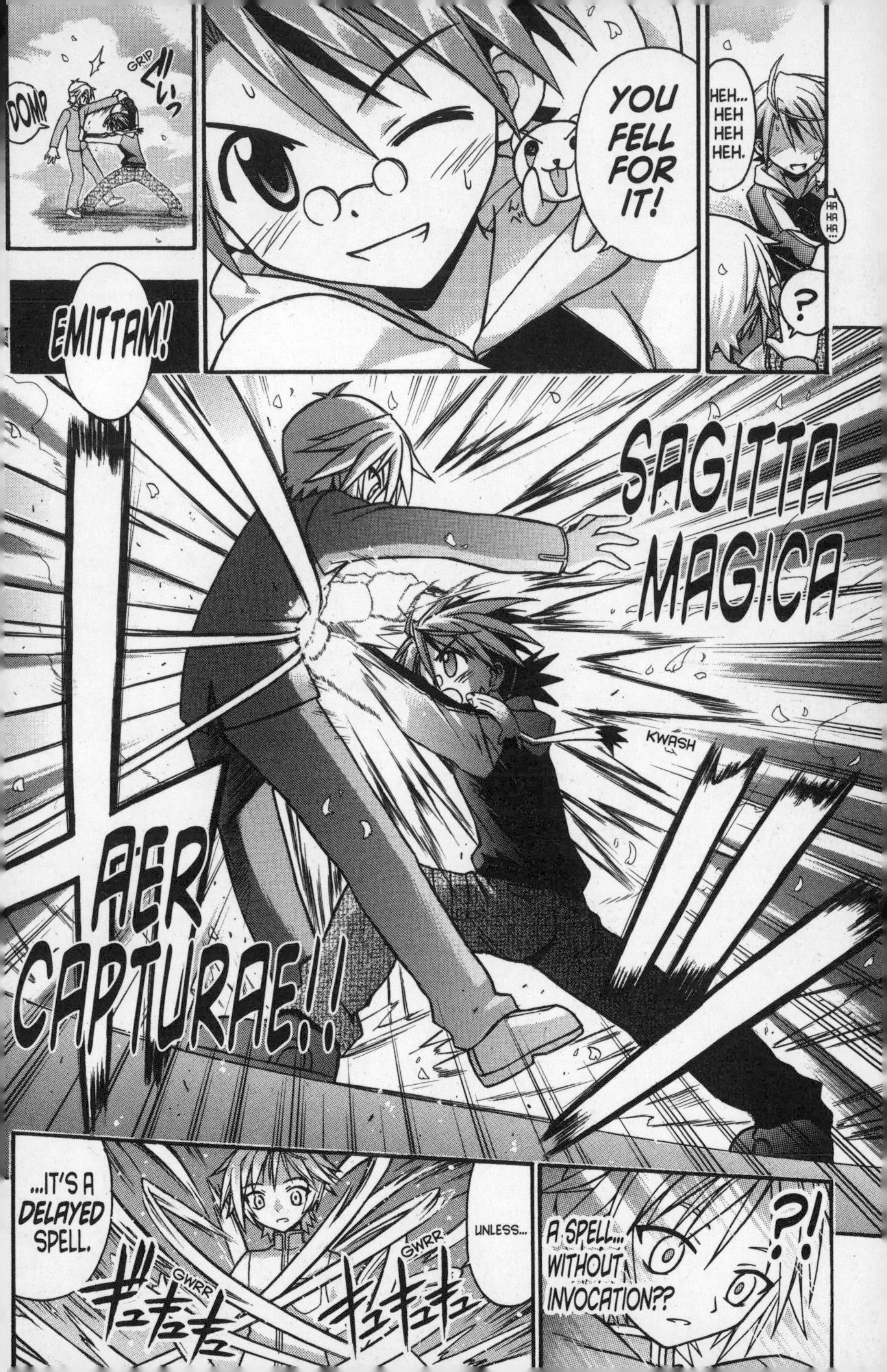
HEH... HEH HEH HEH.
HA HA HA...
?
YOU FELL FOR IT!
GRIP
DOMP
EMITTAM!
SAGITTA MAGICA
KWASH
AER CAPTURAE!!
?!
A SPELL... WITHOUT INVOCATION??
UNLESS...
GWRR
...IT'S A DELAYED SPELL.
GWRR

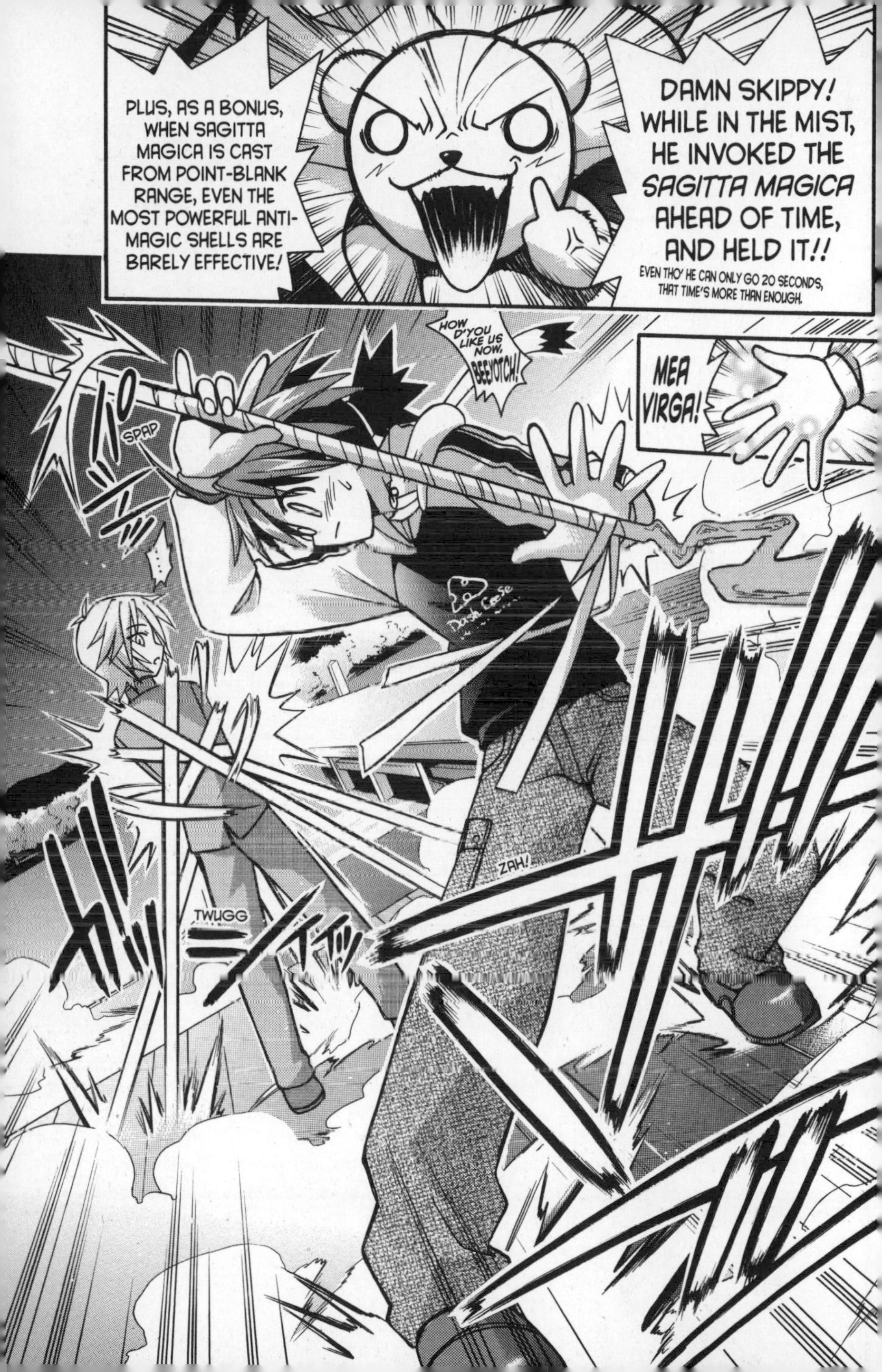
DAMN SKIPPY! WHILE IN THE MIST, HE INVOKED THE *SAGITTA MAGICA* AHEAD OF TIME, AND HELD IT!!
EVEN THO' HE CAN ONLY GO 20 SECONDS, THAT TIME'S MORE THAN ENOUGH.
PLUS, AS A BONUS, WHEN SAGITTA MAGICA IS CAST FROM POINT-BLANK RANGE, EVEN THE MOST POWERFUL ANTI-MAGIC SHELLS ARE BARELY EFFECTIVE!
MEA VIRGA!
HOW D'YOU LIKE US NOW, BEEYOTCH!
SPAP
ZAH!
TWUGG

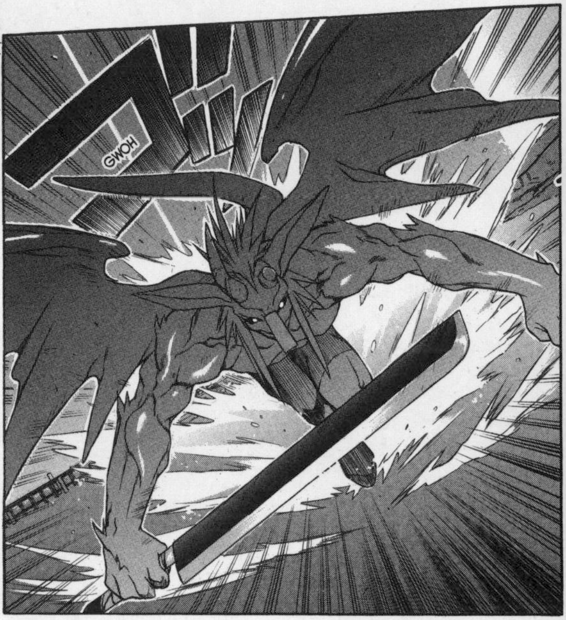
GWOH

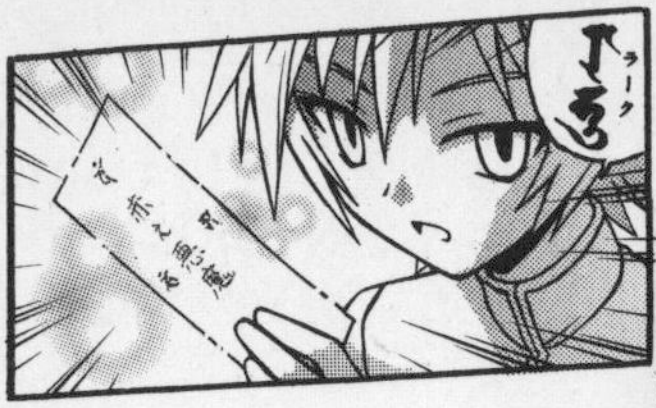

NEGIMA! FORTY-NINTH PERIOD: LEXICON NEGIMARIUM

■

RARK or RAK

In Sanskrit, the word means "devil," and is the spell which the "white-haired youth" invokes to summon the demon Rubicante...a demon of Judeo-Christian origin which appears in Dante's *Inferno.* For it to be summoned by Eastern magic, therefore, the summoner must be puissant, indeed.

■最大加速

MAXIMA ACCELERATIO

Because of the cognates ("maximum" and "acceleration"), it's easy enough to guess at the nature of this spell. Depending on the skill level of the caster, speed can be increased up to 64.2 knots.

■解放

EMITTAM

Recursive or "delayed" spell that recalls a previously uttered incantation. As it's said, "all good things to those who wait," the maximum effectiveness of a given spell is not often realized until some time has passed. Additionally, being able to choose the time of the spell's release allows the caster to await the most opportune moment. Because the casting of a "delayed" spell requires an even higher level of skill, more power is necessary. An even higher-level variant is a delayed spell conditional release, in which certain, specific conditions must be met before the spell is activated.

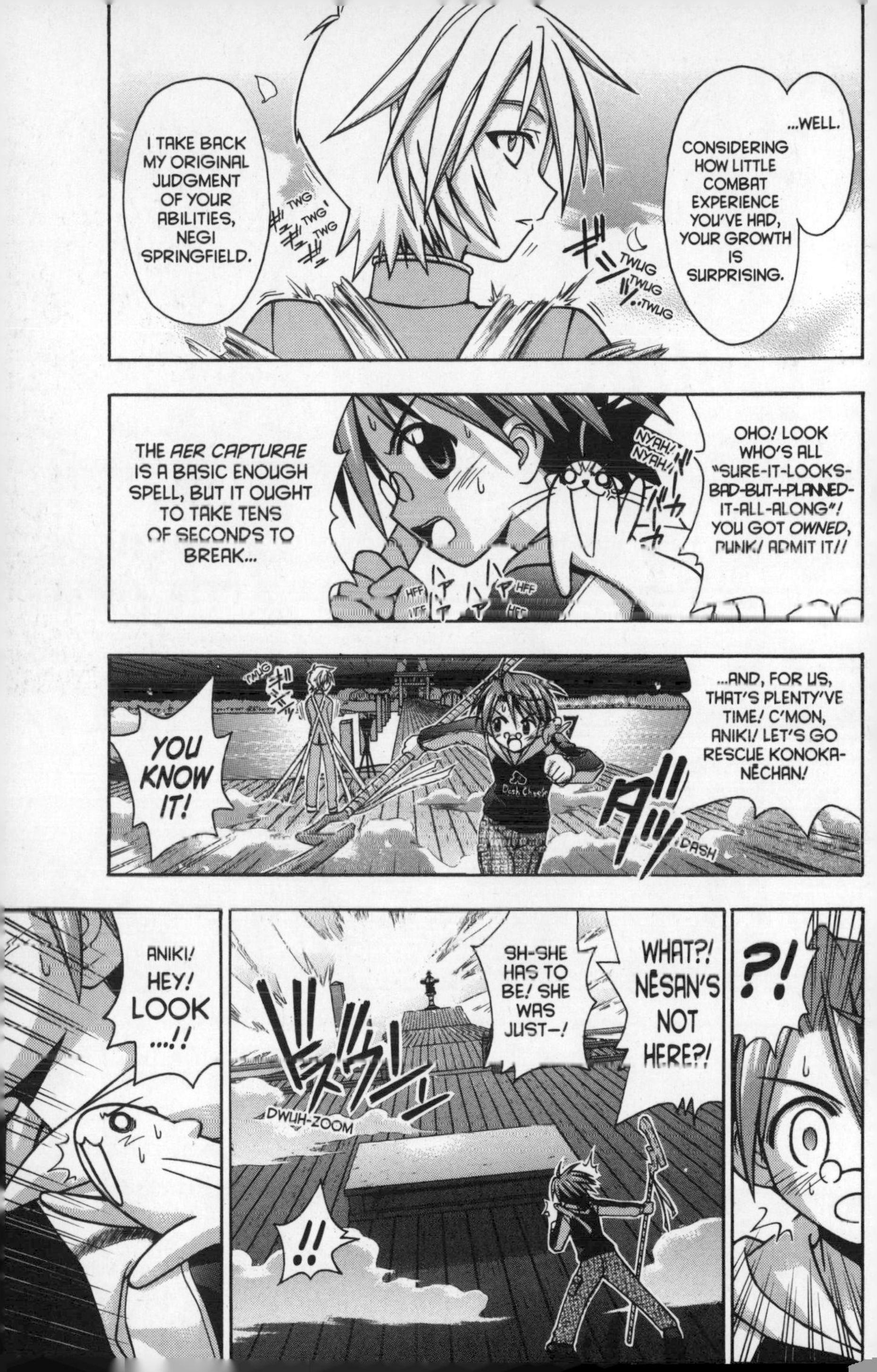
...WELL.
CONSIDERING HOW LITTLE COMBAT EXPERIENCE YOU'VE HAD, YOUR GROWTH IS SURPRISING.
TWUG TWUG TWUG
TWG TWG TWG
I TAKE BACK MY ORIGINAL JUDGMENT OF YOUR ABILITIES, NEGI SPRINGFIELD.
OHO! LOOK WHO'S ALL "SURE-IT-LOOKS-BAD-BUT-I-PLANNED-IT-ALL-ALONG"! YOU GOT OWNED, PUNK! ADMIT IT!!
NYAH! NYAH!
HFF HFF HFF HFF
THE AER CAPTURAE IS A BASIC ENOUGH SPELL, BUT IT OUGHT TO TAKE TENS OF SECONDS TO BREAK...
...AND, FOR US, THAT'S PLENTY'VE TIME! C'MON, ANIKI! LET'S GO RESCUE KONOKA-NÊCHAN!
DASH
TWUG
YOU KNOW IT!
?!
WHAT?! NÊSAN'S NOT HERE?!
SH-SHE HAS TO BE! SHE WAS JUST—!
DWUH-ZOOM
!!
ANIKI! HEY! LOOK ...!!

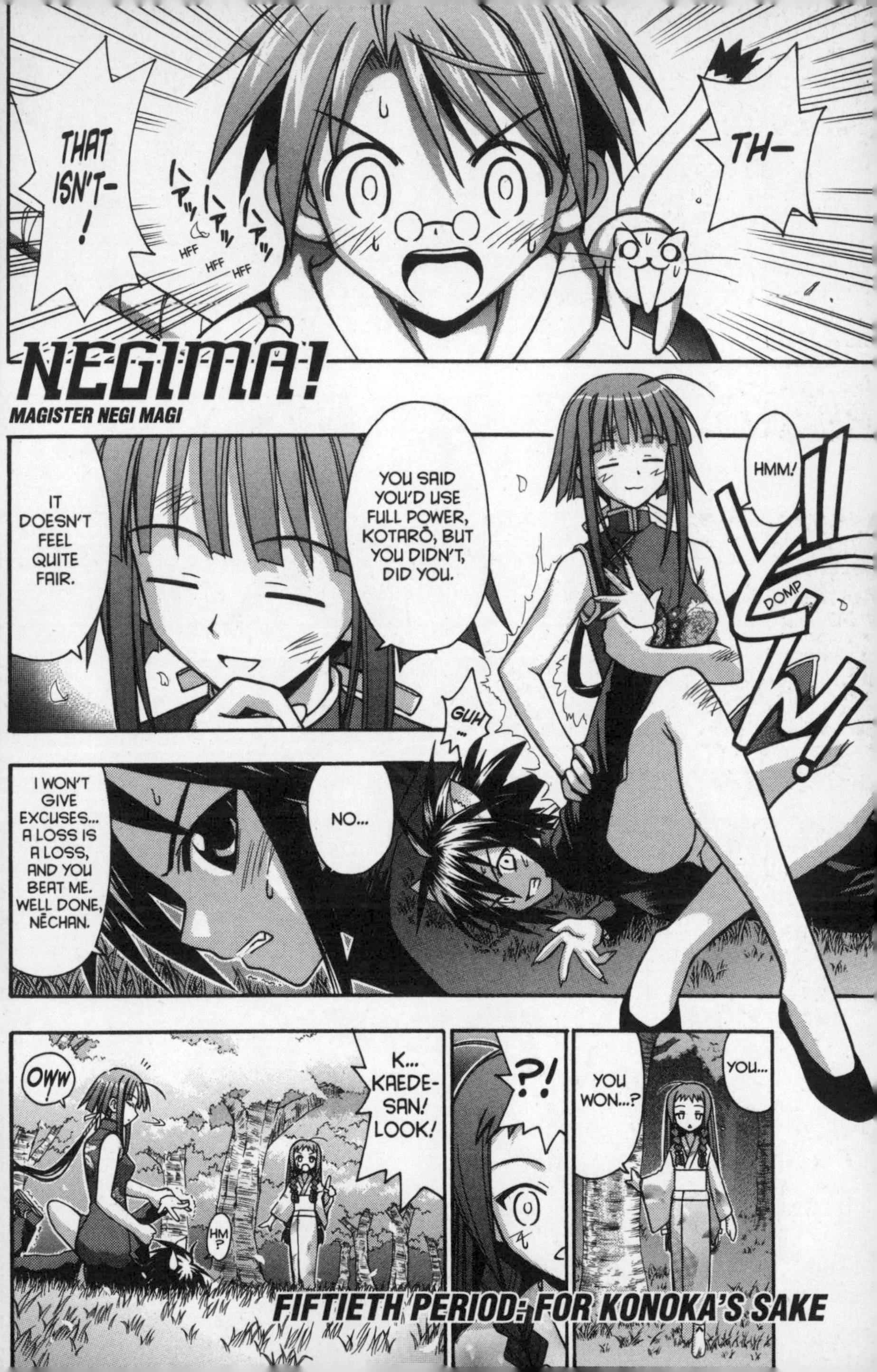
TH-
THAT ISN'T-!
ハアッ ハアッ ハアッ
HFF HFF HFF
NEGIMA!
MAGISTER NEGI MAGI
HMM!
DOMP
GUH...
YOU SAID YOU'D USE FULL POWER, KOTARŌ, BUT YOU DIDN'T, DID YOU.
IT DOESN'T FEEL QUITE FAIR.
NO...
I WON'T GIVE EXCUSES... A LOSS IS A LOSS, AND YOU BEAT ME. WELL DONE, NĒCHAN.
YOU...
YOU WON...?
?!
K... KAEDE-SAN! LOOK!
OWW
HM?
FIFTIETH PERIOD: FOR KONOKA'S SAKE

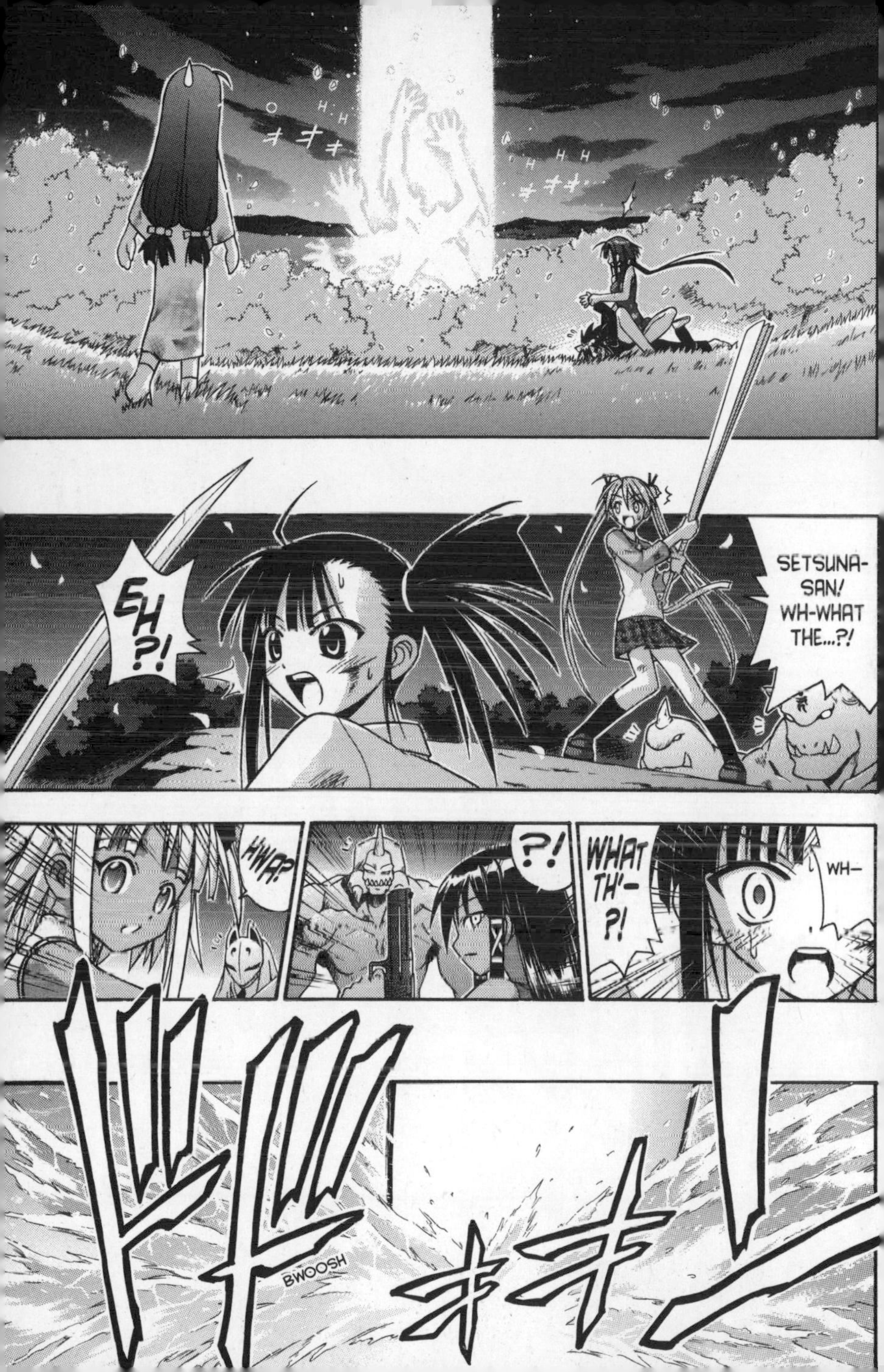
SETSUNA-SAN! WH-WHAT THE...?!
EH?!
WH—
WHAT TH'—?!
?!
HWA?
BWOOSH

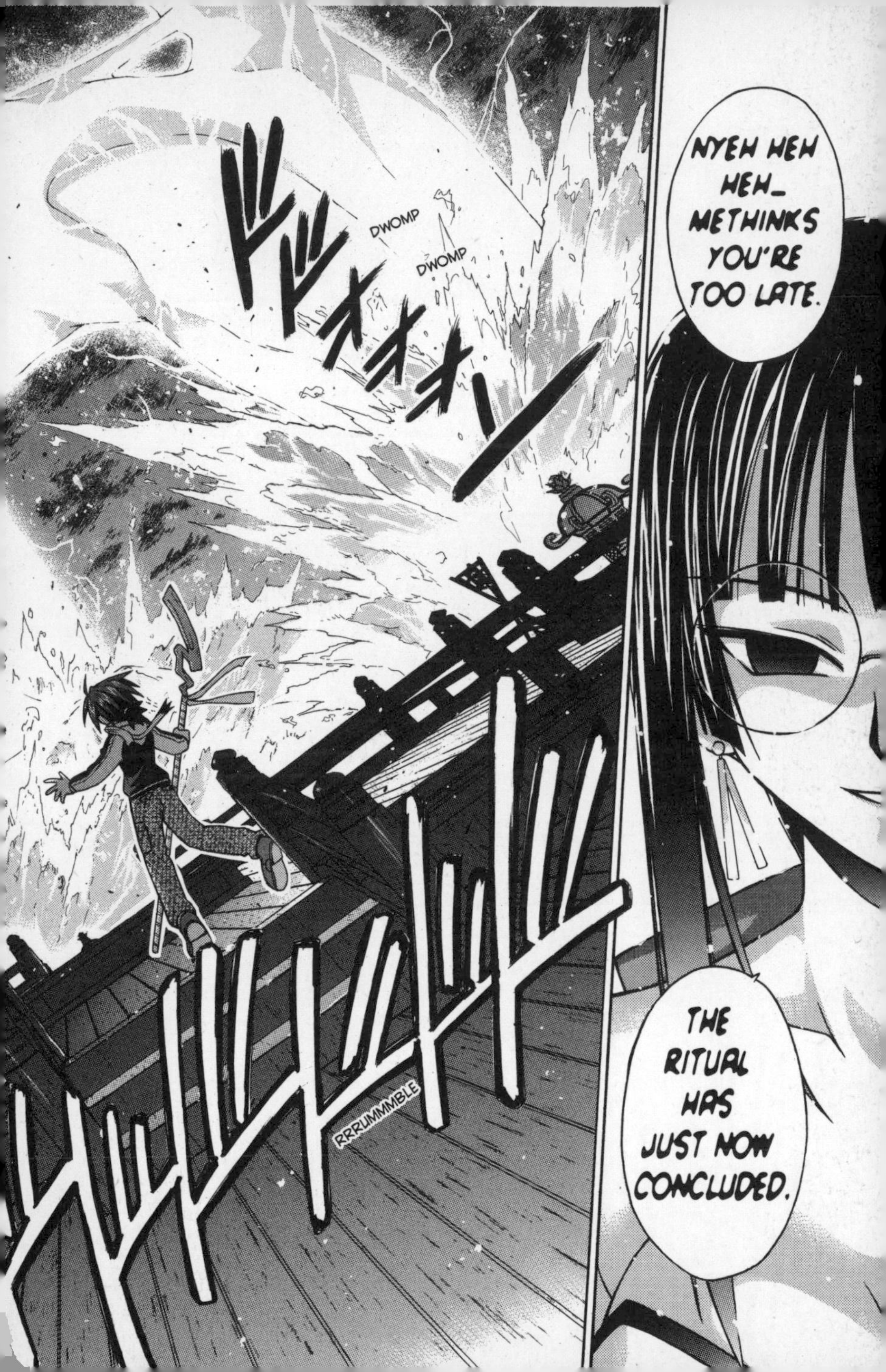
NYEH HEH HEH_ METHINKS YOU'RE TOO LATE.
THE RITUAL HAS JUST NOW CONCLUDED.
ドドオオン
DWOMP
DWOMP
RRRUMMMBLE

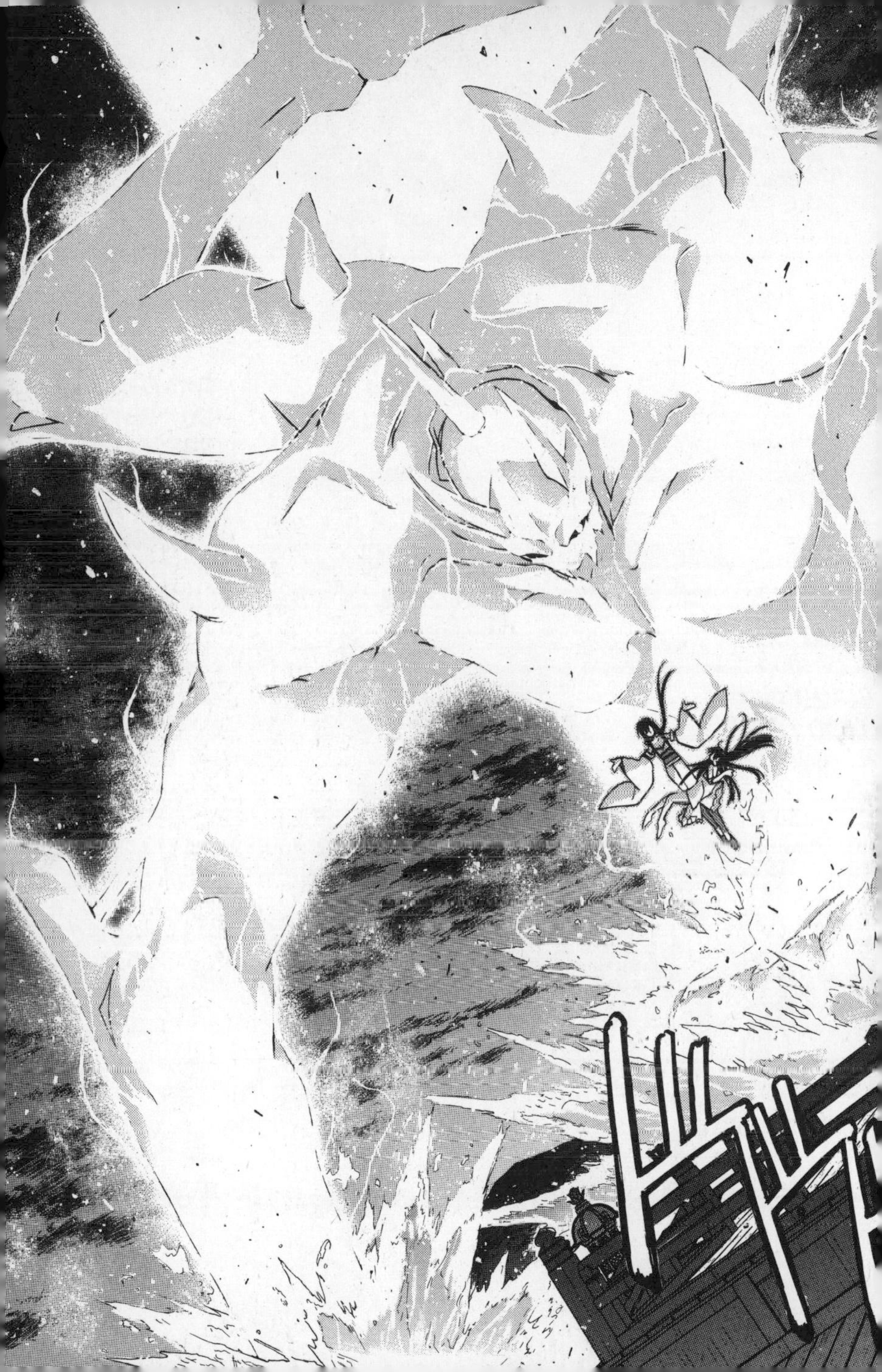

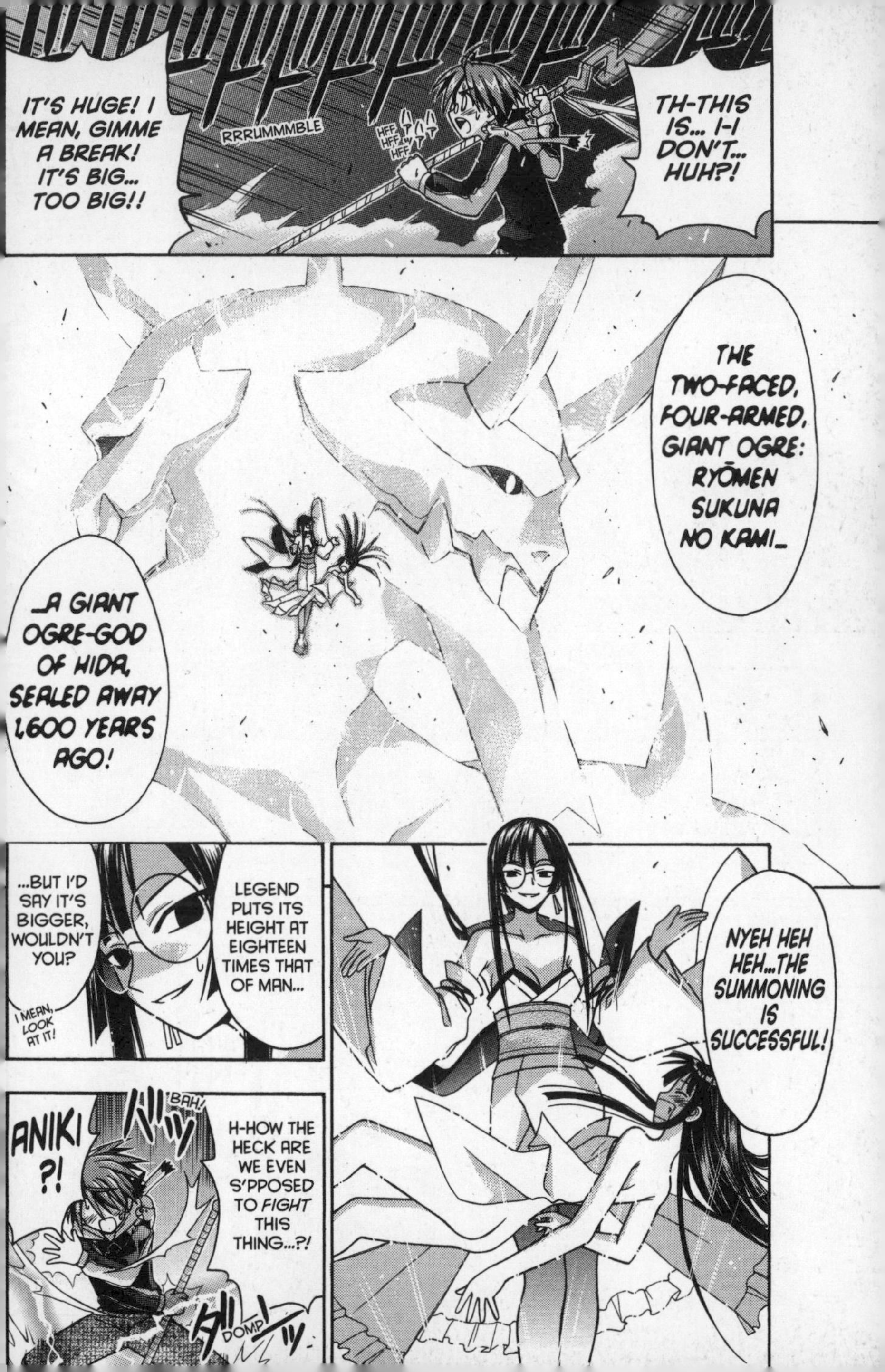
TH-THIS IS... I-I DON'T... HUH?!
HFF HFF HFF
RRRUMMMBLE
IT'S HUGE! I MEAN, GIMME A BREAK! IT'S BIG... TOO BIG!!
THE TWO-FACED, FOUR-ARMED, GIANT OGRE: RYŌMEN SUKUNA NO KAMI...
...A GIANT OGRE-GOD OF HIDA, SEALED AWAY 1,600 YEARS AGO!
NYEH HEH HEH...THE SUMMONING IS SUCCESSFUL!
LEGEND PUTS ITS HEIGHT AT EIGHTEEN TIMES THAT OF MAN...
...BUT I'D SAY IT'S BIGGER, WOULDN'T YOU?
I MEAN, LOOK AT IT!
BAH!
H-HOW THE HECK ARE WE EVEN S'PPOSED TO FIGHT THIS THING...?!
ANIKI ?!
DOMP!

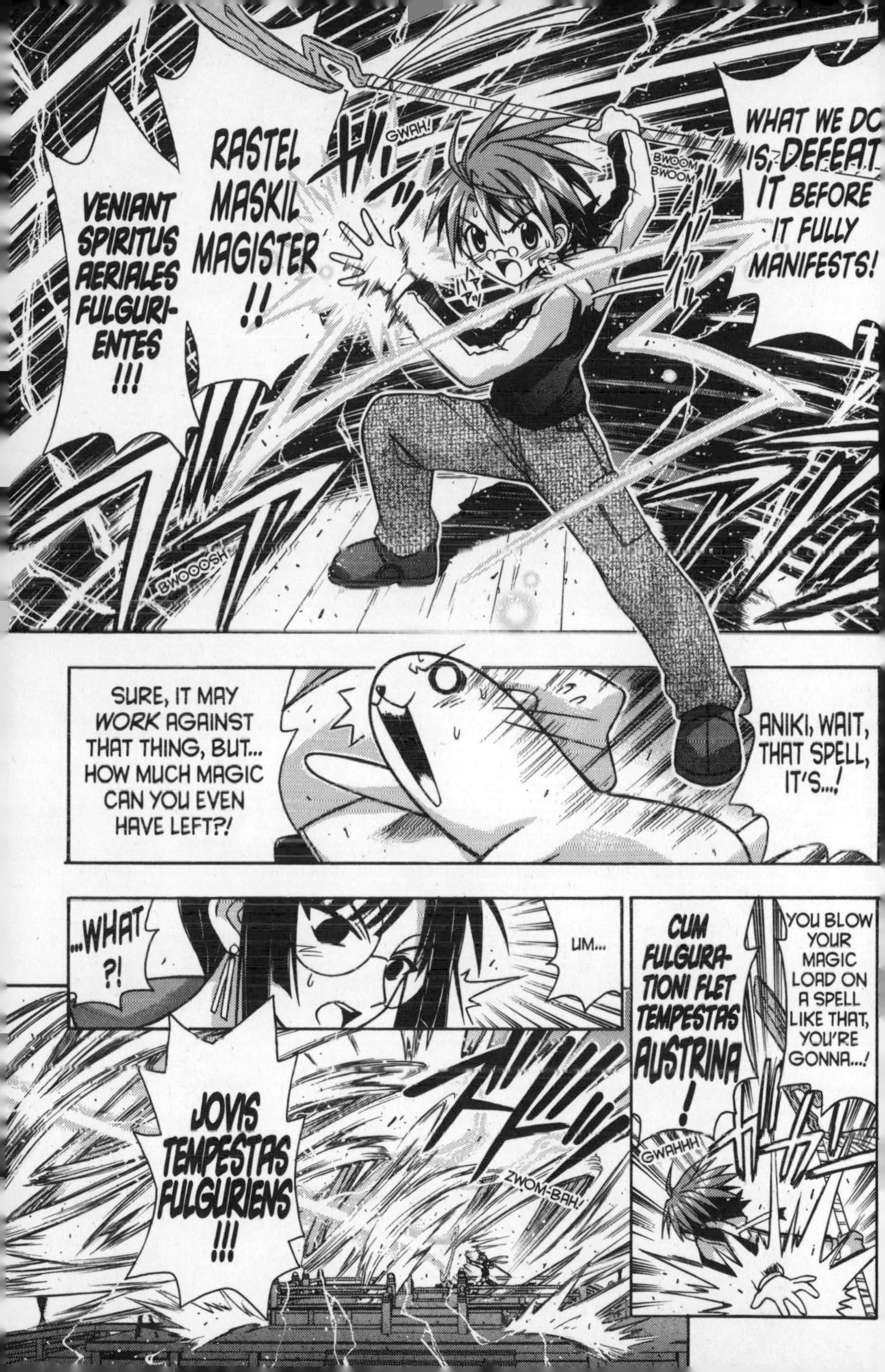
WHAT WE DO IS, DEFEAT IT BEFORE IT FULLY MANIFESTS!
BWOOM BWOOM
GWAH!
RASTEL MASKIL MAGISTER !!
VENIANT SPIRITUS AERIALES FULGURI-ENTES !!!
BWOOOSH
ANIKI, WAIT, THAT SPELL, IT'S...!
SURE, IT MAY WORK AGAINST THAT THING, BUT... HOW MUCH MAGIC CAN YOU EVEN HAVE LEFT?!
YOU BLOW YOUR MAGIC LOAD ON A SPELL LIKE THAT, YOU'RE GONNA...!
CUM FULGURA-TIONI FLET TEMPESTAS AUSTRINA !
GWAHHH
UM...
...WHAT ?!
ZWOM-BAH!
JOVIS TEMPESTAS FULGURIENS !!!

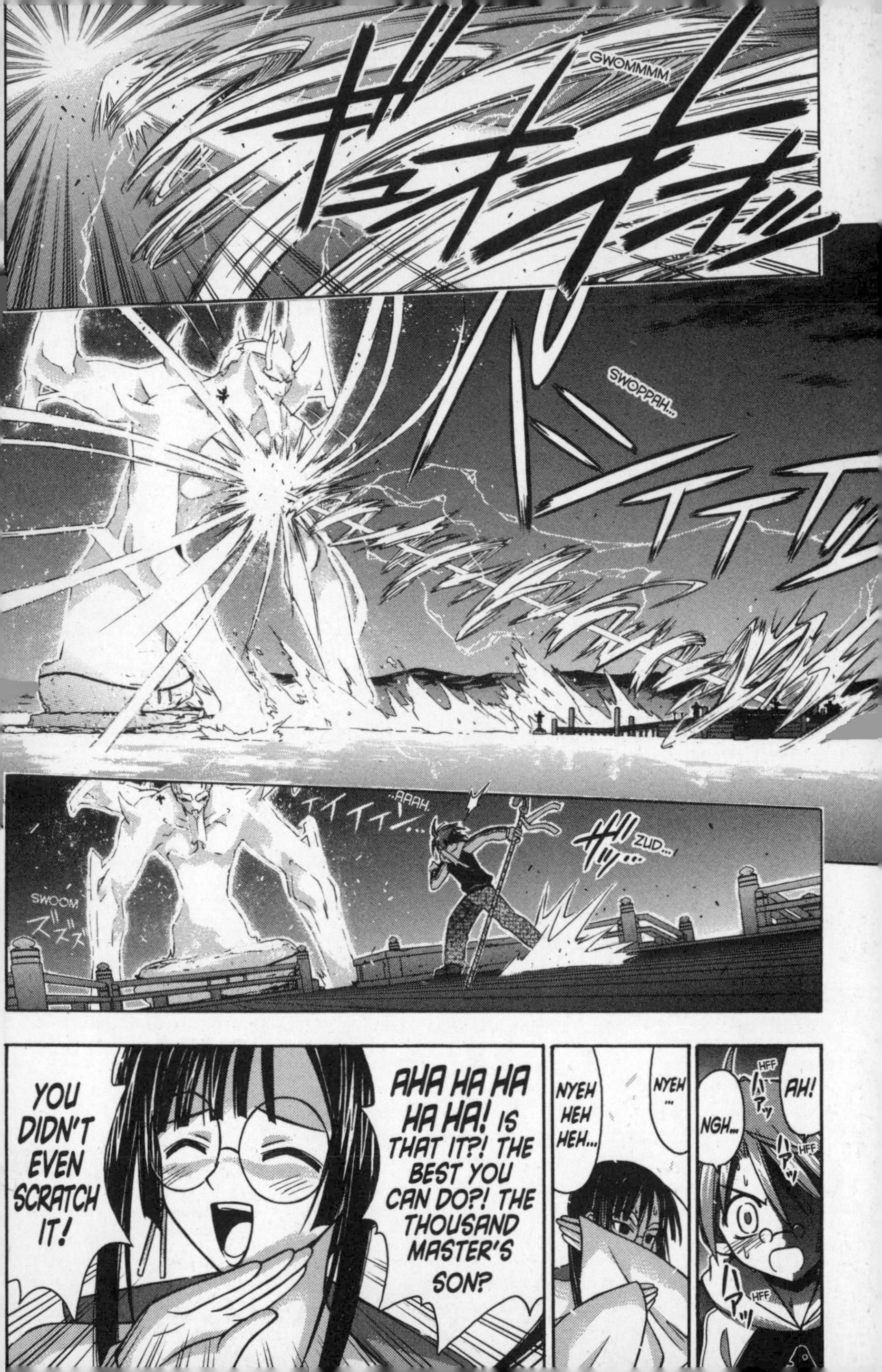
GWOMMMM
SWOPPAH...
ZUD...
...AAAH.
SWOOM
AH!
HFF
NGH...
HFF
HFF
NYEH ...
NYEH HEH HEH...
AHA HA HA HA HA! IS THAT IT?! THE BEST YOU CAN DO?! THE THOUSAND MASTER'S SON?
YOU DIDN'T EVEN SCRATCH IT!

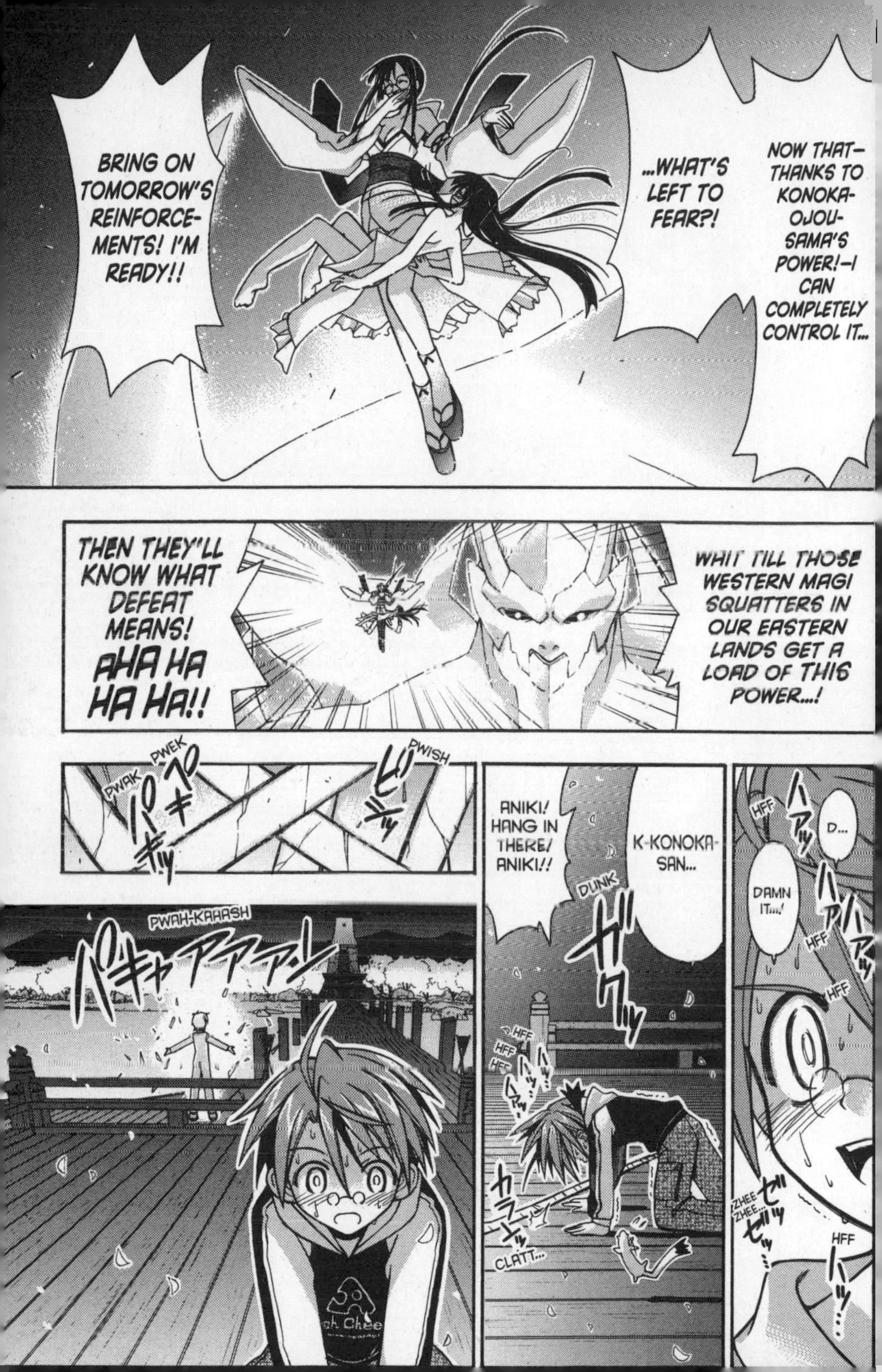

NOW THAT—THANKS TO KONOKA-OJOU-SAMA'S POWER!—I CAN COMPLETELY CONTROL IT...
...WHAT'S LEFT TO FEAR?!
BRING ON TOMORROW'S REINFORCEMENTS! I'M READY!!
WAIT TILL THOSE WESTERN MAGI SQUATTERS IN OUR EASTERN LANDS GET A LOAD OF THIS POWER...!
THEN THEY'LL KNOW WHAT DEFEAT MEANS! AHA HA HA HA!!
HFF
D...
DAMN IT...!
HFF
HFF
ZHEE ZHEE...
HFF
K-KONOKA-SAN...
ANIKI! HANG IN THERE/ ANIKI!!
DUNK
HFF HFF HFF
CLATT...
PWISH
PWEK
PWAK
PWAH-KAAASH

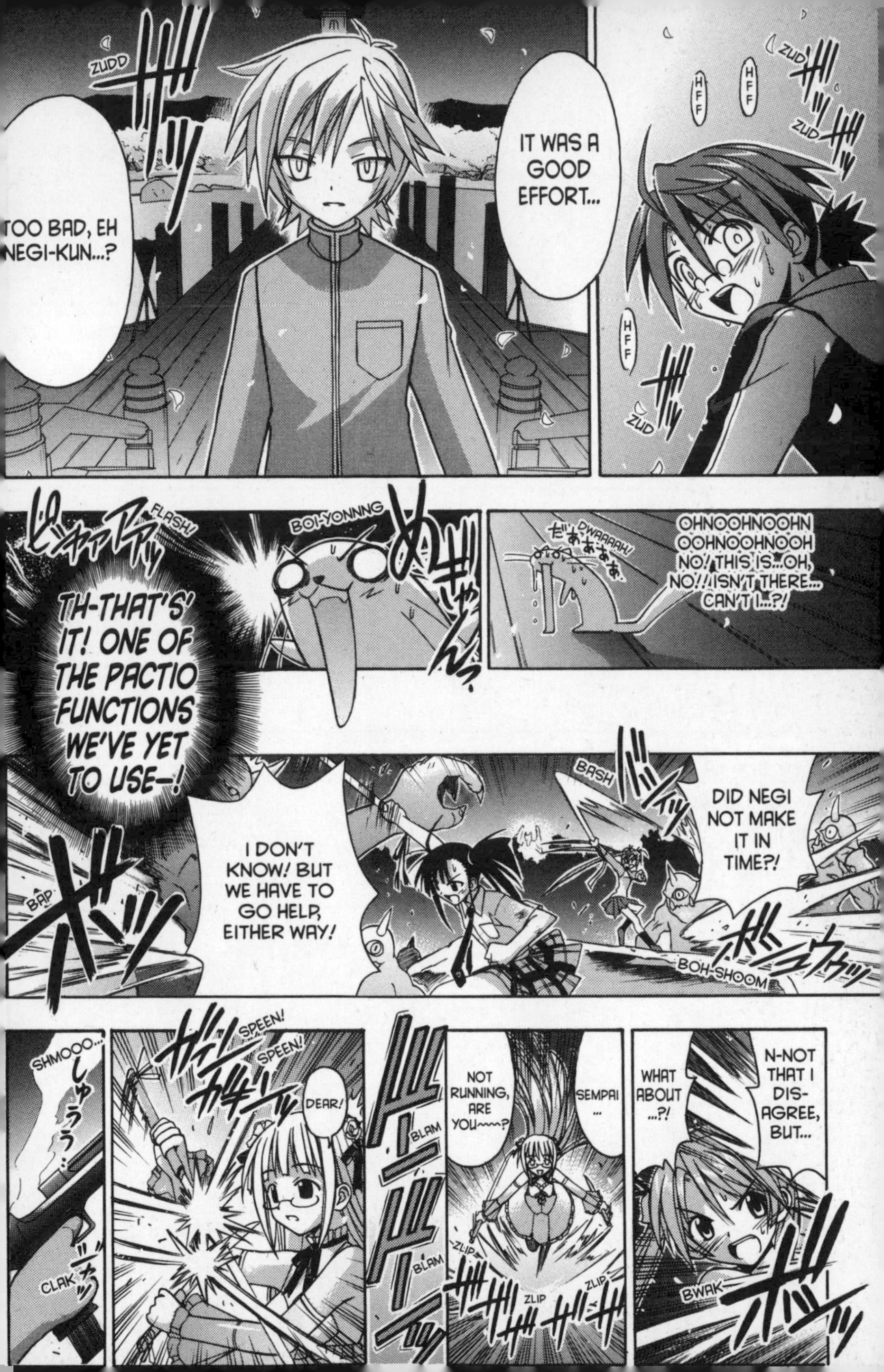
ZUD
HFF
HFF
ZUD
HFF
ZUD
IT WAS A GOOD EFFORT...
ZUDD
TOO BAD, EH NEGI-KUN...?
DWAAAAH!
OHNOOHNOOHN OOHNOOHNOOH NO! THIS IS...OH, NO!! ISN'T THERE... CAN'T I...?!
BOI-YONNNG
FLASH!
TH-THAT'S IT! ONE OF THE PACTIO FUNCTIONS WE'VE YET TO USE–!
BASH
DID NEGI NOT MAKE IT IN TIME?!
BOH-SHOOM
I DON'T KNOW! BUT WE HAVE TO GO HELP, EITHER WAY!
BAP
N-NOT THAT I DIS-AGREE, BUT...
WHAT ABOUT ...?!
BWAK
SEMPAI ...
NOT RUNNING, ARE YOU~~~~?
ZLIP
ZLIP
ZLIP
BLAM
BLAM
DEAR!
SPEEN!
SPEEN!
SHMOOO...
CLAK

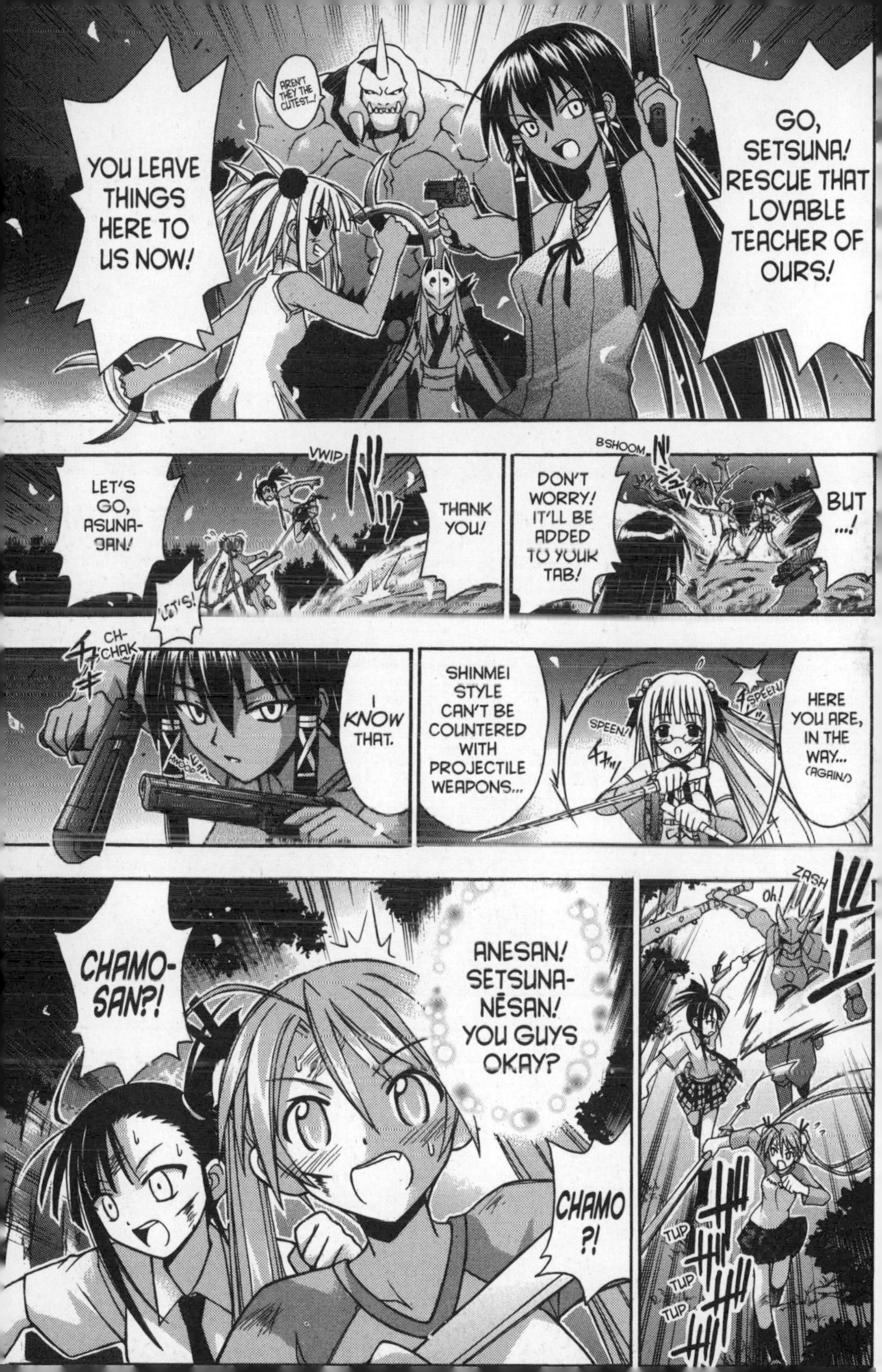
GO, SETSUNA! RESCUE THAT LOVABLE TEACHER OF OURS!
AREN'T THEY THE CUTEST...!
YOU LEAVE THINGS HERE TO US NOW!
BSHOOM
BUT ...!
DON'T WORRY! IT'LL BE ADDED TO YOUR TAB!
THANK YOU!
VWIP
LET'S GO, ASUNA-SAN!
LET'S!
HERE YOU ARE, IN THE WAY... (AGAIN!)
SPEEN!
SPEEN!
SHINMEI STYLE CAN'T BE COUNTERED WITH PROJECTILE WEAPONS...
I KNOW THAT.
CH-CHAK
ZASH
Oh!
TUP
TUP
TUP
ANESAN! SETSUNA-NĒSAN! YOU GUYS OKAY?
CHAMO ?!
CHAMO-SAN?!

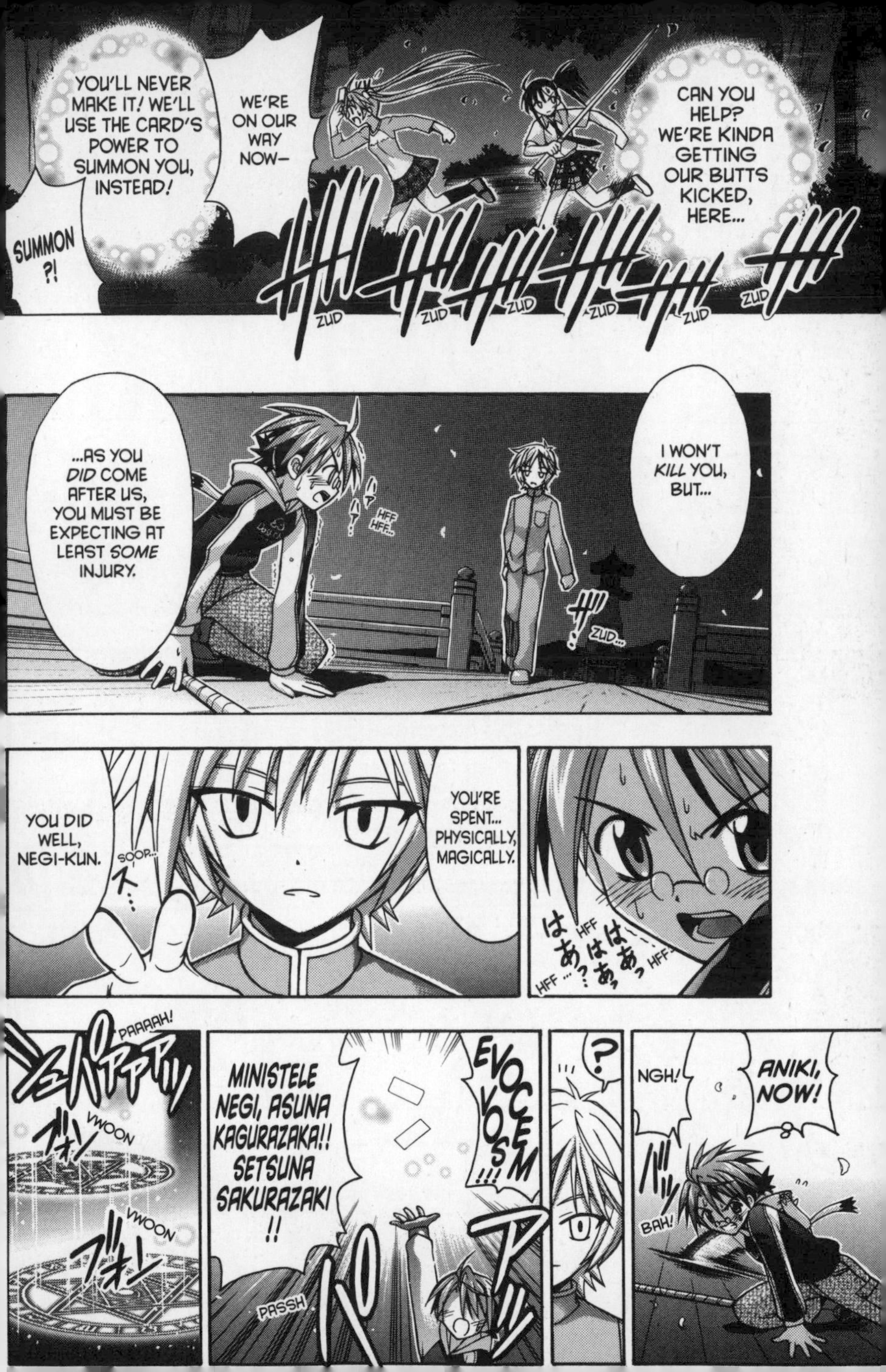
CAN YOU HELP? WE'RE KINDA GETTING OUR BUTTS KICKED, HERE...
WE'RE ON OUR WAY NOW—
YOU'LL NEVER MAKE IT! WE'LL USE THE CARD'S POWER TO SUMMON YOU, INSTEAD!
SUMMON ?!
ZUD
ZUD
ZUD
ZUD
ZUD
ZUD
I WON'T KILL YOU, BUT...
...AS YOU DID COME AFTER US, YOU MUST BE EXPECTING AT LEAST SOME INJURY.
HFF HFF...
ZUD...
HFF HFF... HFF...
YOU'RE SPENT... PHYSICALLY, MAGICALLY.
YOU DID WELL, NEGI-KUN.
SOOP...
ANIKI, NOW!
NGH!
BAH!
?
EVOCEM VOS!!!
MINISTELE NEGI, ASUNA KAGURAZAKA!! SETSUNA SAKURAZAKI!!
PASSH
PAAAAH!
VWOON
VWOON

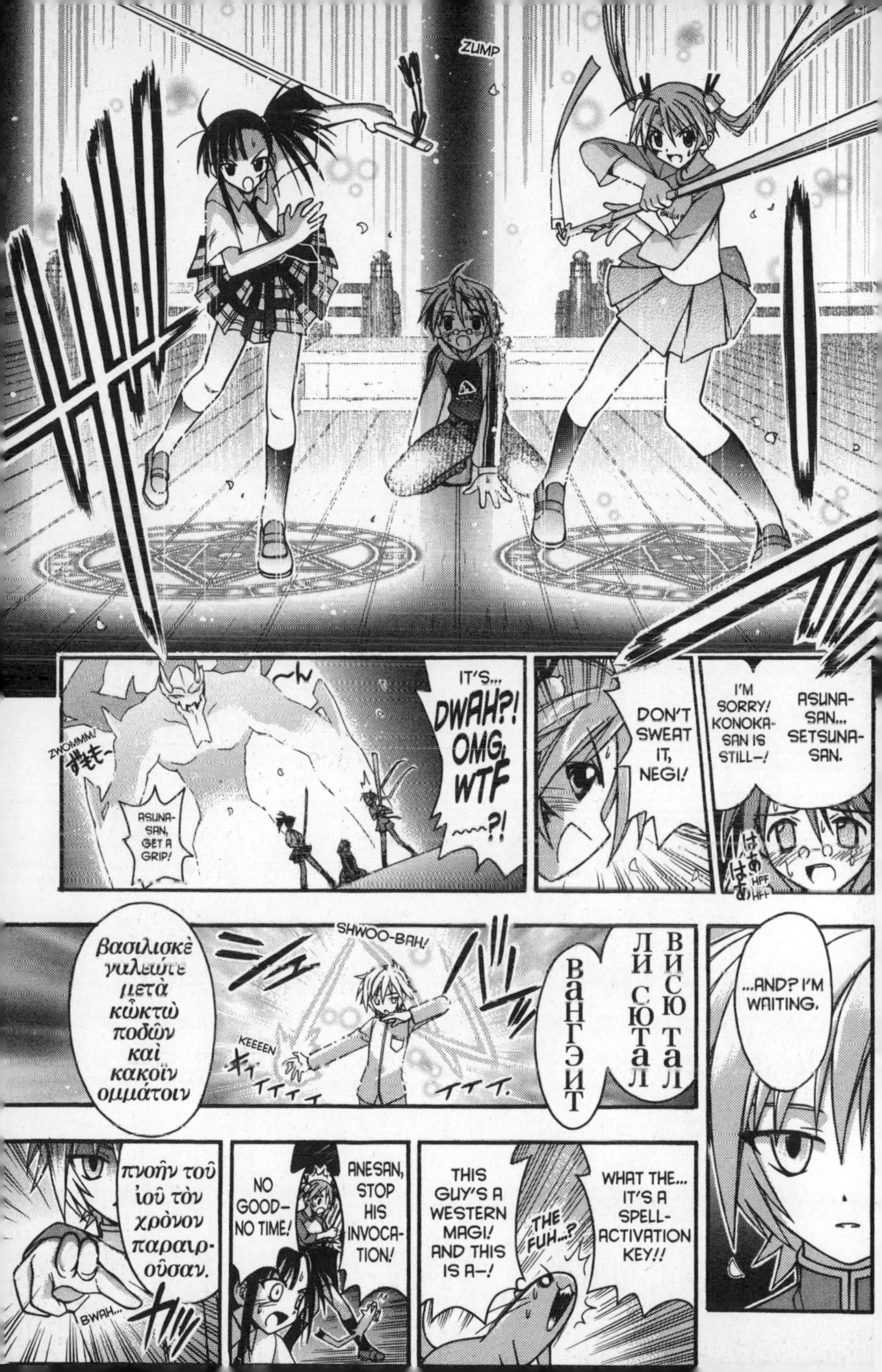
ZUMP
ASUNA-SAN... SETSUNA-SAN.
I'M SORRY! KONOKA-SAN IS STILL–!
HFF HFF
DON'T SWEAT IT, NEGI!
IT'S... DWAH?! OMG, WTF ~~~?!
ZWOMMM!
ASUNA-SAN, GET A GRIP!
...AND? I'M WAITING.
ВИСЮ ТАЛ ЛИ СЮТАЛ ВАНГЭИТ
SHWOO-BAH!
KEEEEN
βασιλισκὲ γαλεώτε μετὰ κῶκτω ποδῶν καὶ κακοῖν ομμάτοιν
WHAT THE... IT'S A SPELL-ACTIVATION KEY!!
THE FUH...?
THIS GUY'S A WESTERN MAGI! AND THIS IS A–!
ANESAN, STOP HIS INVOCATION!
NO GOOD– NO TIME!
πνοὴν τοῦ ἰοῦ τὸν χρόνον παραιρ-οῦσαν.
BWAH...

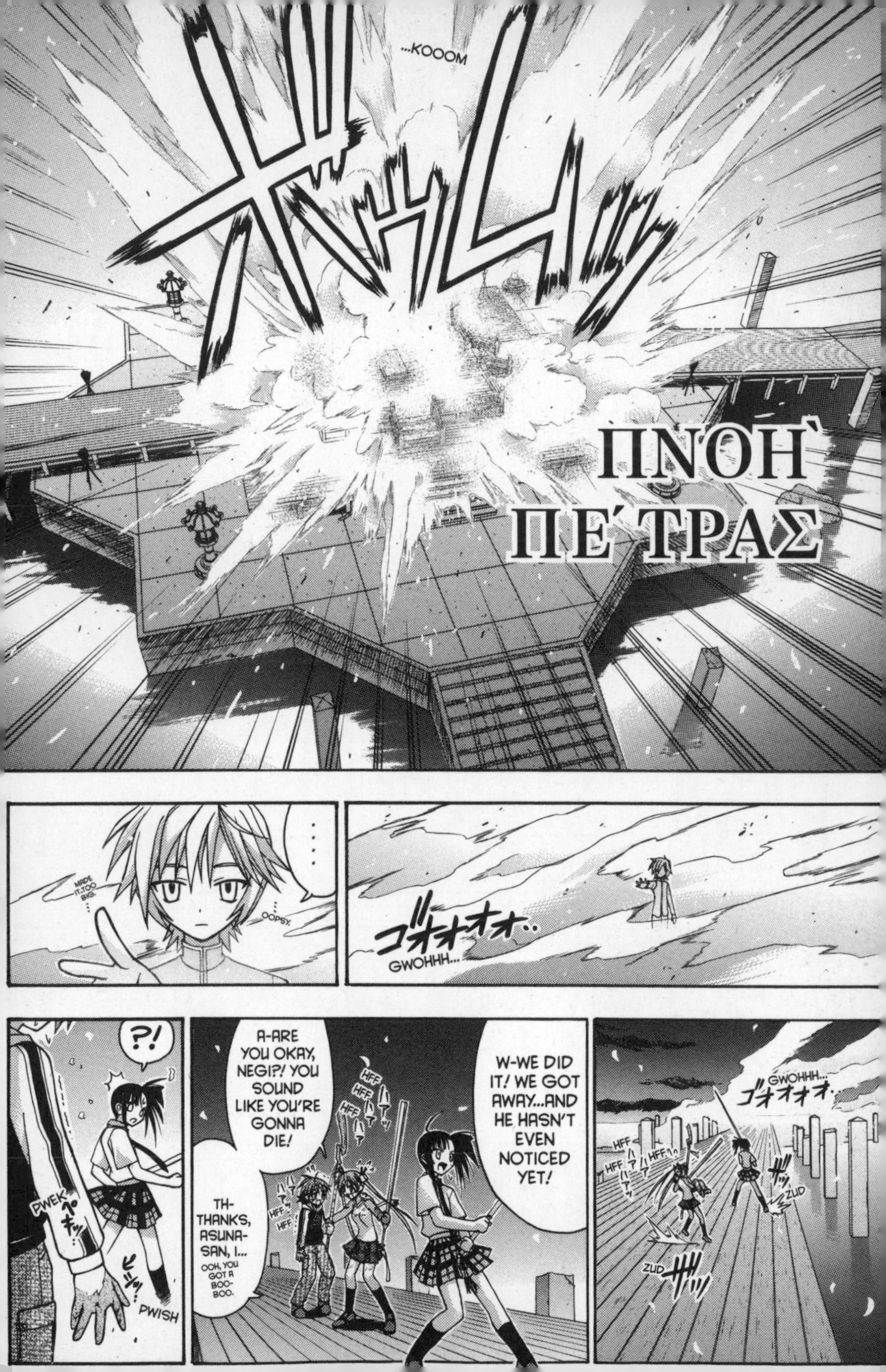

...KOOOM
ΠΝΟῊ ΠΕ΄ΤΡΑΣ
GWOHHH...
ゴオオオオ..
...
MADE IT TOO BIG...
...OOPSY.
GWOHHH...
ゴオオオオ
HFF HFF HFF
ZUD
ZUD
W-WE DID IT! WE GOT AWAY...AND HE HASN'T EVEN NOTICED YET!
A-ARE YOU OKAY, NEGI?! YOU SOUND LIKE YOU'RE GONNA DIE!
HFF HFF HFF
TH-THANKS, ASUNA-SAN, I...
HFF HFF
OOH, YOU GOT A BOO-BOO.
?!
PWEK
PWISH

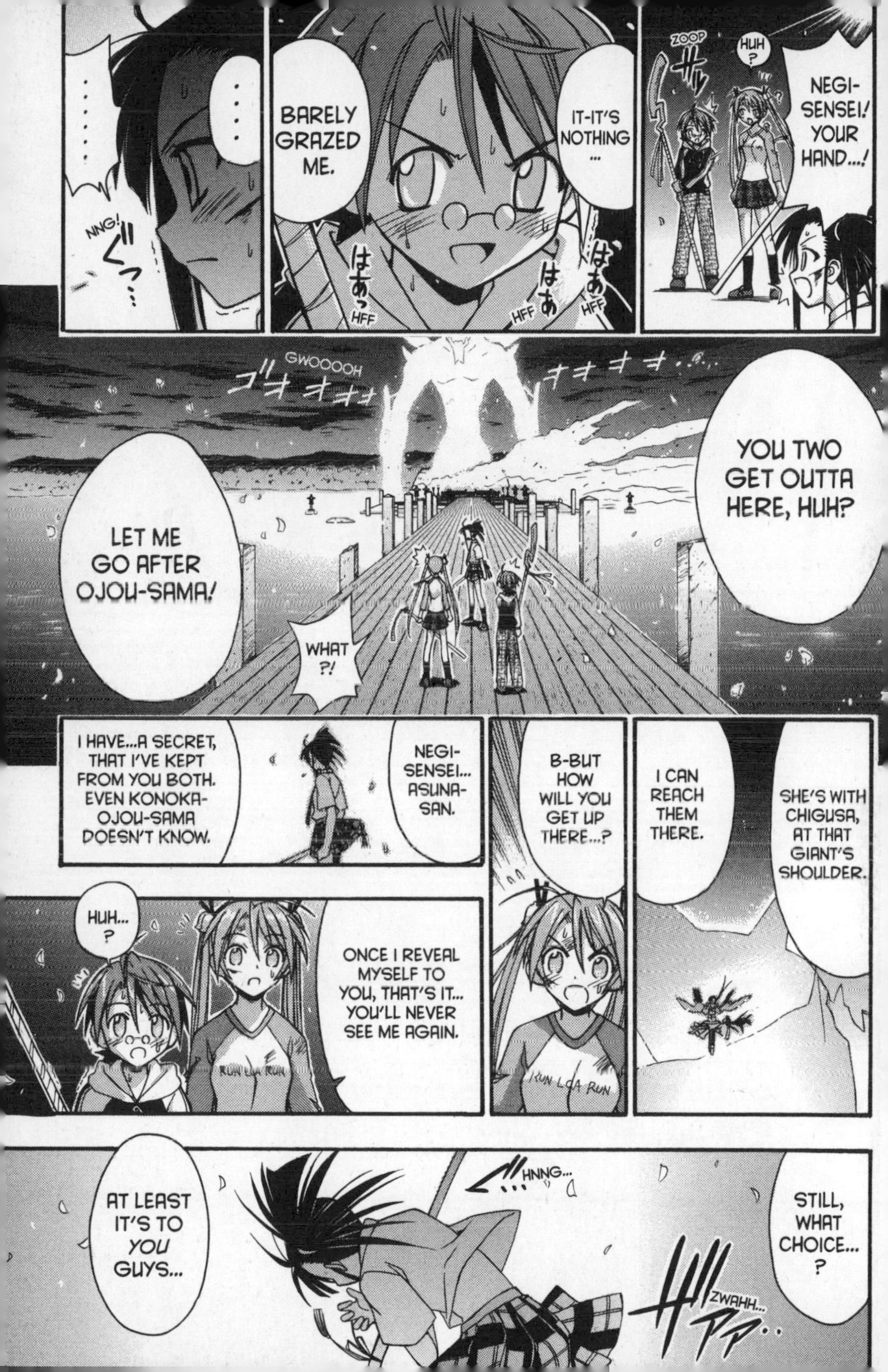
NEGI-SENSEI! YOUR HAND...!
HUH ?
ZOOP
IT-IT'S NOTHING ...
BARELY GRAZED ME.
HFF
HFF
HFF
....
NNG!
YOU TWO GET OUTTA HERE, HUH?
GWOOOOH
LET ME GO AFTER OJOU-SAMA!
WHAT ?!
SHE'S WITH CHIGUSA, AT THAT GIANT'S SHOULDER.
I CAN REACH THEM THERE.
B-BUT HOW WILL YOU GET UP THERE...?
NEGI-SENSEI... ASUNA-SAN.
I HAVE...A SECRET, THAT I'VE KEPT FROM YOU BOTH. EVEN KONOKA-OJOU-SAMA DOESN'T KNOW.
ONCE I REVEAL MYSELF TO YOU, THAT'S IT... YOU'LL NEVER SEE ME AGAIN.
HUH... ?
STILL, WHAT CHOICE... ?
HNNG...
AT LEAST IT'S TO YOU GUYS...
ZWAHH...

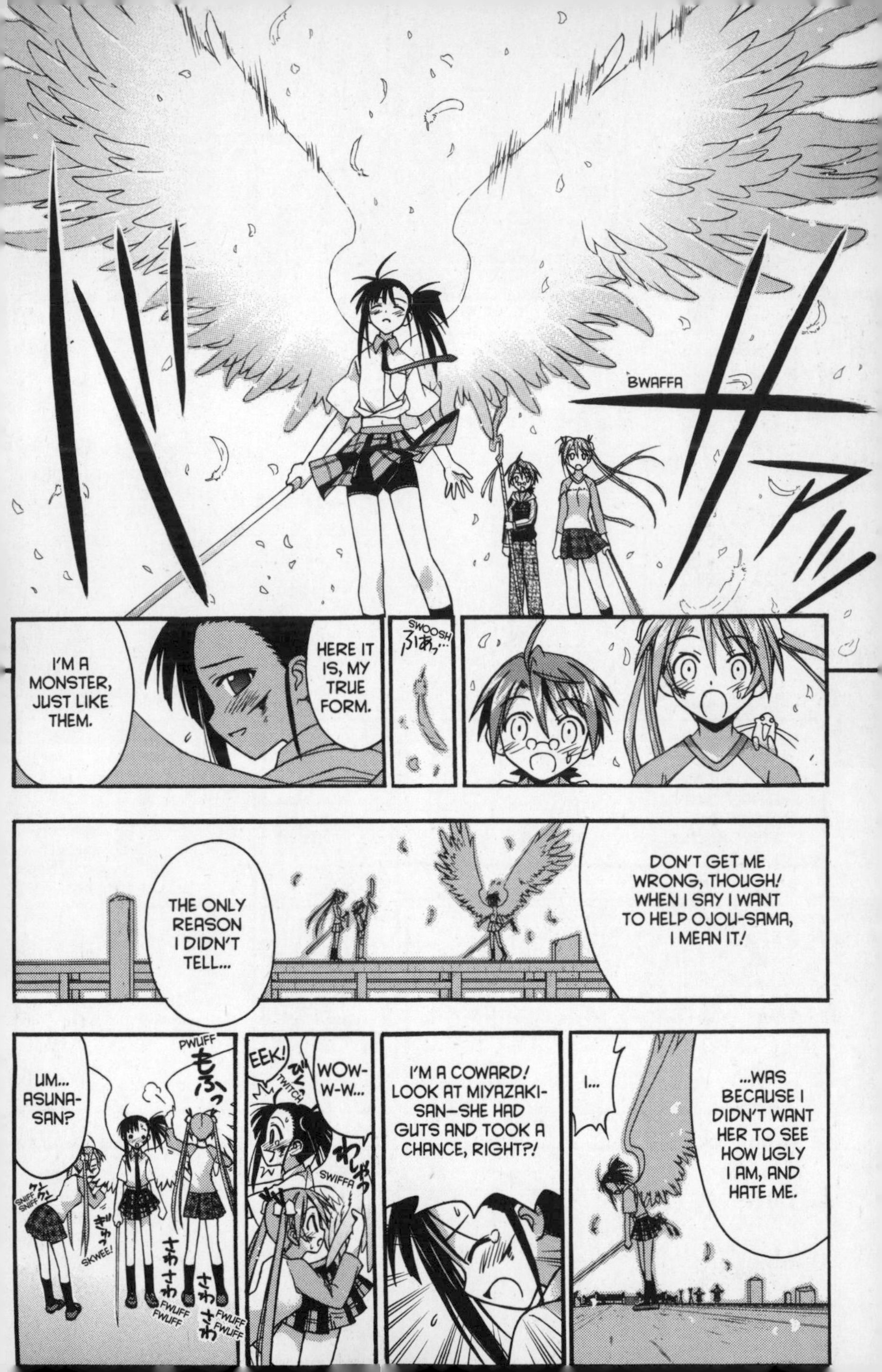
BWAFFA
SWOOSH
ふぁっ…
HERE IT IS, MY TRUE FORM.
I'M A MONSTER, JUST LIKE THEM.
DON'T GET ME WRONG, THOUGH! WHEN I SAY I WANT TO HELP OJOU-SAMA, I MEAN IT!
THE ONLY REASON I DIDN'T TELL...
I...
...WAS BECAUSE I DIDN'T WANT HER TO SEE HOW UGLY I AM, AND HATE ME.
I'M A COWARD! LOOK AT MIYAZAKI-SAN—SHE HAD GUTS AND TOOK A CHANCE, RIGHT?!
WOW-W-W...
EEK!
びくっ
TWITCH
わしゃっ
SWIFFA
PWUFF
もふっ
UM... ASUNA-SAN?
SNIFF SNIFF
SKWEE!
さわさわ
FWUFF FWUFF
さわさわ
FWUFF FWUFF

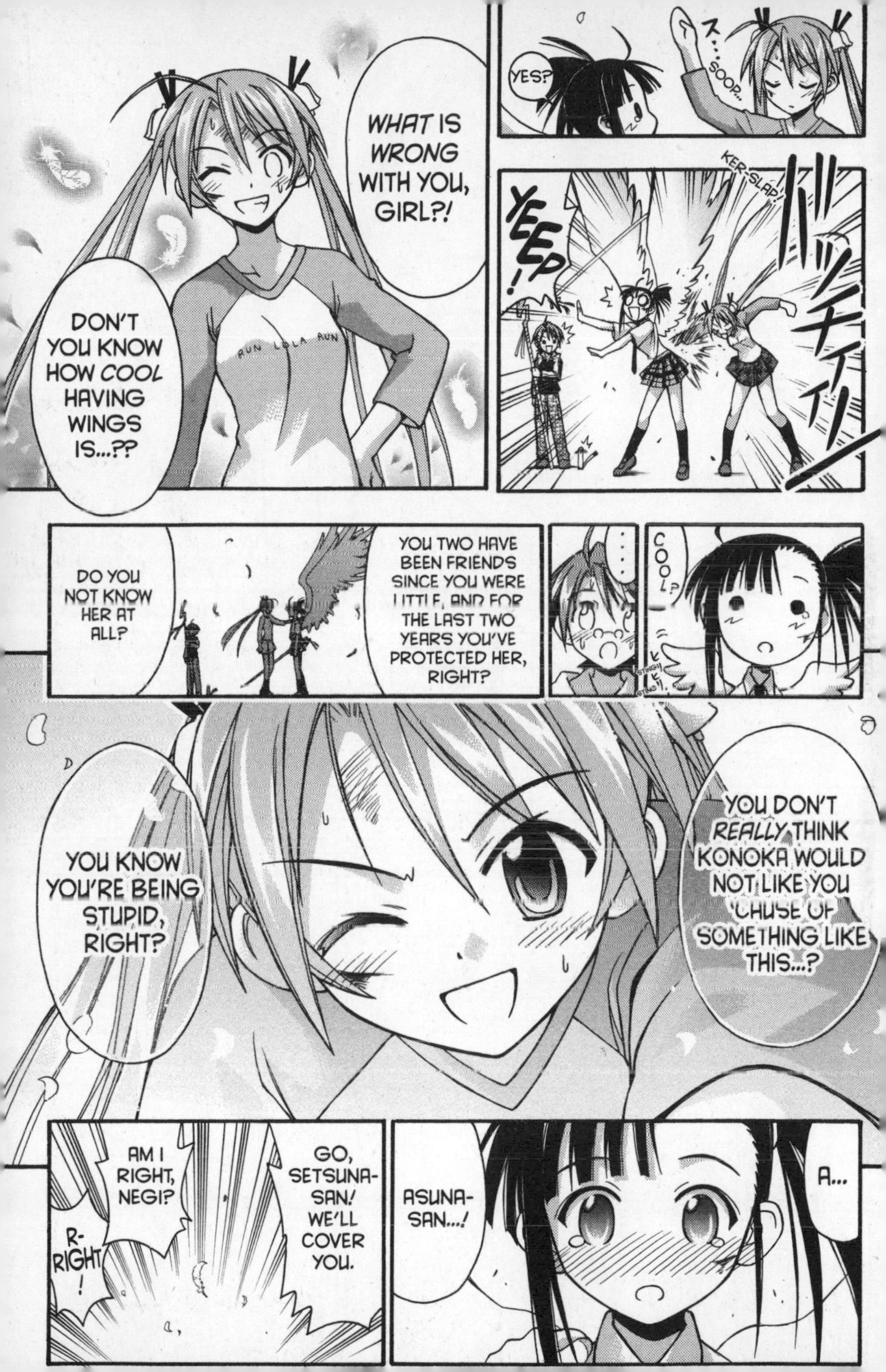
ス…SOOP…
YES?
KER-SLAP!
YEEP!
WHAT IS WRONG WITH YOU, GIRL?!
RUN LOLA RUN
DON'T YOU KNOW HOW COOL HAVING WINGS IS...??
COOL?
STING!! STING!!
...
YOU TWO HAVE BEEN FRIENDS SINCE YOU WERE LITTLE, AND FOR THE LAST TWO YEARS YOU'VE PROTECTED HER, RIGHT?
DO YOU NOT KNOW HER AT ALL?
YOU DON'T REALLY THINK KONOKA WOULD NOT LIKE YOU 'CAUSE OF SOMETHING LIKE THIS...?
YOU KNOW YOU'RE BEING STUPID, RIGHT?
A...
ASUNA-SAN...!
GO, SETSUNA-SAN! WE'LL COVER YOU.
AM I RIGHT, NEGI?
R-RIGHT!

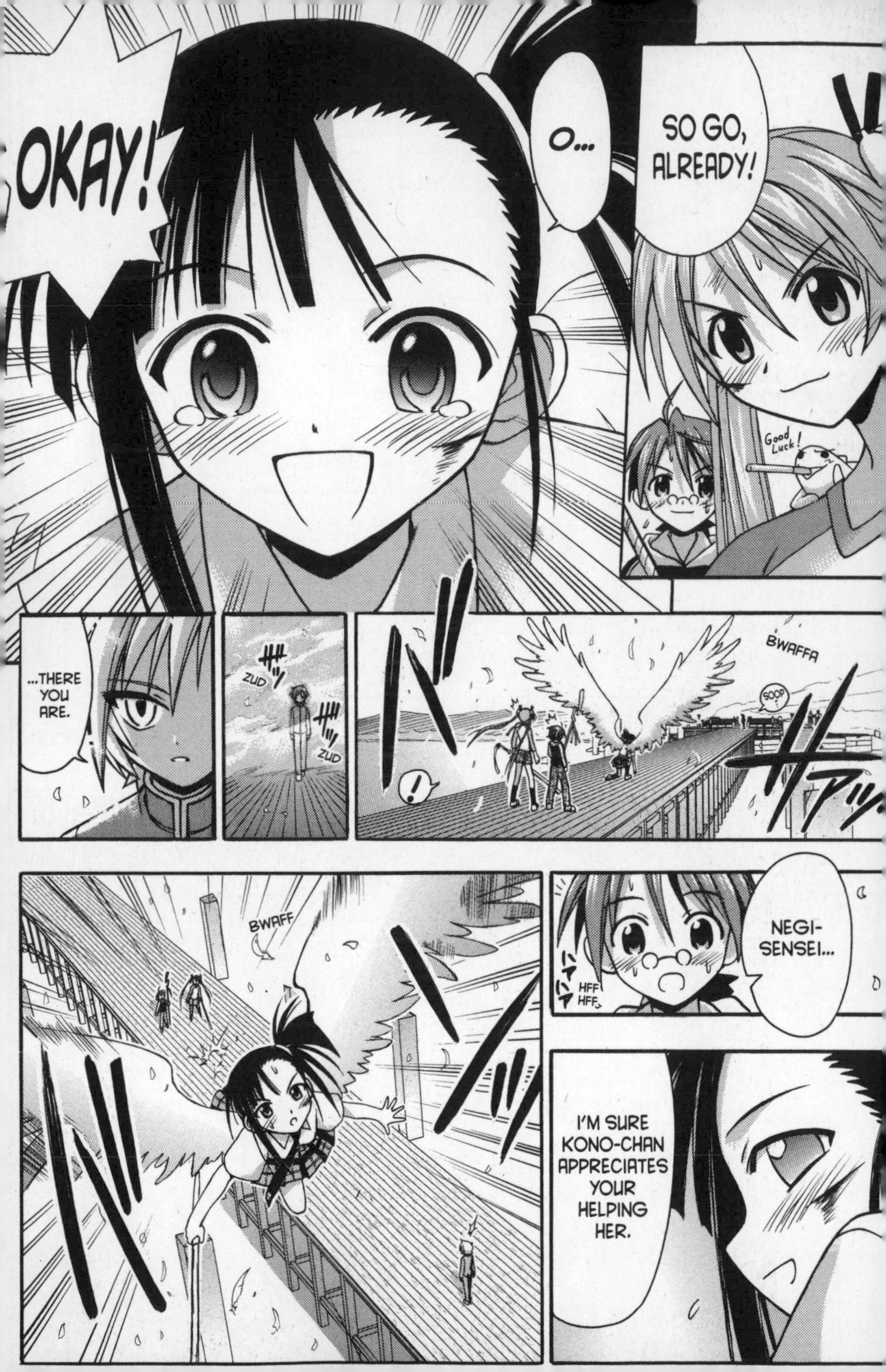
SO GO, ALREADY!
Good Luck!
O...
OKAY!
BWAFFA
SOOP
!
ZUD
ZUD
...THERE YOU ARE.
NEGI-SENSEI...
HFF HFF
I'M SURE KONO-CHAN APPRECIATES YOUR HELPING HER.
BWAFF

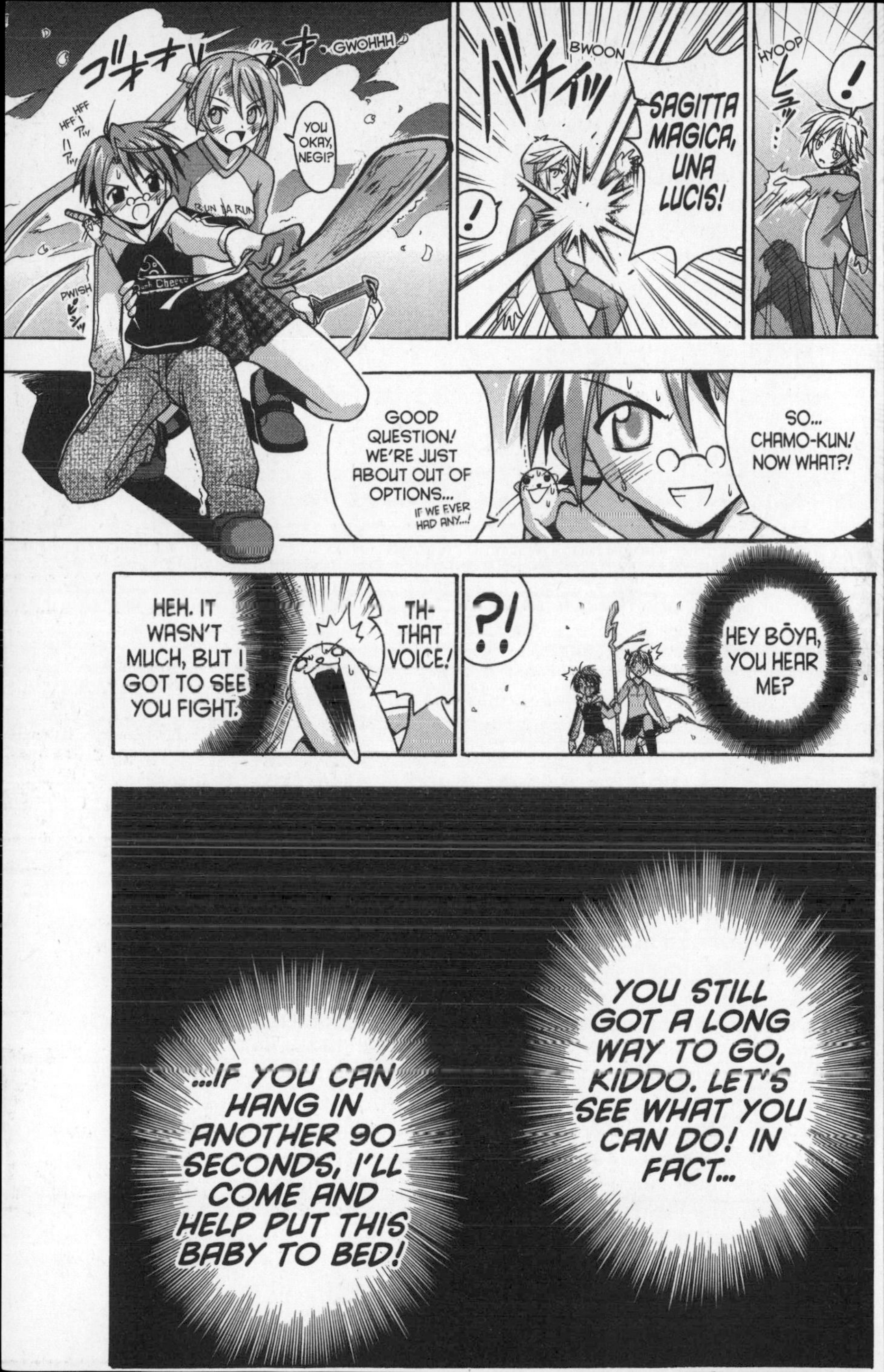

HYOOP
!
BWOON
SAGITTA MAGICA, UNA LUCIS!
!
SO... CHAMO-KUN! NOW WHAT?!
GOOD QUESTION! WE'RE JUST ABOUT OUT OF OPTIONS...
IF WE EVER HAD ANY...!
GWOHHH
YOU OKAY, NEGI!?
HFF HFF
PWISH
HEY BŌYA, YOU HEAR ME?
?!
TH- THAT VOICE!
HEH. IT WASN'T MUCH, BUT I GOT TO SEE YOU FIGHT.
YOU STILL GOT A LONG WAY TO GO, KIDDO. LET'S SEE WHAT YOU CAN DO! IN FACT...
...IF YOU CAN HANG IN ANOTHER 90 SECONDS, I'LL COME AND HELP PUT THIS BABY TO BED!

NEGIMA! FIFTIETH PERIOD: LEXICON NEGIMARIUM

■「召喚、ネギの従者、神楽坂明日菜、桜咲刹那」
エウォケム・ウォース・ミニストラエ・ネギィ・カグラザカアスナ・サクラザキセトゥナ
EVOCEM VOS, MINISTRAE NEGII, CAGRAZACA ASUNA, SACURAZACI SETSUNA

Spell allowing the Magi to summon his or her Ministra from great distances (in this case, Asuna and Setsuna to Negi). To move both living and inanimate objects instantly, across space, a high level of magic is necessary, and yet, considering how weak Negi's condition was at the time of his casting, the card's inherent magical properties must also be considered.

■ヴィシュ・タル・リ・シュタル・ヴァンゲイト
(в и с ю т а л л и с ю т а л в а н г э и т)
VISH TAL LI SHUTAL VANGATE

Spell-activation key for the white-haired youth who calls himself "Fate Averruncus." Apparently well versed in the Eastern Magicks, this Magi commands more than meets the eye.

■「小さき王、八つ足の蜥蜴、邪眼の主よ。時を奪う毒の吐息を。『石の息吹』」
バーシリスケ、ガレオーテ、メタ・コークトー・ポドーン・カイ・カコイン・オンマトイン・ブノエーン・トゥ・イウー・トン・クロノン・パライルーサン ブノエー・ベトラス
(βασιλισκὲ γαλεώτε μετὰ κώκτὼ ποδῶν καὶ κακοῖν ὀμμάτοιν πνοῆν τοῦ ἰοῦ τὸν χρὸνον παραιροῦσαν. ΠΝΟΗ᾽ ΠΕ΄ΤΡΑΣ)
KRONON PARA IRUSAN BUNOE PETRAS
"Little King, Eight-Legged Lizard, Master of the Evil Eye. Gives the poison-breath that steals time: 'Breath of Stone'"

In ancient Greek, *basiliskos* or "basilisk" means "little king"...but of course it's also the name of a mythological creature said to be able to petrify just by looking at someone, or to kill with its poisonous breath. In the case of this particular (high-level) spell, a cloud of gas that petrifies anything with which it comes in contact is created. Invoked in ancient Greek (rather than in Latin, the language in which Negi usually utters his invocations), the practice is believed to originate in the various backgrounds of the western Magi.

In a letter to the Emperor Augustus, the Roman poet Horatius wrote, "*Graecia capta ferum victorem cept et artes intulit agresti Latio* ('Captive Greece captured her fierce captor and brought the arts into uncultured Latium' [Epistulae II.1, 156-157].") Compared to ancient Rome, which used as its main language Latin, the culture of ancient Greece was advanced. For example, Euclid's *Elements,* Plutarch's *Lives,* Strabon's *Geografika,* Ptolemy's *Megale Syntaxis* ("Great Compilation"), the New Testament and more—all considered to be in literature's highest echelons were all written in ancient Greek (even the Hebrew Old Testament was translated into it). During the Middle Ages, when Latin became the standardized language across Europe, the treasures of ancient Greek literature lay dormant, protected by Eastern and Islamic countries, until rediscovered by the humanists of the Renaissance. Therefore, although Latin and ancient Greek are "old" languages, the higher status is seen by many scholar's eyes to belong to ancient Greek (even Negi's Latin spells *Telepathia* and *Nebula Hypnotica* have their roots in it).

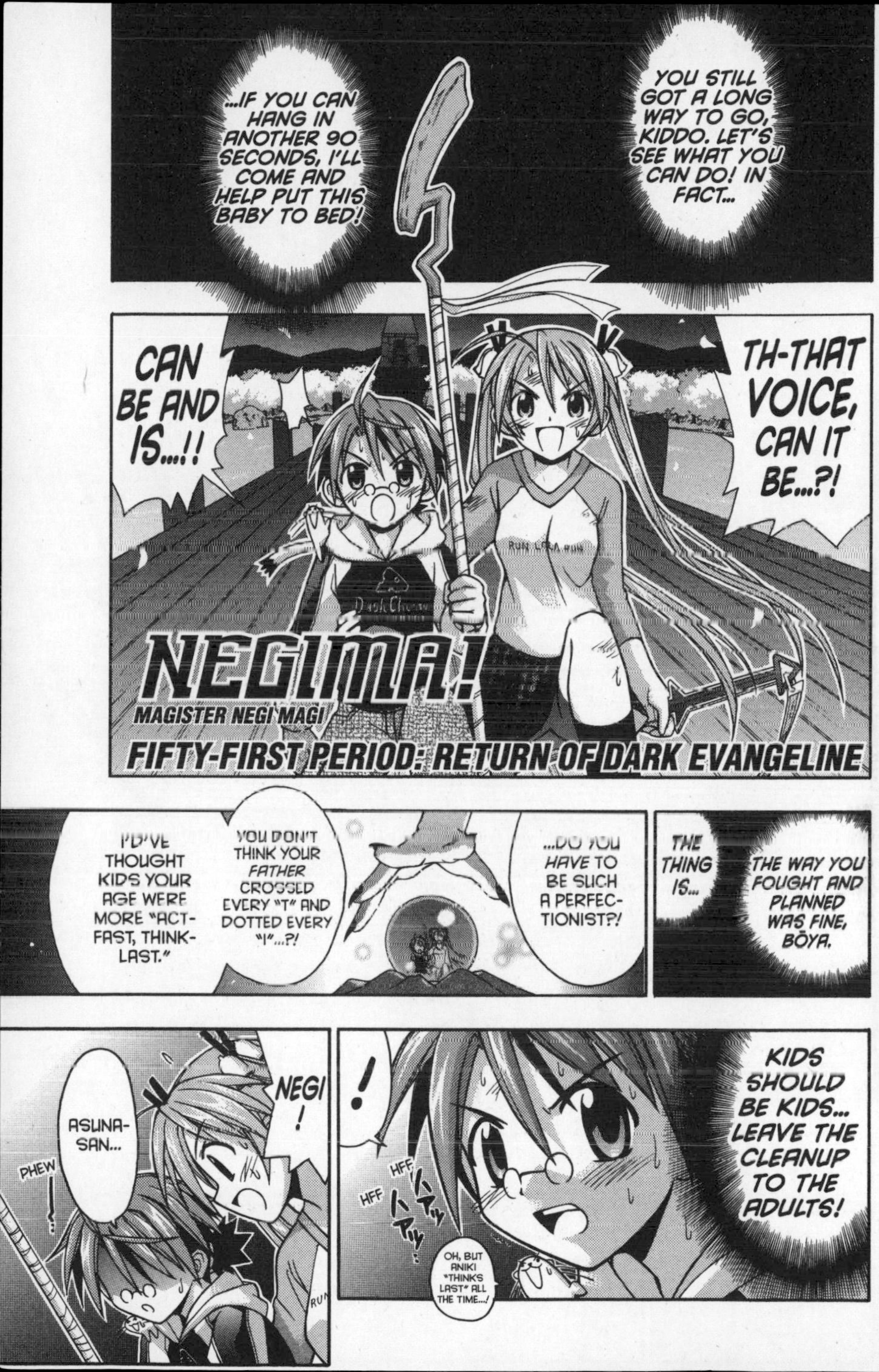

YOU STILL GOT A LONG WAY TO GO, KIDDO. LET'S SEE WHAT YOU CAN DO! IN FACT...
...IF YOU CAN HANG IN ANOTHER 90 SECONDS, I'LL COME AND HELP PUT THIS BABY TO BED!
TH-THAT VOICE, CAN IT BE...?!
CAN BE AND IS...!!
RUN LALA RUN
NEGIMA!
MAGISTER NEGI MAGI
FIFTY-FIRST PERIOD: RETURN OF DARK EVANGELINE
THE THING IS...
THE WAY YOU FOUGHT AND PLANNED WAS FINE, BÖYA.
...DO YOU HAVE TO BE SUCH A PERFECTIONIST?!
YOU DON'T THINK YOUR FATHER CROSSED EVERY "T" AND DOTTED EVERY "I"...?!
I'D'VE THOUGHT KIDS YOUR AGE WERE MORE "ACT-FAST, THINK-LAST."
KIDS SHOULD BE KIDS... LEAVE THE CLEANUP TO THE ADULTS!
!
HFF
ハァッ
HFF
ハァッ
OH, BUT ANIKI "THINKS LAST" ALL THE TIME...!
NEGI!
ASUNA-SAN...
PHEW
RUN

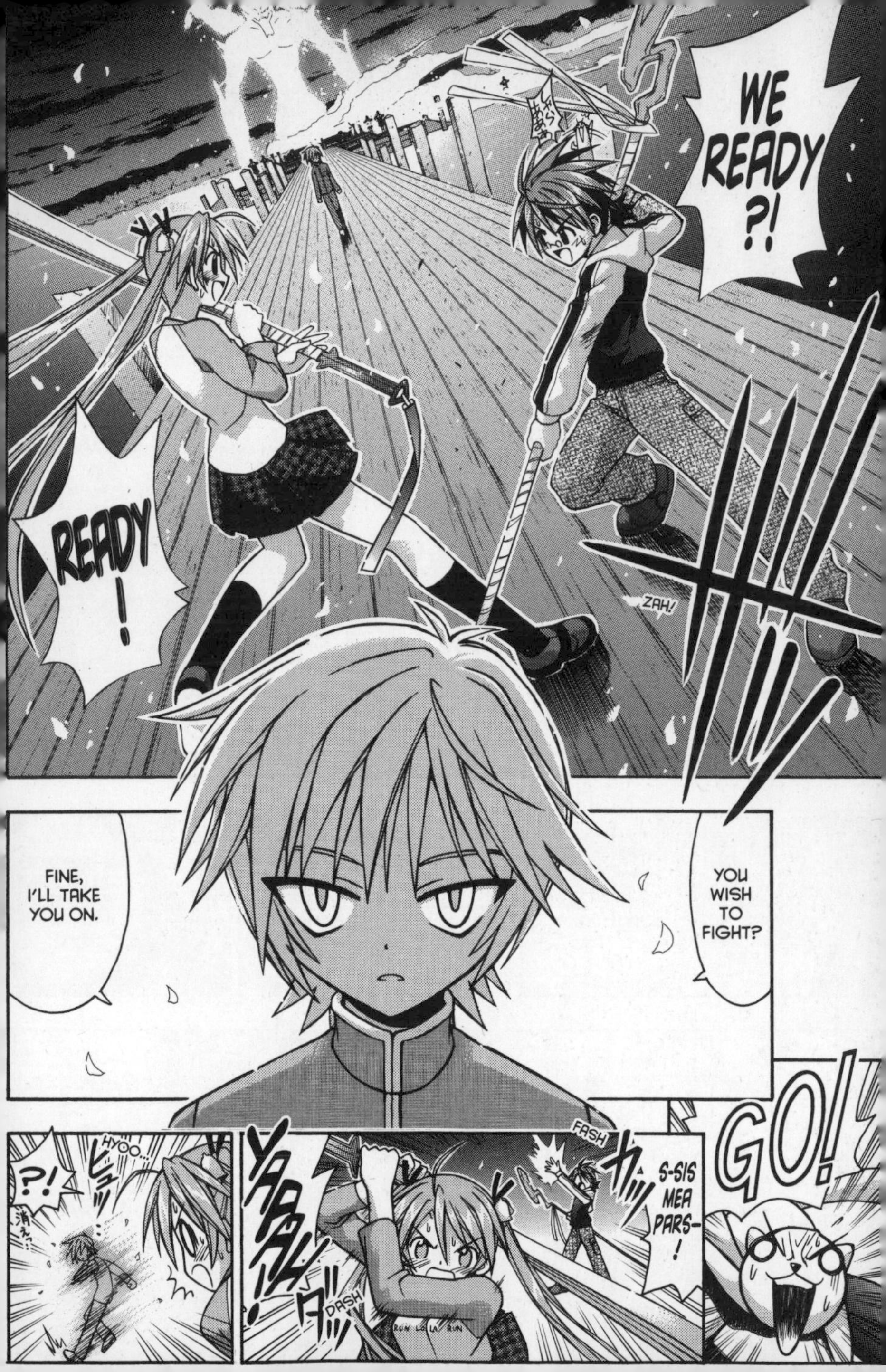

WE READY?!
READY!
ZAH!
YOU WISH TO FIGHT?
FINE, I'LL TAKE YOU ON.
GO!
S-SIS MEA PARS-!
FASH
DASH
HYOO...
?!

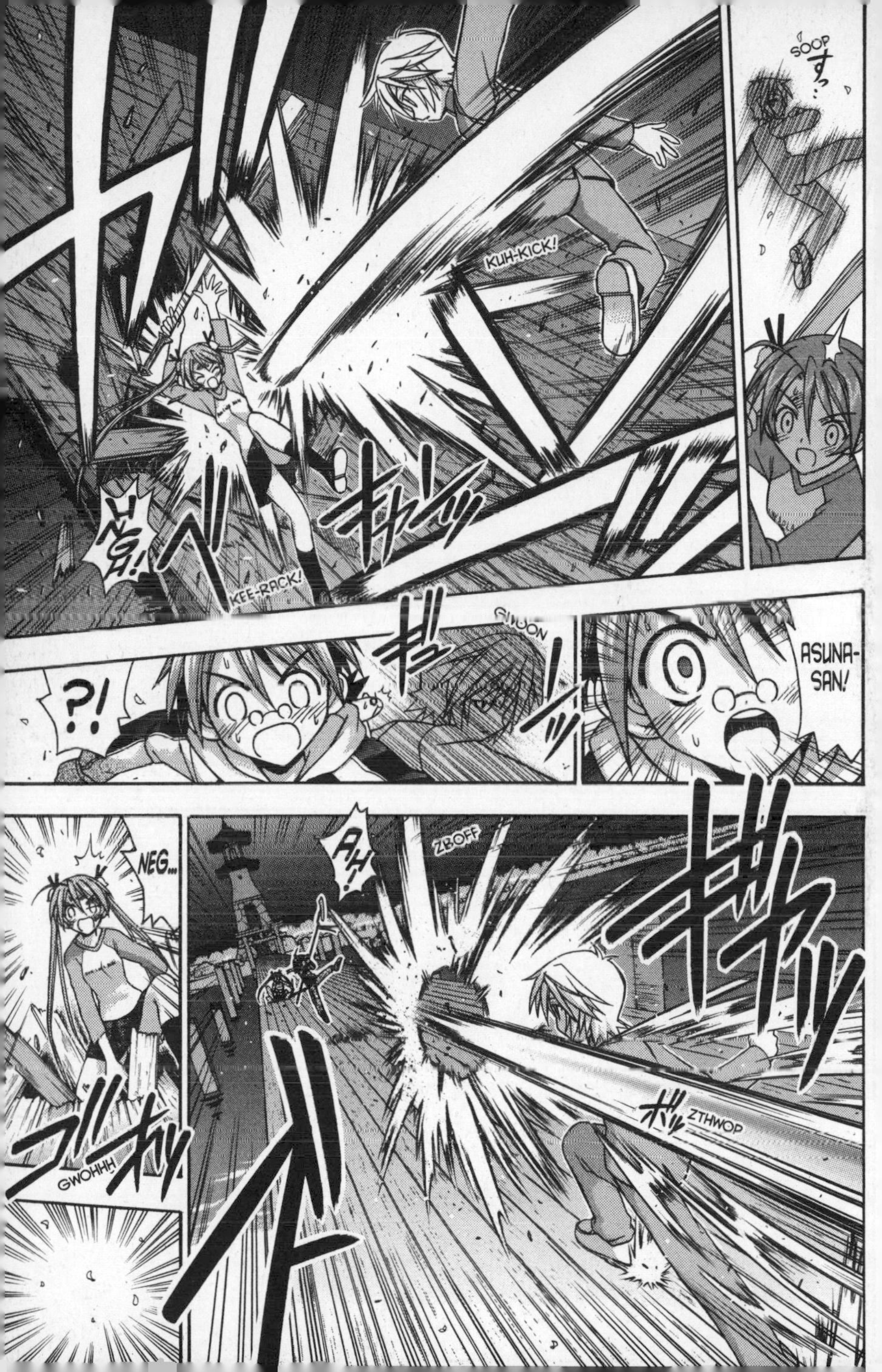
SOOP
すっ
KUH-KICK!
HNGH!
KEE-RACK!
ASUNA-SAN!
GWOON
?!
ZBOFF
AH!
ZTHWOP
NEG...
GWOHHH

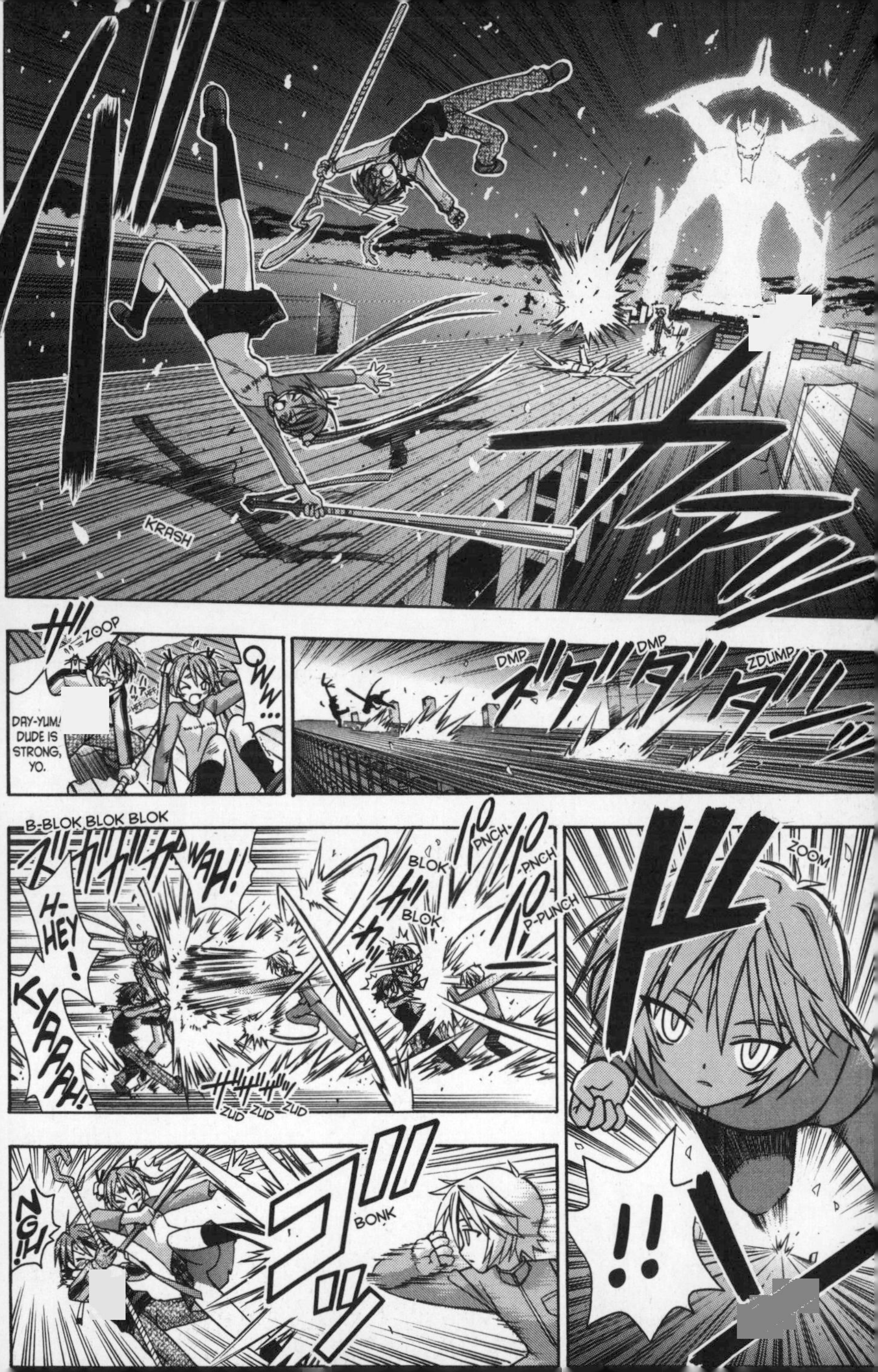
KRASH
DMP
DMP
ZDUMP
ZOOP
QWW...
DAY-YUM! DUDE IS STRONG, YO.
ZOOM
!!
PNCH
PNCH
P-PUNCH
BLOK
BLOK
B-BLOK BLOK BLOK
WAH!
H-HEY!
KYAAAAH!
ZUD ZUD ZUD
BONK
NGH!!

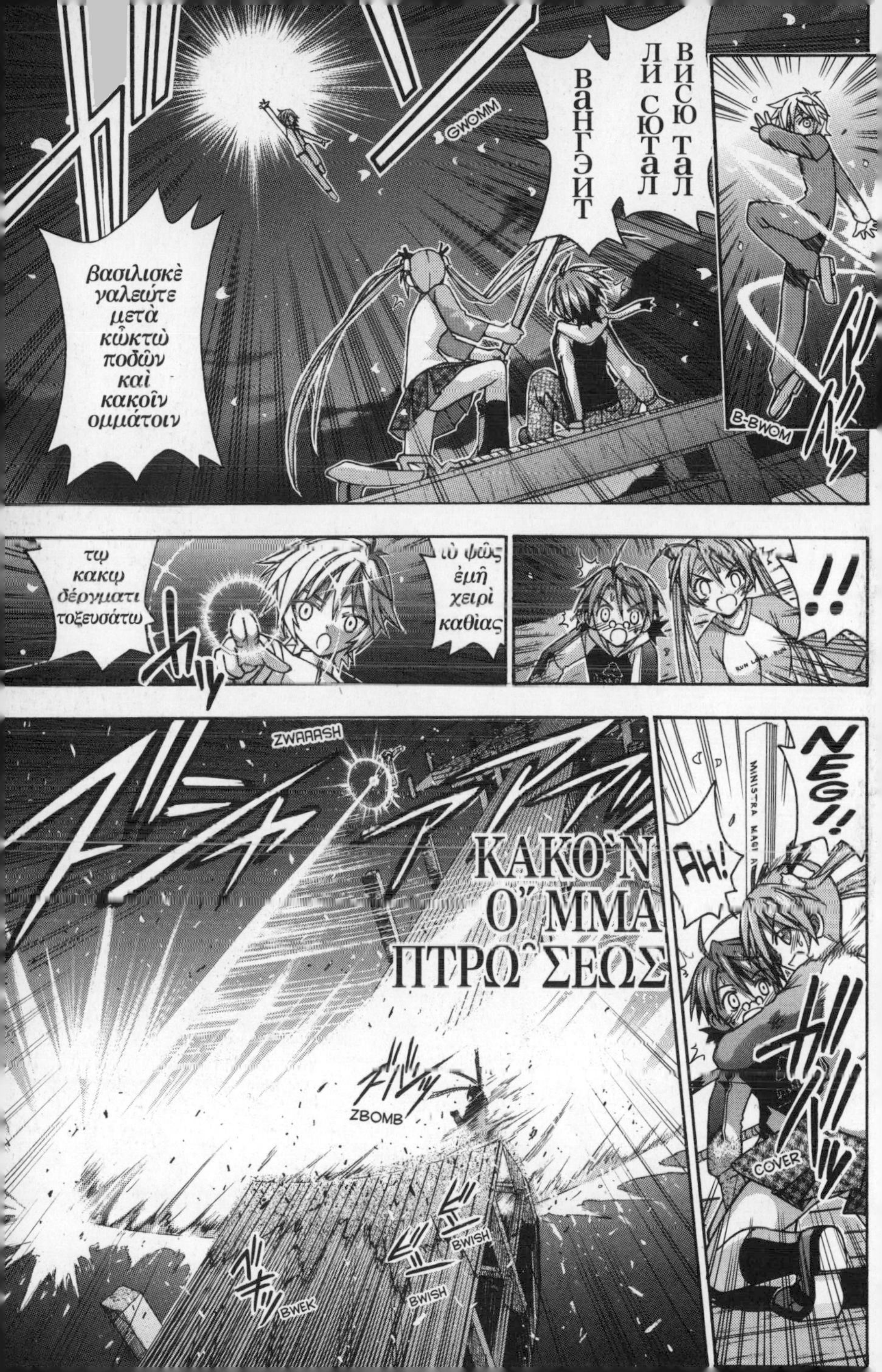
B-BWOM
ВИСЮ ТАЛ ЛИ СЮТАЛ ВАНГЭЙТ
GWOMM
βασιλισκὲ γαλεῶτε μετὰ κῶκτῶ ποδῶν καὶ κακοῖν ομμάτοιν
!!
ιὺ φῶς ἐμῆ χειρὶ καθίας
τῳ κακῳ δέργματι τοξευσάτω
NEGI!!
MINISTRA MAGI
AH!
COVER
ZWAAASH
ΚΑΚΟ'Ν Ο' ΜΜΑ ΠΤΡΩ΄ ΣΕΩΣ
ZBOMB
BWISH
BWISH
BWEK

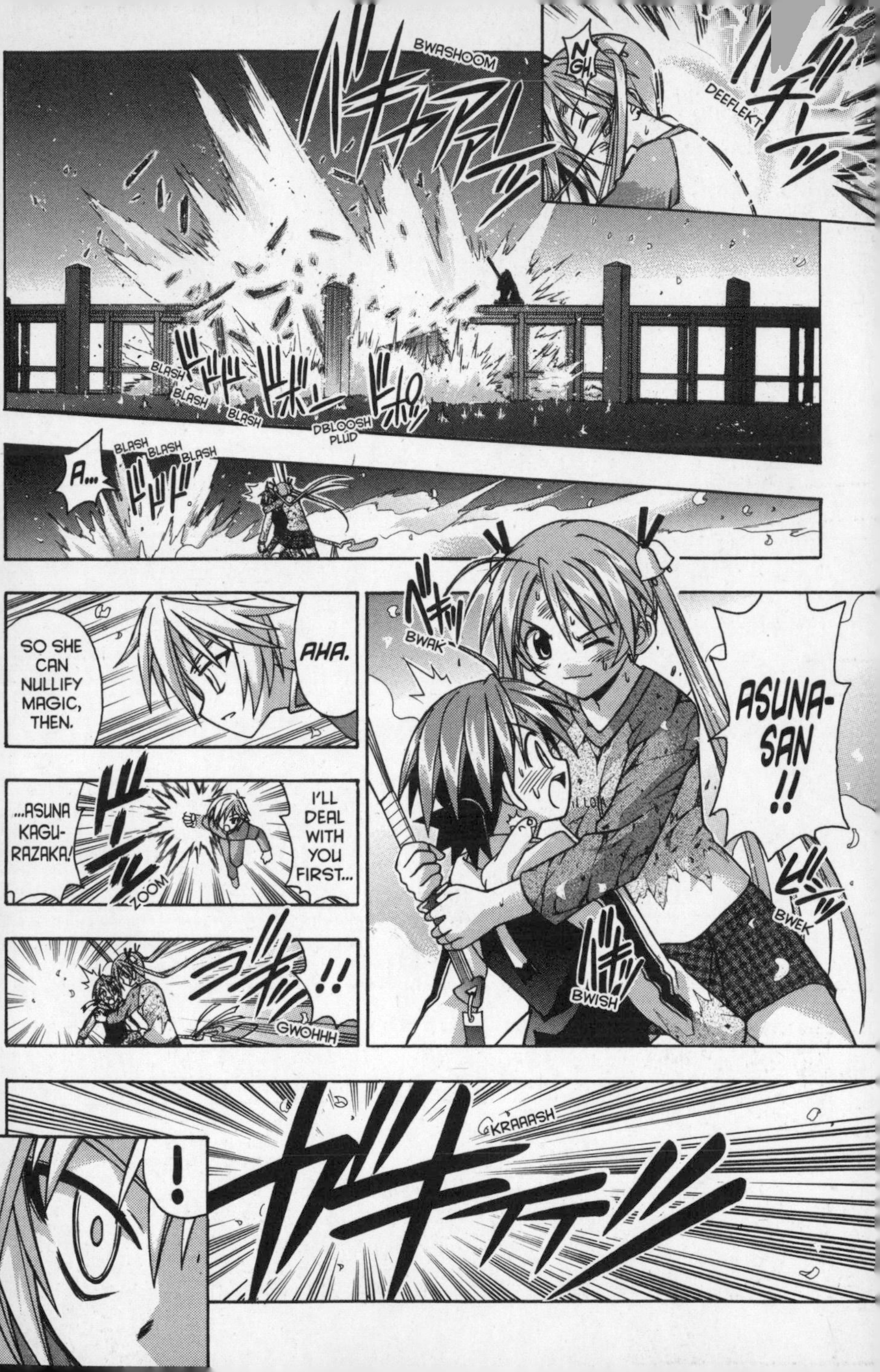

NGH!
DEEFLEKT
BWASHOOM
BLASH
BLASH
BLASH
DBLOOSH
PLUD
BLASH
BLASH
BLASH
A...
BWAK
ASUNA-SAN!!
BWEK
BWISH
AHA.
SO SHE CAN NULLIFY MAGIC, THEN.
I'LL DEAL WITH YOU FIRST...
...ASUNA KAGURAZAKA!
ZOOM
!!
GWOHHH
KRAAASH
!

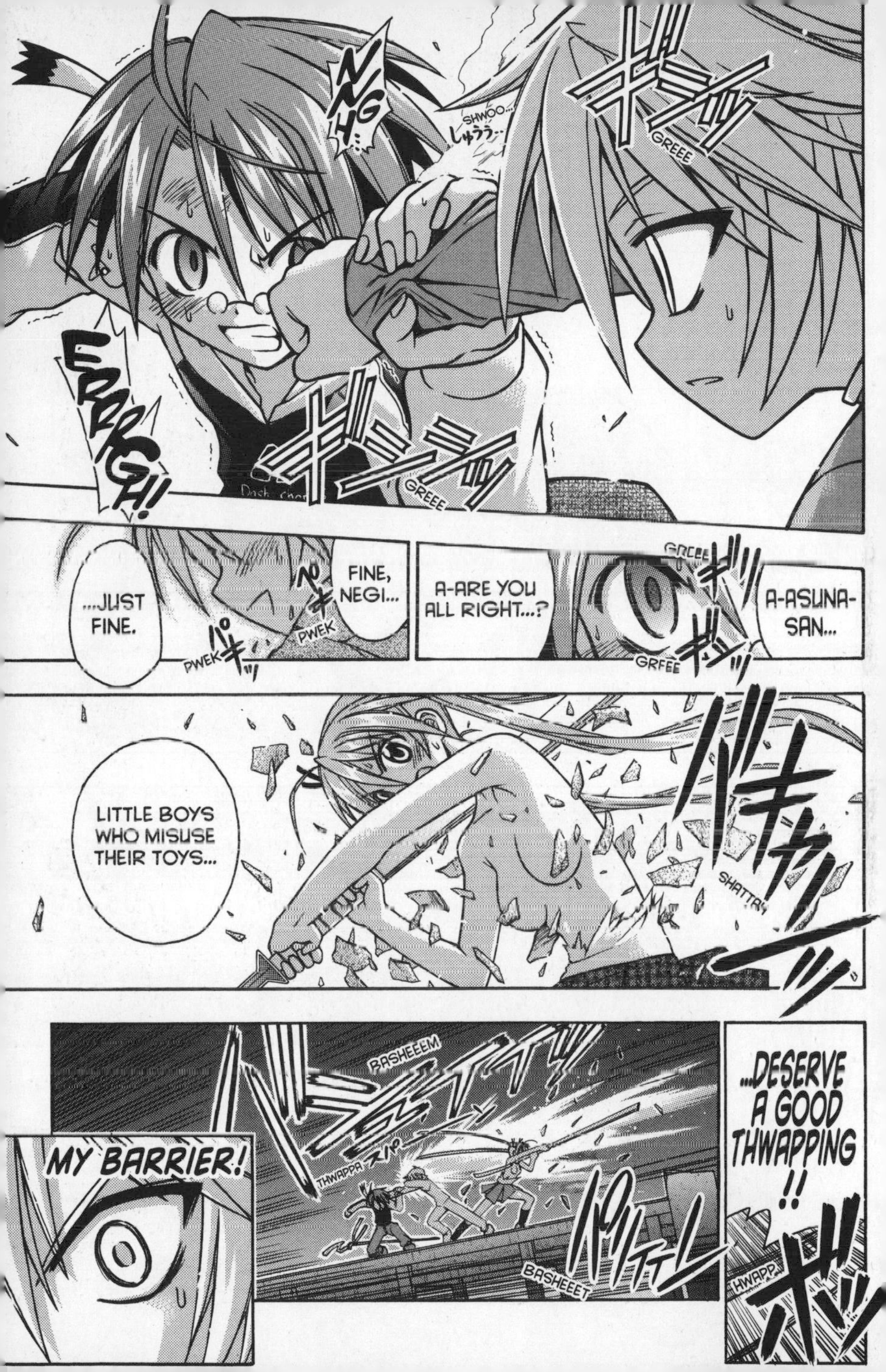
GREEE
SHWOO...
しゅうう...
NNGH...
ERRRGH!
GREEE
A-ASUNA-SAN...
GREEE
GRFEE
A-ARE YOU ALL RIGHT...?
FINE, NEGI...
PWEK
PWEK
...JUST FINE.
SHATTA
LITTLE BOYS WHO MISUSE THEIR TOYS...
...DESERVE A GOOD THWAPPING!!
THWAPP
BASHEEEM
THWAPPA
BASHEEET
MY BARRIER!

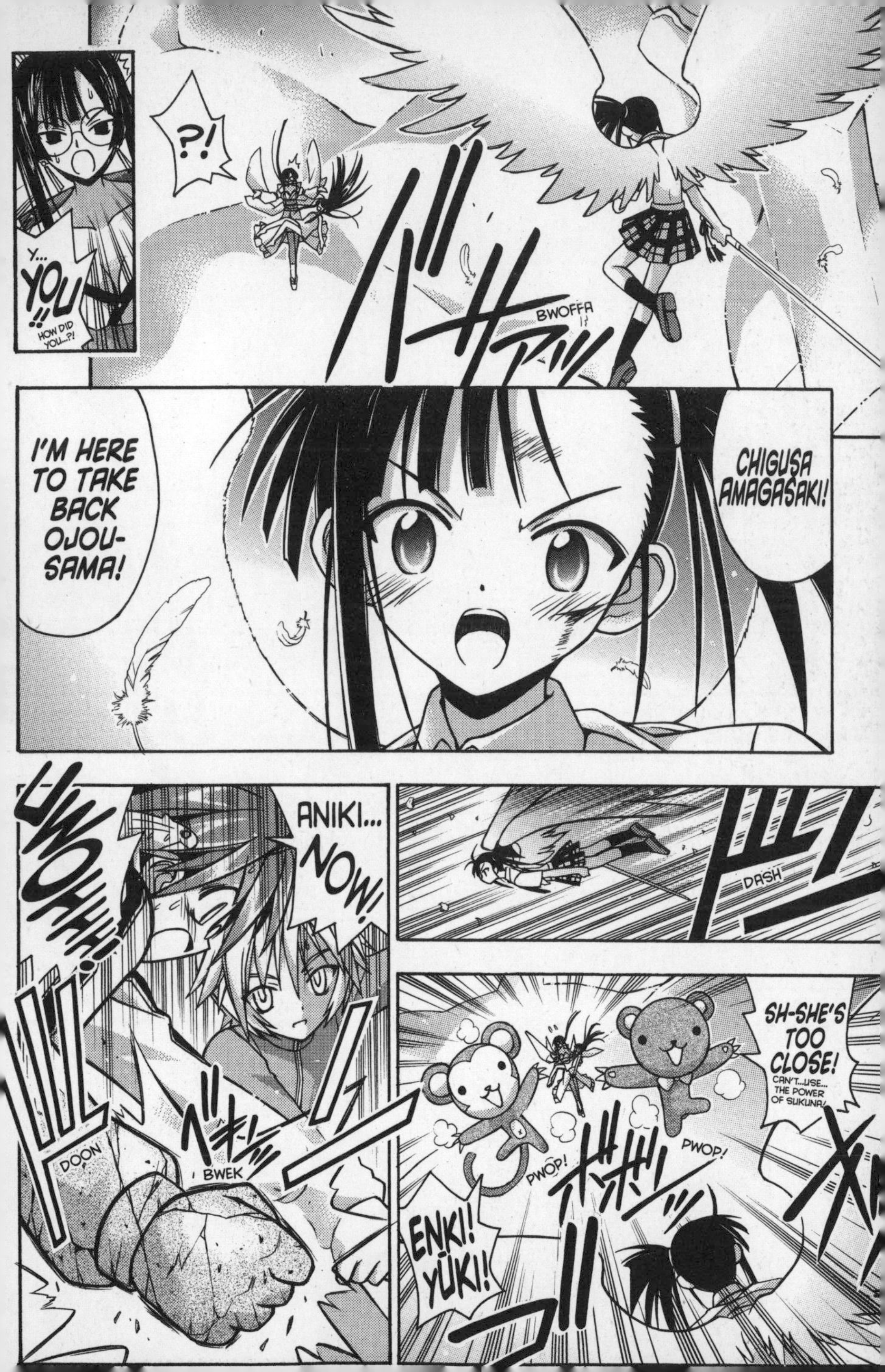
BWOFFA
?!
Y... YOU!!
HOW DID YOU...?!
CHIGUSA AMAGASAKI!
I'M HERE TO TAKE BACK OJOU-SAMA!
DASH
SH-SHE'S TOO CLOSE!
CAN'T...USE... THE POWER OF SUKUNA!
PWOP!
PWOP!
ENKI! YÜKI!
ANIKI... NOW!
BWEK
DOON

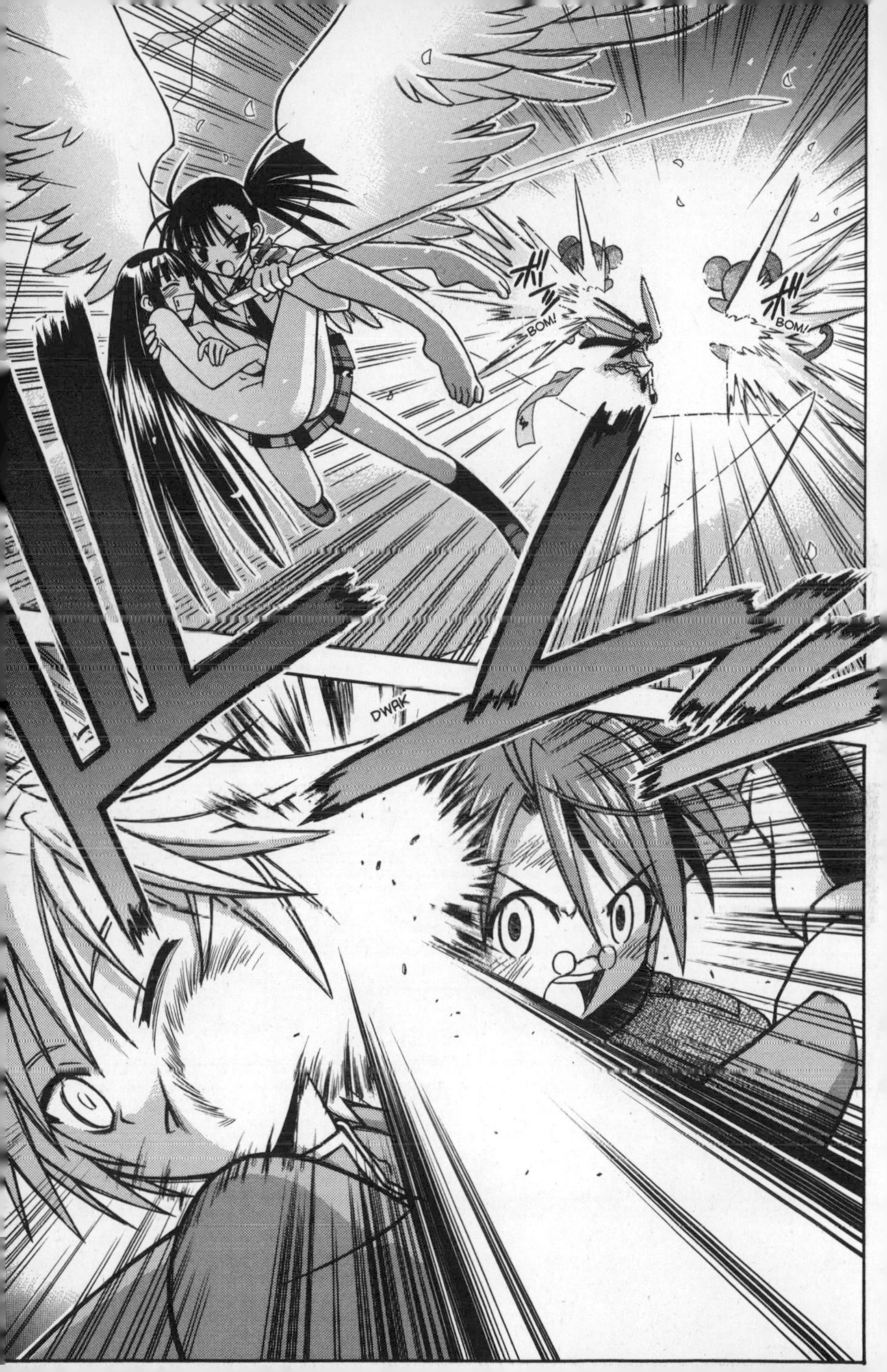
BOM!
BOM!
DWAK

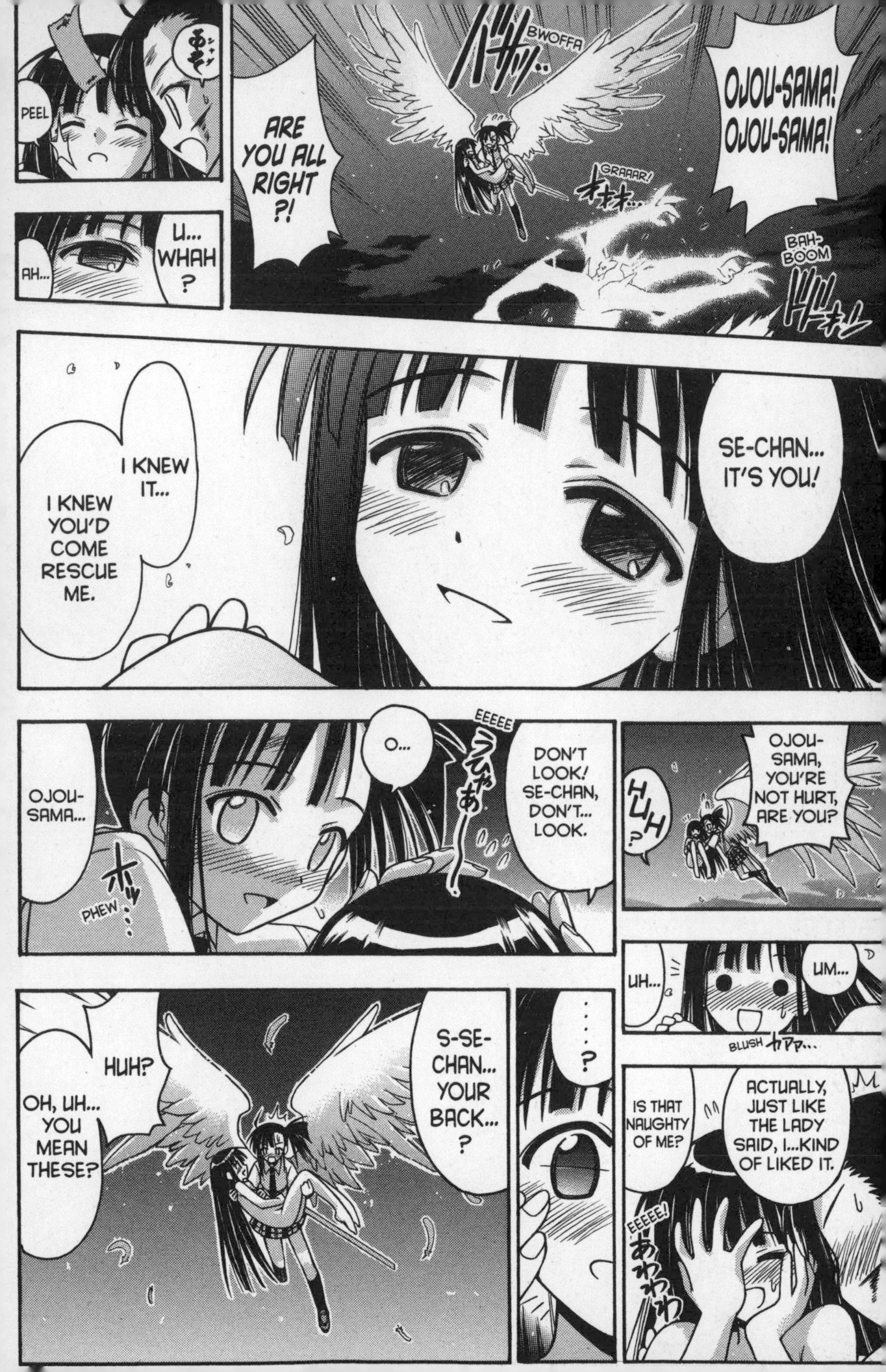
OJOU-SAMA! OJOU-SAMA!
BAH-BOOM
GRAAAR!
BWOFFA
ARE YOU ALL RIGHT ?!
PEEL
U... WHAH ?
AH...
SE-CHAN... IT'S YOU!
I KNEW IT...
I KNEW YOU'D COME RESCUE ME.
OJOU-SAMA, YOU'RE NOT HURT, ARE YOU?
HUH ?
EEEEE
DON'T LOOK! SE-CHAN, DON'T... LOOK.
O...
OJOU-SAMA...
PHEW
UM...
UH...
BLUSH
ACTUALLY, JUST LIKE THE LADY SAID, I...KIND OF LIKED IT.
IS THAT NAUGHTY OF ME?
EEEEE!
...?
S-SE-CHAN... YOUR BACK... ?
HUH?
OH, UH... YOU MEAN THESE?

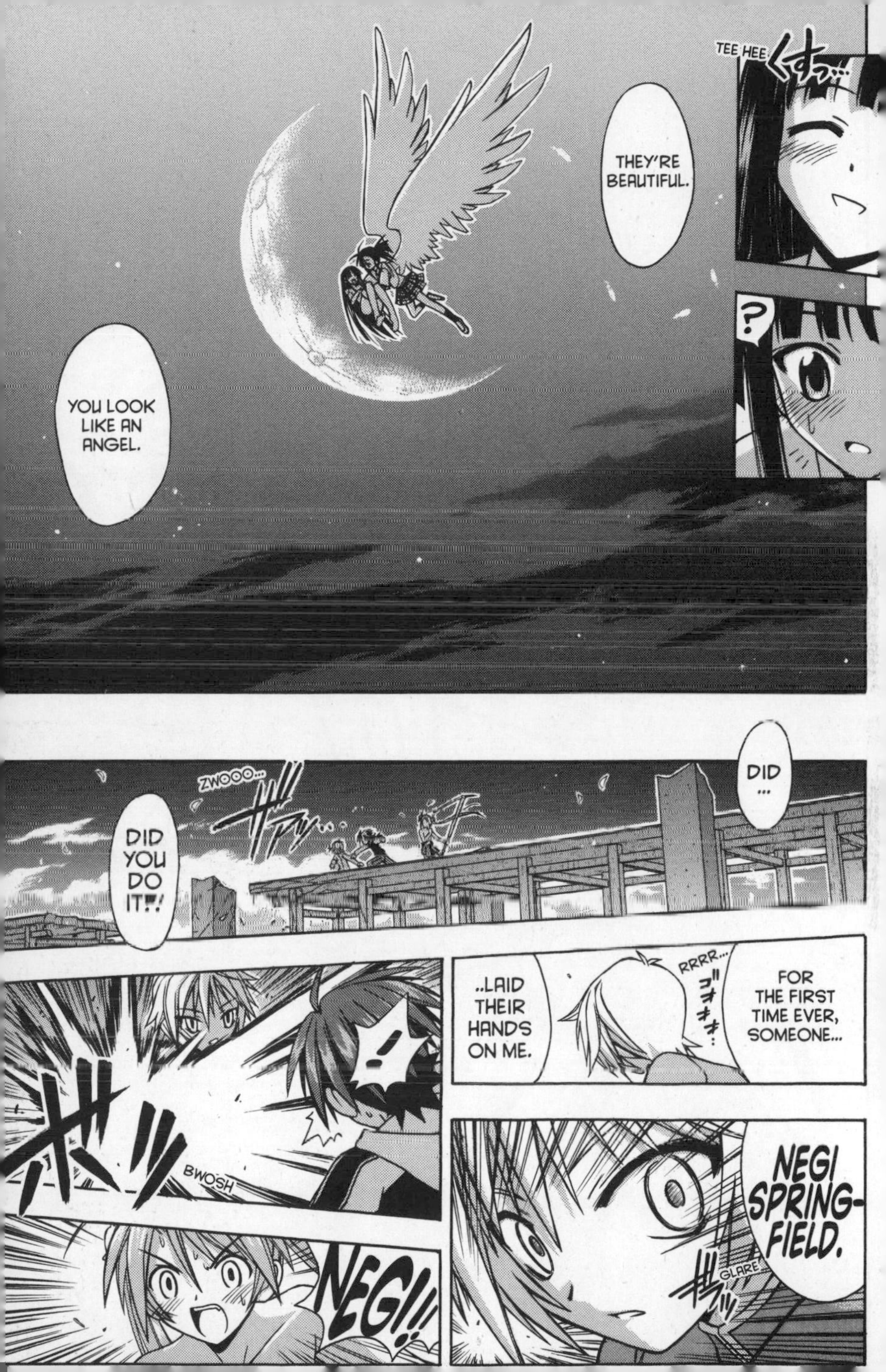
TEE HEE
くすっ…
?
THEY'RE BEAUTIFUL.
YOU LOOK LIKE AN ANGEL.
DID ...
ZWOOO...
DID YOU DO IT!?!
FOR THE FIRST TIME EVER, SOMEONE...
RRRR...
..LAID THEIR HANDS ON ME.
!
BWOSH
NEGI SPRINGFIELD.
GLARE
NEGI!!!

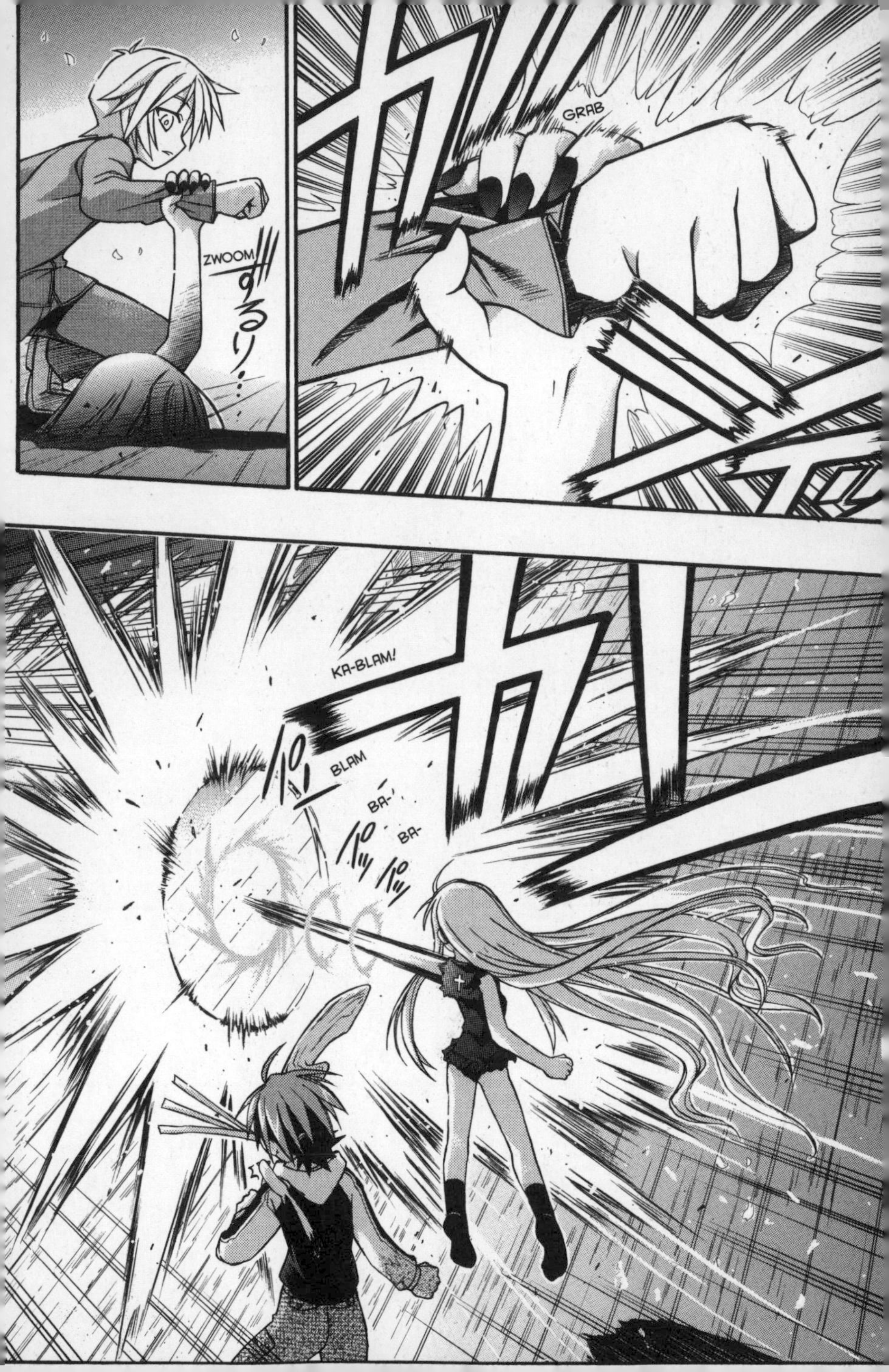
GRAB
ZWOOM
するり…
KA-BLAM!
BLAM
BA-
BA-

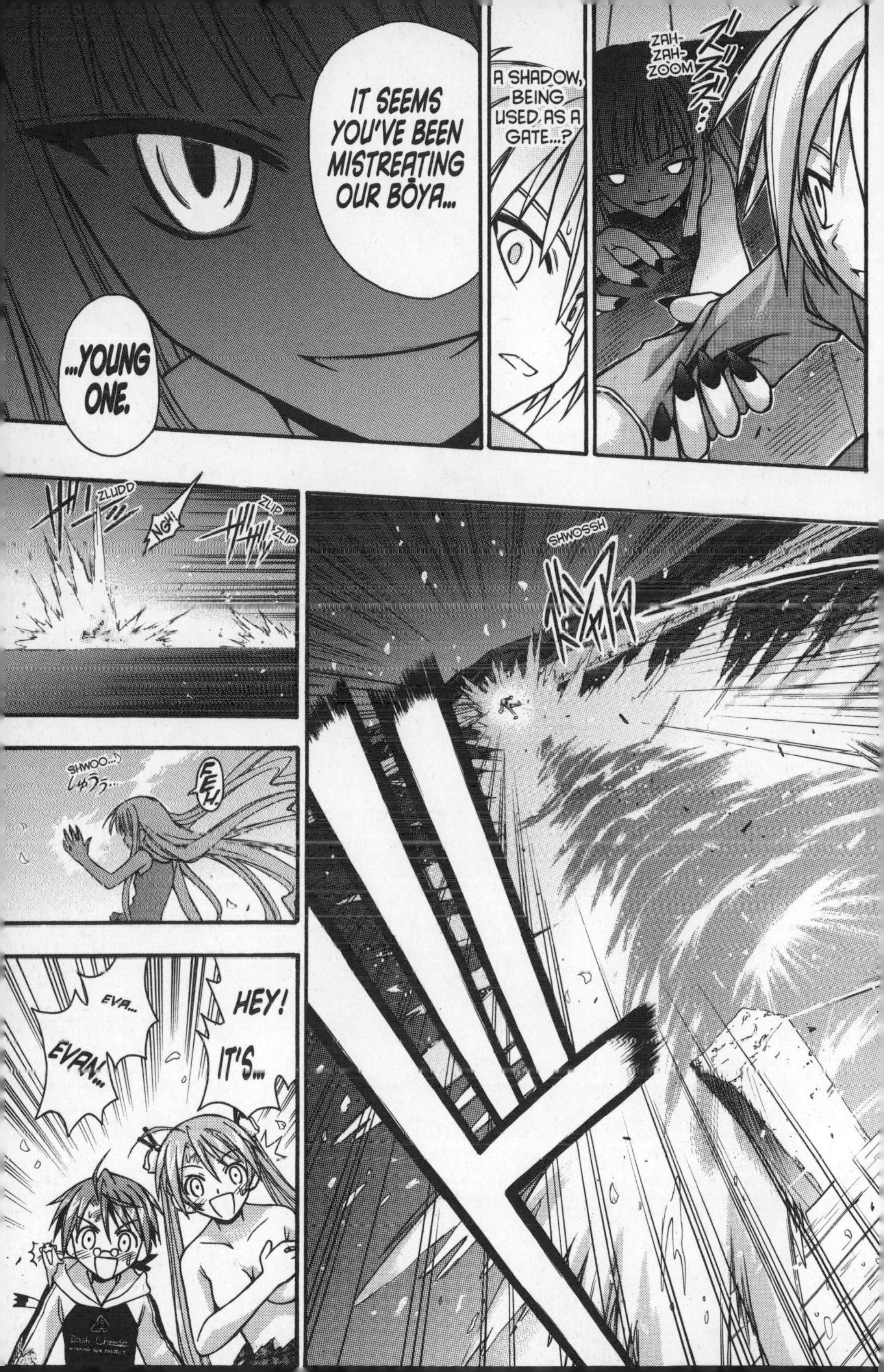

ZAH-ZAH-ZOOM
A SHADOW, BEING USED AS A GATE...?
IT SEEMS YOU'VE BEEN MISTREATING OUR BŌYA...
...YOUNG ONE.
SHWOSSH
ZLUDD
NGH!
ZLIP
ZLIP
SHWOO...
しゅうう...
EEH!
HEY!
EVA...
IT'S...
EVAN!...

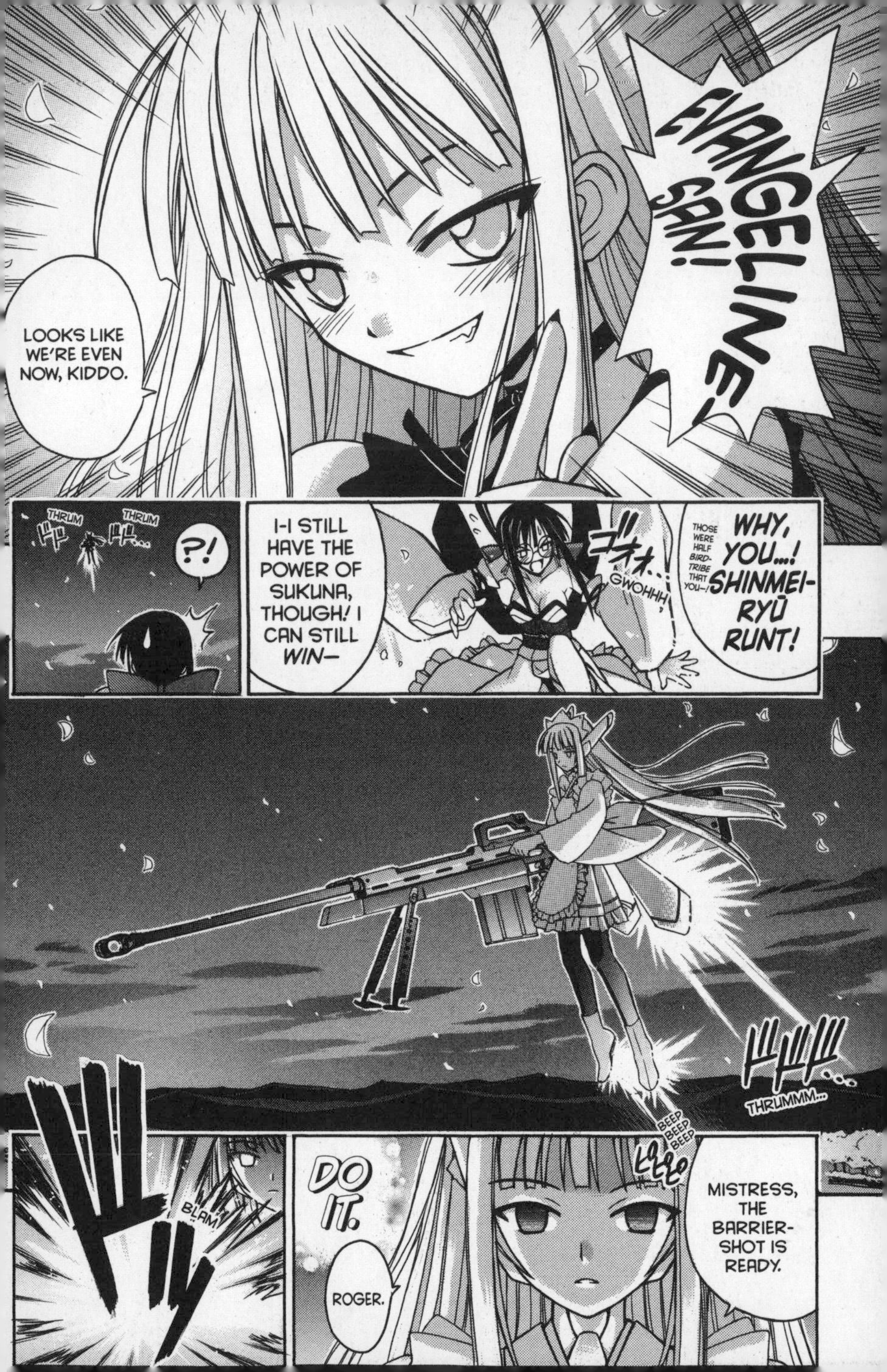
EVANGELINE-SAN!
LOOKS LIKE WE'RE EVEN NOW, KIDDO.
WHY, YOU...! SHINMEI-RYŪ RUNT!
THOSE WERE HALF BIRD-TRIBE THAT YOU—!
GWOHHH
I-I STILL HAVE THE POWER OF SUKUNA, THOUGH! I CAN STILL WIN—
THRUM
THRUM
?!
THRUMMM...
BEEP BEEP BEEP
MISTRESS, THE BARRIER-SHOT IS READY.
DO IT.
ROGER.
BLAM

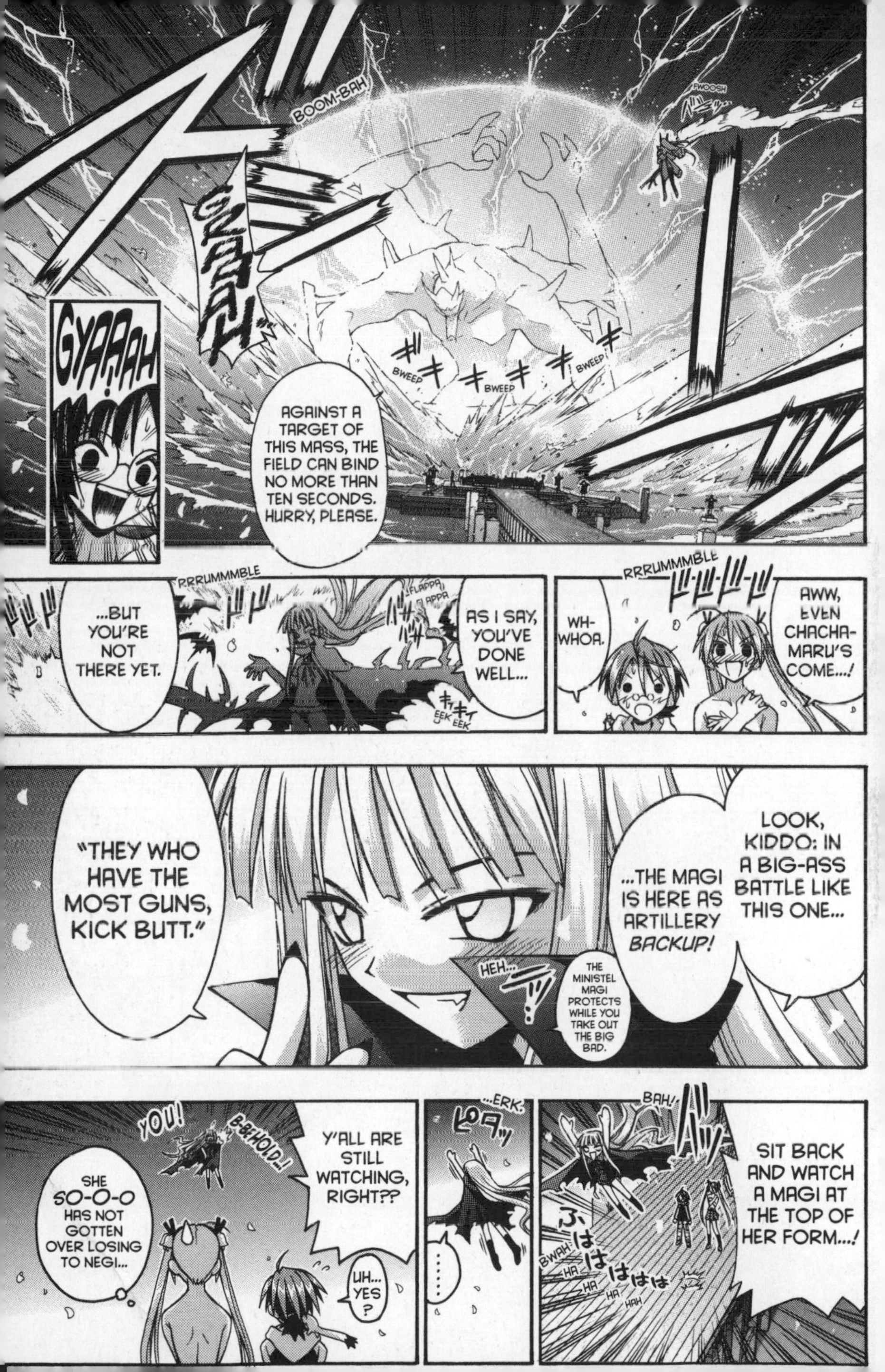
FWOOSH
BOOM-BAH
BWEEP
BWEEP
BWEEP
AGAINST A TARGET OF THIS MASS, THE FIELD CAN BIND NO MORE THAN TEN SECONDS. HURRY, PLEASE.
GYAAAH!
RRRUMMMBLE
AWW, EVEN CHACHA-MARU'S COME...!
WH-WHOA.
RRRUMMMBLE
FLAPPA FLAPPA
AS I SAY, YOU'VE DONE WELL...
EEK EEK
...BUT YOU'RE NOT THERE YET.
LOOK, KIDDO: IN A BIG-ASS BATTLE LIKE THIS ONE...
...THE MAGI IS HERE AS ARTILLERY *BACKUP!*
THE MINISTEL MAGI PROTECTS WHILE YOU TAKE OUT THE BIG BAD.
HEH...
"THEY WHO HAVE THE MOST GUNS, KICK BUTT."
BAH!
SIT BACK AND WATCH A MAGI AT THE TOP OF HER FORM...!
BWAH HA HA HA HAH
...ERK.
......
Y'ALL ARE STILL WATCHING, RIGHT??
B-BEHOLD...!
YOU!
SHE SO-O-O HAS NOT GOTTEN OVER LOSING TO NEGI...
UH... YES?

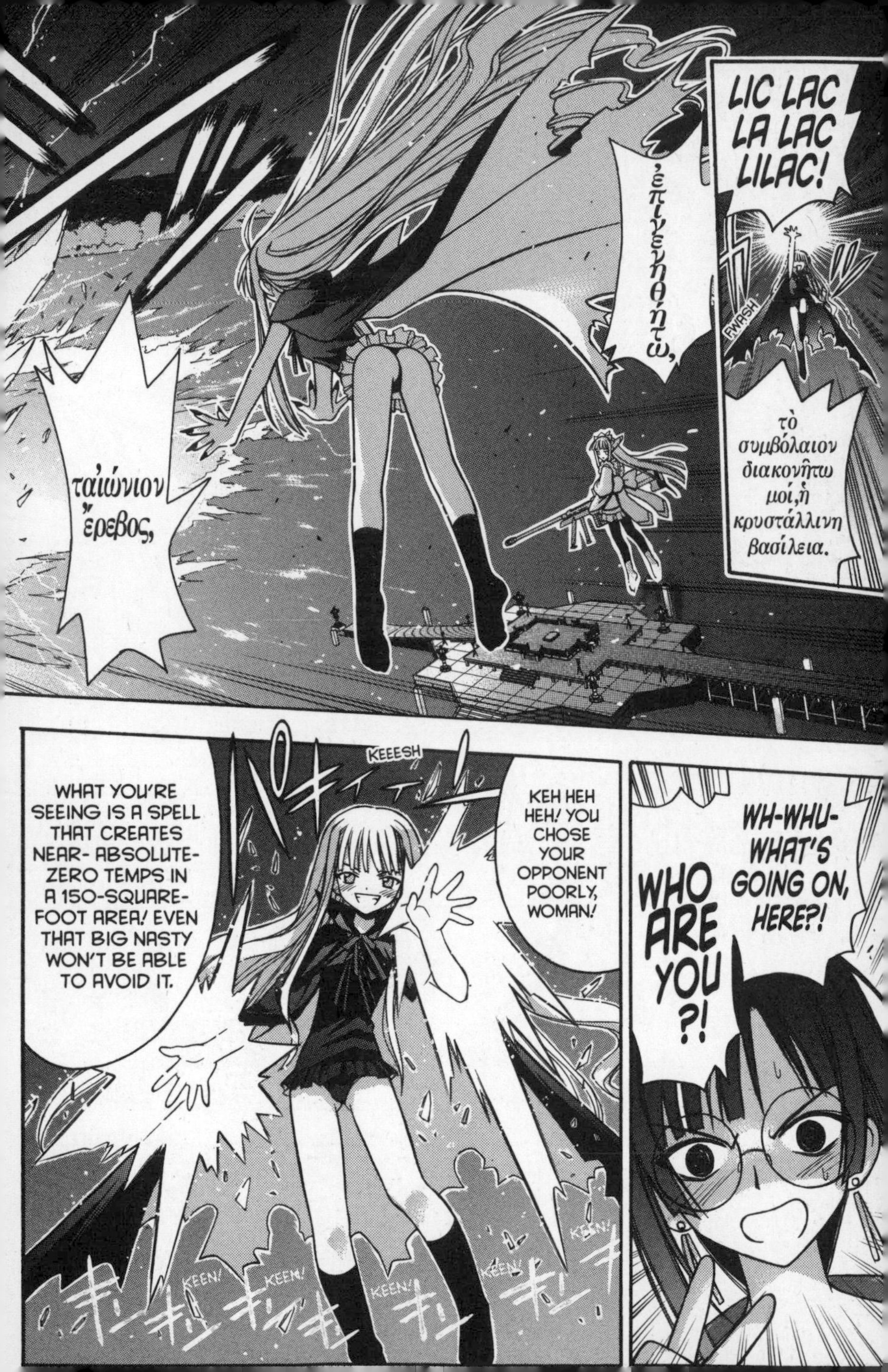
LIC LAC LA LAC LILAC!
FWASH
τὸ συμβόλαιον διακονῆητω μοί, ἡ κρυστάλλινη βασίλεια.
ἐπιγενηθήτω,
ταἰώνιον ἔρεβος,
WH-WHU-WHAT'S GOING ON, HERE?!
WHO ARE YOU?!
KEEESH
KEH HEH HEH! YOU CHOSE YOUR OPPONENT POORLY, WOMAN!
WHAT YOU'RE SEEING IS A SPELL THAT CREATES NEAR- ABSOLUTE-ZERO TEMPS IN A 150-SQUARE-FOOT AREA! EVEN THAT BIG NASTY WON'T BE ABLE TO AVOID IT.
KEEN!
KEEN!
KEEN!
KEEN!
KEEN!

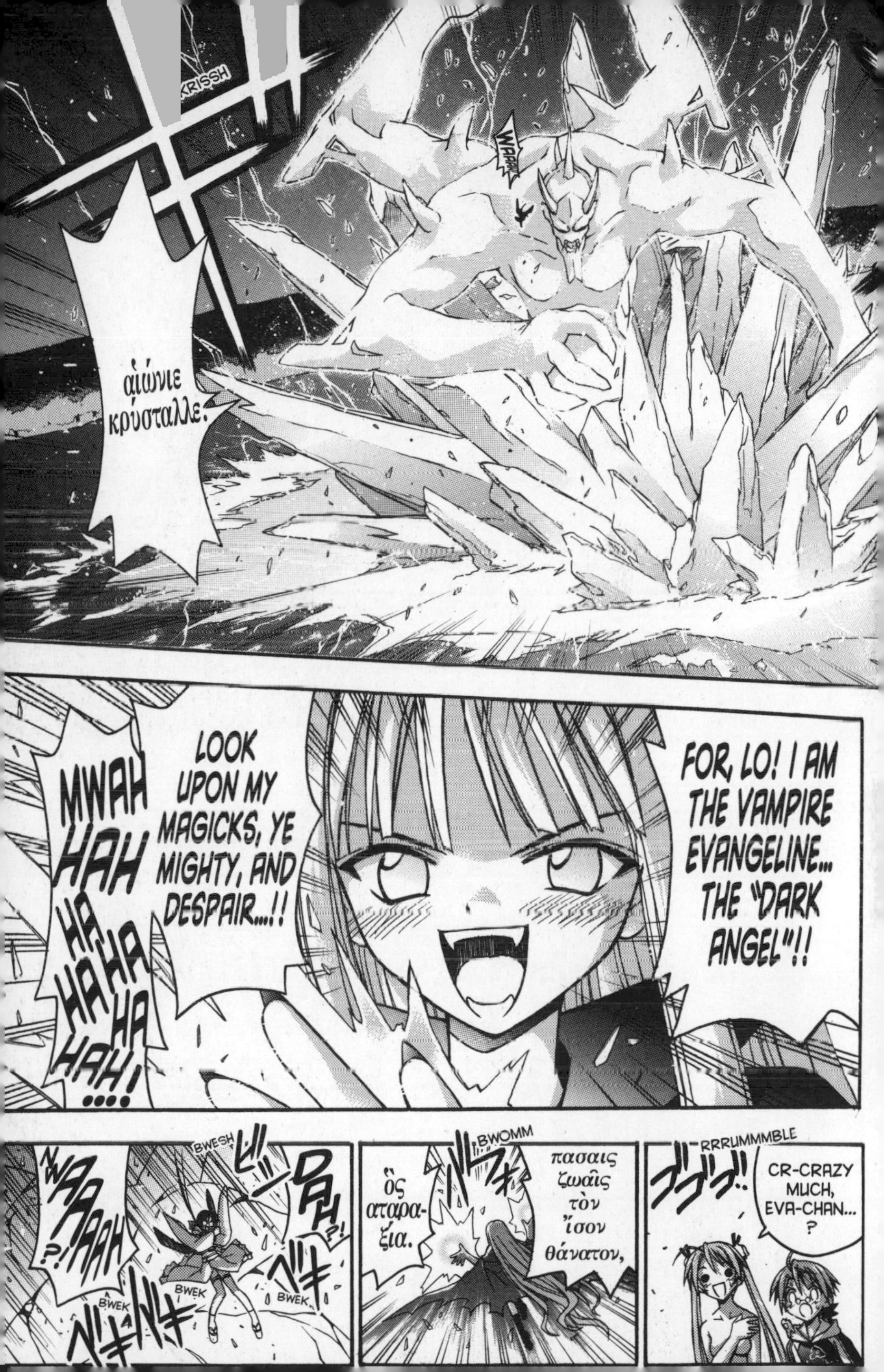
KRISSH
αἰώνιε κρύσταλλε.
FOR, LO! I AM THE VAMPIRE EVANGELINE... THE "DARK ANGEL"!!
LOOK UPON MY MAGICKS, YE MIGHTY, AND DESPAIR...!!
MWAH HAH HA HA HA HA HAH!....
RRRUMMMBLE
CR-CRAZY MUCH, EVA-CHAN...?
BWOMM
πασαις ζωαῖς τὸν ἴσον θάνατον,
ὅς αταραξια.
BWESH
DAH?!
NWAAAAH?!
BWEK
BWEK
BWEK

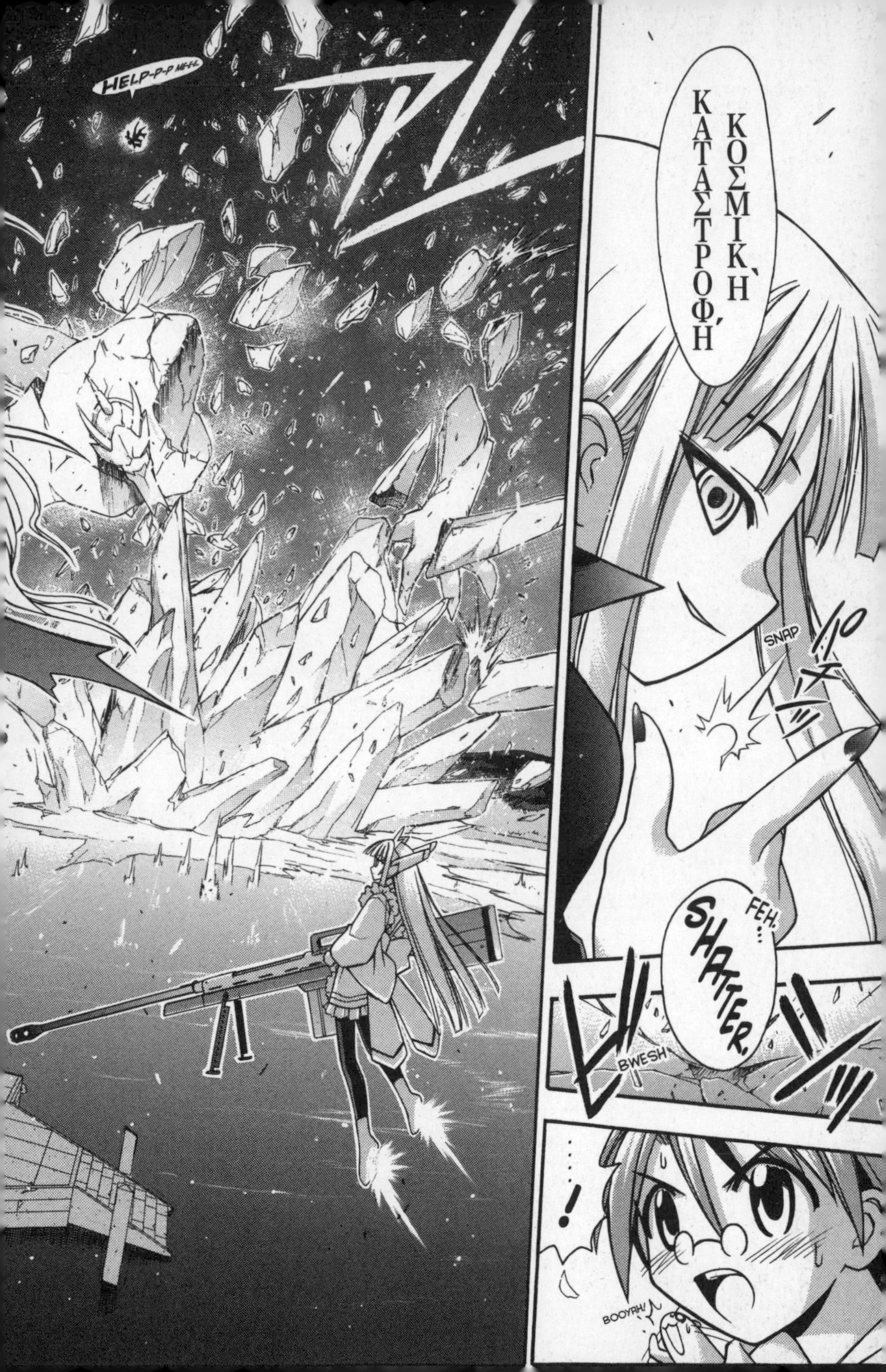
ΚΟΣΜΙΚῊ ΚΑΤΑΣΤΡΟΦΉ
SNAP
FEH...
SHATTER.
BWESH
...!
BOOYAH!
HELP-P-P ME-E-E

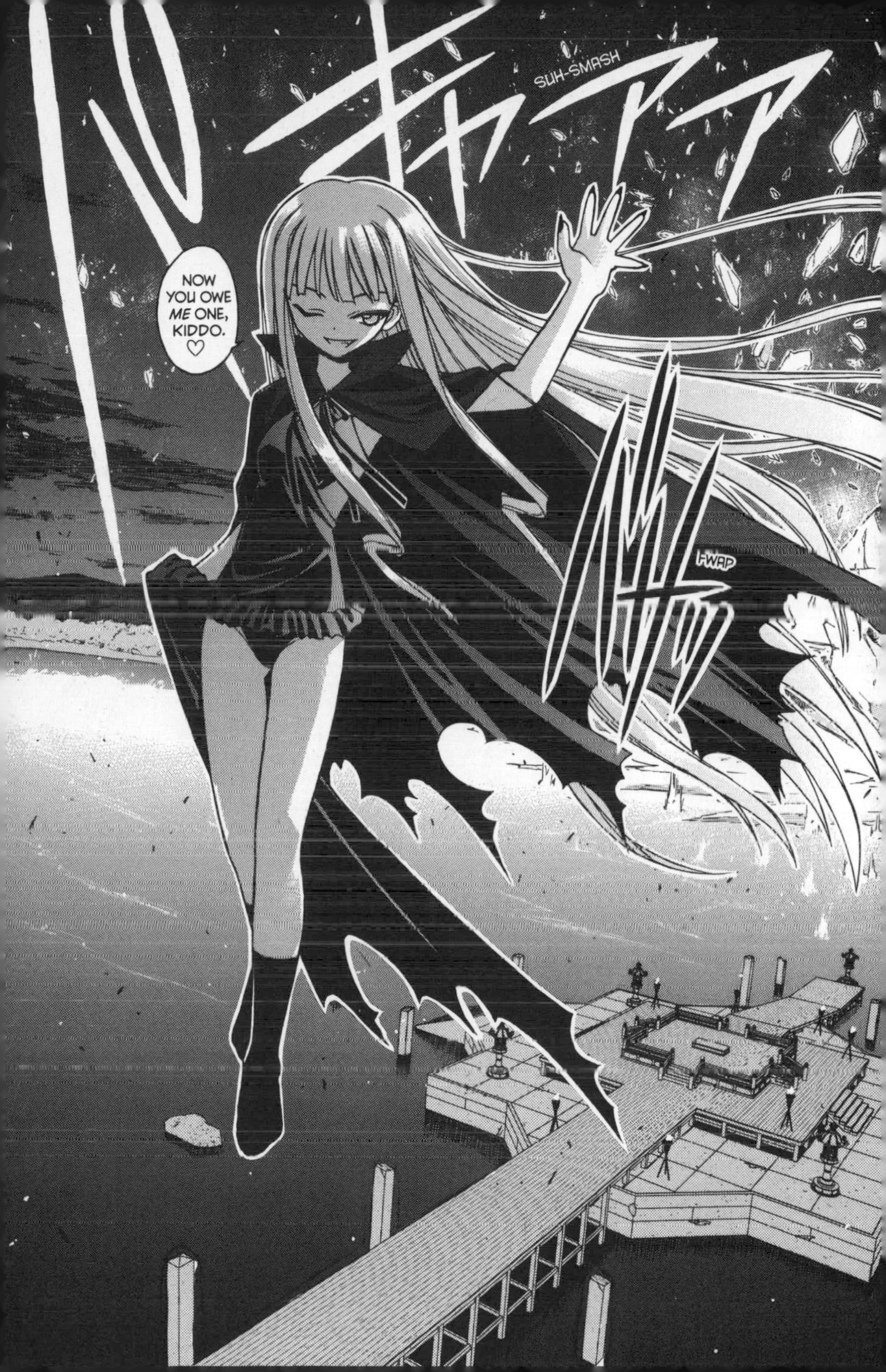
SUH-SMASH
NOW YOU OWE *ME* ONE, KIDDO. ♡
FWAP

■「小さき王、八つ足の蜥蜴、邪眼の主よ。その光、我が手に宿し、禍いなる眼差しで射よ。『石化の邪眼』」

バーシリスケ・ガレオーテ・メタ・コークト・ボドーン・カイ・カコイン・オンマトイン・ト・フォース・エメーイ・ケイリ・カティアース・トーイ・カコーイ・デルグマティ・トクセウサトー カコン・オンマ・ペトロ—セオース

(βασιλισκὲ γαλεῶτε μετὰ κὼκτῶ ποδῶν καὶ κακοῖν ὄμμάτοιν τὸ φῶς ἐμῇ χειρὶ καθίας τῷ κακῷ δέργματι τοξευσάτω.ΚΑΚΟ`Ν Ο¨ΜΜΑ ΠΕΤΡΩ¨ΣΕΩΣ)

BASILSKE GALEOTE, META, KOKTO, BODON KAI KAKOIN ONMATRAIN FORCE EMAY KAIRI KATIARTH TOY KAKOI DELGMAI TOKSEUSATO KAKON OMMA PETROSEOS

"Little King, Eight-Legged Lizard, Master of the Evil Eye. Let your light shine from my hand, release the fire of catastrophe: 'Evil Eye of Petrifaction'"

Spell that emits beam of light from the fingertips, causing the petrifaction of the subject. Perhaps not unsurprisingly, yet another high-level spell, invoked in ancient Greek.

■「契約に従い、我に従え、氷の女王。来れ、とこしえのやみ、えいえんのひょうが。全ての命ある者に等しき死を。其は、安らぎ也。『おわるせかい』」

ト・シュンボライオン・ディアーコネート・モイ・ヘー・クリュスタリネー・バシレイア・エビゲネーテート・タイオーニオン・エレボス・ハイオーニエ・クリュスタレ・バーサイス・ゾーイス・トン・イソン・タナトン・ホス・アタラクシア コズミケー・カタストロフェー

(τὸ συμβόλαιον διακονήτω μοί,ἡ κρυστάλλινη βασίλεια.ἐπιγενηθήτω,ταιώνιον ἔρεβος,αιώνιε κρύσταλλε.πάσαις ζωαῖς τὸν ἴσον θάνατον,ὃς ἀταραξία.ΚΟΣΜΙΚΗ΄ ΚΑΤΑΣΤΡΟΦΗ΄)

TO SHUMBOLION DIAKONOTO MOI HEI KRYSTALINE BASHLEIA EVIGENATO TAIONION ELEBOS HAIONIE KRYSTALE VERSAIS ZOICE TON ISON TANATON HOS ATAKSIA KOZMIKE KATAZROFE

"Upon our pact, do my bidding, O Queen of Ice. Come forth from the never-ending darkness, the eternal glacier, bring death to all that hast life. You are the place of eternal rest: 'The End of the World'"

Magic spell that creates a 150-square-foot area of absolute-zero temperature (-273.150 C; for the sake of comparison, oxygen freezes at -1830 C in one atmosphere, nitrogen at -1960 C, hydrogen at -2530 C, and helium at -268.9 C). At these extreme temperatures, events which do not normally occur in nature begin to happen, such as breakdowns on the atomic level, and super-conductivity. In that sense, although lowering the temperature may seem a simple enough operation, to bypass the laws of thermodynamics takes a powerful Magi.

There is a passage in the spell which references "eternal glacier." At that point, the area of effect is created; not until the final words "end of the world" are uttered is the outcome decided. With the "end of the world" portion of the spell, the opponent is frozen completely, and shattered. A revision to "frozen world," and the target is encased in a virtual pillar of ice. Back in the days when Evangeline had a bounty on her head, she'd use this spell often. For those bounty hunters who wouldn't think twice about killing a seemingly "little" girl (despite her real, chronological age), she would opt instead for "end of the world." Despite all this, while she is trapped within the confines of Mahora Academy, Evangeline's magic is sealed away, and she has no access to the formerly favorite high-level spells she once invoked in ancient Greek.

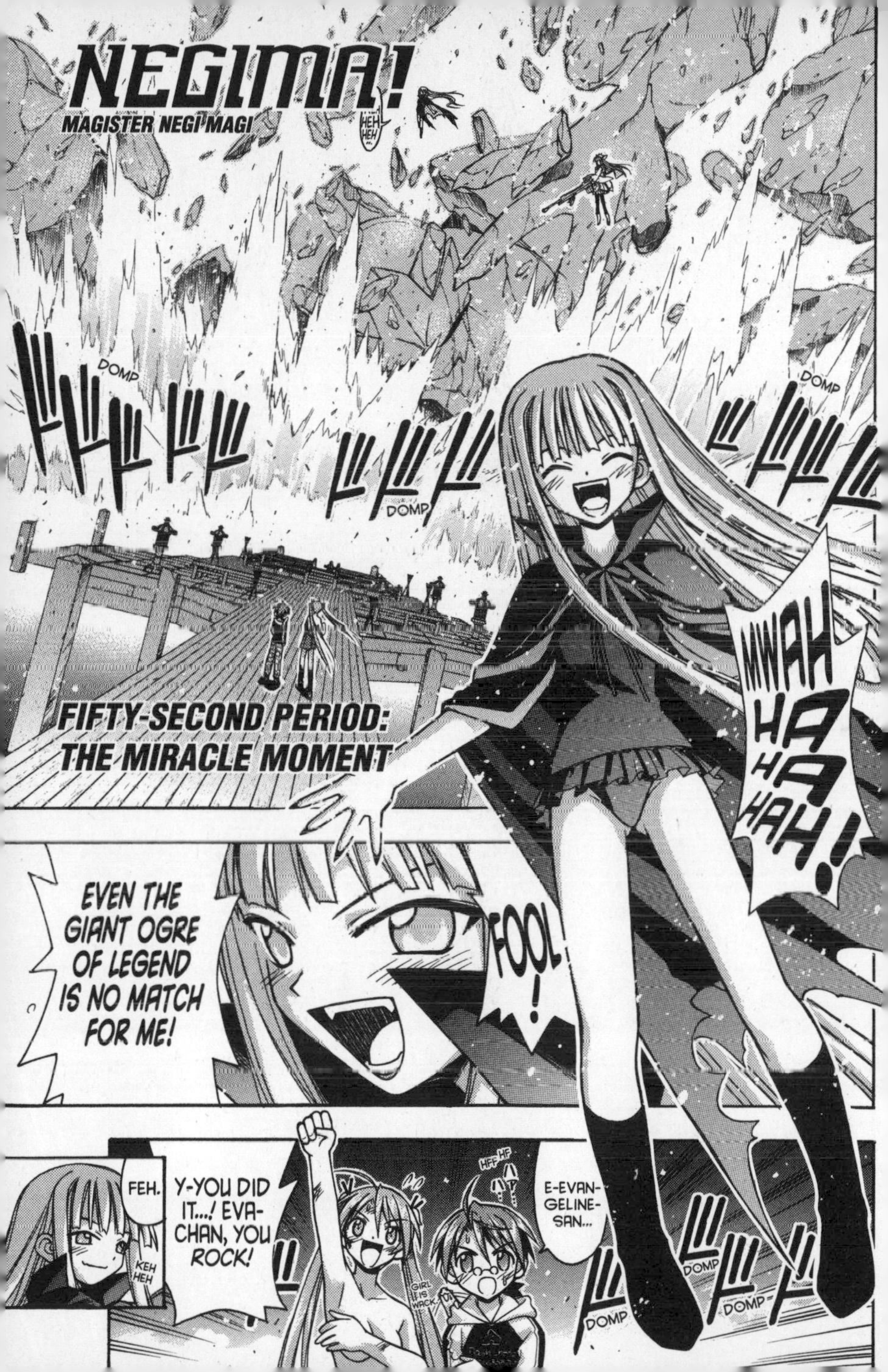
NEGIMA!
MAGISTER NEGI MAGI
HEH HEH
DOMP
DOMP
DOMP
MWAH HA HA HAH!
FIFTY-SECOND PERIOD: THE MIRACLE MOMENT
FOOL!
EVEN THE GIANT OGRE OF LEGEND IS NO MATCH FOR ME!
DOMP
DOMP
DOMP
E-EVAN-GELINE-SAN...
HFF HF
GIRL IS WACK
Y-YOU DID IT...! EVA-CHAN, YOU ROCK!
FEH.
KEH HEH

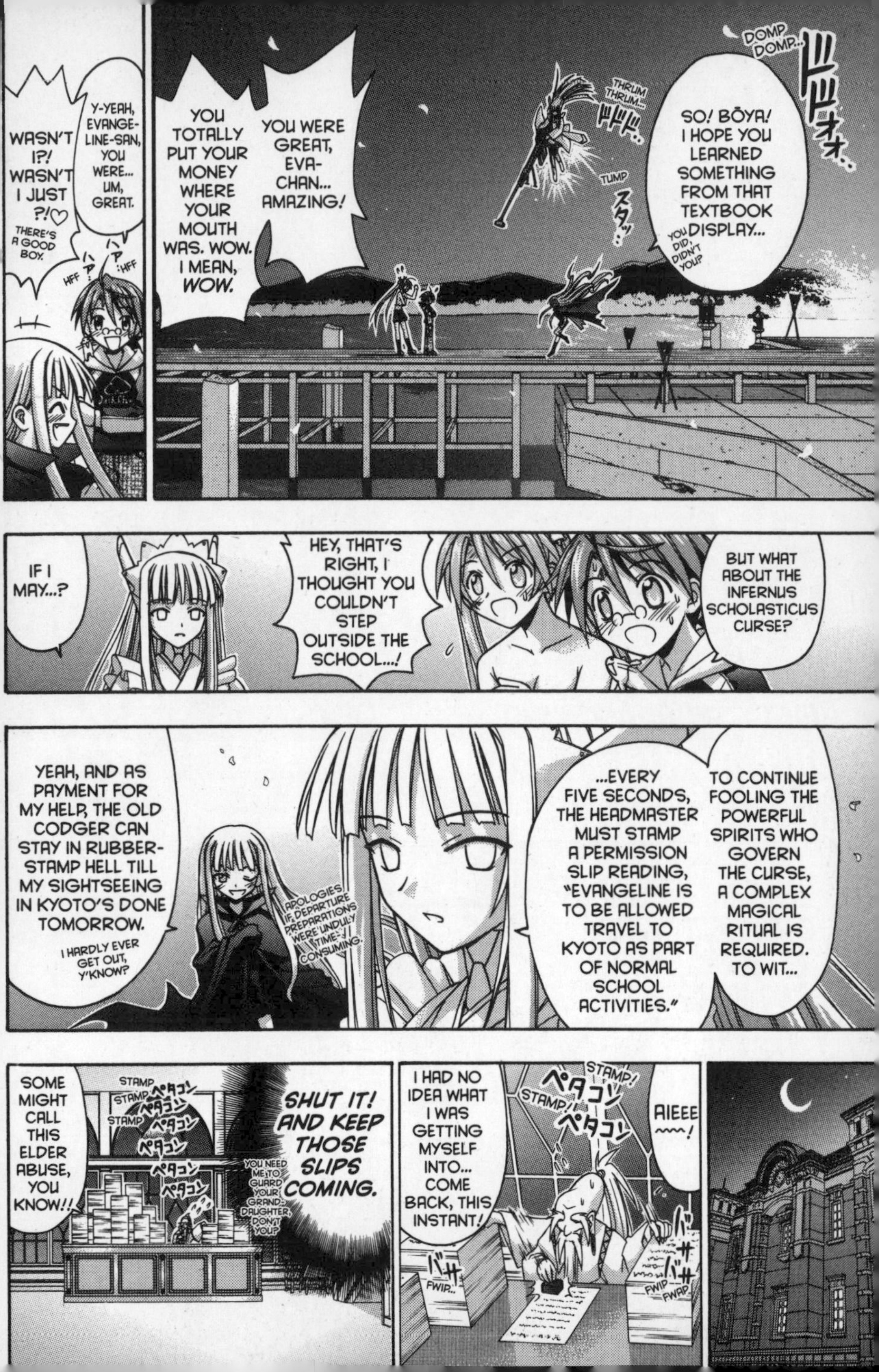
DOMP DOMP...
SO! BŌYA! I HOPE YOU LEARNED SOMETHING FROM THAT TEXTBOOK DISPLAY...
YOU DID, DIDN'T YOU?
THRUM THRUM...
TUMP
YOU WERE GREAT, EVA-CHAN... AMAZING!
YOU TOTALLY PUT YOUR MONEY WHERE YOUR MOUTH WAS. WOW. I MEAN, WOW.
Y-YEAH, EVANGE-LINE-SAN, YOU WERE... UM, GREAT.
WASN'T I?! WASN'T I JUST ?!♡
HFF HFF
THERE'S A GOOD BOY.
BUT WHAT ABOUT THE INFERNUS SCHOLASTICUS CURSE?
HEY, THAT'S RIGHT, I THOUGHT YOU COULDN'T STEP OUTSIDE THE SCHOOL...!
IF I MAY...?
TO CONTINUE FOOLING THE POWERFUL SPIRITS WHO GOVERN THE CURSE, A COMPLEX MAGICAL RITUAL IS REQUIRED. TO WIT...
...EVERY FIVE SECONDS, THE HEADMASTER MUST STAMP A PERMISSION SLIP READING, "EVANGELINE IS TO BE ALLOWED TRAVEL TO KYOTO AS PART OF NORMAL SCHOOL ACTIVITIES."
APOLOGIES IF DEPARTURE PREPARATIONS WERE UNDULY TIME-CONSUMING.
YEAH, AND AS PAYMENT FOR MY HELP, THE OLD CODGER CAN STAY IN RUBBER-STAMP HELL TILL MY SIGHTSEEING IN KYOTO'S DONE TOMORROW.
I HARDLY EVER GET OUT, Y'KNOW?
AIEEE ~~~!
STAMP!
STAMP!
I HAD NO IDEA WHAT I WAS GETTING MYSELF INTO... COME BACK, THIS INSTANT!
FWIP FWAP
FWIP...
SHUT IT! AND KEEP THOSE SLIPS COMING.
YOU NEED ME TO GUARD YOUR GRAND-DAUGHTER, DON'T YOU?
STAMP
STAMP
STAMP
SOME MIGHT CALL THIS ELDER ABUSE, YOU KNOW!!

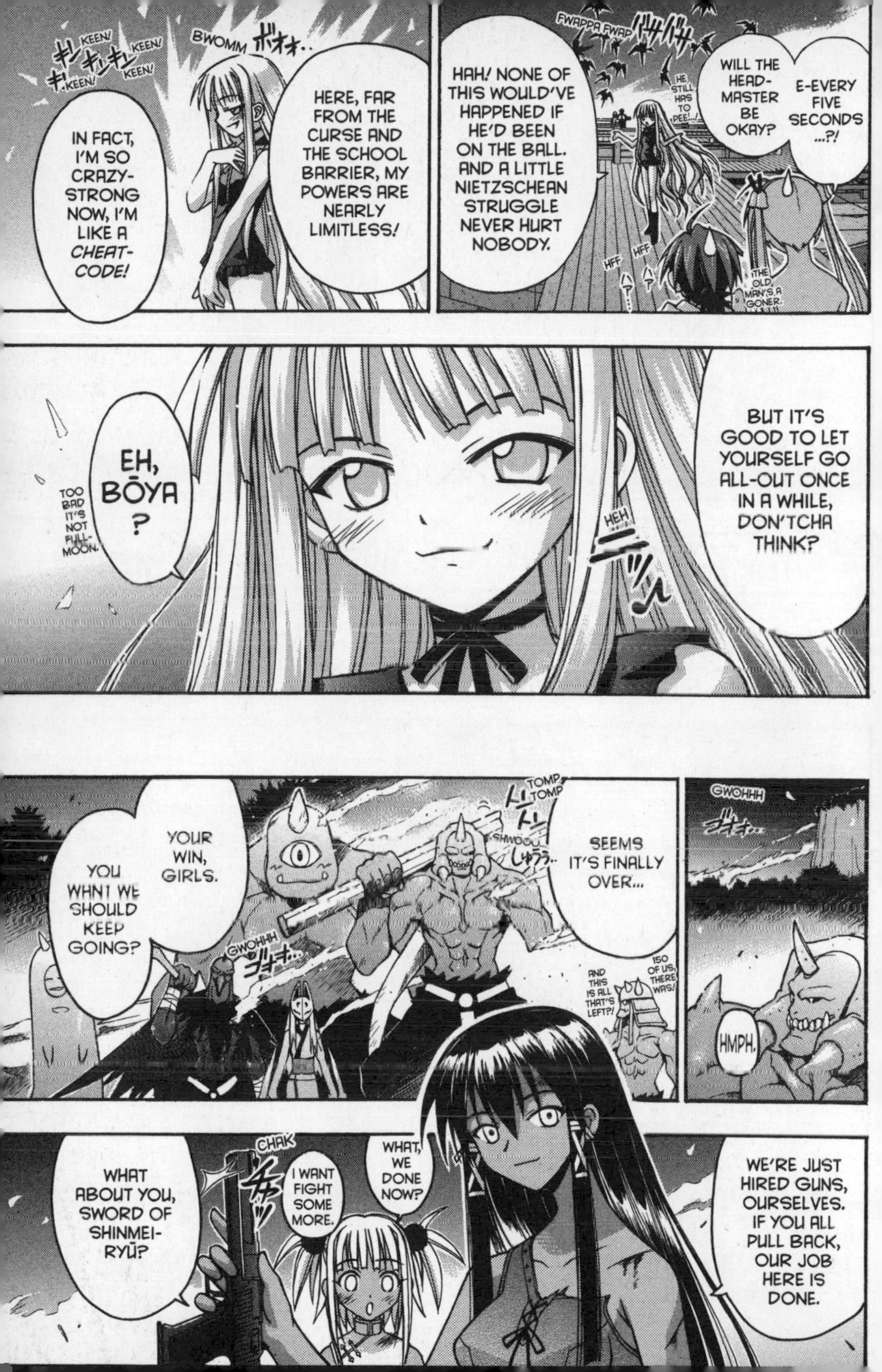
FWAPPA FWAP
WILL THE HEAD-MASTER BE OKAY?
E-EVERY FIVE SECONDS ...?!
HAH! NONE OF THIS WOULD'VE HAPPENED IF HE'D BEEN ON THE BALL. AND A LITTLE NIETZSCHEAN STRUGGLE NEVER HURT NOBODY.
HE STILL HAS TO PEE!...!
HFF HFF
THE OLD MAN'S A GONER.
KEEN! KEEN! KEEN! KEEN!
BWOMM
HERE, FAR FROM THE CURSE AND THE SCHOOL BARRIER, MY POWERS ARE NEARLY LIMITLESS!
IN FACT, I'M SO CRAZY-STRONG NOW, I'M LIKE A CHEAT-CODE!
BUT IT'S GOOD TO LET YOURSELF GO ALL-OUT ONCE IN A WHILE, DON'TCHA THINK?
HEH
EH, BŌYA?
TOO BAD IT'S NOT FULL-MOON.
GWOHHH
HMPH.
SEEMS IT'S FINALLY OVER...
TOMP TOMP
SHWOOO
150 OF US, THERE WAS!
AND THIS IS ALL THAT'S LEFT?!
YOUR WIN, GIRLS.
YOU WANT WE SHOULD KEEP GOING?
GWOHHH
WE'RE JUST HIRED GUNS, OURSELVES. IF YOU ALL PULL BACK, OUR JOB HERE IS DONE.
WHAT, WE DONE NOW?
I WANT FIGHT SOME MORE.
CHAK
WHAT ABOUT YOU, SWORD OF SHINMEI-RYŪ?

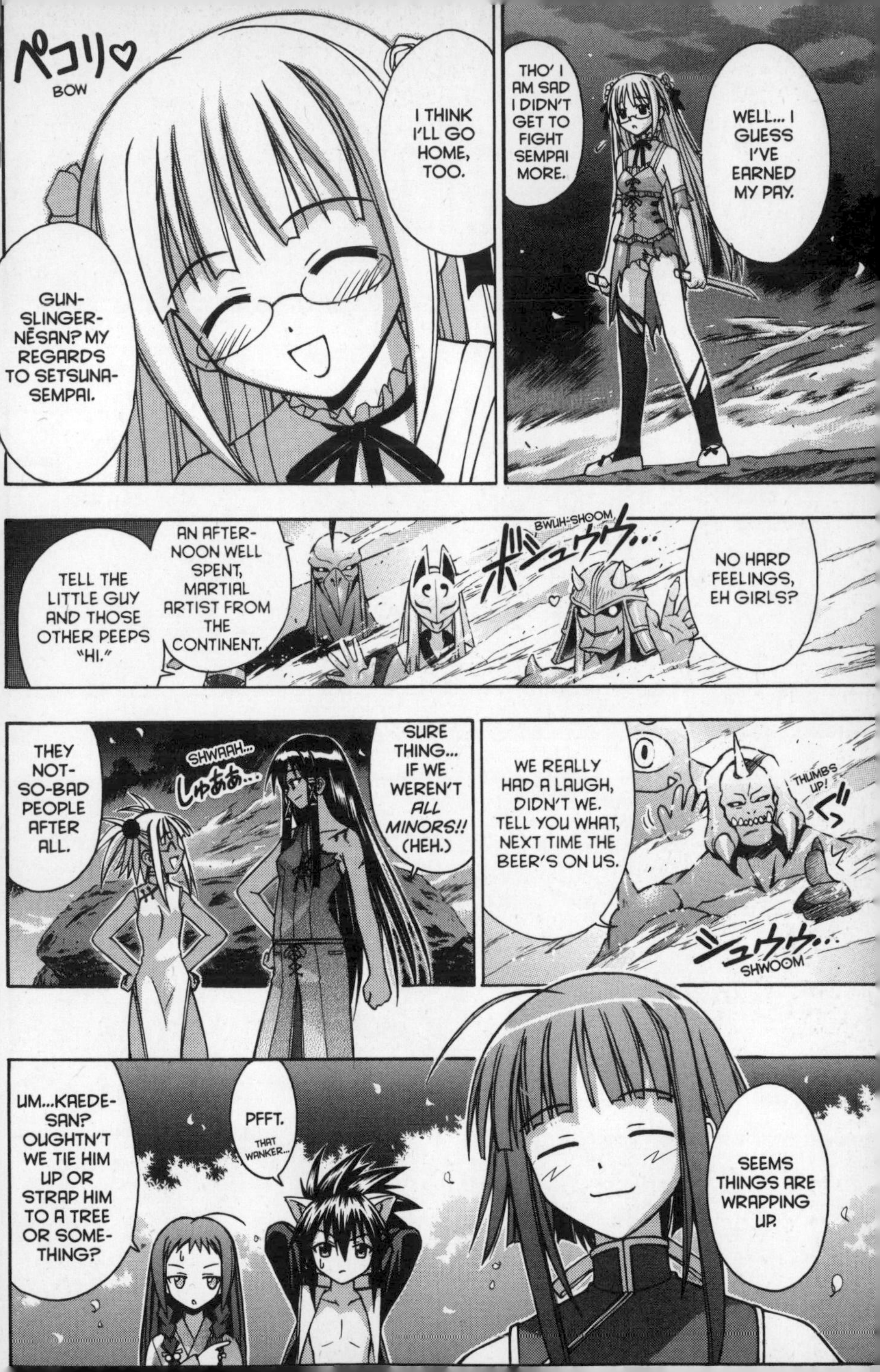
WELL... I GUESS I'VE EARNED MY PAY.
THO' I AM SAD I DIDN'T GET TO FIGHT SEMPAI MORE.
I THINK I'LL GO HOME, TOO.
ペコリ♡
BOW
GUN-SLINGER-NĒSAN? MY REGARDS TO SETSUNA-SEMPAI.
NO HARD FEELINGS, EH GIRLS?
BWUH-SHOOM
ボシュウウ...
AN AFTER-NOON WELL SPENT, MARTIAL ARTIST FROM THE CONTINENT.
TELL THE LITTLE GUY AND THOSE OTHER PEEPS "HI."
THUMBS UP!
WE REALLY HAD A LAUGH, DIDN'T WE. TELL YOU WHAT, NEXT TIME THE BEER'S ON US.
シュウウ...
SHWOOM
SURE THING... IF WE WEREN'T *ALL MINORS!!* (HEH.)
SHWAAH...
しゅあぁ...
THEY NOT-SO-BAD PEOPLE AFTER ALL.
SEEMS THINGS ARE WRAPPING UP.
PFFT.
THAT WANKER...
UM...KAEDE-SAN? OUGHTN'T WE TIE HIM UP OR STRAP HIM TO A TREE OR SOME-THING?

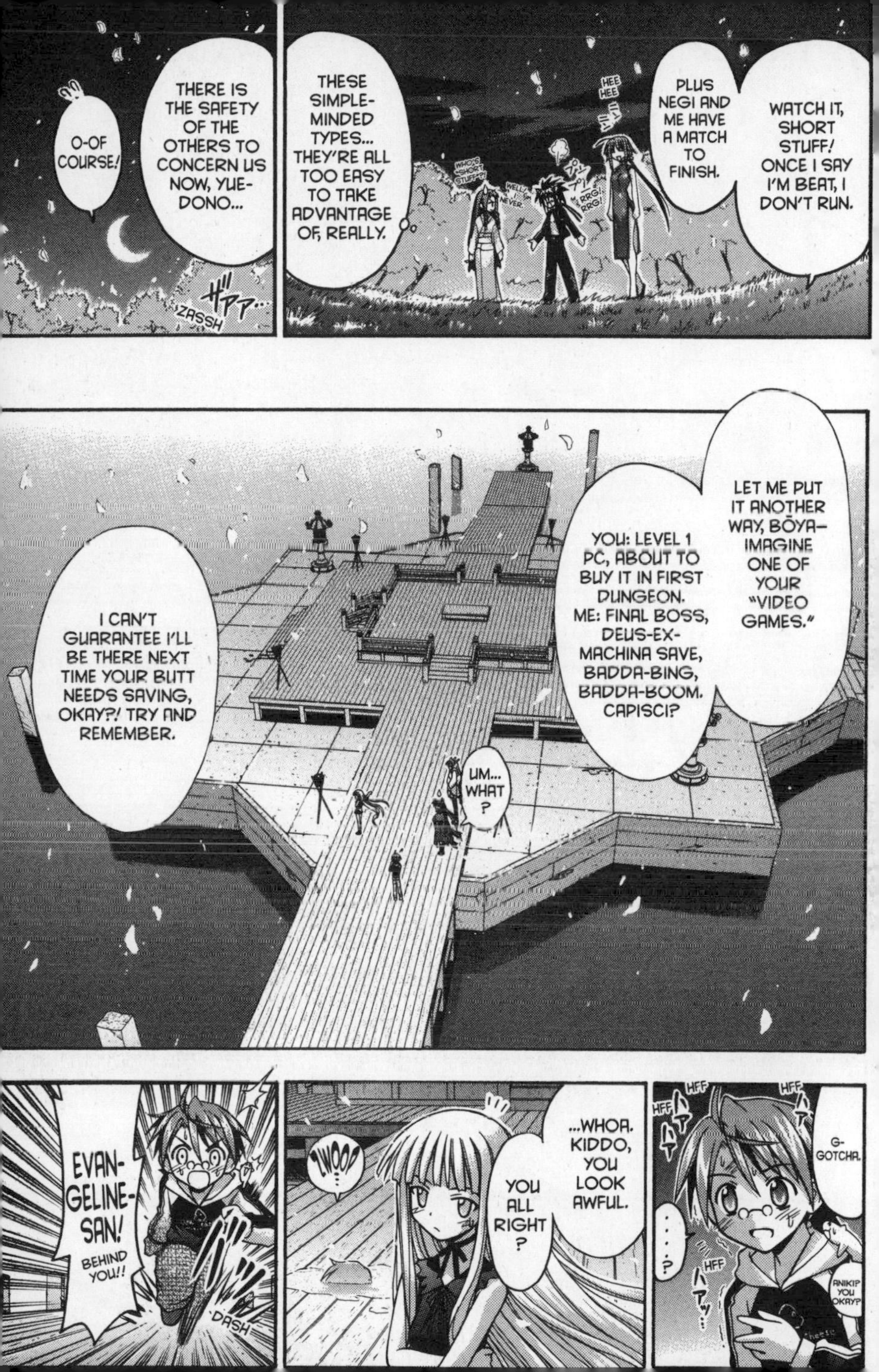
WATCH IT, SHORT STUFF! ONCE I SAY I'M BEAT, I DON'T RUN.
PLUS NEGI AND ME HAVE A MATCH TO FINISH.
HEE HEE
RRG! RRG!
WHO'S SHORT STUFF?!
WELL, I NEVER.
THESE SIMPLE-MINDED TYPES... THEY'RE ALL TOO EASY TO TAKE ADVANTAGE OF, REALLY.
THERE IS THE SAFETY OF THE OTHERS TO CONCERN US NOW, YUE-DONO...
O-OF COURSE!
ZASSH
LET ME PUT IT ANOTHER WAY, BŌYA— IMAGINE ONE OF YOUR "VIDEO GAMES."
YOU: LEVEL 1 PC, ABOUT TO BUY IT IN FIRST DUNGEON. ME: FINAL BOSS, DEUS-EX-MACHINA SAVE, BADDA-BING, BADDA-BOOM. CAPISCI?
UM... WHAT?
I CAN'T GUARANTEE I'LL BE THERE NEXT TIME YOUR BUTT NEEDS SAVING, OKAY?! TRY AND REMEMBER.
HFF
HFF
G-GOTCHA.
HFF
HFF
...?
ANIKI? YOU OKAY?
...WHOA. KIDDO, YOU LOOK AWFUL.
YOU ALL RIGHT?
ZWOOP
EVAN-GELINE-SAN!
BEHIND YOU!!
DASH

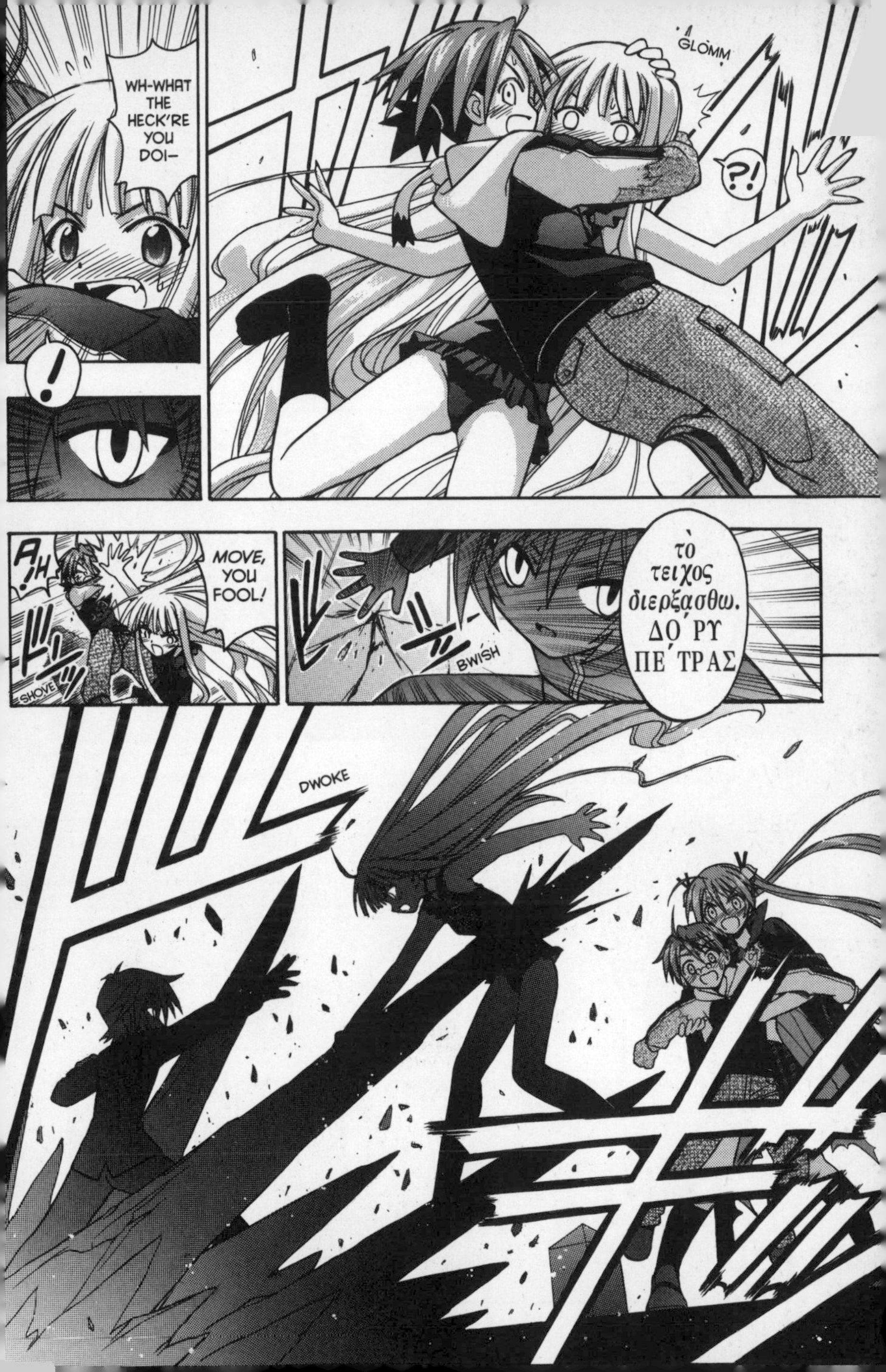
GLOMM
?!
WH-WHAT THE HECK'RE YOU DOI—
!
τὸ τεῖχος διερξάσθω. ΔΌΡΥ ΠΈΤΡΑΣ
BWISH
MOVE, YOU FOOL!
AH!
SHOVE
DWOKE

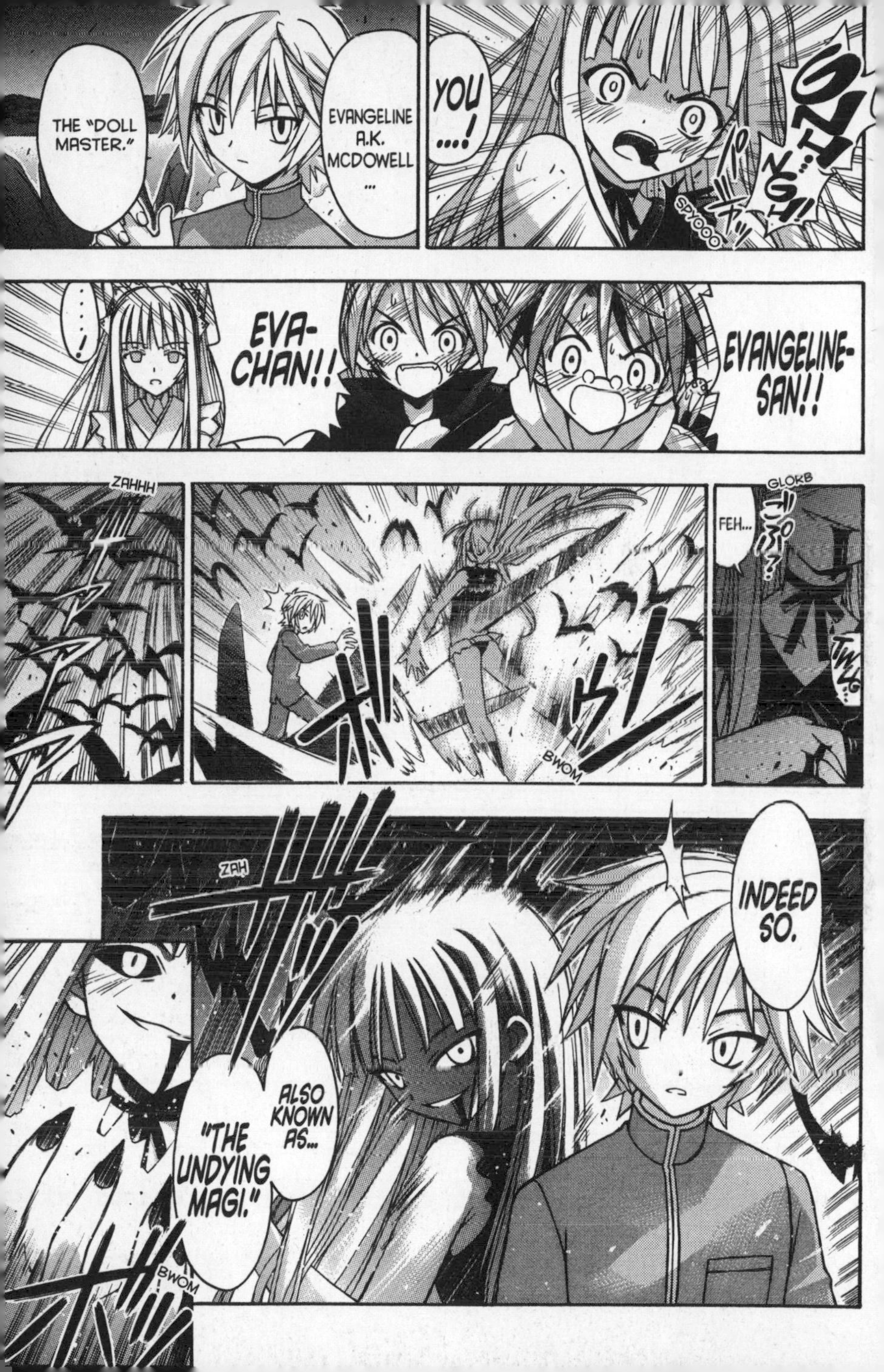
OHH... NGH!!
YOU ....!
SPYOOO
EVANGELINE A.K. MCDOWELL ...
THE "DOLL MASTER."
EVANGELINE-SAN!!
EVA-CHAN!!
......!
GLOKB
FEH...
TWUG
BWOM
ZAHHH
INDEED SO.
ZAH
ALSO KNOWN AS...
"THE UNDYING MAGI."
BWOM

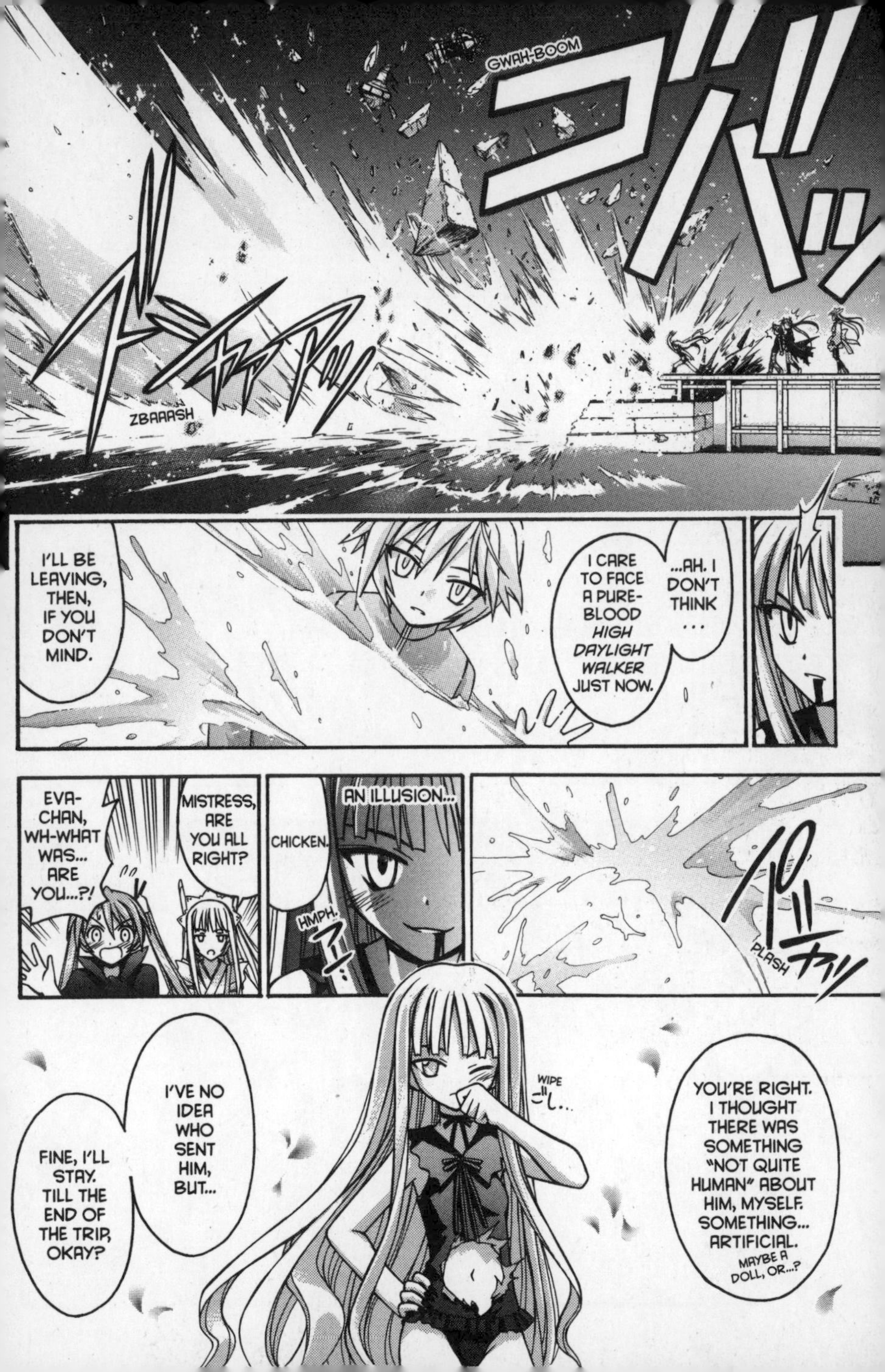
GWAH-BOOM
ZBAAASH
...AH. I DON'T THINK . . .
I CARE TO FACE A PURE-BLOOD HIGH DAYLIGHT WALKER JUST NOW.
I'LL BE LEAVING, THEN, IF YOU DON'T MIND.
PLASH
AN ILLUSION...
CHICKEN.
HMPH.
MISTRESS, ARE YOU ALL RIGHT?
EVA-CHAN, WH-WHAT WAS... ARE YOU...?!
YOU'RE RIGHT. I THOUGHT THERE WAS SOMETHING "NOT QUITE HUMAN" ABOUT HIM, MYSELF. SOMETHING... ARTIFICIAL.
MAYBE A DOLL, OR...?
WIPE
I'VE NO IDEA WHO SENT HIM, BUT...
FINE, I'LL STAY. TILL THE END OF THE TRIP, OKAY?

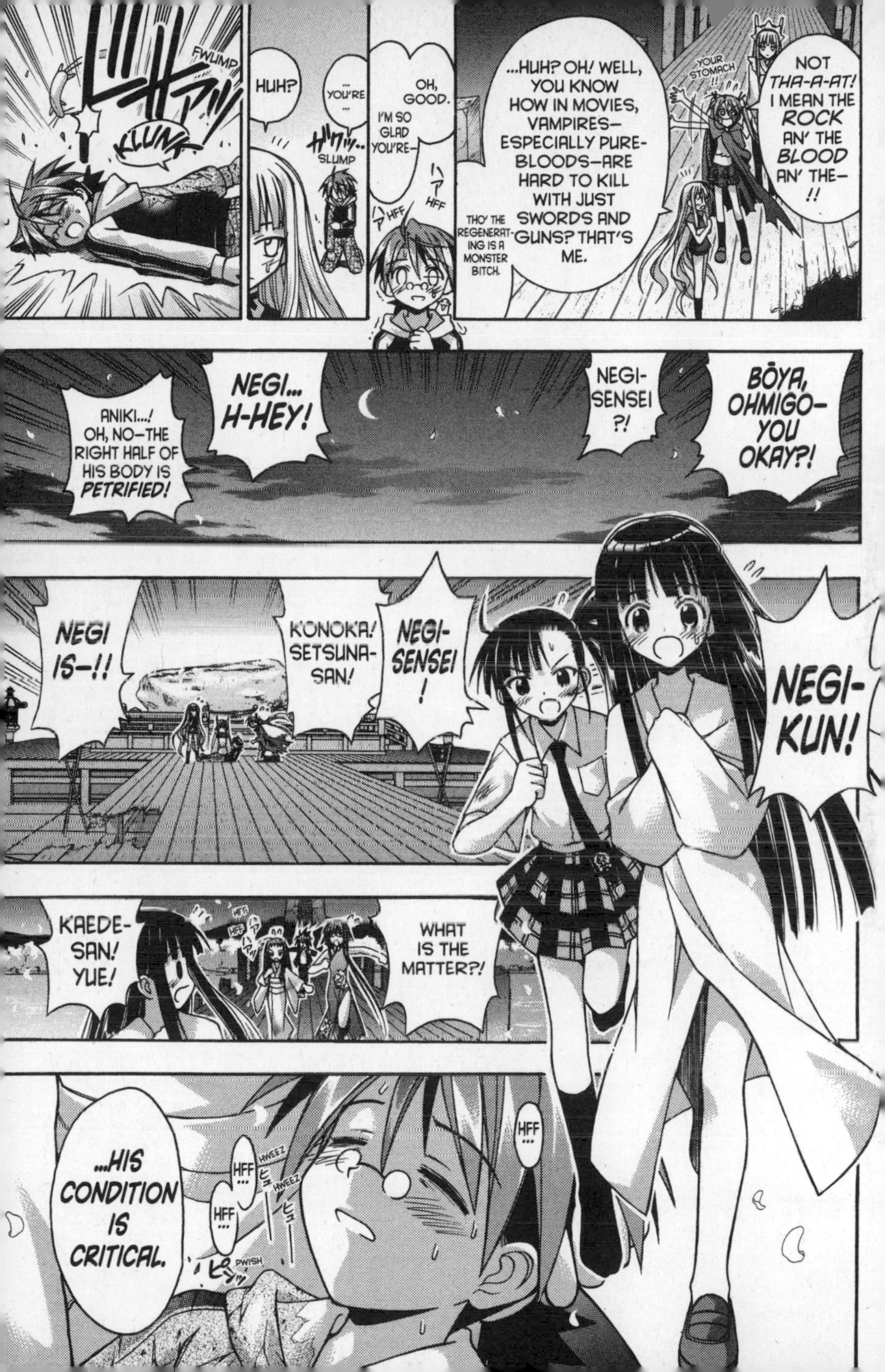
YOUR STOMACH !!
NOT THA-A-AT! I MEAN THE ROCK AN' THE BLOOD AN' THE— !!
...HUH? OH! WELL, YOU KNOW HOW IN MOVIES, VAMPIRES—ESPECIALLY PURE-BLOODS—ARE HARD TO KILL WITH JUST SWORDS AND GUNS? THAT'S ME.
THO' THE REGENERATING IS A MONSTER BITCH.
OH, GOOD. I'M SO GLAD YOU'RE—
... YOU'RE ...
HUH?
HFF
HFF
SLUMP
FWUMP
KLUNK
BÖYA, OHMIGO-YOU OKAY?!
NEGI-SENSEI ?!
NEGI... H-HEY!
ANIKI...! OH, NO—THE RIGHT HALF OF HIS BODY IS PETRIFIED!
NEGI-KUN!
NEGI-SENSEI !
KONOKA! SETSUNA-SAN!
NEGI IS—!!
WHAT IS THE MATTER?!
HFF
HFF
KAEDE-SAN! YUE!
HFF ...
HWEEZ
HWEEZ
HFF ...
HFF ...
PWISH
...HIS CONDITION IS CRITICAL.

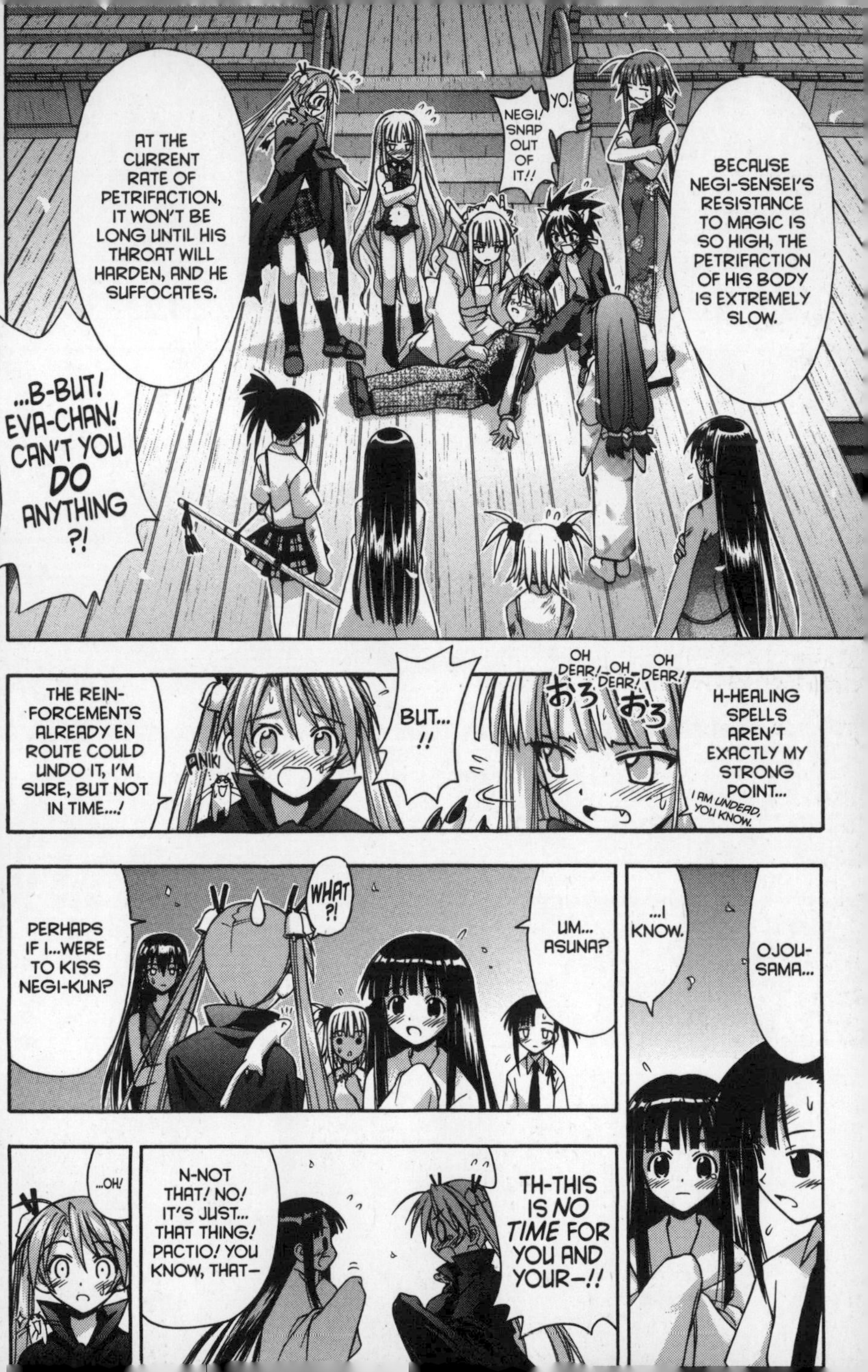
BECAUSE NEGI-SENSEI'S RESISTANCE TO MAGIC IS SO HIGH, THE PETRIFACTION OF HIS BODY IS EXTREMELY SLOW.
YO!
NEGI! SNAP OUT OF IT!!
AT THE CURRENT RATE OF PETRIFACTION, IT WON'T BE LONG UNTIL HIS THROAT WILL HARDEN, AND HE SUFFOCATES.
...B-BUT! EVA-CHAN! CAN'T YOU DO ANYTHING ?!
H-HEALING SPELLS AREN'T EXACTLY MY STRONG POINT...
I AM UNDEAD, YOU KNOW.
OH DEAR! OH DEAR! OH DEAR!
おろ おろ
BUT... !!
ANIKI
THE REIN-FORCEMENTS ALREADY EN ROUTE COULD UNDO IT, I'M SURE, BUT NOT IN TIME...!
OJOU-SAMA...
...I KNOW.
UM... ASUNA?
WHAT ?!
PERHAPS IF I...WERE TO KISS NEGI-KUN?
TH-THIS IS NO TIME FOR YOU AND YOUR-!!
N-NOT THAT! NO! IT'S JUST... THAT THING! PACTIO! YOU KNOW, THAT-
...OH!

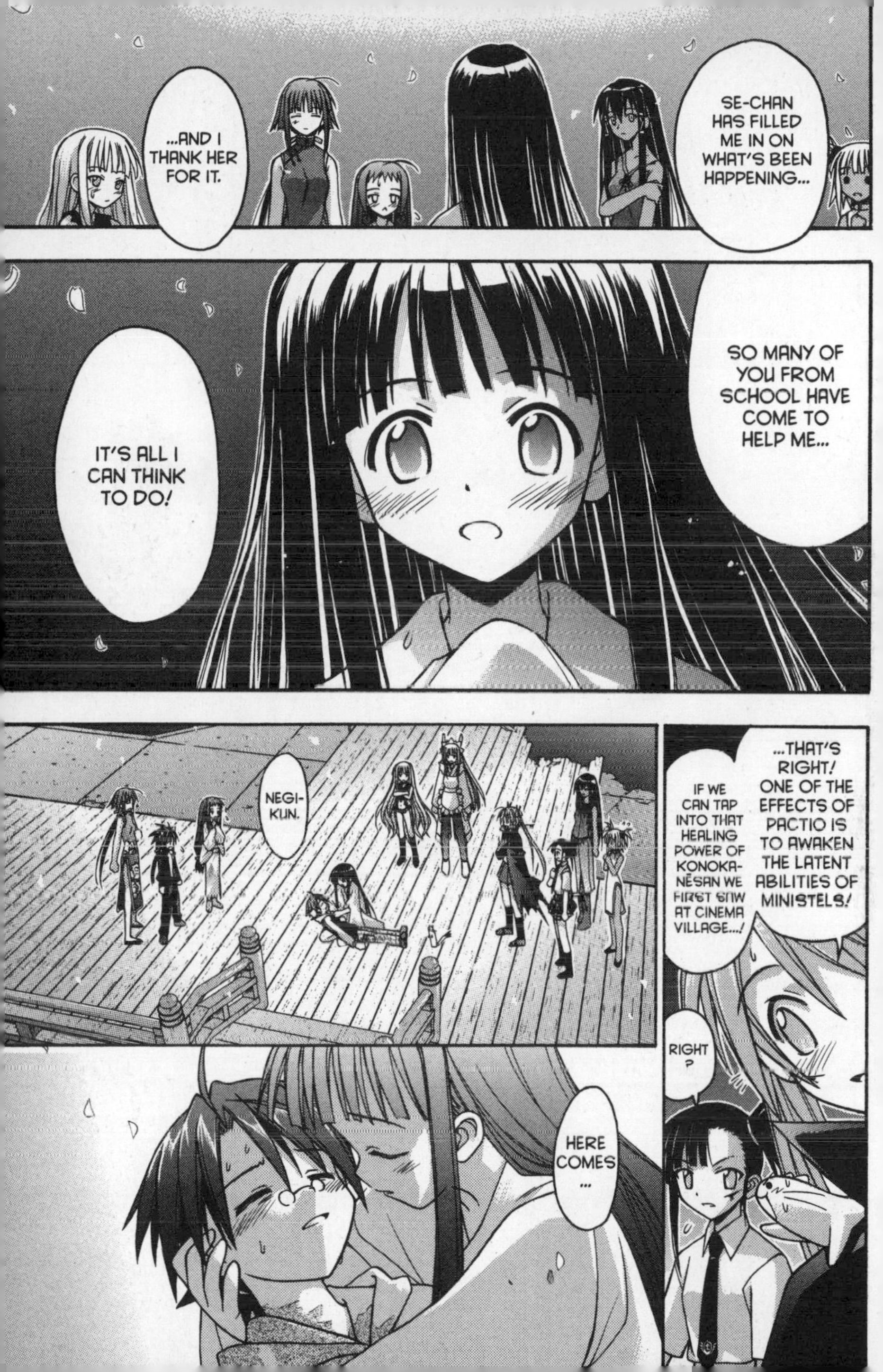
SE-CHAN HAS FILLED ME IN ON WHAT'S BEEN HAPPENING...
...AND I THANK HER FOR IT.
SO MANY OF YOU FROM SCHOOL HAVE COME TO HELP ME...
IT'S ALL I CAN THINK TO DO!
...THAT'S RIGHT! ONE OF THE EFFECTS OF PACTIO IS TO AWAKEN THE LATENT ABILITIES OF MINISTELS!
IF WE CAN TAP INTO THAT HEALING POWER OF KONOKA-NÉSAN WE FIRST SAW AT CINEMA VILLAGE...!
RIGHT?
NEGI-KUN.
HERE COMES ...

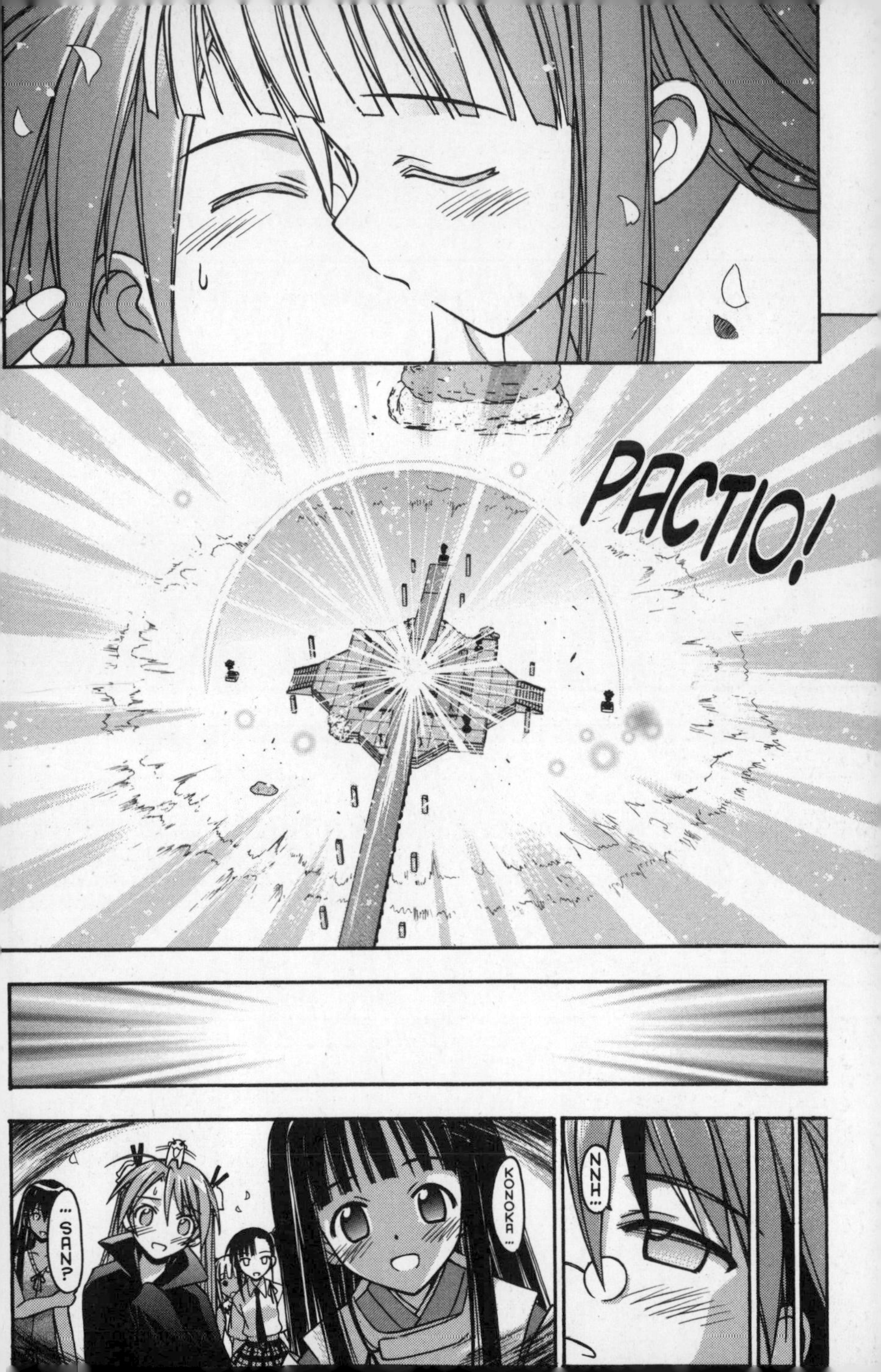
PACTIO!
NNH...!
KONOKA...
...SAN?

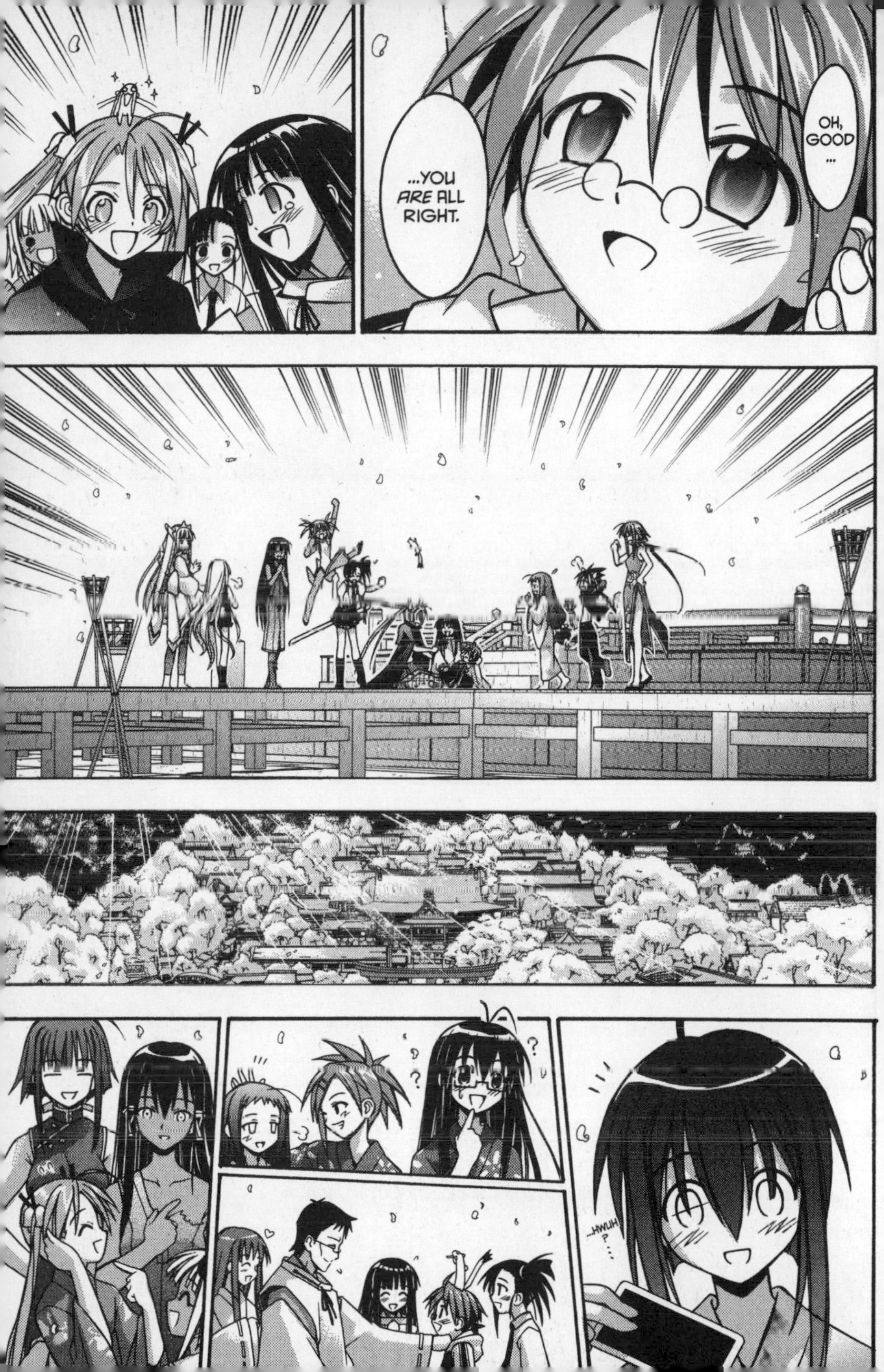
OH, GOOD ...
...YOU ARE ALL RIGHT.
...HWUH ?...

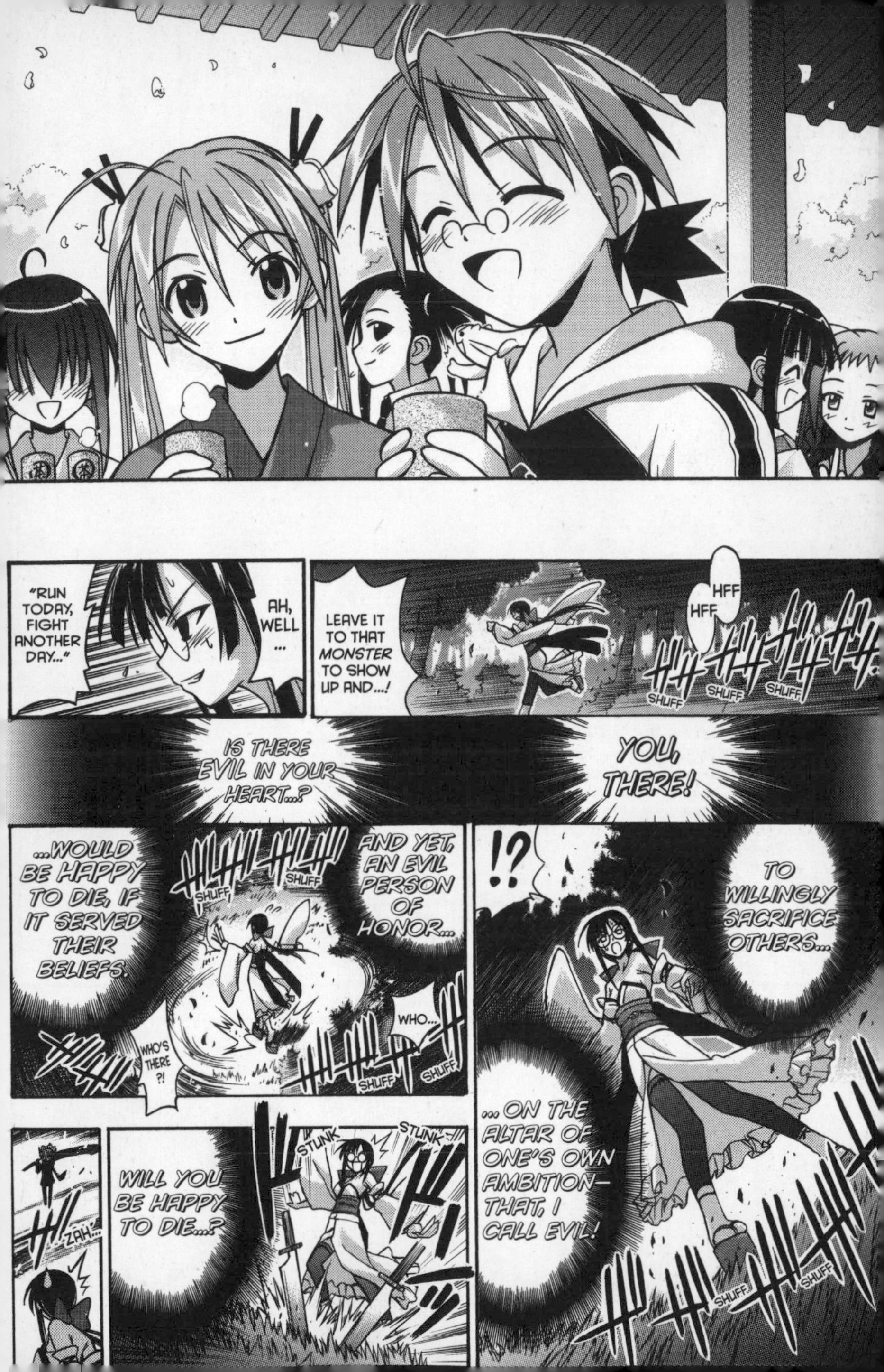
HFF
HFF
SHUFF
SHUFF
SHUFF
LEAVE IT TO THAT MONSTER TO SHOW UP AND...!
AH, WELL ...
"RUN TODAY, FIGHT ANOTHER DAY..."
YOU, THERE!
IS THERE EVIL IN YOUR HEART...?
!?
TO WILLINGLY SACRIFICE OTHERS...
...ON THE ALTAR OF ONE'S OWN AMBITION—THAT, I CALL EVIL!
SHUFF
SHUFF
AND YET, AN EVIL PERSON OF HONOR...
...WOULD BE HAPPY TO DIE, IF IT SERVED THEIR BELIEFS.
SHUFF
SHUFF
WHO...
WHO'S THERE ?!
SHUFF
SHUFF
STUNK
STUNK
WILL YOU BE HAPPY TO DIE...?
ZAH...

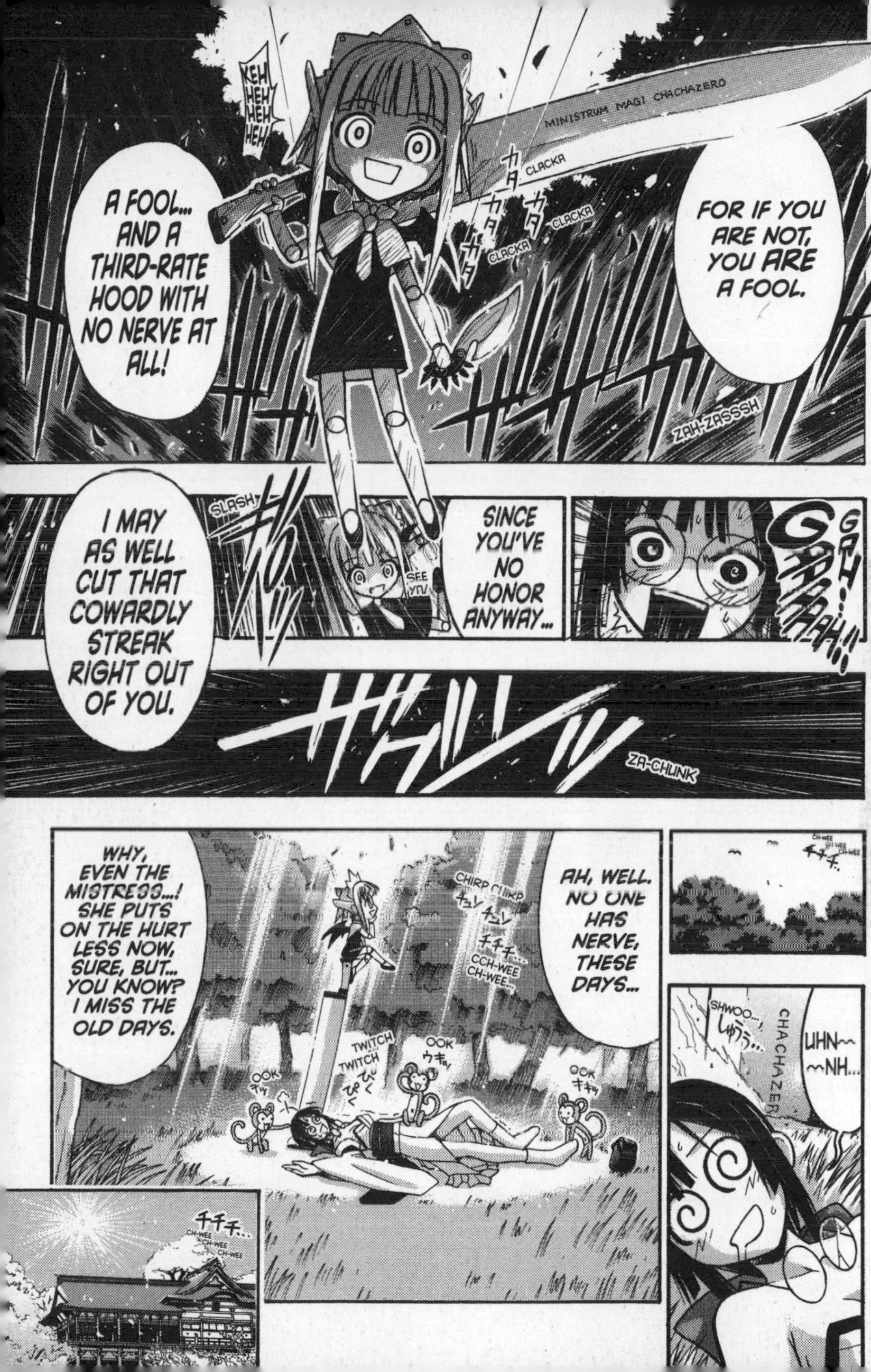
FOR IF YOU ARE NOT, YOU ARE A FOOL.
MINISTRUM MAGI CHACHAZERO
KEH HEH HEH HEH
A FOOL... AND A THIRD-RATE HOOD WITH NO NERVE AT ALL!
CLACKA
CLACKA
CLACKA
ZAH-ZASSSH
GAH...
GRAAAAH!!
SINCE YOU'VE NO HONOR ANYWAY...
SEE YA!
SLASH
I MAY AS WELL CUT THAT COWARDLY STREAK RIGHT OUT OF YOU.
ZA-CHUNK
CH-WEE CH-WEE CH-WEE
SHWOO...
CHACHAZERO
UHN~~NH...
AH, WELL. NO ONE HAS NERVE, THESE DAYS...
CHIRP CHIRP
CCH-WEE CH-WEE...
WHY, EVEN THE MISTRESS...! SHE PUTS ON THE HURT LESS NOW, SURE, BUT... YOU KNOW? I MISS THE OLD DAYS.
OOK
OOK
TWITCH TWITCH
OOK
CH-WEE CH-WEE CH-WEE

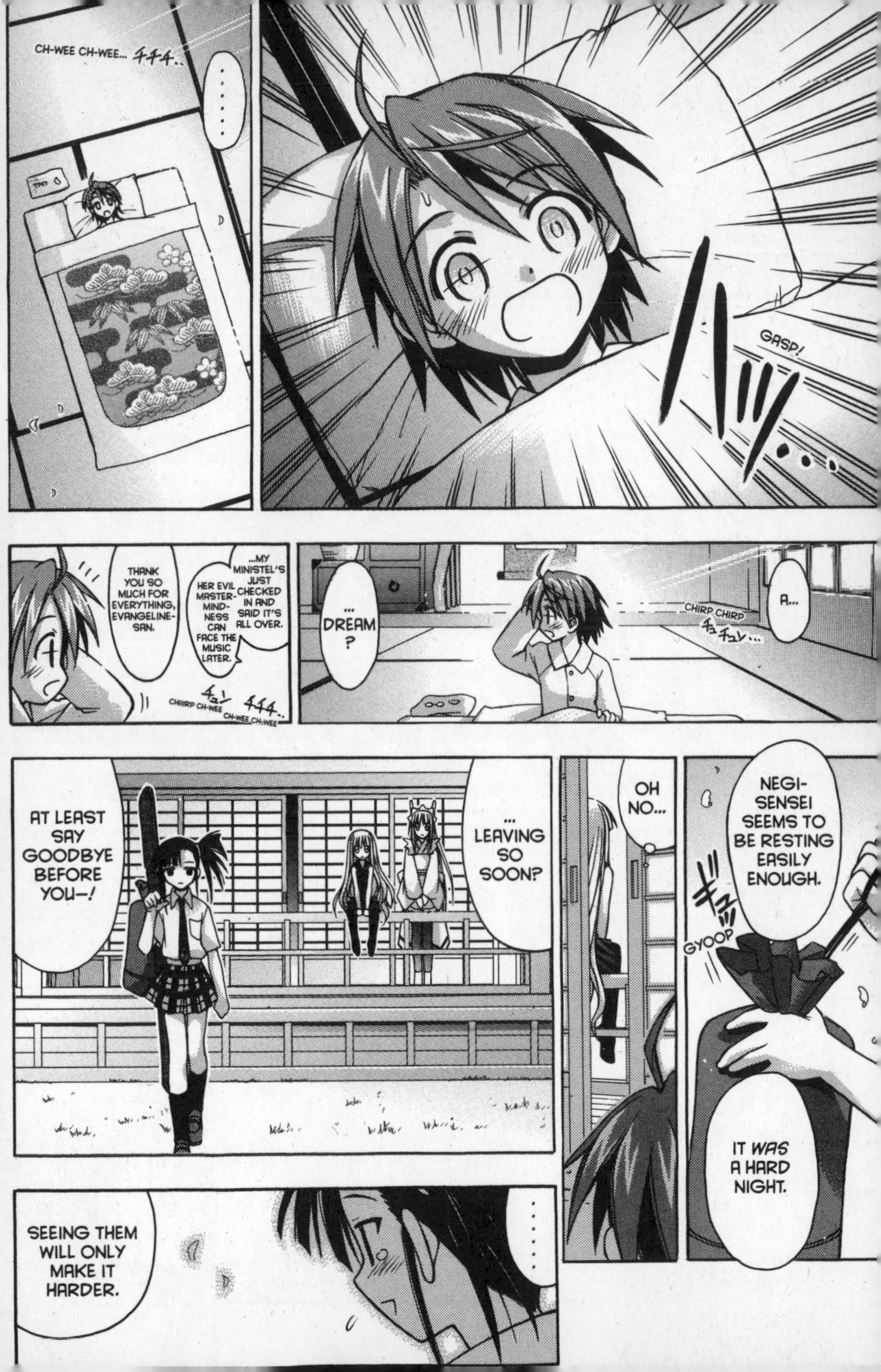
GASP!
ハッ...
CH-WEE CH-WEE... チチチ..
......
A...
CHIRP CHIRP
チュチュン...
...DREAM?
...MY MINISTEL'S JUST CHECKED IN AND SAID IT'S ALL OVER.
HER EVIL MASTER-MINDNESS CAN FACE THE MUSIC LATER.
THANK YOU SO MUCH FOR EVERYTHING, EVANGELINE-SAN.
チュン CHIIIRP CH-WEE
チチチ.. CH-WEE CH-WEE
NEGI-SENSEI SEEMS TO BE RESTING EASILY ENOUGH.
GYOOP
IT WAS A HARD NIGHT.
OH NO...
...LEAVING SO SOON?
AT LEAST SAY GOODBYE BEFORE YOU–!
......
SEEING THEM WILL ONLY MAKE IT HARDER.

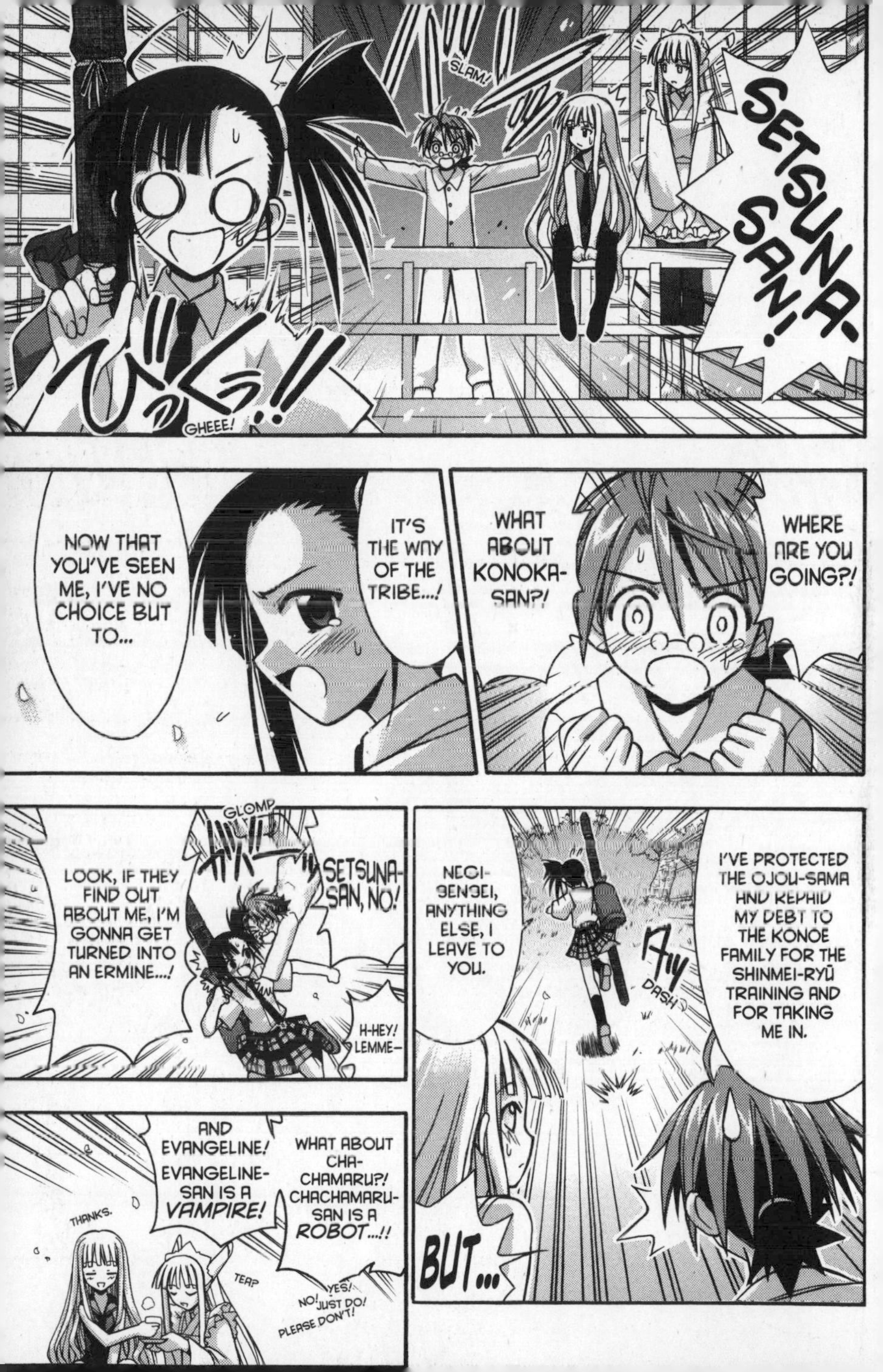
SETSUNA-SAN!
SLAM!
GHEEE!
WHERE ARE YOU GOING?!
WHAT ABOUT KONOKA-SAN?!
IT'S THE WAY OF THE TRIBE...!
NOW THAT YOU'VE SEEN ME, I'VE NO CHOICE BUT TO...
I'VE PROTECTED THE OJOU-SAMA AND REPAID MY DEBT TO THE KONOE FAMILY FOR THE SHINMEI-RYŪ TRAINING AND FOR TAKING ME IN.
DASH
NEGI-SENSEI, ANYTHING ELSE, I LEAVE TO YOU.
BUT...
GLOMP
SETSUNA-SAN, NO!
LOOK, IF THEY FIND OUT ABOUT ME, I'M GONNA GET TURNED INTO AN ERMINE...!
H-HEY! LEMME—
WHAT ABOUT CHA-CHAMARU?! CHACHAMARU-SAN IS A ROBOT...!!
AND EVANGELINE! EVANGELINE-SAN IS A VAMPIRE!
YES! JUST DO!
NO! PLEASE DON'T!
TEA?
THANKS.

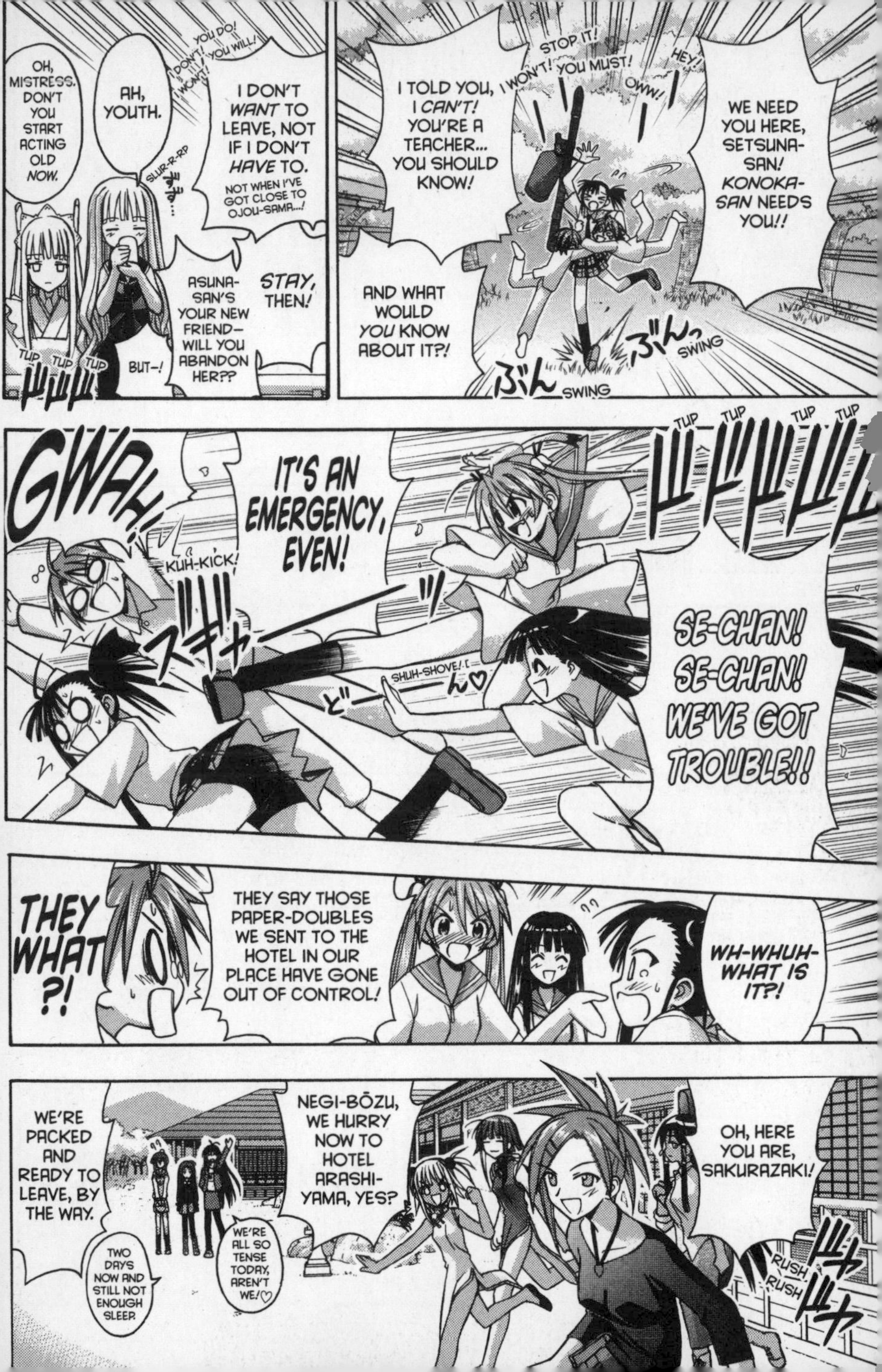
WE NEED YOU HERE, SETSUNA-SAN! KONOKA-SAN NEEDS YOU!!
HEY!
OWW!
YOU MUST!
STOP IT!
I WON'T!
I TOLD YOU, I CAN'T! YOU'RE A TEACHER... YOU SHOULD KNOW!
AND WHAT WOULD YOU KNOW ABOUT IT?!
SWING
SWING
I DON'T WANT TO LEAVE, NOT IF I DON'T HAVE TO. NOT WHEN I'VE GOT CLOSE TO OJOU-SAMA...!
YOU DO! YOU WILL!
I DON'T! I WON'T!
STAY, THEN!
ASUNA-SAN'S YOUR NEW FRIEND— WILL YOU ABANDON HER??
BUT—!
AH, YOUTH.
SLUR-R-RP
OH, MISTRESS. DON'T YOU START ACTING OLD NOW.
TUP TUP TUP
TUP TUP TUP TUP
SE-CHAN! SE-CHAN! WE'VE GOT TROUBLE!!
IT'S AN EMERGENCY, EVEN!
SHUH-SHOVE!♡
KUH-KICK!
GWAH!!
WH-WHUH-WHAT IS IT?!
THEY SAY THOSE PAPER-DOUBLES WE SENT TO THE HOTEL IN OUR PLACE HAVE GONE OUT OF CONTROL!
THEY WHAT?!
OH, HERE YOU ARE, SAKURAZAKI!
RUSH RUSH
NEGI-BŌZU, WE HURRY NOW TO HOTEL ARASHI-YAMA, YES?
WE'RE ALL SO TENSE TODAY, AREN'T WE!♡
WE'RE PACKED AND READY TO LEAVE, BY THE WAY.
TWO DAYS NOW AND STILL NOT ENOUGH SLEEP.

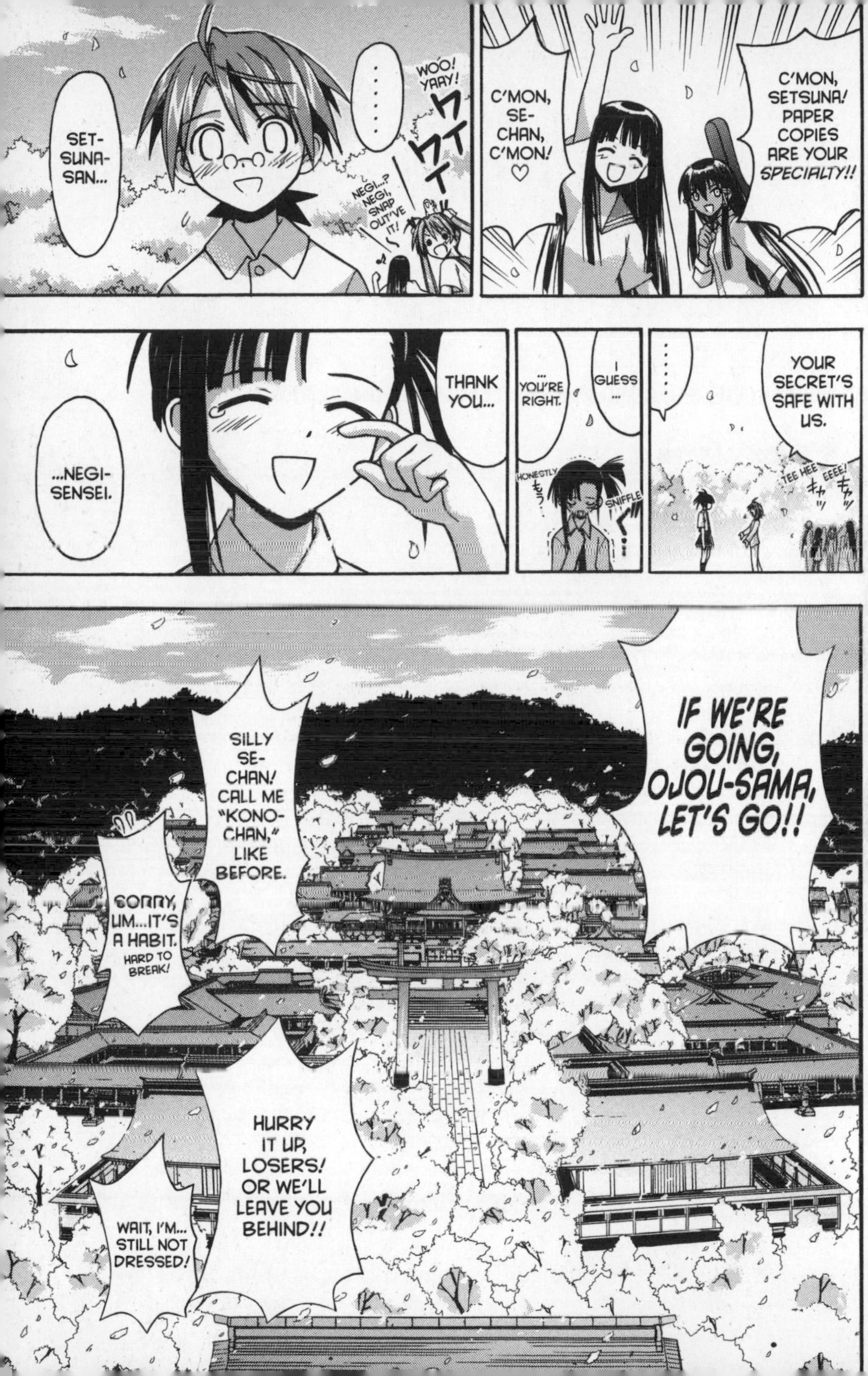
C'MON, SETSUNA! PAPER COPIES ARE YOUR SPECIALTY!!
C'MON, SE-CHAN, C'MON! ♡
......
WOO! YAAY!
NEGI...? NEGI, SNAP OUT'VE IT!
SET-SUNA-SAN...
YOUR SECRET'S SAFE WITH US.
......
TEE HEE キャッ
EEEE! キャッ
I GUESS...
...YOU'RE RIGHT.
HONESTLY もう…
SNIFFLE
THANK YOU...
...NEGI-SENSEI.
IF WE'RE GOING, OJOU-SAMA, LET'S GO!!
SILLY SE-CHAN! CALL ME "KONO-CHAN," LIKE BEFORE.
SORRY, UM...IT'S A HABIT. HARD TO BREAK!
HURRY IT UP, LOSERS! OR WE'LL LEAVE YOU BEHIND!!
WAIT, I'M... STILL NOT DRESSED!

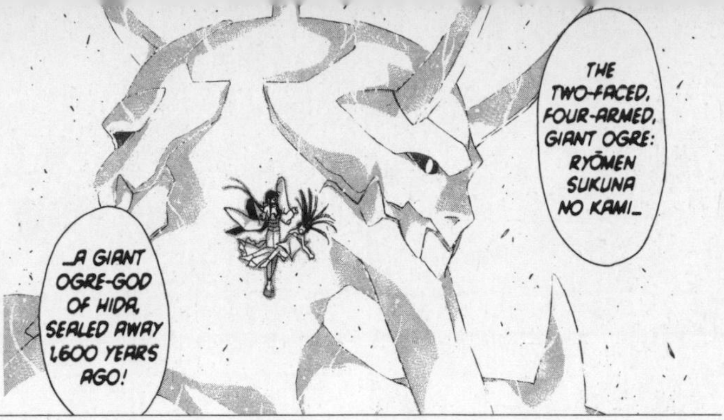
THE TWO-FACED, FOUR-ARMED, GIANT OGRE: RYÔMEN SUKUNA NO KAMI...
...A GIANT OGRE-GOD OF HIDA, SEALED AWAY 1,600 YEARS AGO!

NEGIMA! FIFTY-SECOND PERIOD: LEXICON NEGIMARIUM

■「障壁突破『石の槍』」

ト•テイコス•ディエルクサストー ドリュ•ペトラス

(τὸ τεῖχος διερξάσθω.ΔΟ΄ΡΥ ΠΕ΄ΤΡΑΣ)

BTO TICOS DIELKSATO DRU PETROSE

"Magic Wall-Breaker: 'Spear of Stone'"

Ordinarily, this spell (named "Spear of Stone") causes a sharp pillar of stone to appear and attack the target. In this variation, however, spell-breaking properties are added in order to better penetrate a spell-caster's protective barrier. The barrier of a powerful Magi is often complex and multilayered; because of this, before the Magi can cast spells of their own, they would need to first cancel their own barriers—which for safety reasons would be impossible. However, in the case of the "white-haired youth," he first invoked a complex cancellation spell ahead of time and then, immediately after using a "gate" to get close to Evangeline, deployed the cancellation spell *and* the "Spear of Stone" simultaneously. (You could say that his attack consisted of a cancellation spell + gate spell + attack spell + delay spell.) Only a Magi of extremely high skill could pull off such a feat.

■ RYÔMEN SUKUNA NO KAMI

In the Nihonshoki, the reign of the 16th Emperor, Ôsazaki no Mikoto, is recounted, and in the eleventh book, there is this entry: "In the Year 65, there was a man who came to the land of Hida, who said his name was Sukuna. Although he had but one body, he had two faces—one in front, and one on his back. Although he had knees, he had no heels. In his four hands, two wielded swords, while the other two carried bows. Because he refused to follow the orders of the Emperor, the warrior Rikuma Nekotakebu of Naniwa was sent to dispatch him. Sukuna fought back but was defeated and sealed away in a cave where a shrine was erected. Also known as 'Takano Uchi,' the soldier who defeated Sukuna is well known for his military tactics." In this actual history of *Ryômen no Sukuna,* no mention is made of his size; it is unknown whether or not he is a giant. In the area of Hida, in Gifu Prefecture, Sukuna is considered a giant demon-god...and yet, the locals do not consider him to be a doer of evil.

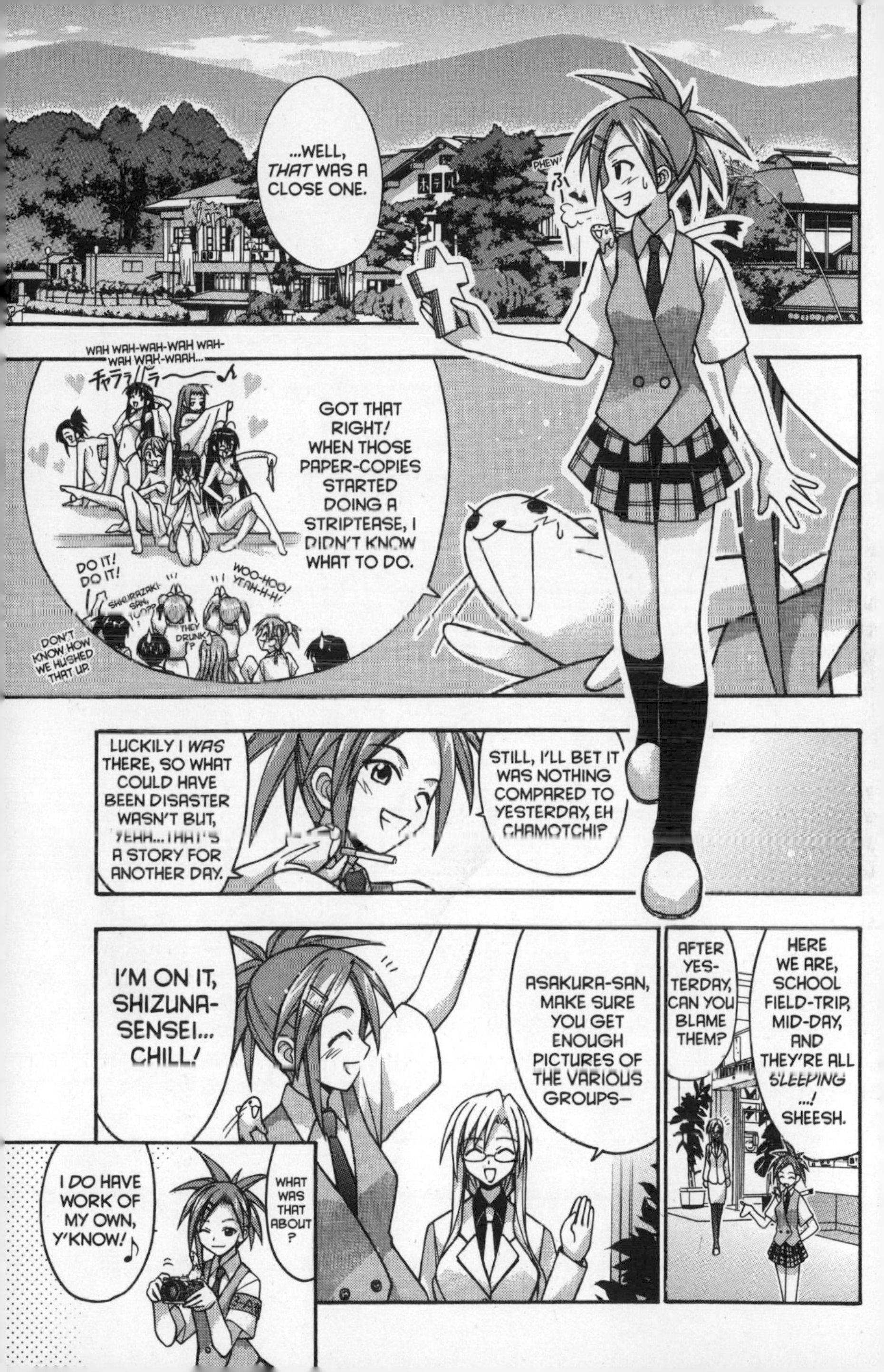
...WELL, *THAT* WAS A CLOSE ONE.
PHEW
GOT THAT RIGHT! WHEN THOSE PAPER-COPIES STARTED DOING A STRIPTEASE, I DIDN'T KNOW WHAT TO DO.
WAH WAH-WAH-WAH WAH-WAH WAH-WAAH...
DO IT! DO IT!
WOO-HOO! YEAH-H-H!
THEY DRUNK?
DON'T KNOW HOW WE HUSHED THAT UP.
STILL, I'LL BET IT WAS NOTHING COMPARED TO YESTERDAY, EH CHAMOTCHI?
LUCKILY I *WAS* THERE, SO WHAT COULD HAVE BEEN DISASTER WASN'T BUT, YEAH... THAT'S A STORY FOR ANOTHER DAY.
HERE WE ARE, SCHOOL FIELD-TRIP, MID-DAY, AND THEY'RE ALL *SLEEPING* ...! SHEESH.
AFTER YES-TERDAY, CAN YOU BLAME THEM?
ASAKURA-SAN, MAKE SURE YOU GET ENOUGH PICTURES OF THE VARIOUS GROUPS—
I'M ON IT, SHIZUNA-SENSEI... CHILL!
WHAT WAS THAT ABOUT?
I *DO* HAVE WORK OF MY OWN, Y'KNOW! ♪

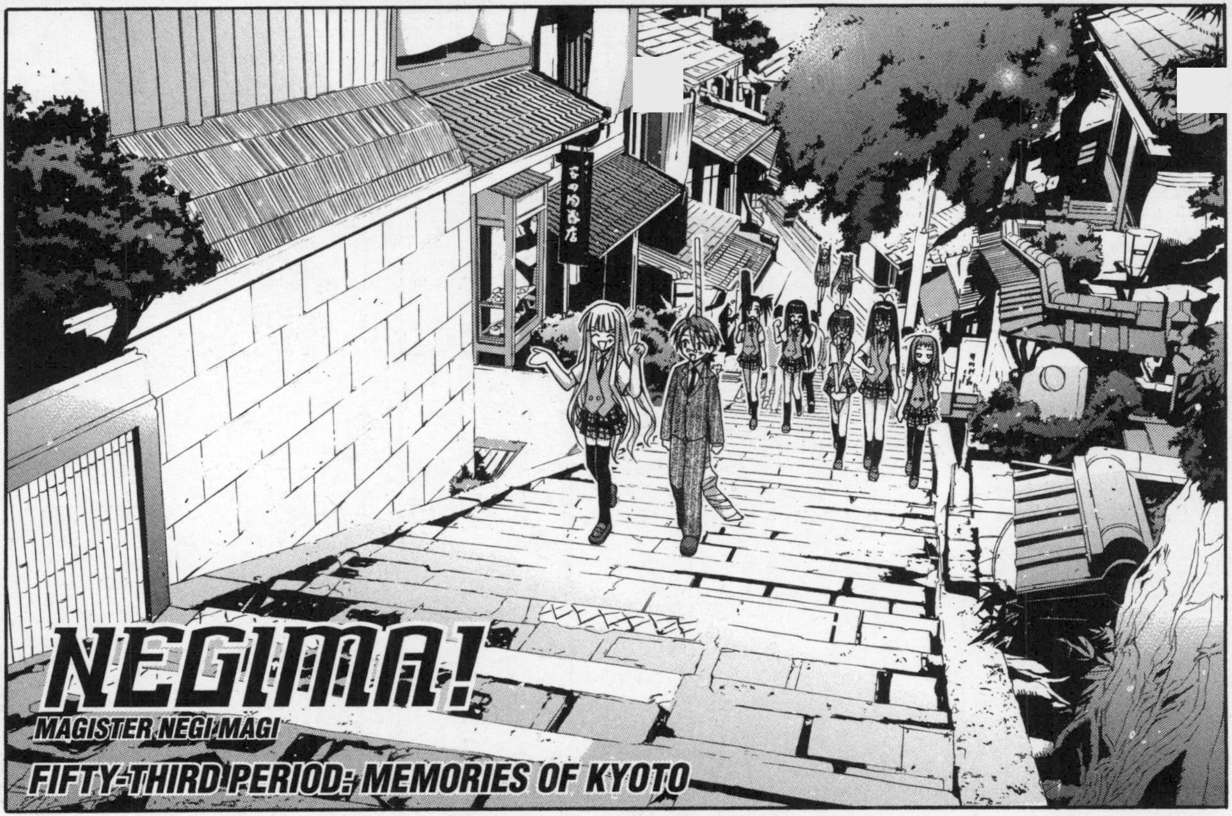
NEGIMA!
MAGISTER NEGI MAGI
FIFTY-THIRD PERIOD: MEMORIES OF KYOTO

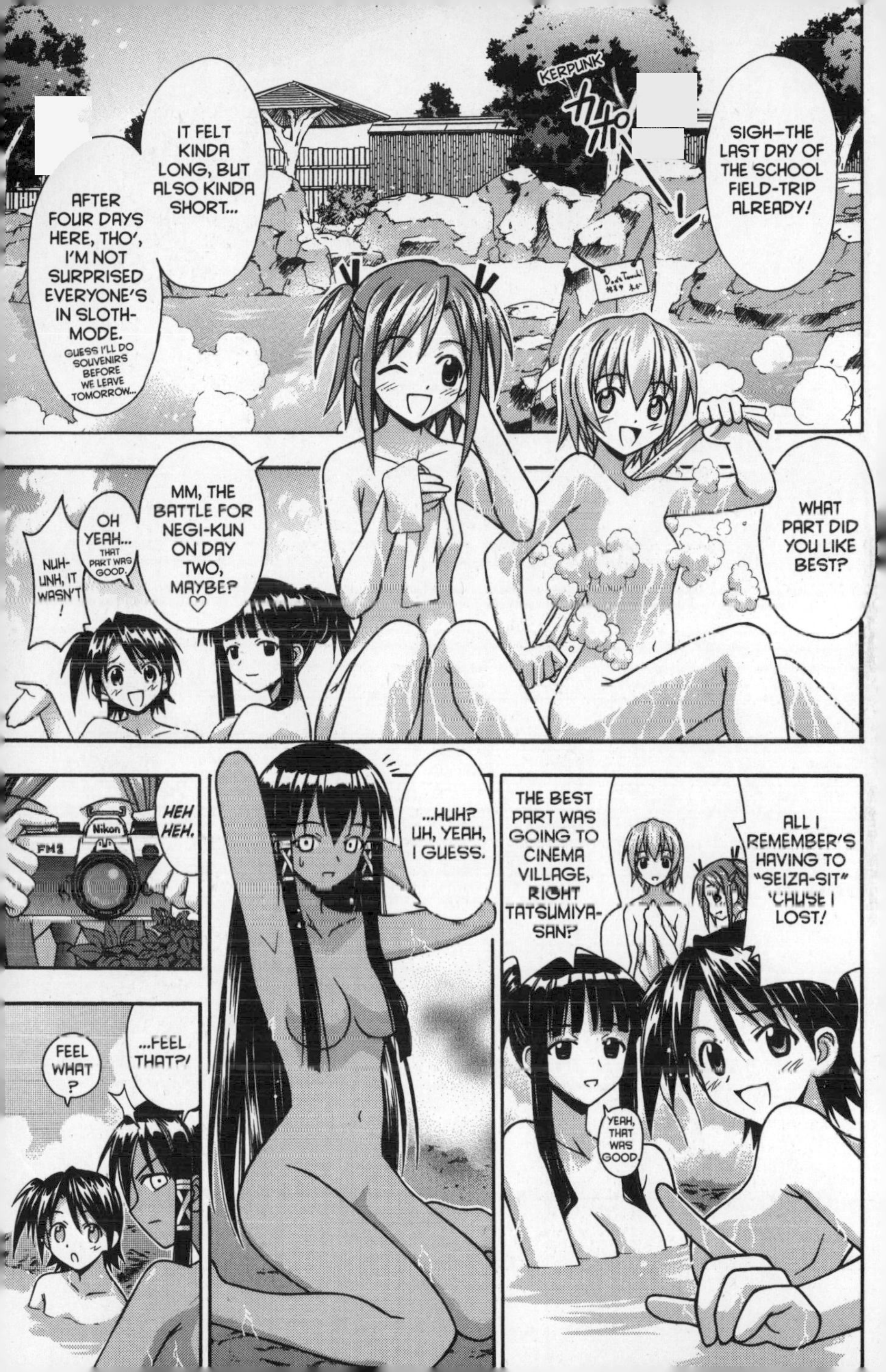
SIGH—THE LAST DAY OF THE SCHOOL FIELD-TRIP ALREADY!
KERPUNK
IT FELT KINDA LONG, BUT ALSO KINDA SHORT...
AFTER FOUR DAYS HERE, THO', I'M NOT SURPRISED EVERYONE'S IN SLOTH-MODE.
GUESS I'LL DO SOUVENIRS BEFORE WE LEAVE TOMORROW...
WHAT PART DID YOU LIKE BEST?
MM, THE BATTLE FOR NEGI-KUN ON DAY TWO, MAYBE? ♡
OH YEAH... THAT PART WAS GOOD.
NUH-UNH, IT WASN'T!
ALL I REMEMBER'S HAVING TO "SEIZA-SIT" 'CAUSE I LOST!
THE BEST PART WAS GOING TO CINEMA VILLAGE, RIGHT TATSUMIYA-SAN?
YEAH, THAT WAS GOOD.
...HUH? UH, YEAH, I GUESS.
HEH HEH.
Nikon
FM2
...FEEL THAT?!
FEEL WHAT?

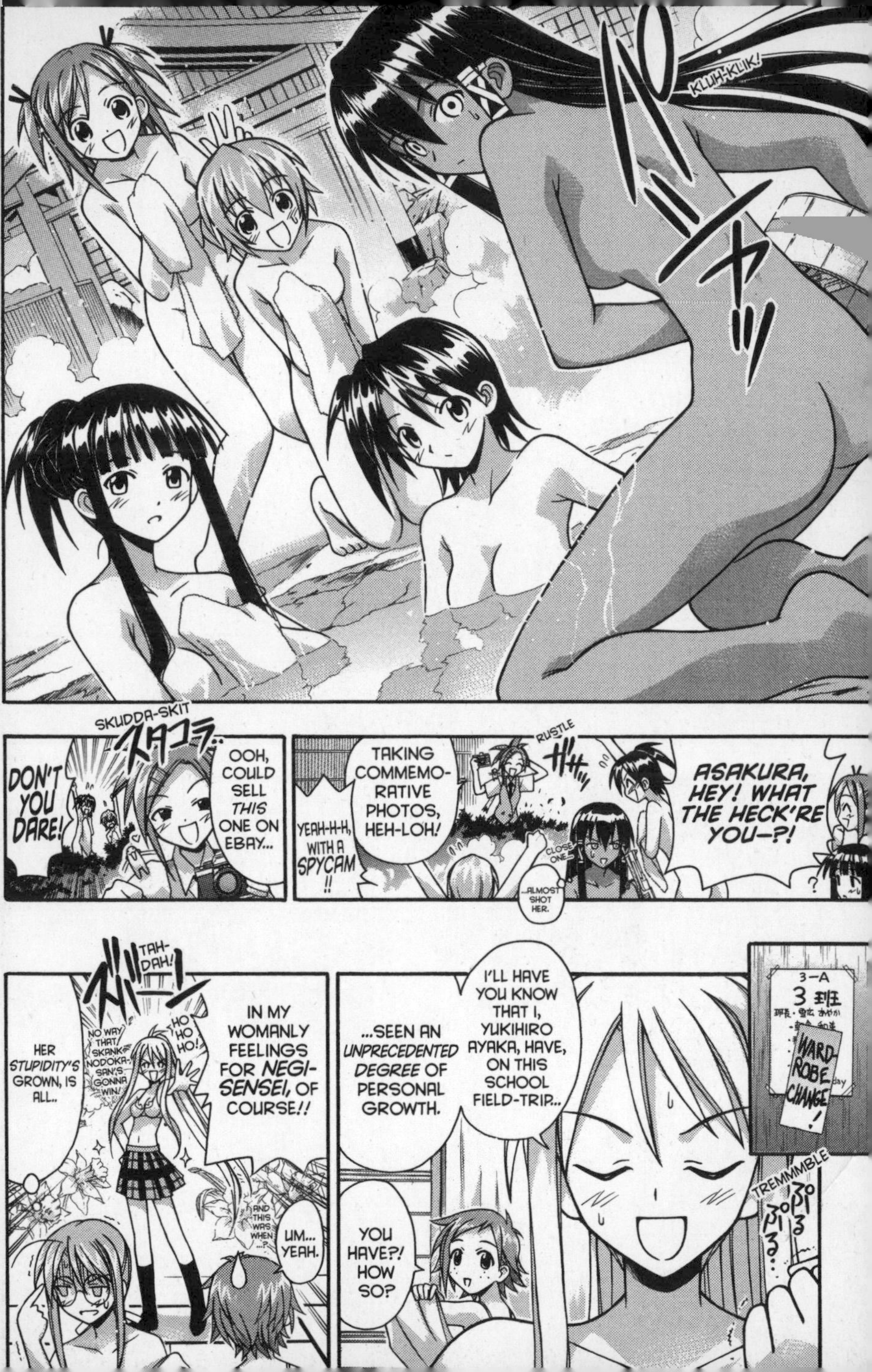
KLUH-KLIK!
ASAKURA, HEY! WHAT THE HECK'RE YOU—?!
RUSTLE
CLOSE ONE...
...ALMOST SHOT HER.
TAKING COMMEMORATIVE PHOTOS, HEH-LOH!
YEAH-H-H, WITH A SPYCAM!!
SKUDDA-SKIT
OOH, COULD SELL THIS ONE ON EBAY...
DON'T YOU DARE!
3-A
3班
WARD-ROBE CHANGE!
TREMMMBLE
I'LL HAVE YOU KNOW THAT I, YUKIHIRO AYAKA, HAVE, ON THIS SCHOOL FIELD-TRIP...
...SEEN AN UNPRECEDENTED DEGREE OF PERSONAL GROWTH.
YOU HAVE?! HOW SO?
TAH-DAH!
HO HO HO!
IN MY WOMANLY FEELINGS FOR NEGI-SENSEI, OF COURSE!!
NO WAY THAT SKANK NODOKA-SAN'S GONNA WIN!
HER STUPIDITY'S GROWN, IS ALL..
AND THIS WAS WHEN...?
UM... YEAH.

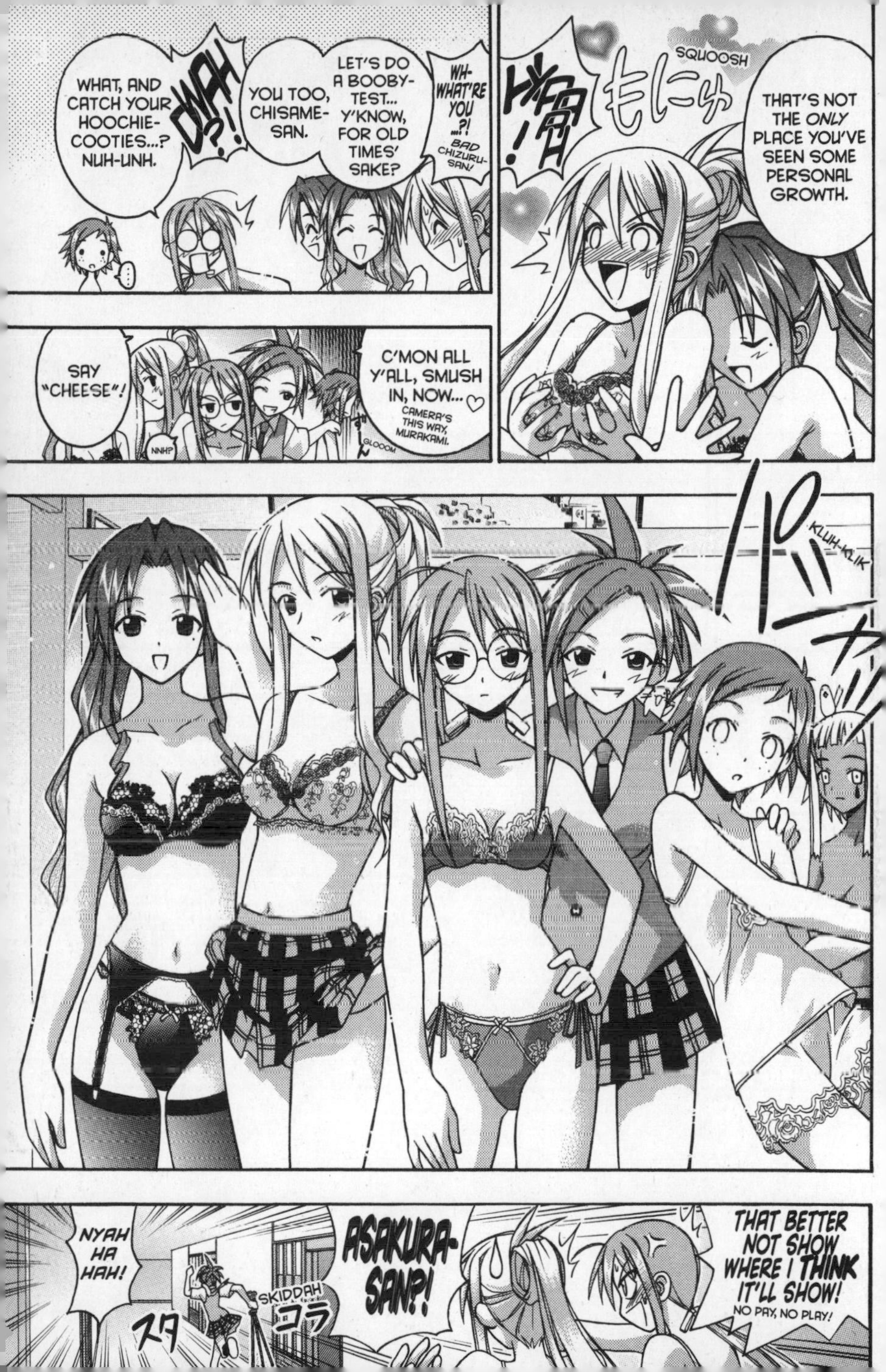
もにゅ
SQUOOSH
THAT'S NOT THE *ONLY* PLACE YOU'VE SEEN SOME PERSONAL GROWTH.
WH-WHAT'RE YOU ?!
BAD CHIZURU-SAN!
LET'S DO A BOOBY-TEST... Y'KNOW, FOR OLD TIMES' SAKE?
YOU TOO, CHISAME-SAN.
DWAH ?!
WHAT, AND CATCH YOUR HOOCHIE-COOTIES...? NUH-UNH.
...
C'MON ALL Y'ALL, SMUSH IN, NOW... ♡
CAMERA'S THIS WAY, MURAKAMI.
GLOOOM
NNH?
SAY "CHEESE"!
KLUH-KLIK
THAT BETTER NOT SHOW WHERE I **THINK** IT'LL SHOW!
NO PAY, NO PLAY!
ASAKURA-SAN?!
コラ
SKIDDAH
スタ
NYAH HA HAH!

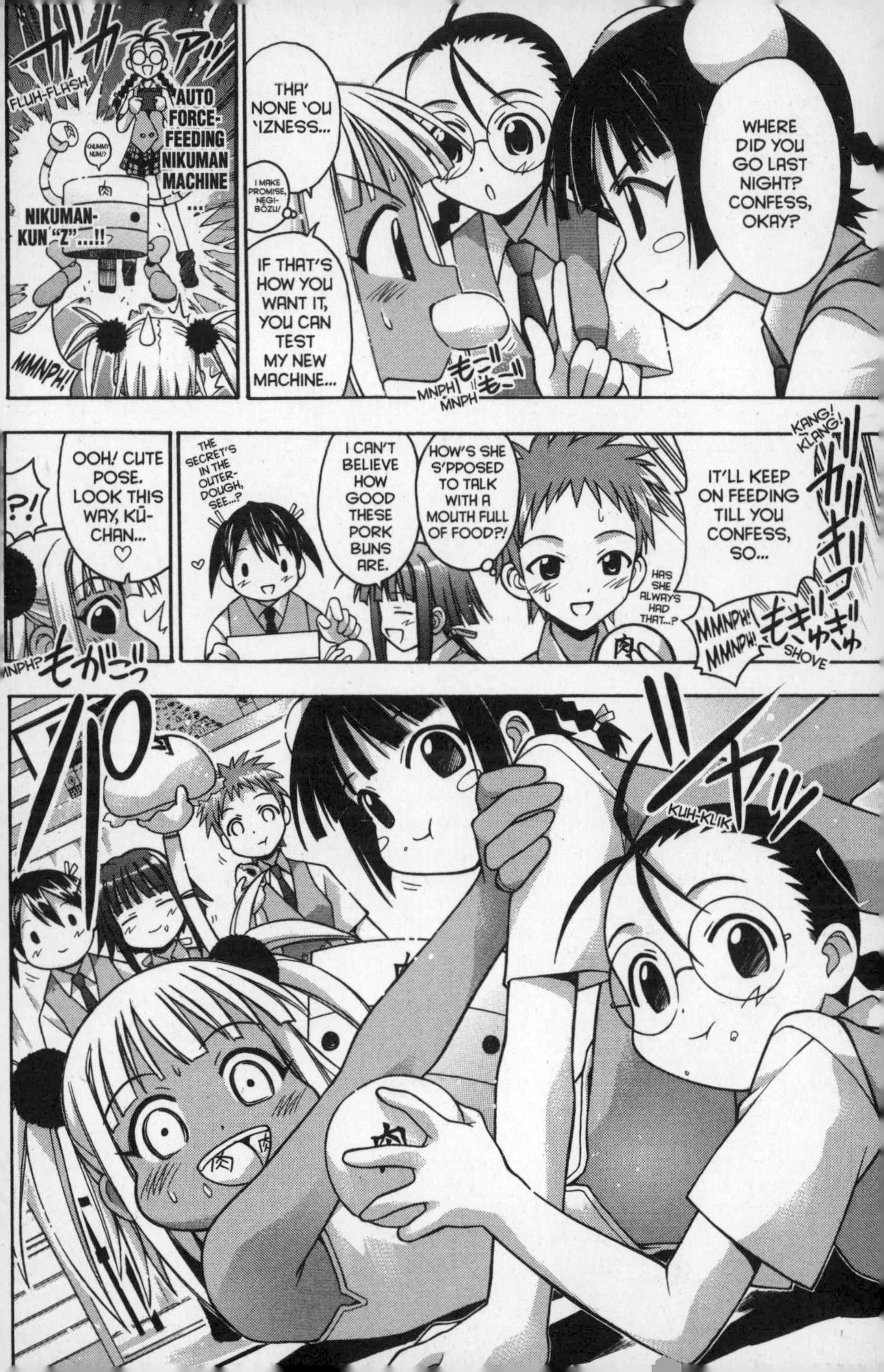
WHERE DID YOU GO LAST NIGHT? CONFESS, OKAY?
THA' NONE 'OU 'IZNESS...
I MAKE PROMISE, NEGI-BŌZU!
IF THAT'S HOW YOU WANT IT, YOU CAN TEST MY NEW MACHINE...
MNPH MNPH
FLUH-FLASH
AUTO FORCE-FEEDING NIKUMAN MACHINE
NUMMY NUM
...
NIKUMAN-KUN "Z"...!!
MMNPH!
KANG! KLANG!
IT'LL KEEP ON FEEDING TILL YOU CONFESS, SO...
HAS SHE ALWAYS HAD THAT...?
MMNPH! MMNPH!
SHOVE
HOW'S SHE S'PPOSED TO TALK WITH A MOUTH FULL OF FOOD?!
I CAN'T BELIEVE HOW GOOD THESE PORK BUNS ARE.
THE SECRET'S IN THE OUTER-DOUGH, SEE...?
OOH! CUTE POSE. LOOK THIS WAY, KŪ-CHAN... ♡
?!
MNPH?
KUH-KLIK

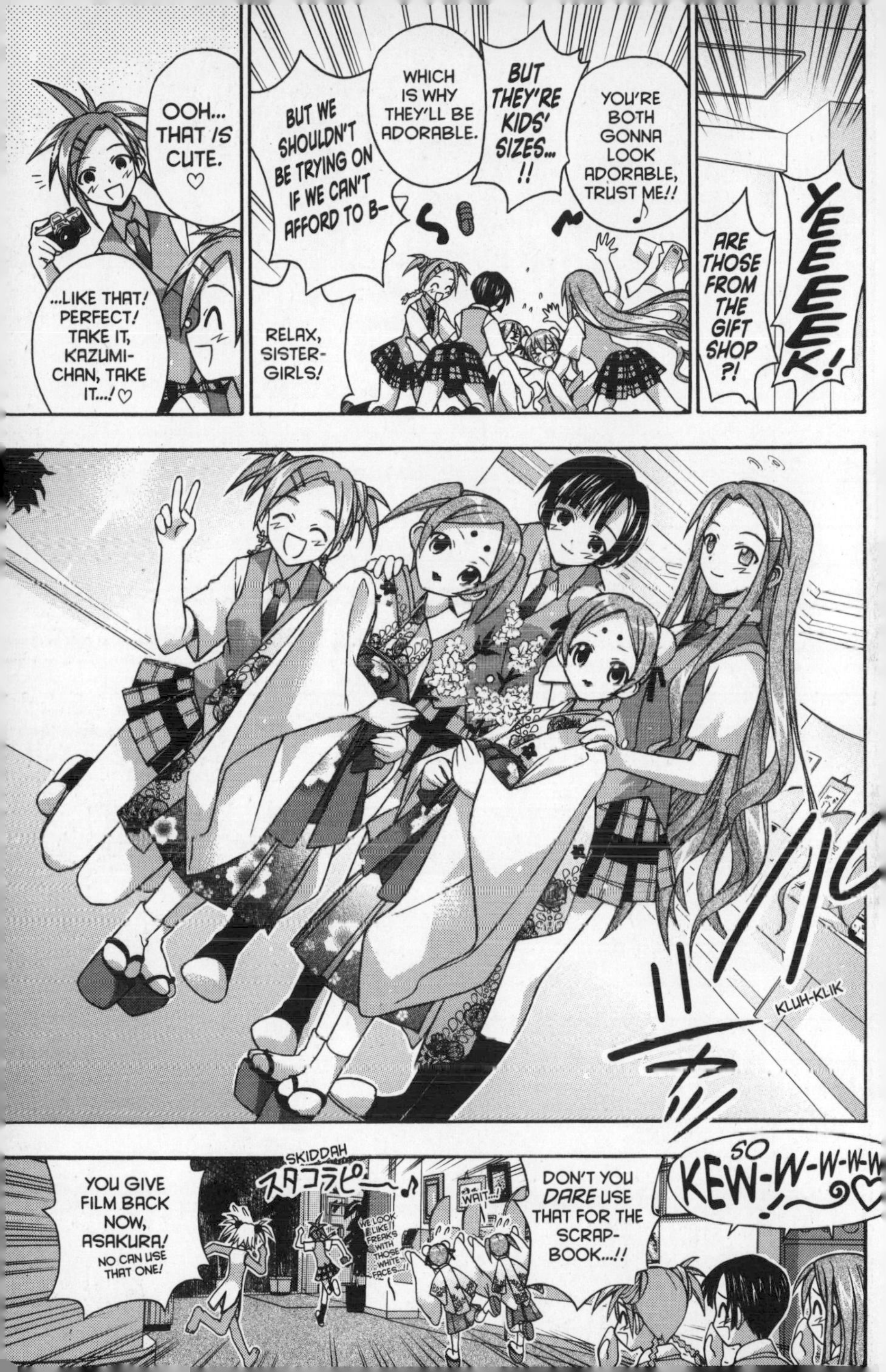
YEEEEK!
ARE THOSE FROM THE GIFT SHOP?!
YOU'RE BOTH GONNA LOOK ADORABLE, TRUST ME!!
BUT THEY'RE KIDS' SIZES...!!
WHICH IS WHY THEY'LL BE ADORABLE.
BUT WE SHOULDN'T BE TRYING ON IF WE CAN'T AFFORD TO B-
RELAX, SISTER-GIRLS!
OOH... THAT IS CUTE. ♡
...LIKE THAT! PERFECT! TAKE IT, KAZUMI-CHAN, TAKE IT...! ♡
KLUH-KLIK
SO KEW-W-W-W-W!~♡
DON'T YOU DARE USE THAT FOR THE SCRAP-BOOK...!!
WAIT...!
WE LOOK LIKE FREAKS WITH THOSE WHITE FACES...!!
SKIDDAH
スタコラピー~♪
YOU GIVE FILM BACK NOW, ASAKURA!
NO CAN USE THAT ONE!

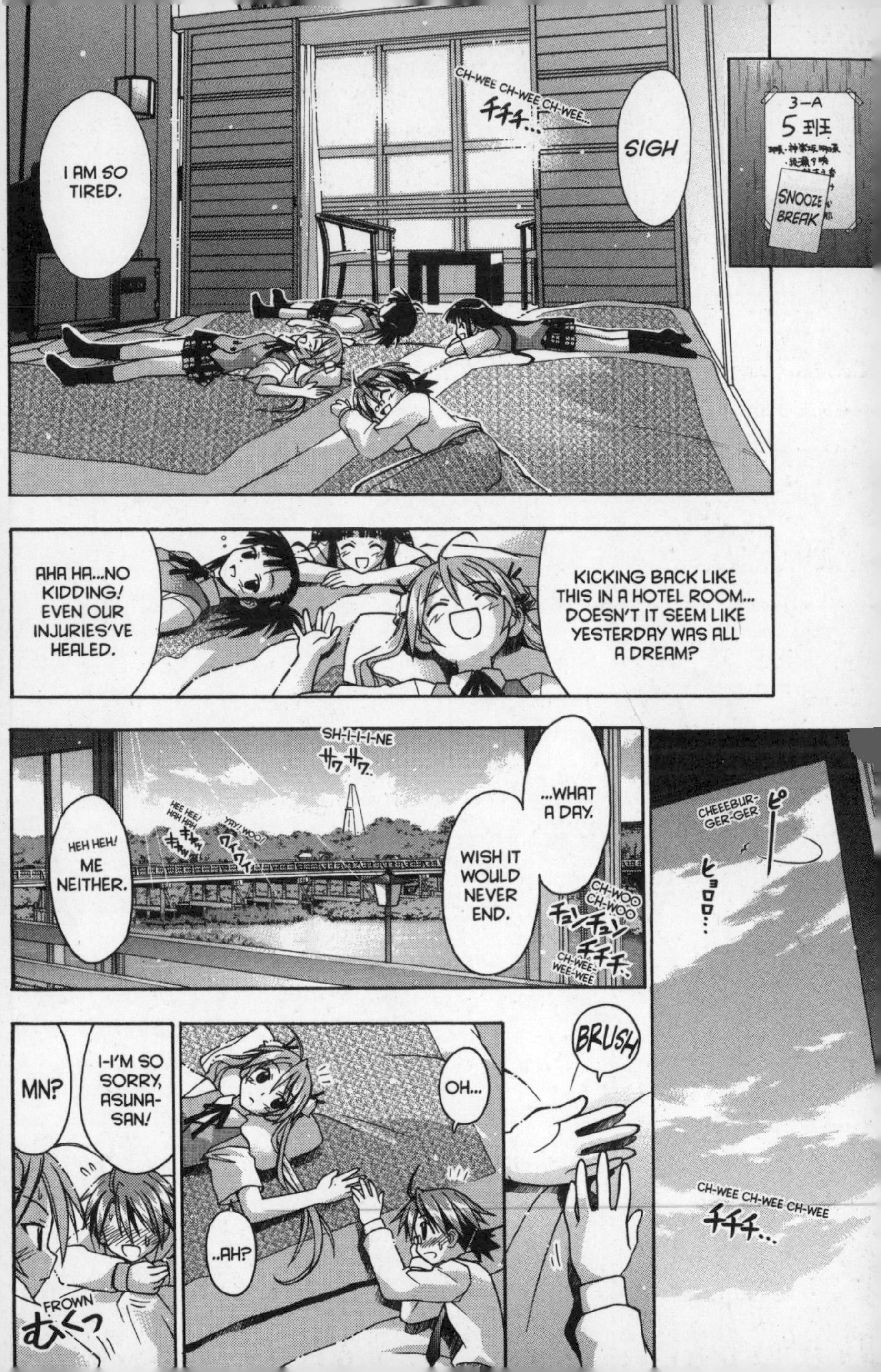
3-A
5班
SNOOZE BREAK
SIGH
CH-WEE CH-WEE CH-WEE...
チチチ...
I AM SO TIRED.
KICKING BACK LIKE THIS IN A HOTEL ROOM... DOESN'T IT SEEM LIKE YESTERDAY WAS ALL A DREAM?
AHA HA...NO KIDDING! EVEN OUR INJURIES'VE HEALED.
CHEEEBUR-GER-GER
ピー
ヒョロロ...
BRUSH
CH-WEE CH-WEE CH-WEE
チチチ...
...WHAT A DAY.
WISH IT WOULD NEVER END.
CH-WOO CH-WOO
チュンチュン
チチチ
CH-WEE-WEE-WEE
SH-I-I-I-NE
サワサワ
YAY! WOO!
ワイワイ
HEE HEE! HAH HAH
キャッキャッ
HEH HEH! ME NEITHER.
OH...
..AH?
I-I'M SO SORRY, ASUNA-SAN!
MN?
FROWN
むくっ

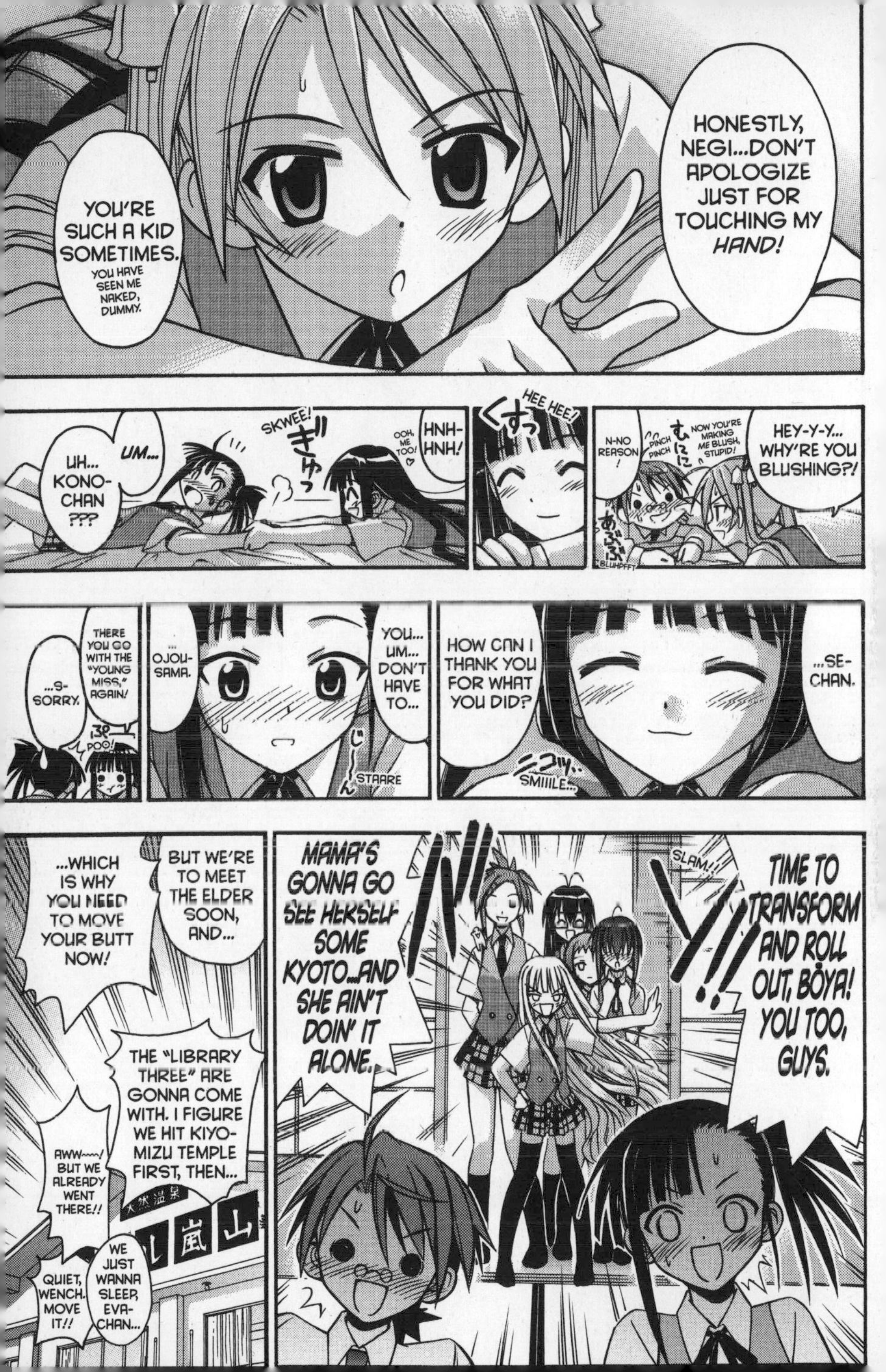
HONESTLY, NEGI...DON'T APOLOGIZE JUST FOR TOUCHING MY HAND!
YOU'RE SUCH A KID SOMETIMES.
YOU HAVE SEEN ME NAKED, DUMMY.
HEY-Y-Y... WHY'RE YOU BLUSHING?!
NOW YOU'RE MAKING ME BLUSH, STUPID!
むにに
PINCH PINCH
N-NO REASON!
あぶぶ
BLUHPFFT
くすっ
HEE HEE!
HNH-HNH!
OOH, ME TOO!
ぎゅっ
SKWEE!
UM...
UH... KONO-CHAN???
...SE-CHAN.
HOW CAN I THANK YOU FOR WHAT YOU DID?
ニコッ
SMIIILE...
YOU... UM... DON'T HAVE TO...
...OJOU-SAMA.
じーん
STAARE
THERE YOU GO WITH THE "YOUNG MISS," AGAIN!
...S-SORRY.
ぷー
POO!
TIME TO TRANSFORM AND ROLL OUT, BÔYA! YOU TOO, GUYS.
SLAM!
MAMA'S GONNA GO SEE HERSELF SOME KYOTO...AND SHE AIN'T DOIN' IT ALONE.
BUT WE'RE TO MEET THE ELDER SOON, AND...
...WHICH IS WHY YOU NEED TO MOVE YOUR BUTT NOW!
THE "LIBRARY THREE" ARE GONNA COME WITH. I FIGURE WE HIT KIYO-MIZU TEMPLE FIRST, THEN...
AWW~~! BUT WE ALREADY WENT THERE!!
WE JUST WANNA SLEEP, EVA-CHAN...
QUIET, WENCH. MOVE IT!!
天然温泉
嵐山

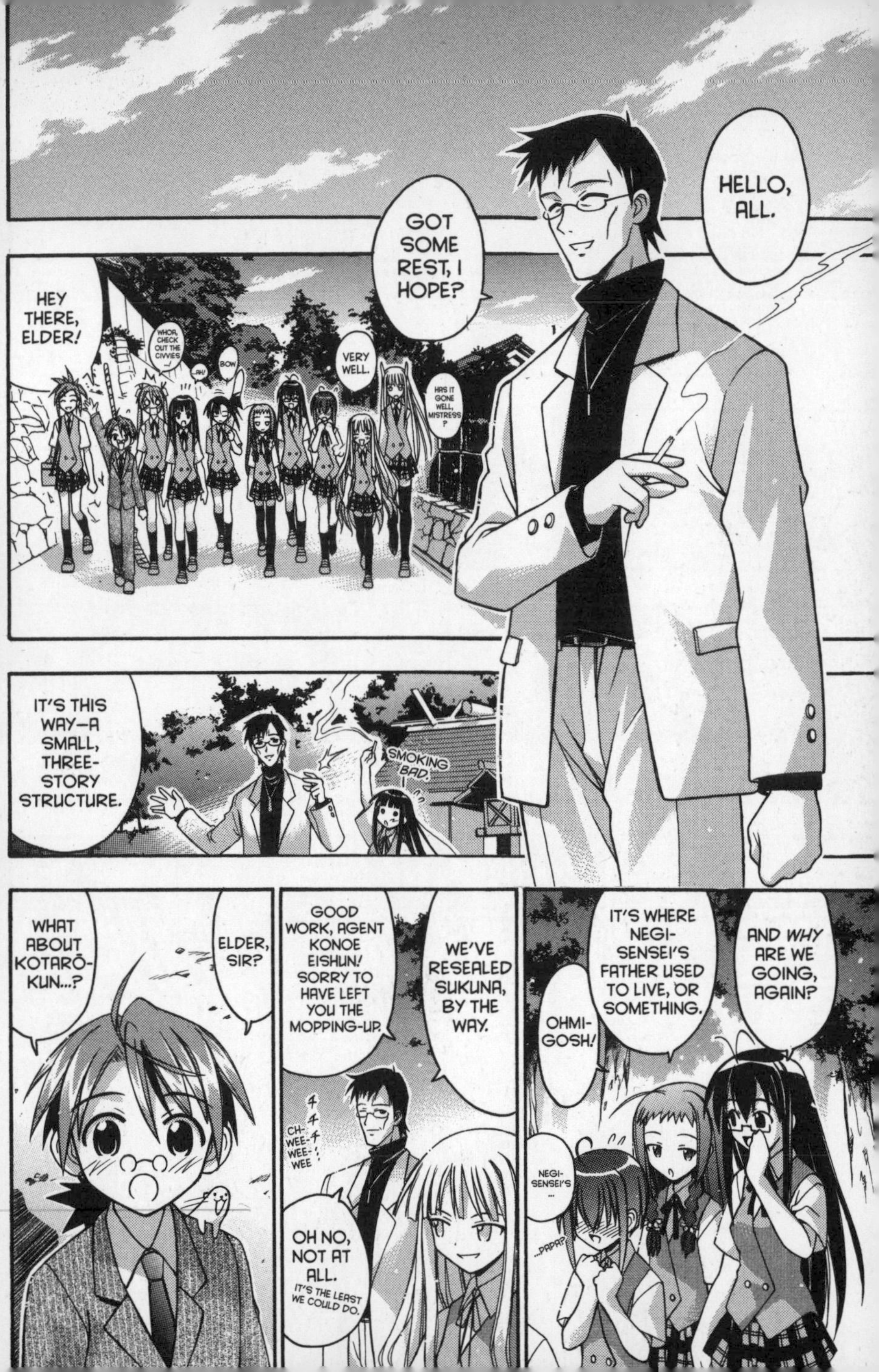
HELLO, ALL.
GOT SOME REST, I HOPE?
HAS IT GONE WELL, MISTRESS?
VERY WELL.
BOW
AH!
WHOA, CHECK OUT THE CIVVIES
HEY THERE, ELDER!
SMOKING BAD.
IT'S THIS WAY—A SMALL, THREE-STORY STRUCTURE.
AND WHY ARE WE GOING, AGAIN?
IT'S WHERE NEGI-SENSEI'S FATHER USED TO LIVE, OR SOMETHING.
OHMI-GOSH!
NEGI-SENSEI'S ...
...PAPA?
WE'VE RESEALED SUKUNA, BY THE WAY.
GOOD WORK, AGENT KONOE EISHUN! SORRY TO HAVE LEFT YOU THE MOPPING-UP.
CH-WEE-WEE-WEE
OH NO, NOT AT ALL.
IT'S THE LEAST WE COULD DO.
ELDER, SIR?
WHAT ABOUT KOTARŌ-KUN...?

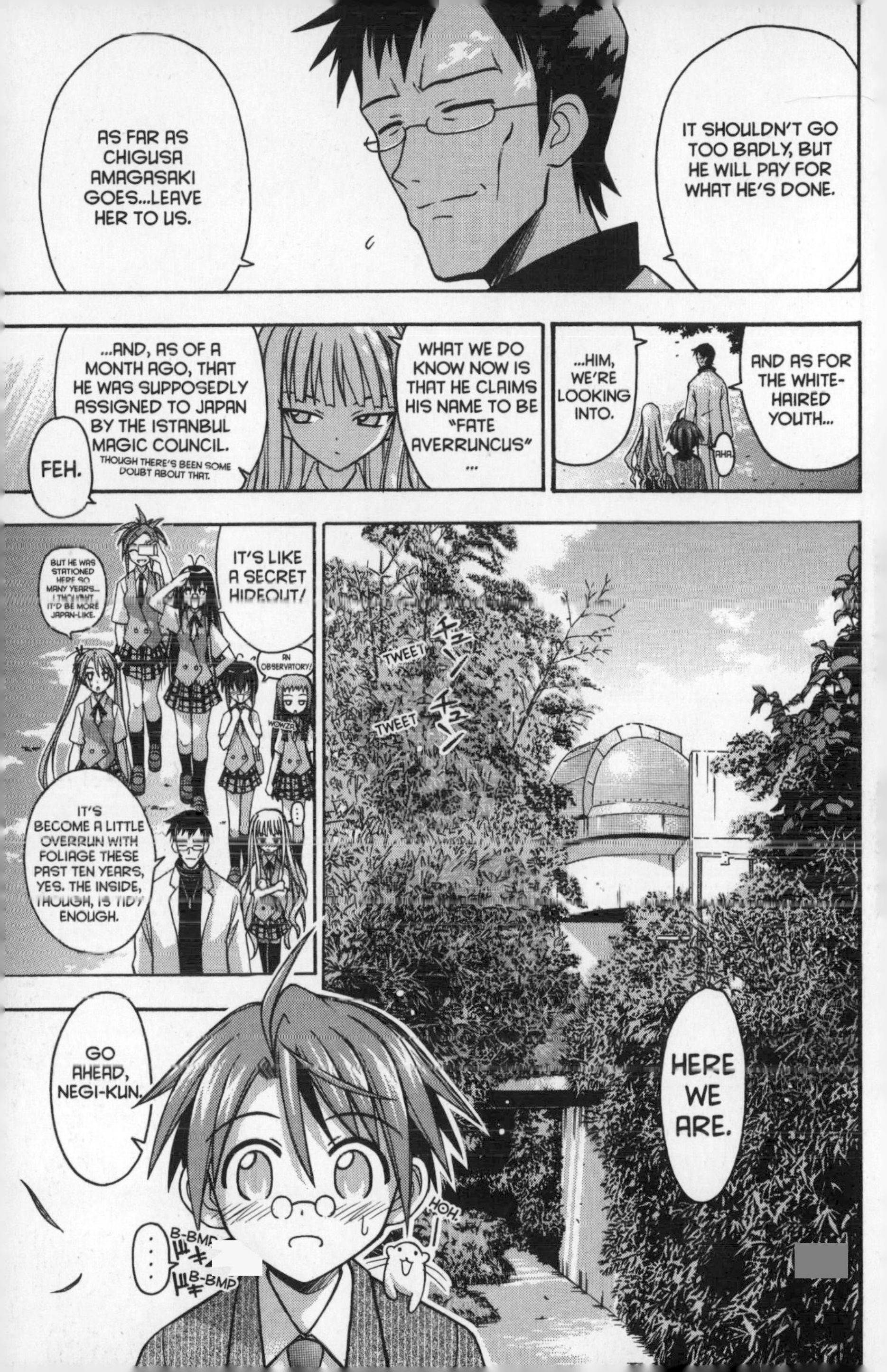
IT SHOULDN'T GO TOO BADLY, BUT HE WILL PAY FOR WHAT HE'S DONE.
AS FAR AS CHIGUSA AMAGASAKI GOES...LEAVE HER TO US.
AND AS FOR THE WHITE-HAIRED YOUTH...
...HIM, WE'RE LOOKING INTO.
AHA.
WHAT WE DO KNOW NOW IS THAT HE CLAIMS HIS NAME TO BE "FATE AVERRUNCUS"...
...AND, AS OF A MONTH AGO, THAT HE WAS SUPPOSEDLY ASSIGNED TO JAPAN BY THE ISTANBUL MAGIC COUNCIL.
THOUGH THERE'S BEEN SOME DOUBT ABOUT THAT.
FEH.
TWEET
TWEET
IT'S LIKE A SECRET HIDEOUT!
BUT HE WAS STATIONED HERE SO MANY YEARS... I THOUGHT IT'D BE MORE JAPAN-LIKE.
AN OBSERVATORY!
WOWZA
...
IT'S BECOME A LITTLE OVERRUN WITH FOLIAGE THESE PAST TEN YEARS, YES. THE INSIDE, THOUGH, IS TIDY ENOUGH.
HERE WE ARE.
HOH.
GO AHEAD, NEGI-KUN.
B-BMP
B-BMP
....

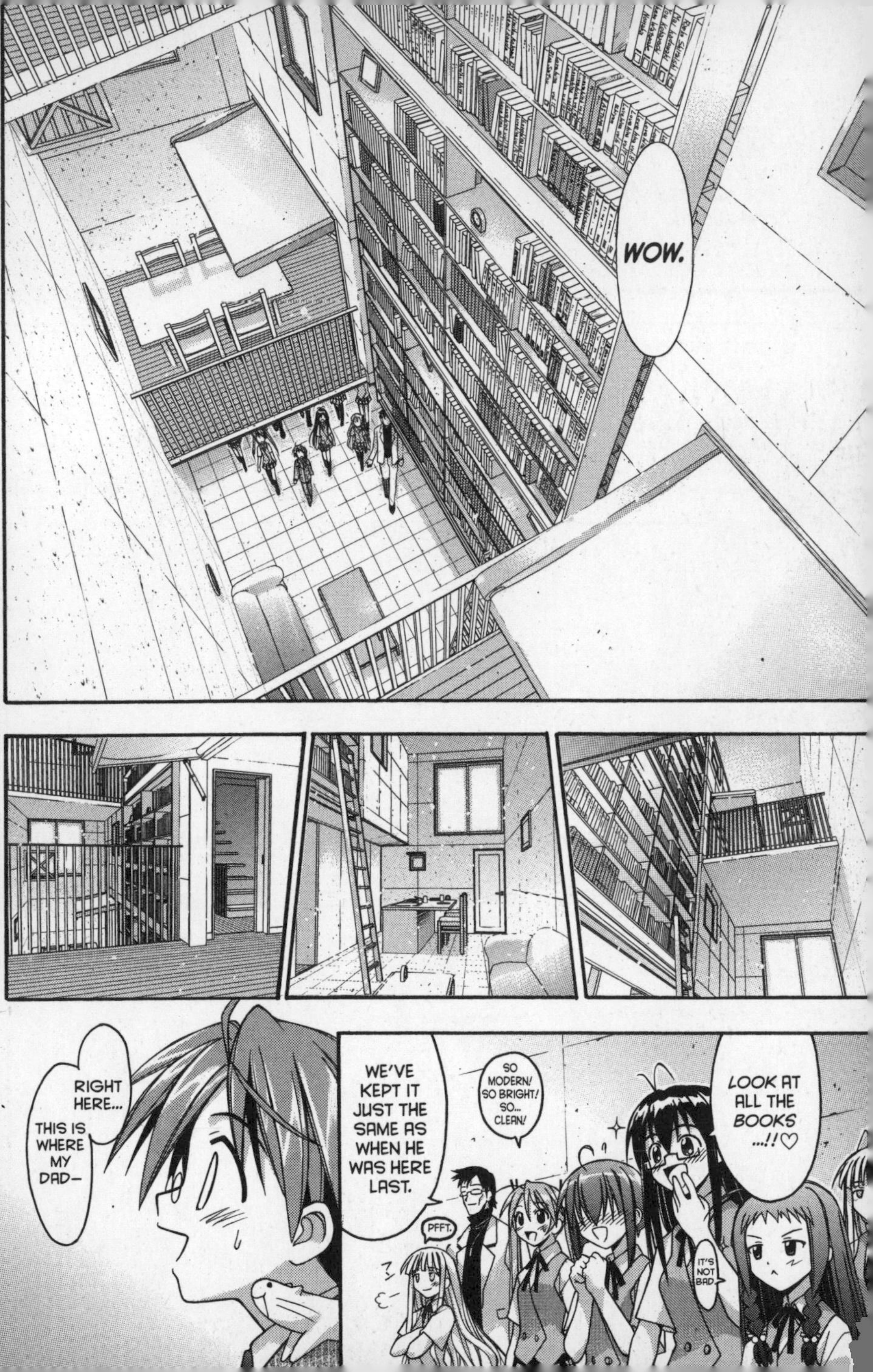
WOW.
LOOK AT ALL THE BOOKS ...!!♡
SO MODERN! SO BRIGHT! SO... CLEAN!
WE'VE KEPT IT JUST THE SAME AS WHEN HE WAS HERE LAST.
IT'S NOT BAD.
PFFT.
RIGHT HERE...
THIS IS WHERE MY DAD—

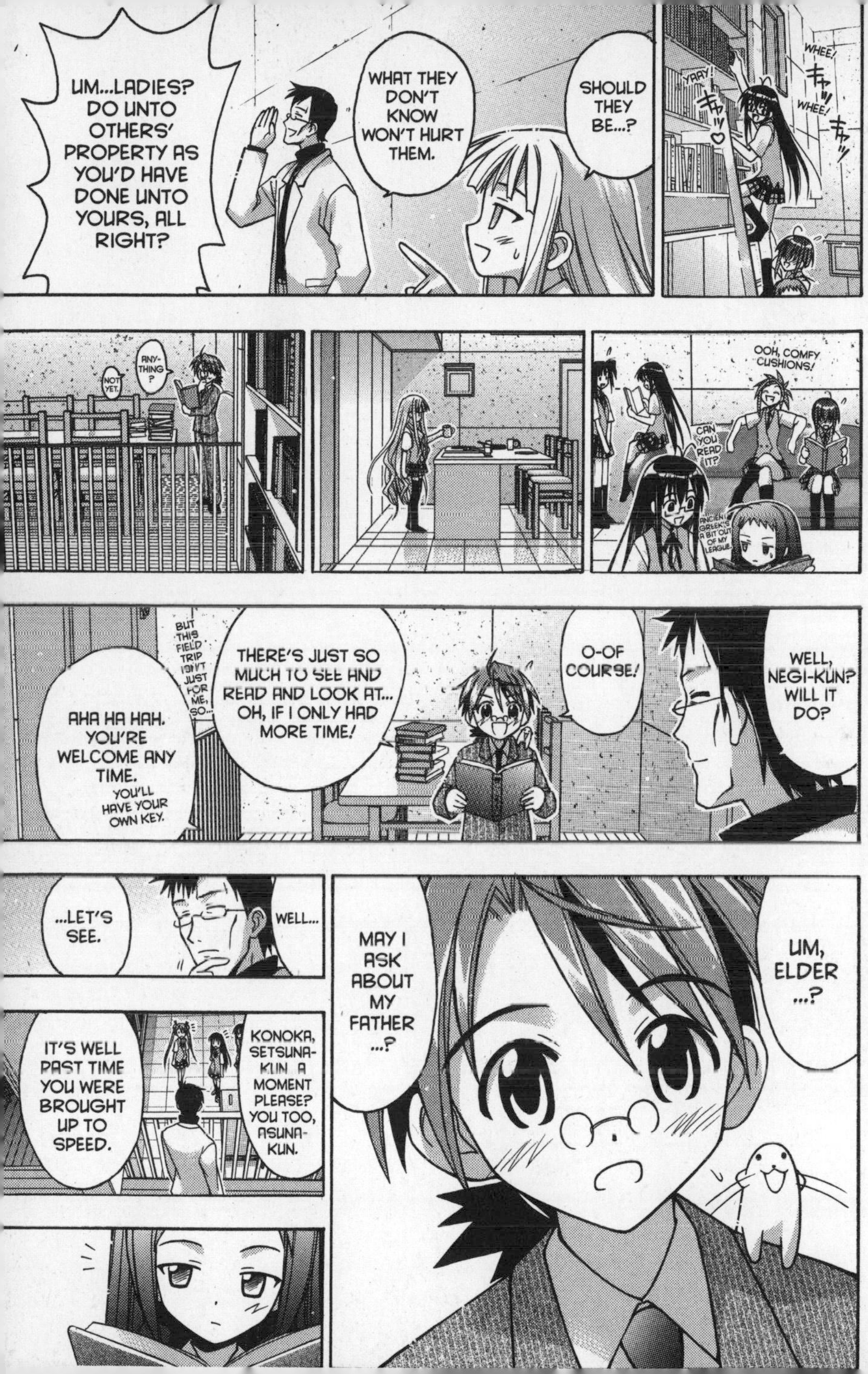
WHEE!
YAAY!
WHEE!
SHOULD THEY BE...?
WHAT THEY DON'T KNOW WON'T HURT THEM.
UM...LADIES? DO UNTO OTHERS' PROPERTY AS YOU'D HAVE DONE UNTO YOURS, ALL RIGHT?
OOH, COMFY CUSHIONS!
CAN YOU READ IT?
ANCIENT GREEK'S A BIT OUT OF MY LEAGUE.
ANY-THING?
NOT YET.
WELL, NEGI-KUN? WILL IT DO?
O-OF COURSE!
THERE'S JUST SO MUCH TO SEE AND READ AND LOOK AT... OH, IF I ONLY HAD MORE TIME!
BUT THIS FIELD TRIP ISN'T JUST FOR ME, SO...
AHA HA HAH. YOU'RE WELCOME ANY TIME.
YOU'LL HAVE YOUR OWN KEY.
UM, ELDER ...?
MAY I ASK ABOUT MY FATHER ...?
WELL...
...LET'S SEE.
KONOKA, SETSUNA-KUN, A MOMENT PLEASE? YOU TOO, ASUNA-KUN.
IT'S WELL PAST TIME YOU WERE BROUGHT UP TO SPEED.

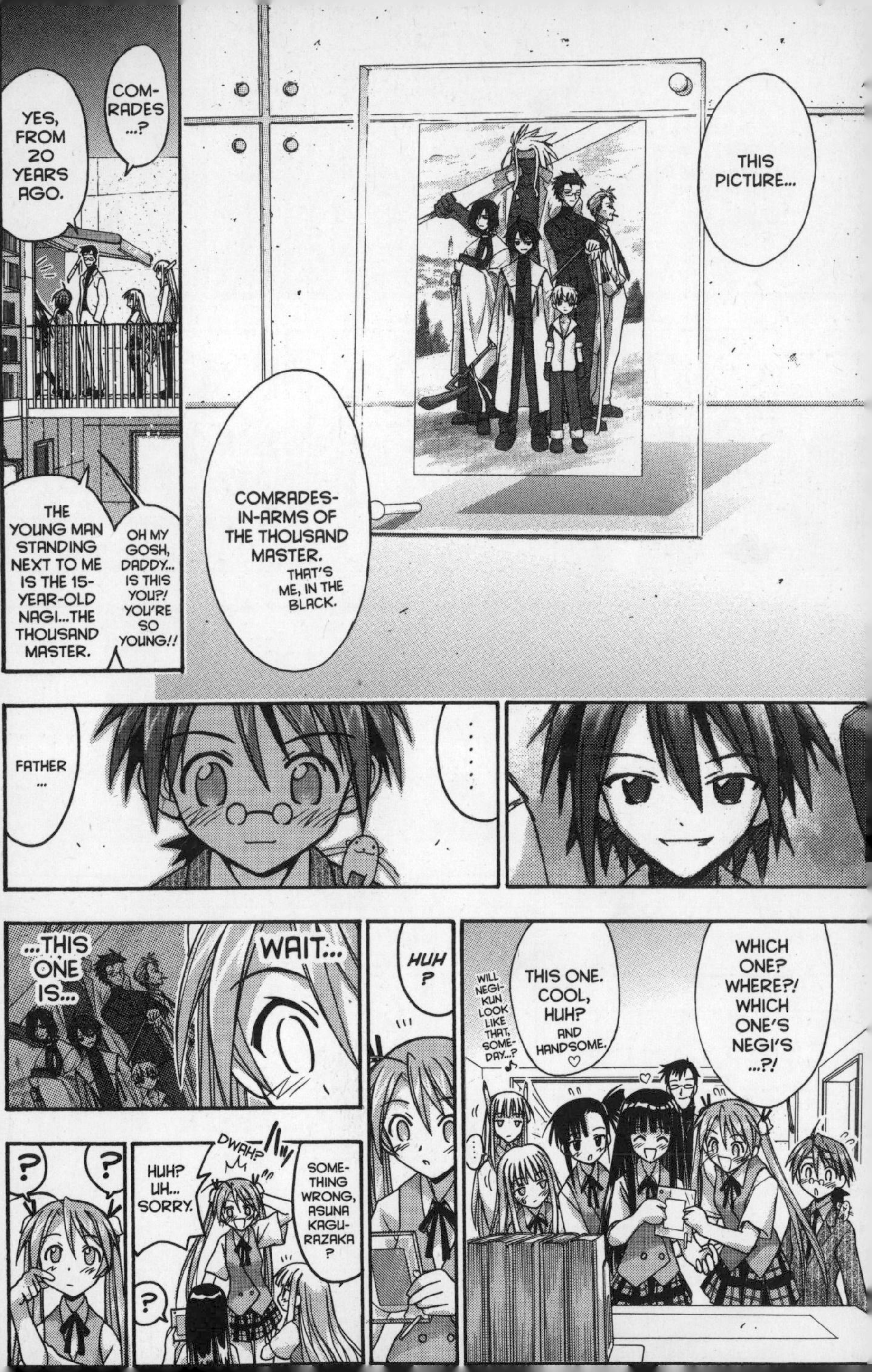
THIS PICTURE...
COMRADES-IN-ARMS OF THE THOUSAND MASTER.
THAT'S ME, IN THE BLACK.
COM-RADES ...?
YES, FROM 20 YEARS AGO.
OH MY GOSH, DADDY... IS THIS YOU?! YOU'RE SO YOUNG!!
THE YOUNG MAN STANDING NEXT TO ME IS THE 15-YEAR-OLD NAGI...THE THOUSAND MASTER.
......
FATHER ...
WHICH ONE? WHERE?! WHICH ONE'S NEGI'S ...?!
THIS ONE. COOL, HUH? AND HANDSOME. ♡
WILL NEGI-KUN LOOK LIKE THAT, SOME-DAY...?
HUH ?
WAIT...
...THIS ONE IS...
SOME-THING WRONG, ASUNA KAGU-RAZAKA ?
DWAH?!
HUH? UH... SORRY.
?
?
?

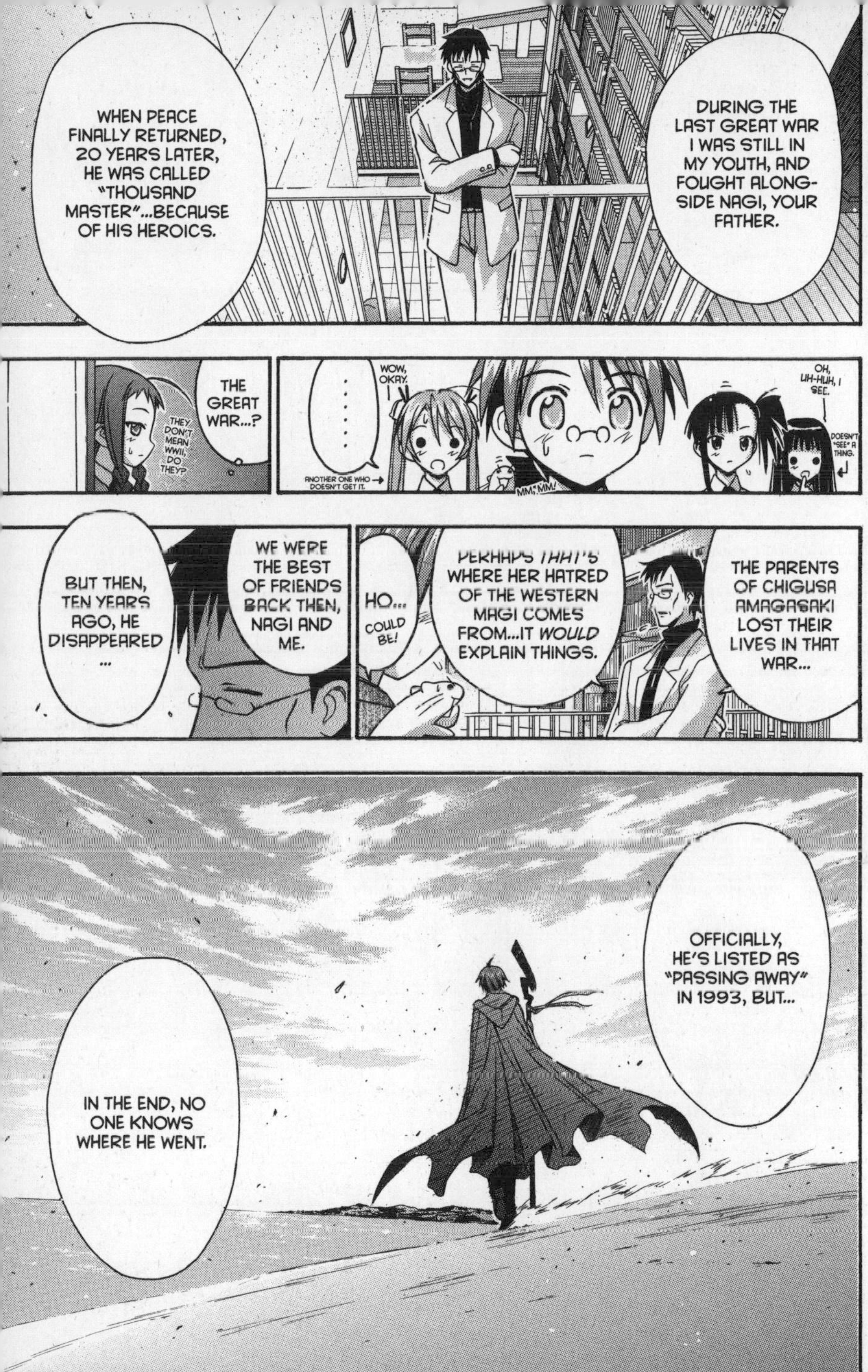
DURING THE LAST GREAT WAR I WAS STILL IN MY YOUTH, AND FOUGHT ALONG-SIDE NAGI, YOUR FATHER.
WHEN PEACE FINALLY RETURNED, 20 YEARS LATER, HE WAS CALLED "THOUSAND MASTER"...BECAUSE OF HIS HEROICS.
OH, UH-HUH, I SEE.
DOESN'T "SEE" A THING.
MM, MM!
WOW, OKAY.
......
ANOTHER ONE WHO DOESN'T GET IT.
THE GREAT WAR...?
THEY DON'T MEAN WWII, DO THEY?
THE PARENTS OF CHIGUSA AMAGASAKI LOST THEIR LIVES IN THAT WAR...
PERHAPS THAT'S WHERE HER HATRED OF THE WESTERN MAGI COMES FROM...IT WOULD EXPLAIN THINGS.
HO...
COULD BE!
WE WERE THE BEST OF FRIENDS BACK THEN, NAGI AND ME.
BUT THEN, TEN YEARS AGO, HE DISAPPEARED...
OFFICIALLY, HE'S LISTED AS "PASSING AWAY" IN 1993, BUT...
IN THE END, NO ONE KNOWS WHERE HE WENT.

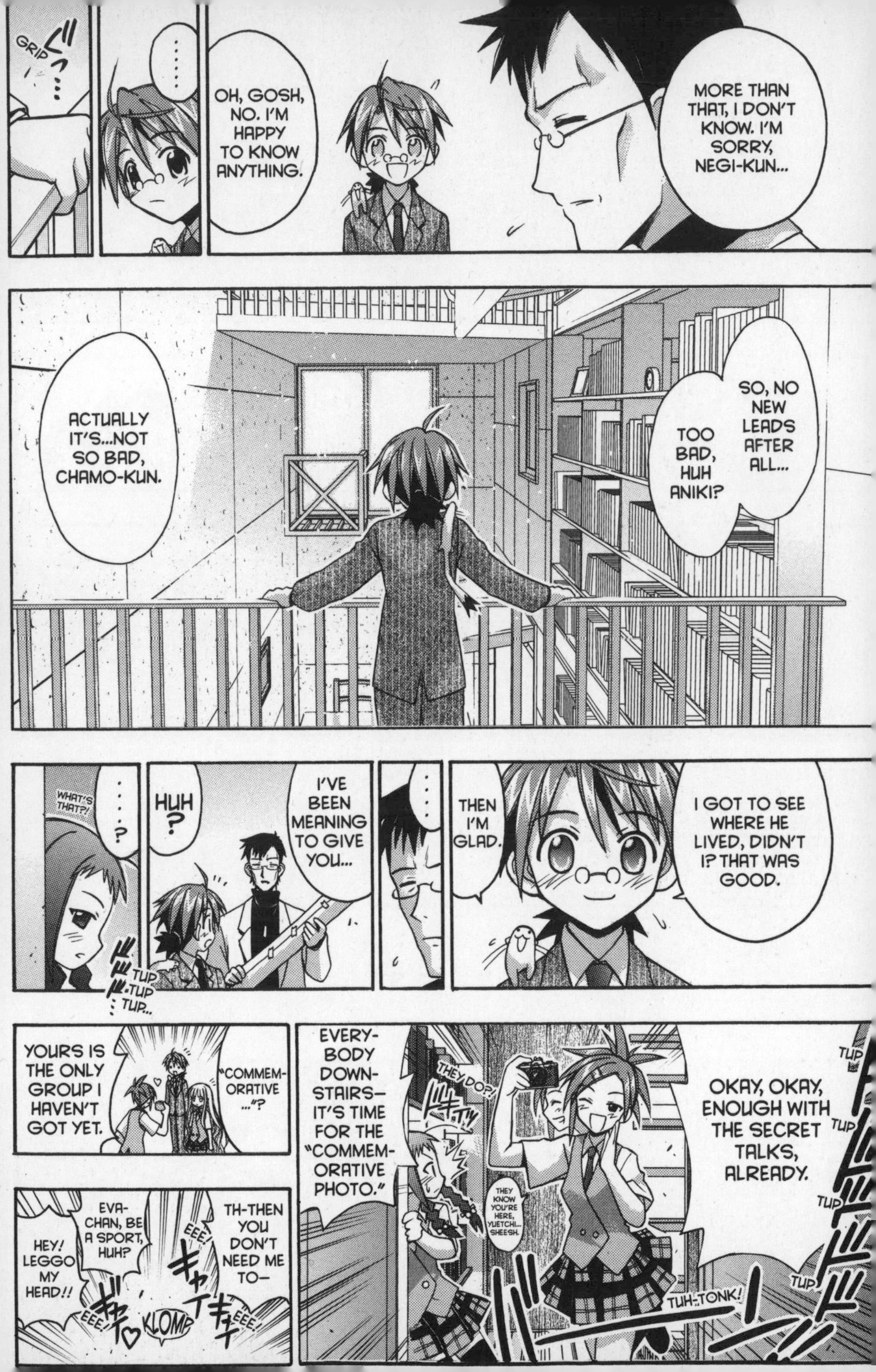
MORE THAN THAT, I DON'T KNOW. I'M SORRY, NEGI-KUN...
OH, GOSH, NO. I'M HAPPY TO KNOW ANYTHING.
......
GRIP
SO, NO NEW LEADS AFTER ALL...
TOO BAD, HUH ANIKI?
ACTUALLY IT'S...NOT SO BAD, CHAMO-KUN.
I GOT TO SEE WHERE HE LIVED, DIDN'T I? THAT WAS GOOD.
.....
THEN I'M GLAD.
I'VE BEEN MEANING TO GIVE YOU...
HUH ?
....?
WHAT'S THAT?!
TUP TUP TUP...
TUP
TUP
OKAY, OKAY, ENOUGH WITH THE SECRET TALKS, ALREADY.
TUP
TUP
THEY DO?!
THEY KNOW YOU'RE HERE, YUETCHI... SHEESH.
EVERY-BODY DOWN-STAIRS— IT'S TIME FOR THE "COMMEM-ORATIVE PHOTO."
TUH-TONK!
"COMMEM-ORATIVE ..."?
YOURS IS THE ONLY GROUP I HAVEN'T GOT YET.
TH-THEN YOU DON'T NEED ME TO—
EVA-CHAN, BE A SPORT, HUH?
EEE!
HEY! LEGGO MY HEAD!!
EEE!
KLOMP
EEE!

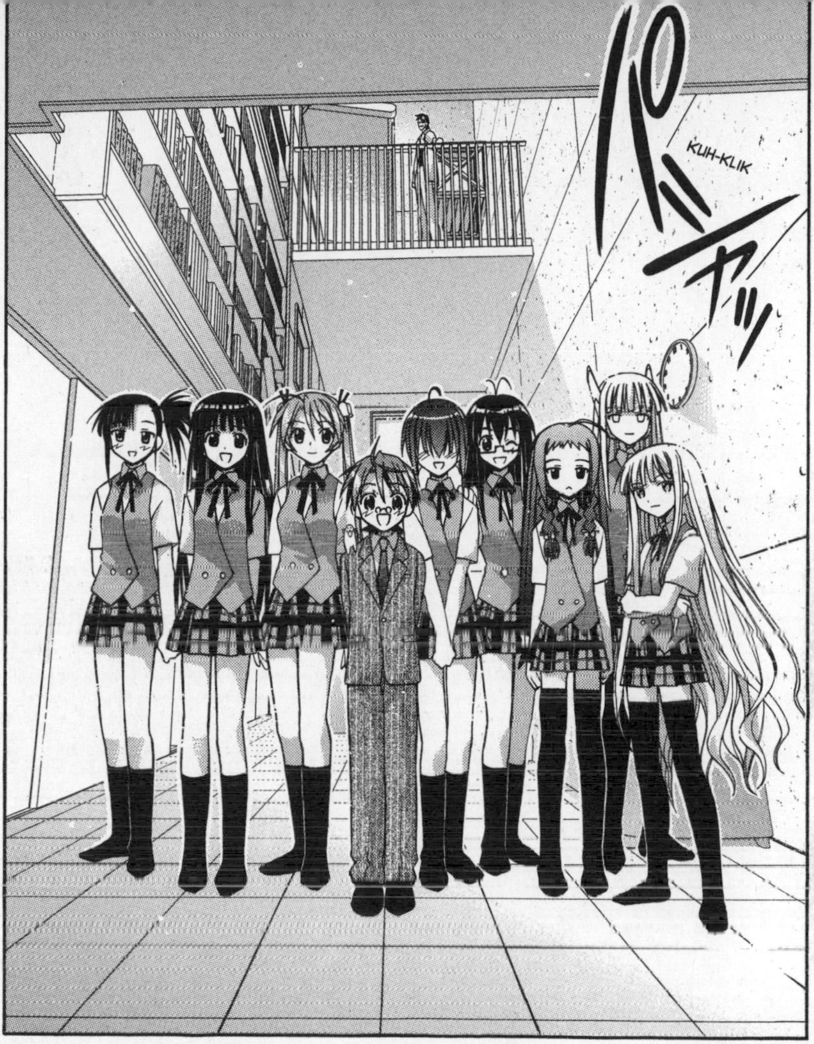
パシャッ
KUH-KLIK
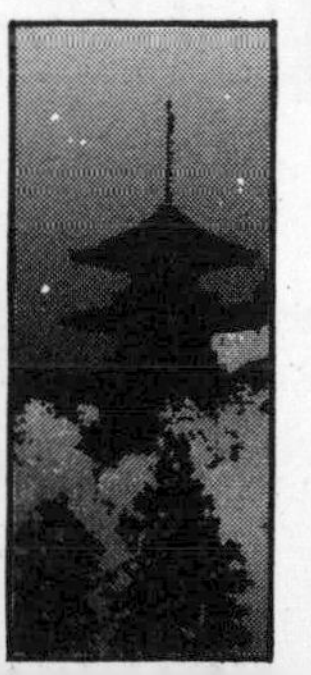
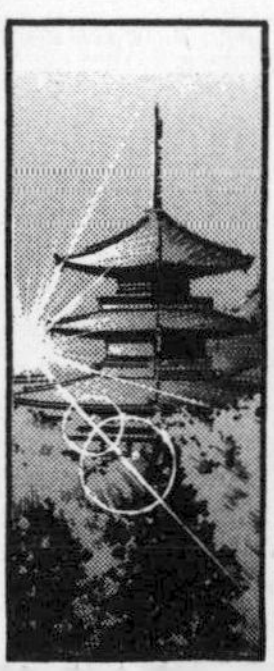
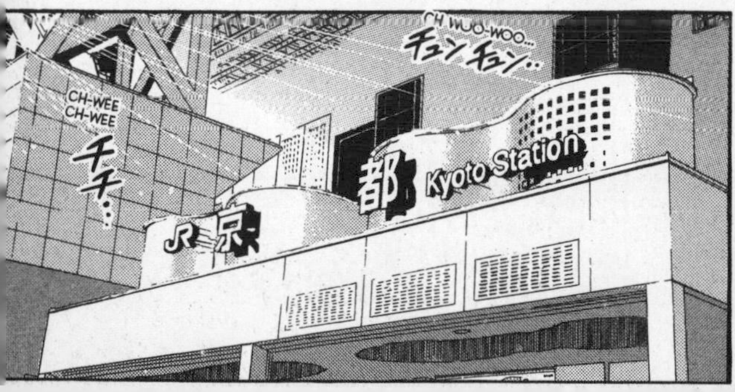
CH WUO-WOO...
チュンチュン..
CH-WEE
CH-WEE
チチ...
JR 京都 Kyoto Station

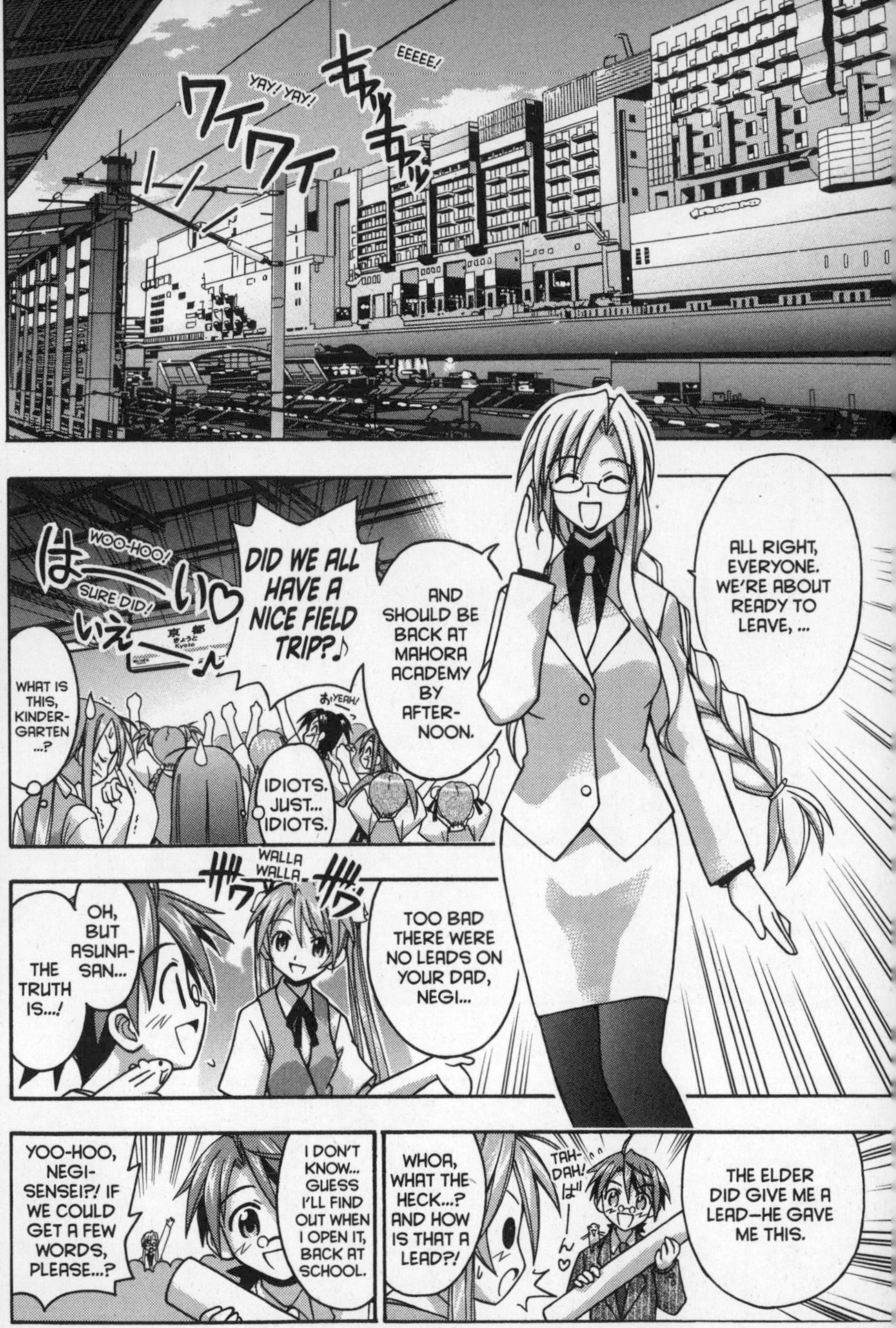
EEEEE!
YAY! YAY!
ALL RIGHT, EVERYONE. WE'RE ABOUT READY TO LEAVE, ...
AND SHOULD BE BACK AT MAHORA ACADEMY BY AFTERNOON.
DID WE ALL HAVE A NICE FIELD TRIP?♪
WOO-HOO!
SURE DID!
YEAH!
IDIOTS. JUST... IDIOTS.
WHAT IS THIS, KINDERGARTEN ...?
WALLA WALLA
TOO BAD THERE WERE NO LEADS ON YOUR DAD, NEGI...
OH, BUT ASUNA-SAN...
THE TRUTH IS...!
THE ELDER DID GIVE ME A LEAD—HE GAVE ME THIS.
TAH-DAH!
WHOA, WHAT THE HECK...? AND HOW IS THAT A LEAD?!
I DON'T KNOW... GUESS I'LL FIND OUT WHEN I OPEN IT, BACK AT SCHOOL.
YOO-HOO, NEGI-SENSEI?! IF WE COULD GET A FEW WORDS, PLEASE...?

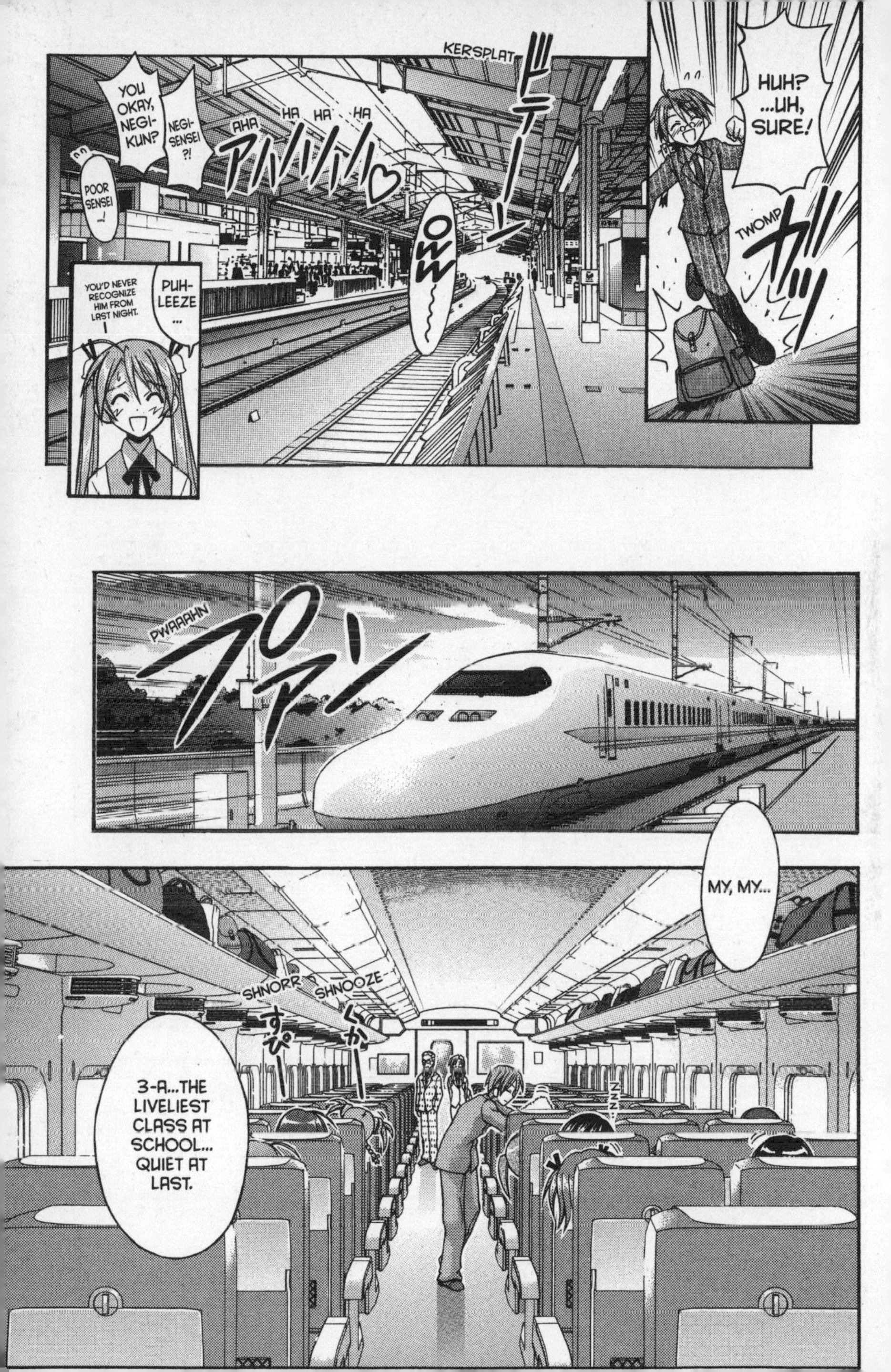
HUH? ...UH, SURE!
TWOMP
ガッ
KERSPLAT
OWW~
AHA HA HA HA
YOU OKAY, NEGI-KUN?
NEGI-SENSEI?!
POOR SENSEI...!
PUH-LEEZE...
YOU'D NEVER RECOGNIZE HIM FROM LAST NIGHT.
PWAAAHN
プァン
MY, MY...
SHNOOZE
SHNORR
ZZZ
3-A...THE LIVELIEST CLASS AT SCHOOL... QUIET AT LAST.

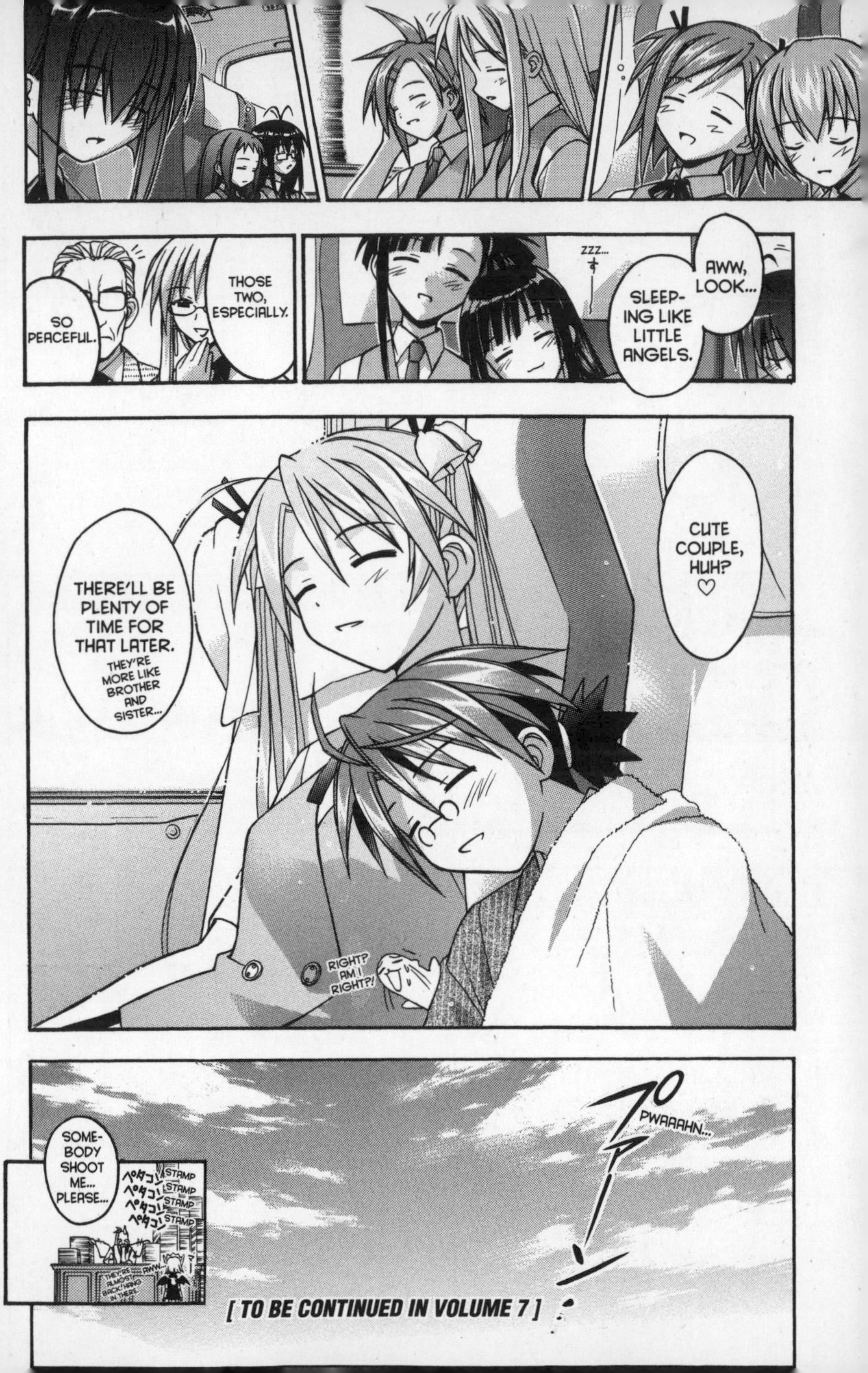
ZZZ...
AWW, LOOK...
SLEEP-ING LIKE LITTLE ANGELS.
THOSE TWO, ESPECIALLY.
SO PEACEFUL.
CUTE COUPLE, HUH? ♡
THERE'LL BE PLENTY OF TIME FOR THAT LATER.
THEY'RE MORE LIKE BROTHER AND SISTER...
RIGHT? AM I RIGHT?!
PWAAAHN...
SOME-BODY SHOOT ME... PLEASE...
STAMP
STAMP
STAMP
STAMP
AWW...
[TO BE CONTINUED IN VOLUME 7]

- STAFF -

Ken Akamatsu
Takashi Takemoto
Kenichi Nakamura
Masaki Ohyama
Keiichi Yamashita
Chigusa Amagasaki
Takaaki Miyahara

Thanks To

Ran Ayanaga

NEGIMA!

PRELIMINARY CHARACTER DESIGNS ROUGH SKETCHES

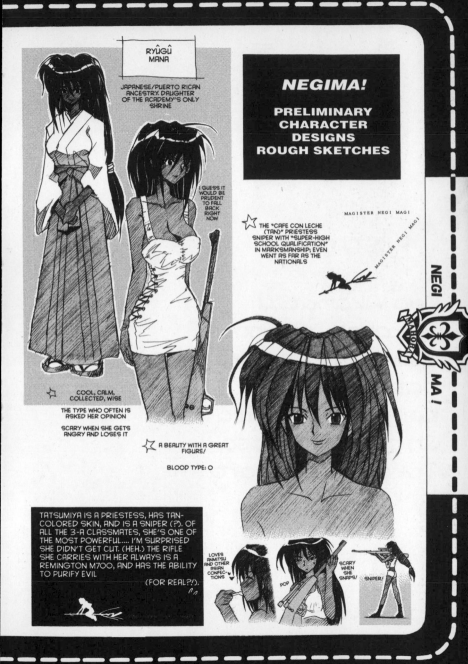

RYÛGÛ MANA

JAPANESE/PUERTO RICAN ANCESTRY. DAUGHTER OF THE ACADEMY'S ONLY SHRINE

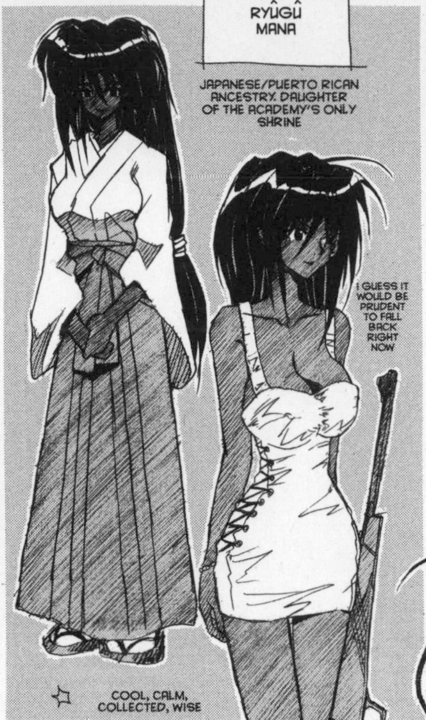
I GUESS IT WOULD BE PRUDENT TO FALL BACK RIGHT NOW

☆ COOL, CALM, COLLECTED, WISE

THE TYPE WHO OFTEN IS ASKED HER OPINION

SCARY WHEN SHE GETS ANGRY AND LOSES IT

☆ THE "CAFE CON LECHE (TAN)" PRIESTESS SNIPER WITH "SUPER-HIGH SCHOOL QUALIFICATION" IN MARKSMANSHIP; EVEN WENT AS FAR AS THE NATIONALS

MAGISTER NEGI MAGI

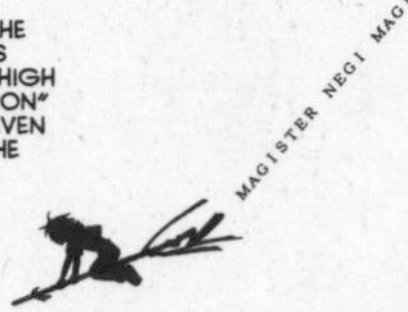
MAGISTER NEGI MAGI

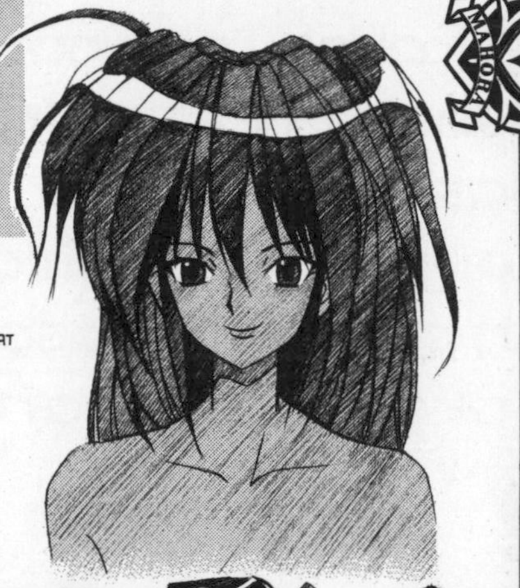

☆ A BEAUTY WITH A GREAT FIGURE!

BLOOD TYPE: O

TATSUMIYA IS A PRIESTESS, HAS TAN-COLORED SKIN, AND IS A SNIPER (?). OF ALL THE 3-A CLASSMATES, SHE'S ONE OF THE MOST POWERFUL.... I'M SURPRISED SHE DIDN'T GET CUT. (HEH.) THE RIFLE SHE CARRIES WITH HER ALWAYS IS A REMINGTON M700, AND HAS THE ABILITY TO PURIFY EVIL

(FOR REAL?!).

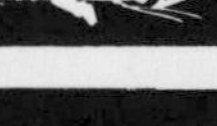

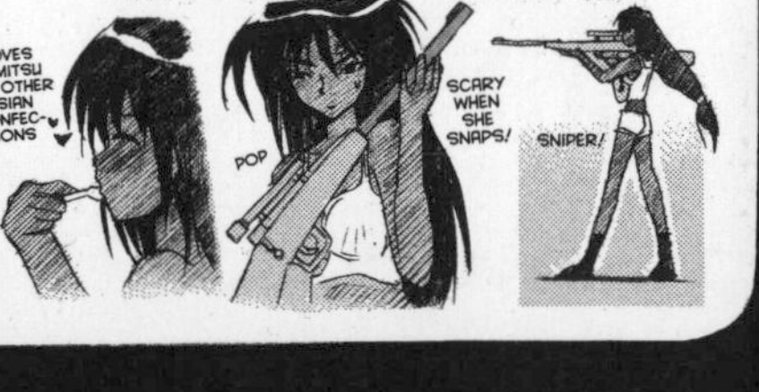
SNIPER!
SCARY WHEN SHE SNAPS!
POP
LOVES ANMITSU AND OTHER ASIAN CONFECTIONS

THE "WHITE-HAIRED YOUTH" WAS DESIGNED BY RAN AYANAGA. HE'S CUTE! HE MAY... OR MAY NOT... BECOME NEGI'S NEMESIS. HE SEEMS LIKE A MAJOR CHARACTER EITHER WAY, THOUGH, DOESN'T HE?

I DO HOPE YOU ENJOYED THE "SCHOOL FIELD TRIP" STORY ARC. NEGI MATURES SO MUCH IN IT, I HAD A GREAT TIME WITH THE DRAWING— AKAMATSU.

とはまた 赤松

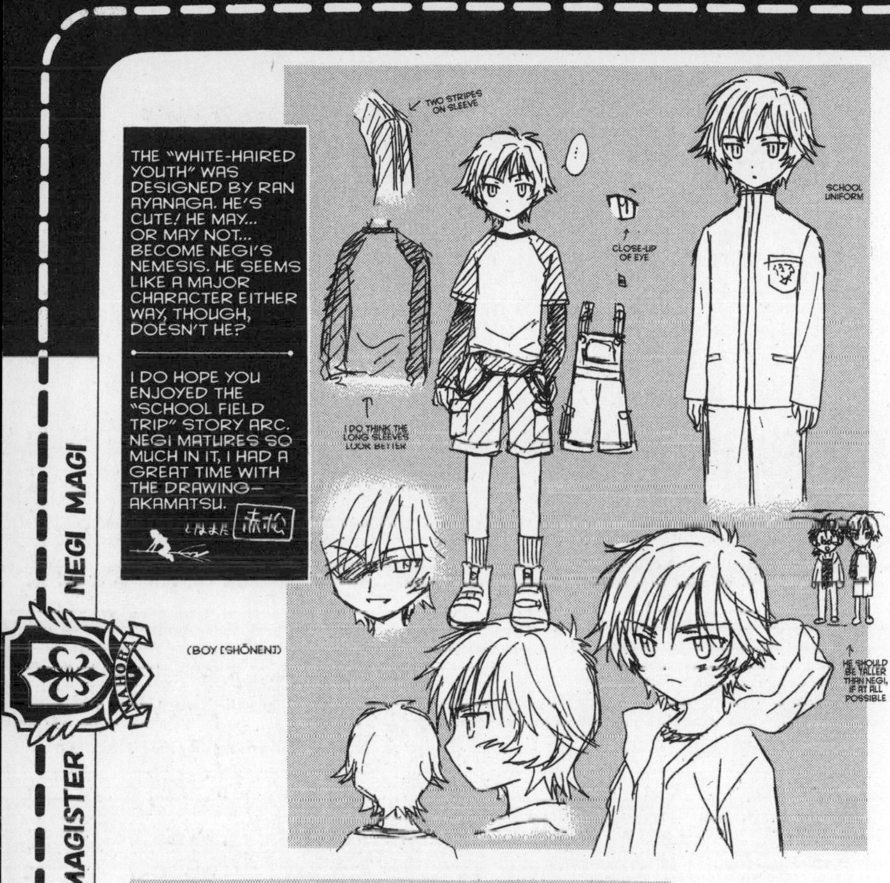

TWO STRIPES ON SLEEVE
...
I DO THINK THE LONG SLEEVES LOOK BETTER
CLOSE-UP OF EYE
SCHOOL UNIFORM
(BOY [SHŌNEN])
HE SHOULD BE TALLER THAN NEGI, IF AT ALL POSSIBLE

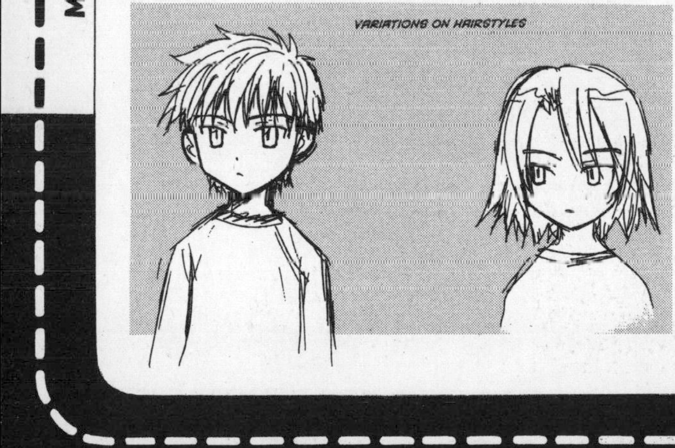

VARIATIONS ON HAIRSTYLES
TOO GIRLISH?
BOB-CUT, AS USUAL

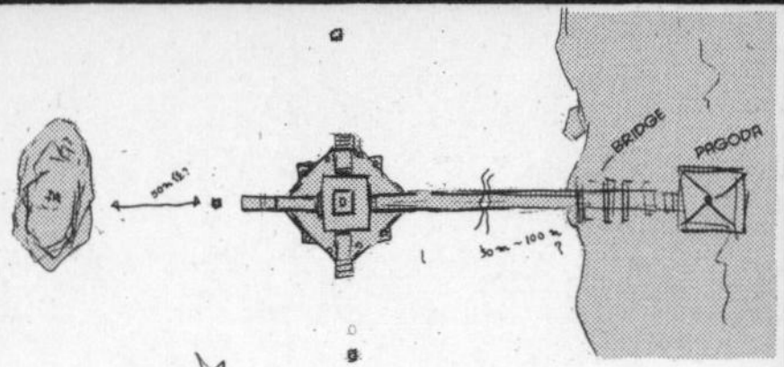
BRIDGE
PAGODA

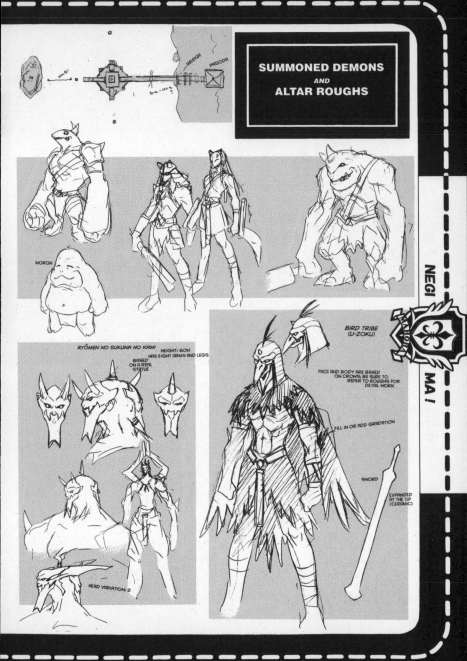

SUMMONED DEMONS
AND
ALTAR ROUGHS

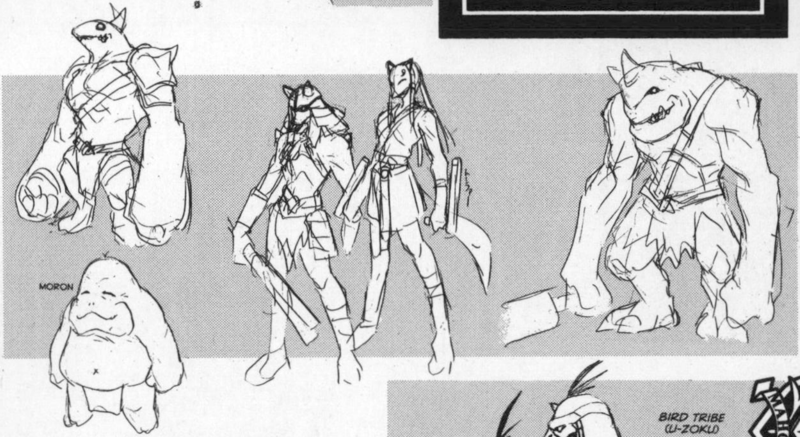
MORON

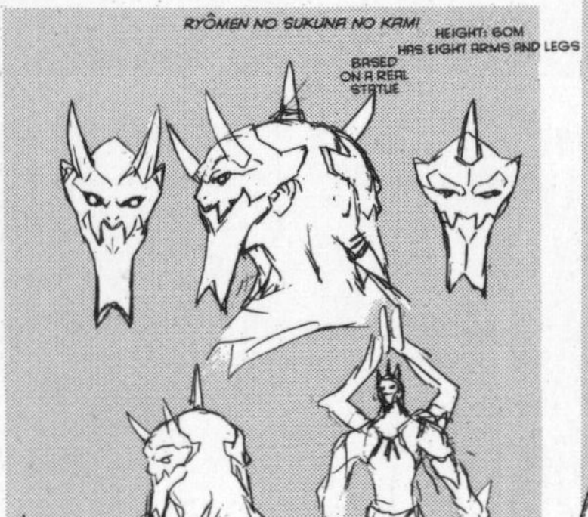
RYÔMEN NO SUKUNA NO KAMI
HEIGHT: 60M
HAS EIGHT ARMS AND LEGS
BASED ON A REAL STATUE
HEAD VARIATION: 2

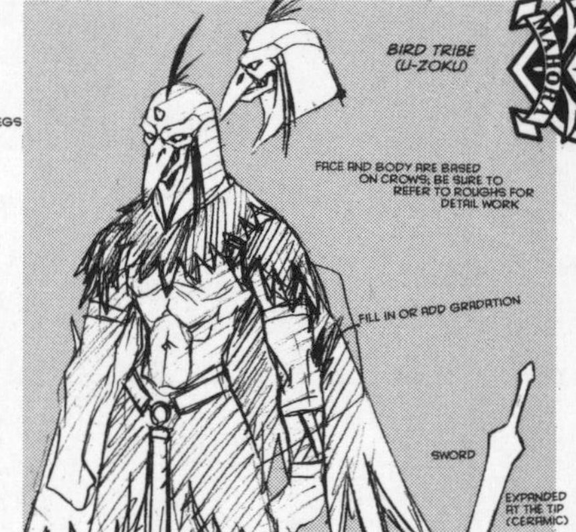
BIRD TRIBE (U-ZOKU)
FACE AND BODY ARE BASED ON CROWS; BE SURE TO REFER TO ROUGHS FOR DETAIL WORK
FILL IN OR ADD GRADATION
SWORD
EXPANDED AT THE TIP (CERAMIC)

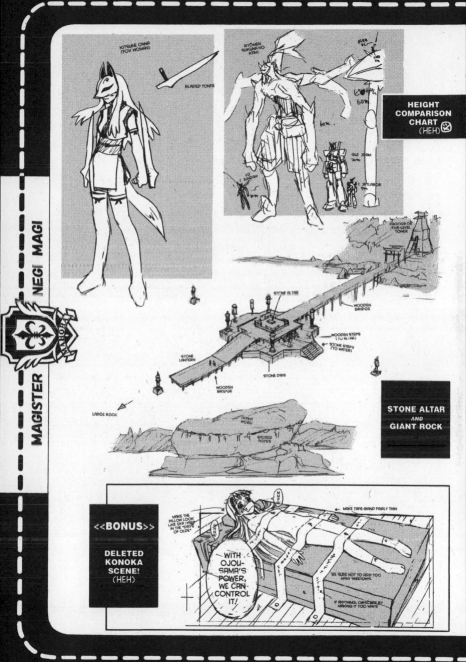

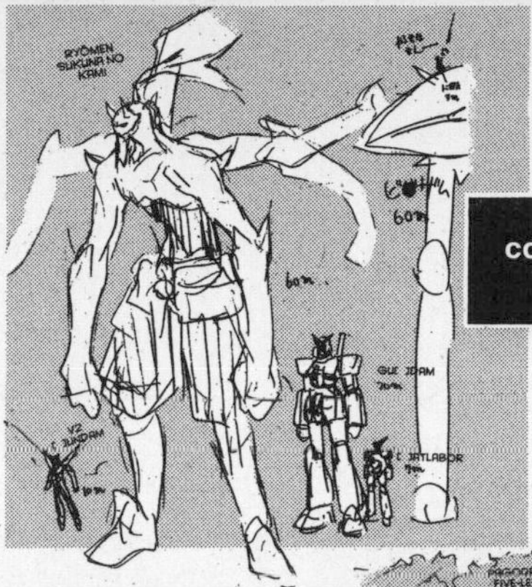
RYŌMEN SUKUNA NO KAMI

HEIGHT COMPARISON CHART (HEH)

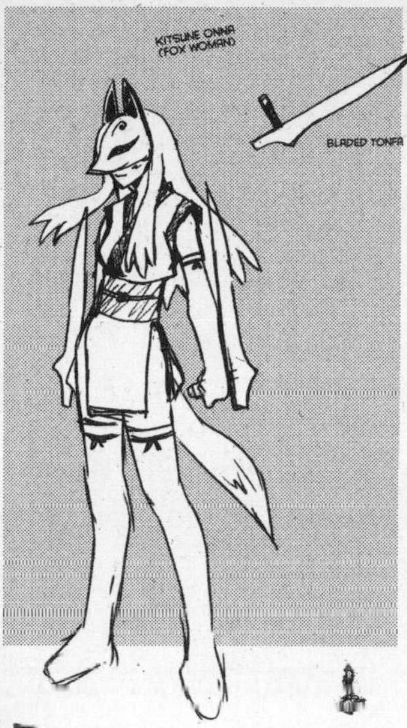
KITSUNE ONNA (FOX WOMAN)
BLADED TONFA

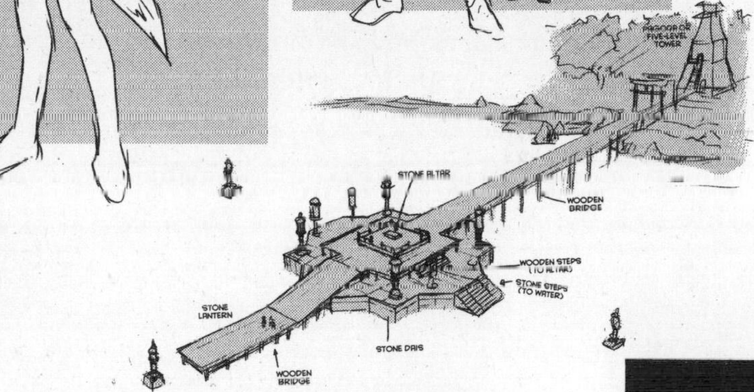
PAGODA OR FIVE-LEVEL TOWER
STONE ALTAR
WOODEN BRIDGE
WOODEN STEPS (TO ALTAR)
STONE STEPS (TO WATER)
STONE LANTERN
STONE DAIS
WOODEN BRIDGE
LARGE ROCK

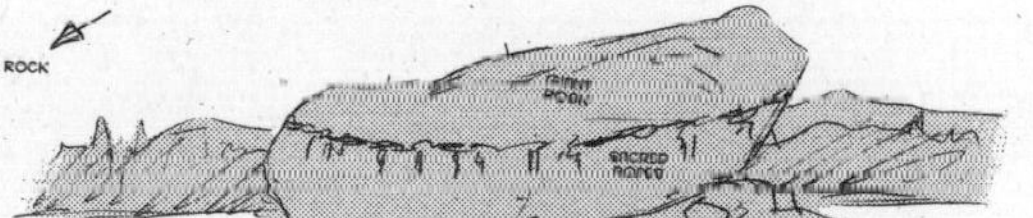

STONE ALTAR AND GIANT ROCK

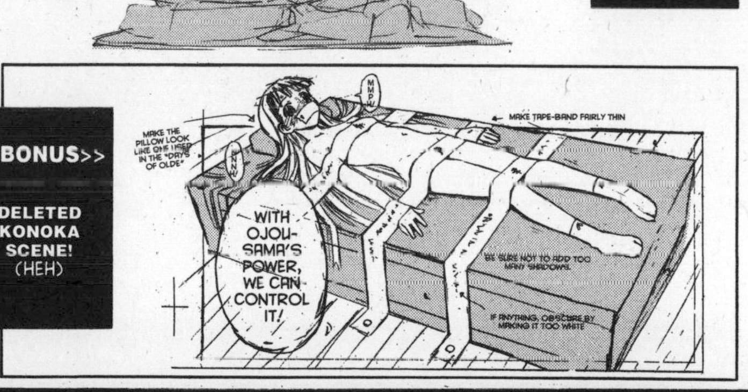
MMPH
MAKE TAPE-BAND FAIRLY THIN
MAKE THE PILLOW LOOK LIKE ONE USED IN THE "DAYS OF OLDE"
NNN
WITH OJOU-SAMA'S POWER, WE CAN CONTROL IT!
BE SURE NOT TO ADD TOO MANY SHADOWS.
IF ANYTHING, OBSCURE BY MAKING IT TOO WHITE

<<BONUS>>

DELETED KONOKA SCENE! (HEH)

About the Creator

Negima! is only Ken Akamatsu's third manga, although he started working in the field in 1994 with *AI Ga Tomaranai* (released in the U.S. with the title *A.I. Love You*). Like all of Akamatsu's work to date, it was published in Kodansha's *Shonen Magazine*. *AI Ga Tomaranai* ran for five years before concluding in 1999. In 1998, however, Akamatsu began the work that would make him one of the most popular manga artists in Japan: *Love Hina*. *Love Hina* ran for four years, and before its conclusion in 2002, it would cause Akamatsu to be granted the prestigious Manga of the Year award from Kodansha, as well as going on to become one of the bestselling manga in the United States.

Translation Notes

Japanese is a tricky language for most Westerners, and translation is often more art than science. For your edification and reading pleasure, here are notes on some of the places where we could have gone in a different direction in our translation of the work, or where a Japanese cultural reference is used.

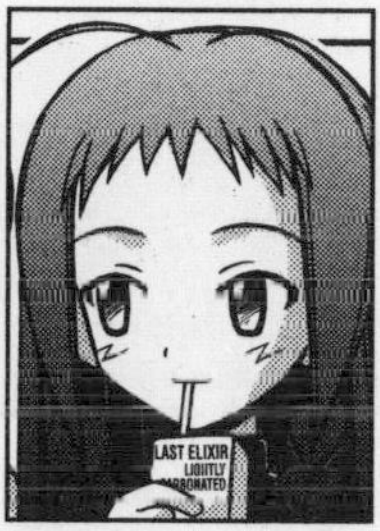
LAST ELIXIR
LIGHTLY

Last Elixir, page 6

One of the items you can get in the Final Fantasy series of RPG games, Last Elixir is a high-powered tonic which heals both the HP (hit points) and MP (magic points) of the entire party. Yet another in the continuing saga of Yue's strange soft drinks.

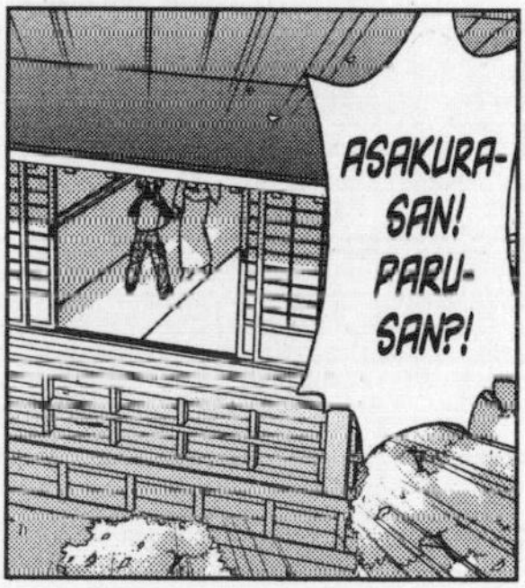
ASAKURA-SAN! PARU-SAN?!

Paru-san, page 28

Because of the way the romanization works out, this Haruna nickname could be "Pal" or it could be "Paru"—short of asking the author his personal preference, either is correct.

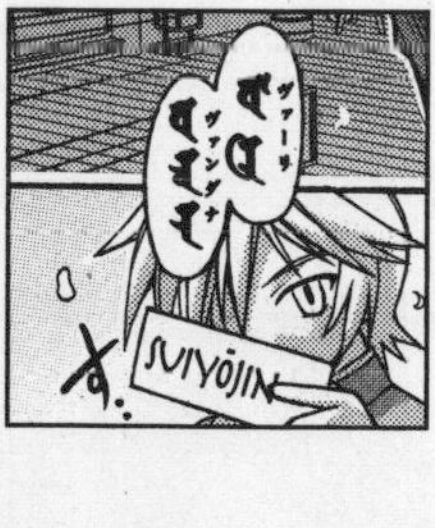
SUIYÔJIN

Suiyôjin, page 43

Literally, "water-demon circle."

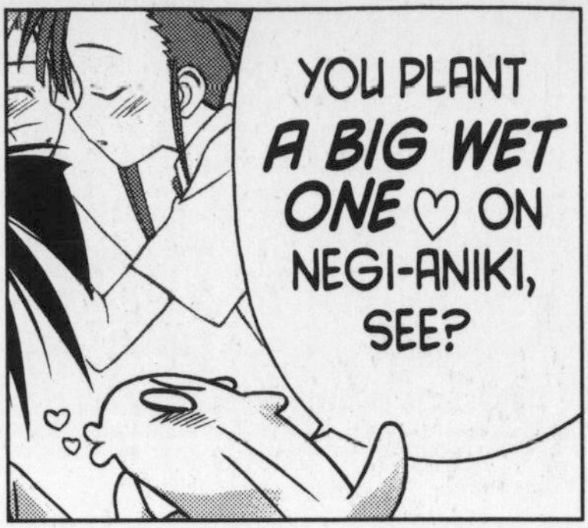
YOU PLANT A BIG WET ONE ♡ ON NEGI-ANIKI, SEE?

Aniki/Nêsan/Anesan, page 53

Terms of high respect and respectful familiarity, the honorifics *"Aniki/Nêsan/Anesan"* come out to "Older Brother," "Older Sister" (more familiar), and "Older Sister" (more formal). As well-known sobriquets within the *Yakuza* patois, Chamo-kun's use of them adds a dimension to his character.

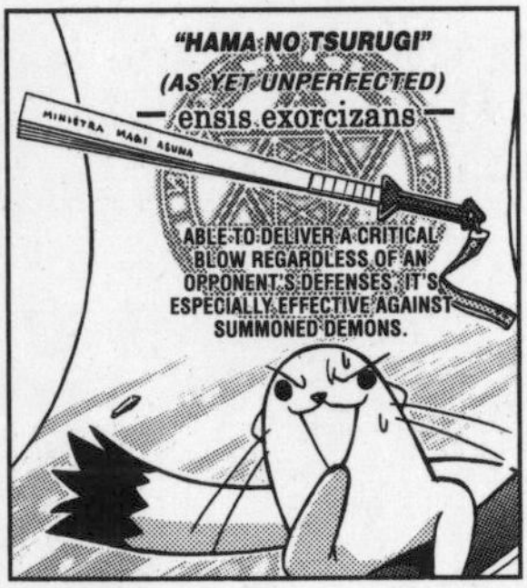
"HAMA NO TSURUGI"
(AS YET UNPERFECTED)
—ensis exorcizans—
MINISTRA MAGI ASUNA
ABLE TO DELIVER A CRITICAL BLOW REGARDLESS OF AN OPPONENT'S DEFENSES. IT'S ESPECIALLY EFFECTIVE AGAINST SUMMONED DEMONS.

Hama no Tsurugi, page 63

Literally, "Sword of Demon-Dispelling." Since it's not in its completed form, however, it appears as a *harisen*—an item constructed of a piece of paper, repeatedly folded back upon itself like a fan, with a handle bound by tape. *Harisen* are a staple sight-gag in Japanese comedy shows, and are used to give the offending parties a hearty smack upside the head.

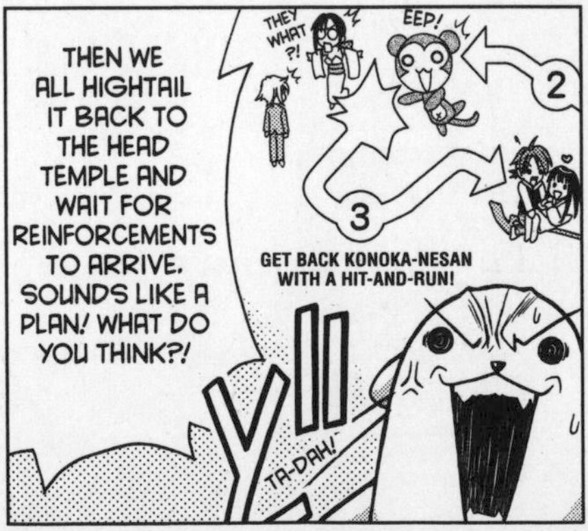
EEP!
2
THEY WHAT ?!
THEN WE ALL HIGHTAIL IT BACK TO THE HEAD TEMPLE AND WAIT FOR REINFORCEMENTS TO ARRIVE. SOUNDS LIKE A PLAN! WHAT DO YOU THINK?!
3
GET BACK KONOKA-NESAN WITH A HIT-AND-RUN!
TA-DAH!

Head Temple, page 64

The Japanese term is "Sohonzan" and is the name given to the main (head) temple of a Buddhist sect.

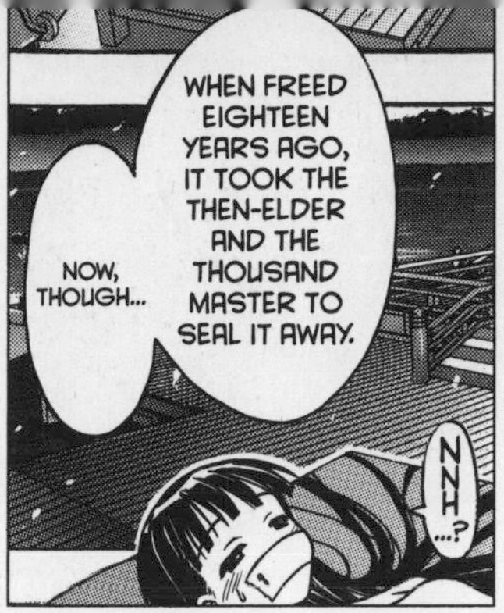
WHEN FREED EIGHTEEN YEARS AGO, IT TOOK THE THEN-ELDER AND THE THOUSAND MASTER TO SEAL IT AWAY.
NOW, THOUGH...
NNH ...?

Elder, page 70

The Japanese term is "osa" (which can be translated as "Chief"), but given the fantasy feel of the series, it seems that in this instance, "Elder" works better.

Hyakuretsu Okazani, page 74

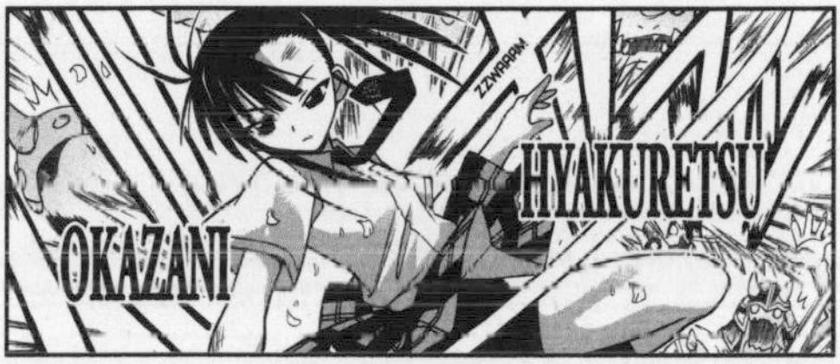
HYAKURETSU
OKAZANI

Literally, "One Hundred-Strike Cherry Blossom Cut"...and it still sounds much cooler in the Japanese.

Inugami, page 77

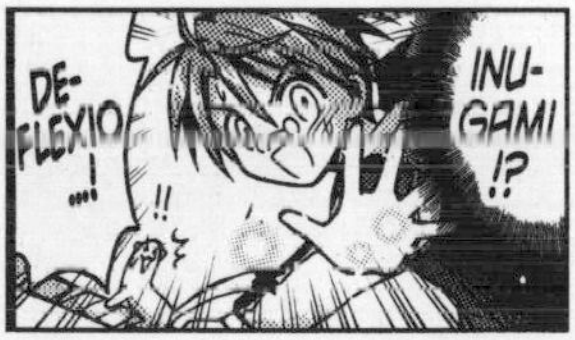
INU-GAMI !?
DE-FLEXIO ...!

Dog-like demons (from *inu*, "dog" + "*-gami*" or "*-kami*," spirits or gods) invoked by those desperate for vengeance. Because they're known to turn on the summoner just as easily, those who would use the Inugami to wreak their revenge should be prepared for that fury to be turned back on them.

Raimeiken, page 81

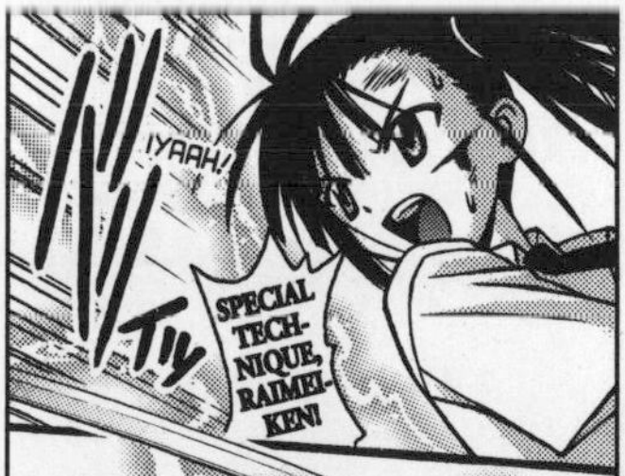
IYAAH!
SPECIAL TECH-NIQUE, RAIMEI-KEN!

Another of Setsuna's special attacks. Literally translates to "Thunder-Clap Sword."

Matiponchuan, page 102

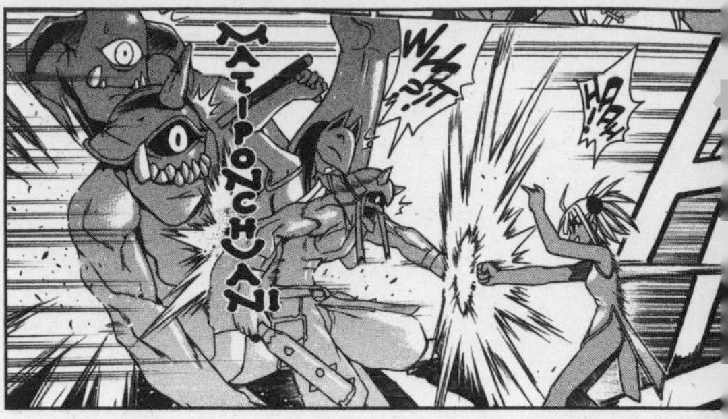
MATIPONCHUAN!

(Japanese reading of the phonetic Chinese.) The user builds up *ki* or *chi* in their "gut," unleashing it along with a mid-level punch to create an explosive impact on the opponent. Rendered in Japanese as "Batei Hôken," *batei* means "horse's hoof," while *hôken* means "mid-level punch."

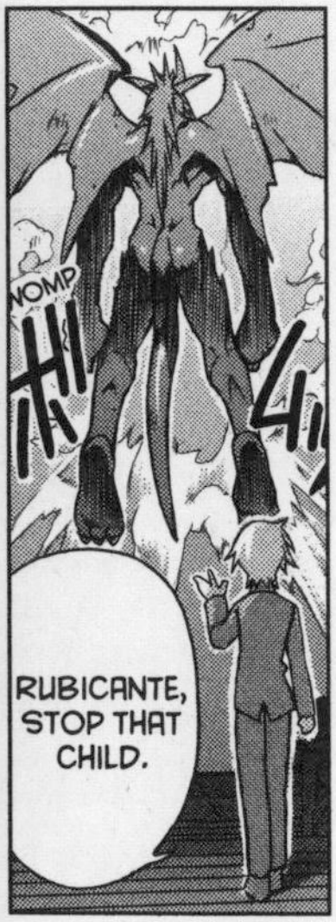
RUBICANTE, STOP THAT CHILD.

Rubicante, page 107

Fate's demonic minion. The name originates from a demon appearing in Dante's "Inferno," and refers to the color of its fury—blood red.

Seiza, page 177

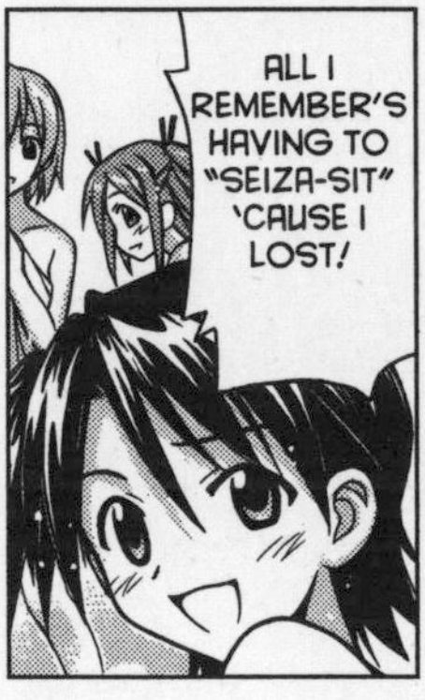
ALL I REMEMBER'S HAVING TO "SEIZA-SIT" 'CAUSE I LOST!

In Japanese, the word *seiza* is made up of the characters for "correct" and "sit" and refers to the position used in the tea ceremony and in Zen meditation. It involves folding the lower legs under your thighs, and if you're not used to it, it can be very uncomfortable if maintained for prolonged periods.

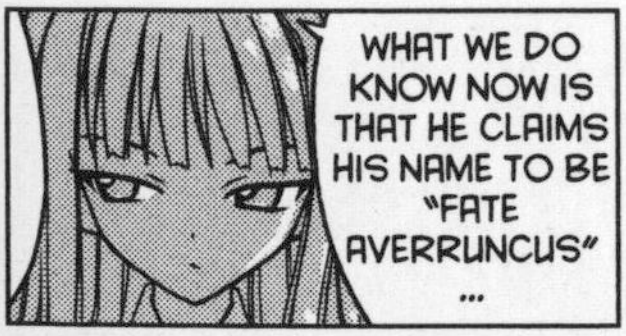
WHAT WE DO KNOW NOW IS THAT HE CLAIMS HIS NAME TO BE "FATE AVERRUNCUS" ...

Fate Averruncus, page 185

The name of the "white-haired youth." The Roman god of aversion, "Averruncus" is said to help in avoiding calamity, while also bringing forth good fortune. In other references, Averruncus is known as the god of childbirth.

A Gallery of *Negima!* Cover Sketches

As a special treat, we're including here the artwork printed beneath the dust jacket of each Japanese edition of *Negima!* These are the sketches which eventually became the full-color covers for Volumes 1 to 6.

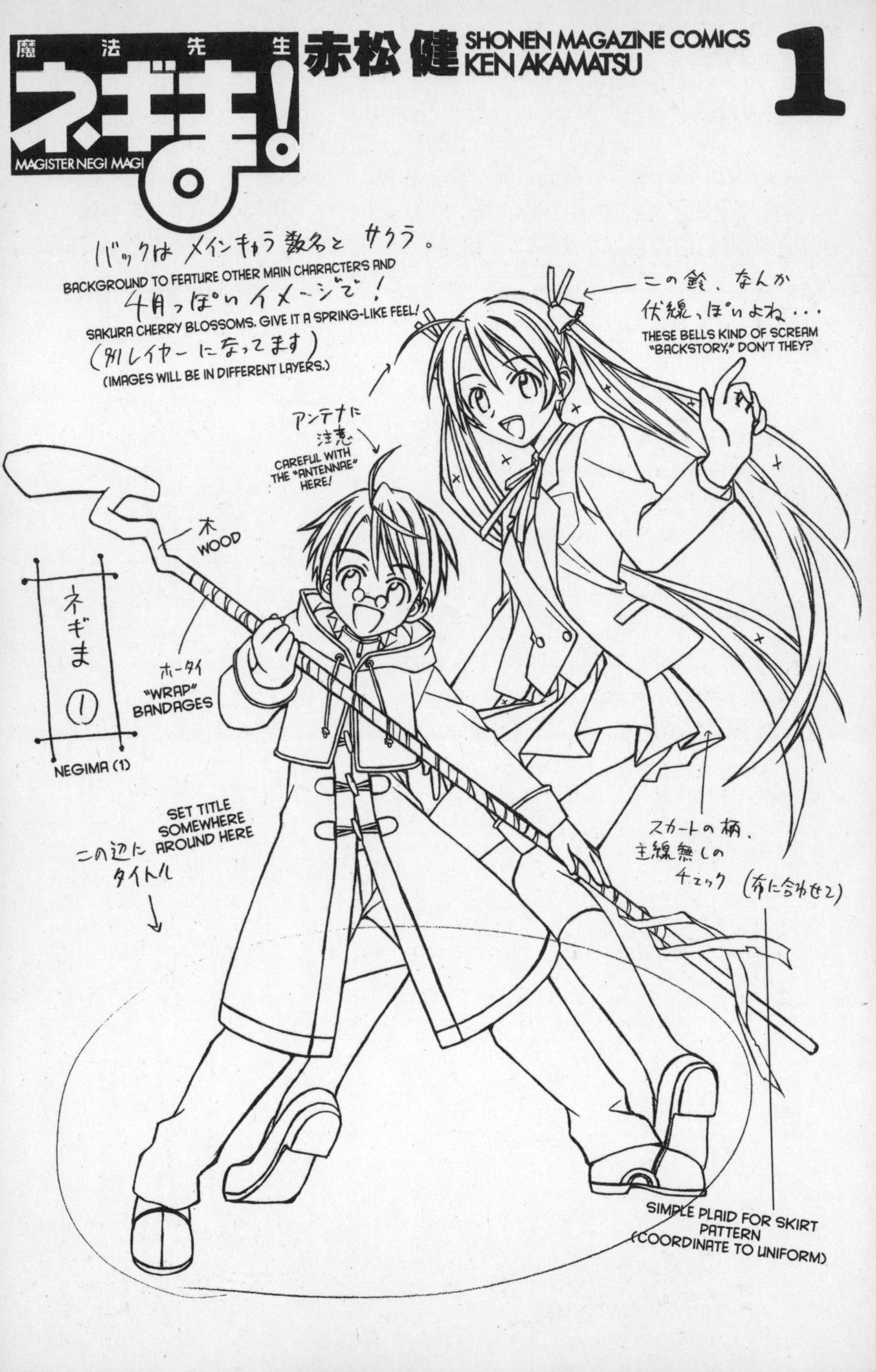

魔法先生
ネギま！
MAGISTER NEGI MAGI
赤松 健
SHONEN MAGAZINE COMICS
KEN AKAMATSU
1
バックは メインキャラ数名と サクラ。
BACKGROUND TO FEATURE OTHER MAIN CHARACTERS AND
4月っぽいイメージで！
SAKURA CHERRY BLOSSOMS. GIVE IT A SPRING-LIKE FEEL!
（別レイヤーになってます）
(IMAGES WILL BE IN DIFFERENT LAYERS.)
この鈴、なんか
伏線っぽいよね・・・
THESE BELLS KIND OF SCREAM "BACKSTORY," DON'T THEY?
アンテナに
注意
CAREFUL WITH THE "ANTENNAE" HERE!
木
WOOD
ネギま
①
NEGIMA (1)
ホータイ
"WRAP" BANDAGES
SET TITLE SOMEWHERE AROUND HERE
この辺に
タイトル
スカートの柄、
主線無しの
チェック（布に合わせて）
SIMPLE PLAID FOR SKIRT PATTERN (COORDINATE TO UNIFORM)

キャラ解説

CHARACTER PROFILE

㉗ 宮崎のどか（本屋）

㉗ NODOKA MIYAZAKI (A.K.A. "BOOKSTORE-GIRL, OR LIBRARY-GIRL")

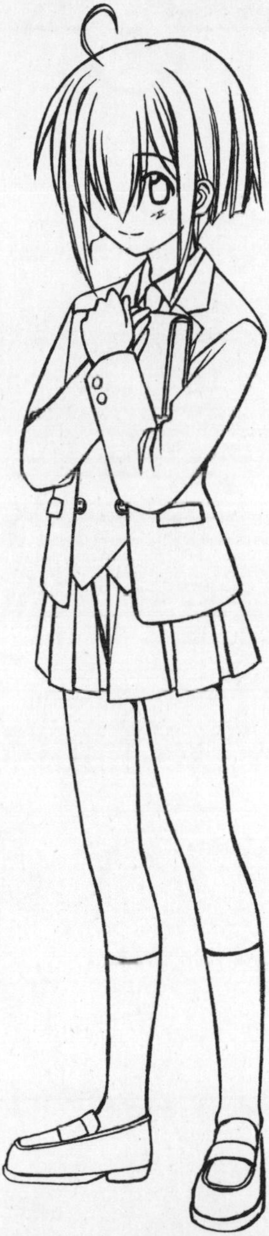

こいつのイメージは もろ「しのぶ」

INSPIRATION FOR THIS CHARACTER IS FROM [LOVE HINA

なんですけど（笑）、あれより もっと

CHARACTER] "SHINOBU," ACTUALLY. (HEH.) NODOKA,

ひっこみ思案で 自分に自信が

THOUGH, IS EVEN MORE WITHDRAWN, AND TENDS

ない キャラなんです。

TO BE UNSURE OF HERSELF.

そこで、「メガネっ娘」より更に

THINK OF HER AS AN "EVOLVED" FORM OF MEGANEKKO

進歩した「前髪っ娘」という

("GIRL WITH GLASSES"), DESIGNED WITH THE TITLE MAEGAMIKKO

概念を導入して デザインして

("GIRL WITH LONG HAIR FALLING INTO BANGS") IN MIND.

みました！

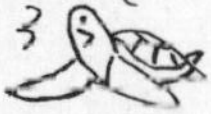

萌えっ

HUMINA HUMINA

うわー！？

WOWZA!

スタイルとかは あんまりよくないです。

NOTHING TO WRITE HOME ABOUT IN THE FIGURE DEPARTMENT—

けっこう気にしてるっぽいです。

A SENSITIVE SUBJECT TO HER.

赤松

(AKAMATSU)

2巻目も よろしく お願いいたします〜。

PLEASE LOOK FORWARD TO VOL. 2

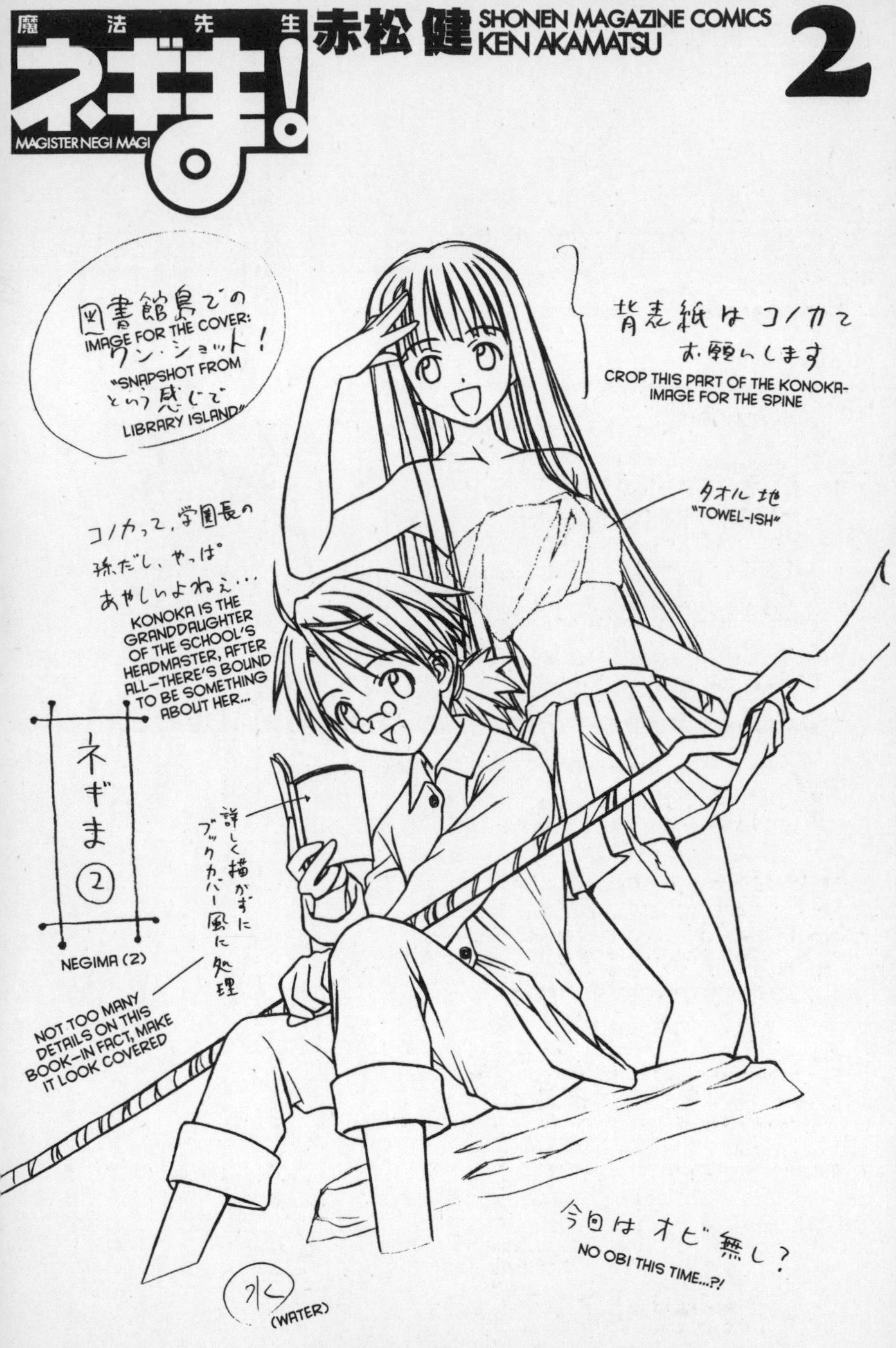
魔法先生
ネギま!
MAGISTER NEGI MAGI
赤松 健
SHONEN MAGAZINE COMICS
KEN AKAMATSU
2
図書館島での
ワン・ショット！
という感じで
IMAGE FOR THE COVER: "SNAPSHOT FROM LIBRARY ISLAND"
背表紙はコノカで
お願いします
CROP THIS PART OF THE KONOKA-IMAGE FOR THE SPINE
タオル地
"TOWEL-ISH"
コノカって、学園長の
孫だし、やっぱ
あやしいよねぇ…
KONOKA IS THE GRANDDAUGHTER OF THE SCHOOL'S HEADMASTER, AFTER ALL—THERE'S BOUND TO BE SOMETHING ABOUT HER...
ネギま ②
NEGIMA (2)
詳しく描かずに
ブックカバー風に処理
NOT TOO MANY DETAILS ON THIS BOOK—IN FACT, MAKE IT LOOK COVERED
今回は オビ無し？
NO OBI THIS TIME...?!
水
(WATER)

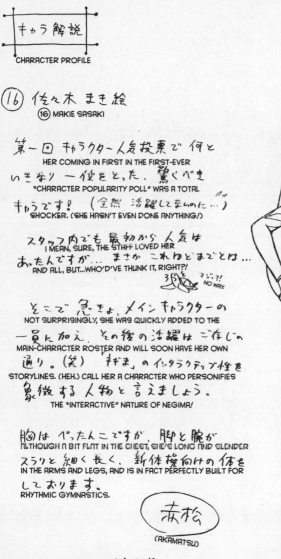

キャラ解説

CHARACTER PROFILE

⑯ 佐々木 まき絵
⑯ MAKIE SASAKI

第一回 キャラクター人気投票で 何と
HER COMING IN FIRST IN THE FIRST-EVER

いきなり 一位をとった、驚くべき
"CHARACTER POPULARITY POLL" WAS A TOTAL

キャラです！（全然 活躍して ないのに…）
SHOCKER. (SHE HASN'T EVEN DONE ANYTHING!)

スタッフ内でも 最初から 人気は
I MEAN, SURE, THE STAFF LOVED HER

あったんですが… まさか これほどまでとは…
AND ALL, BUT...WHO'D'VE THUNK IT, RIGHT?!

マジ?!
NO WAY.

そこで 急きょ、メインキャラクターの
NOT SURPRISINGLY, SHE WAS QUICKLY ADDED TO THE

一員に加え、その後の活躍は ご存じの
MAIN-CHARACTER ROSTER AND WILL SOON HAVE HER OWN

通り。（笑）「ネギま」の インタラクティブ性を
STORYLINES. (HEH.) CALL HER A CHARACTER WHO PERSONIFIES

象徴する 人物と 言えましょう。
THE "INTERACTIVE" NATURE OF NEGIMA!

胸は ぺったんこですが、脚と腕が
ALTHOUGH A BIT FLAT IN THE CHEST, SHE'S LONG AND SLENDER

スラッと 細く 長く、新体操向けの 体を
IN THE ARMS AND LEGS, AND IS IN FACT PERFECTLY BUILT FOR

しております。
RHYTHMIC GYMNASTICS.

赤松
(AKAMATSU)

それでは また 3巻で… ♪
SEE YOU IN VOL. 3....!

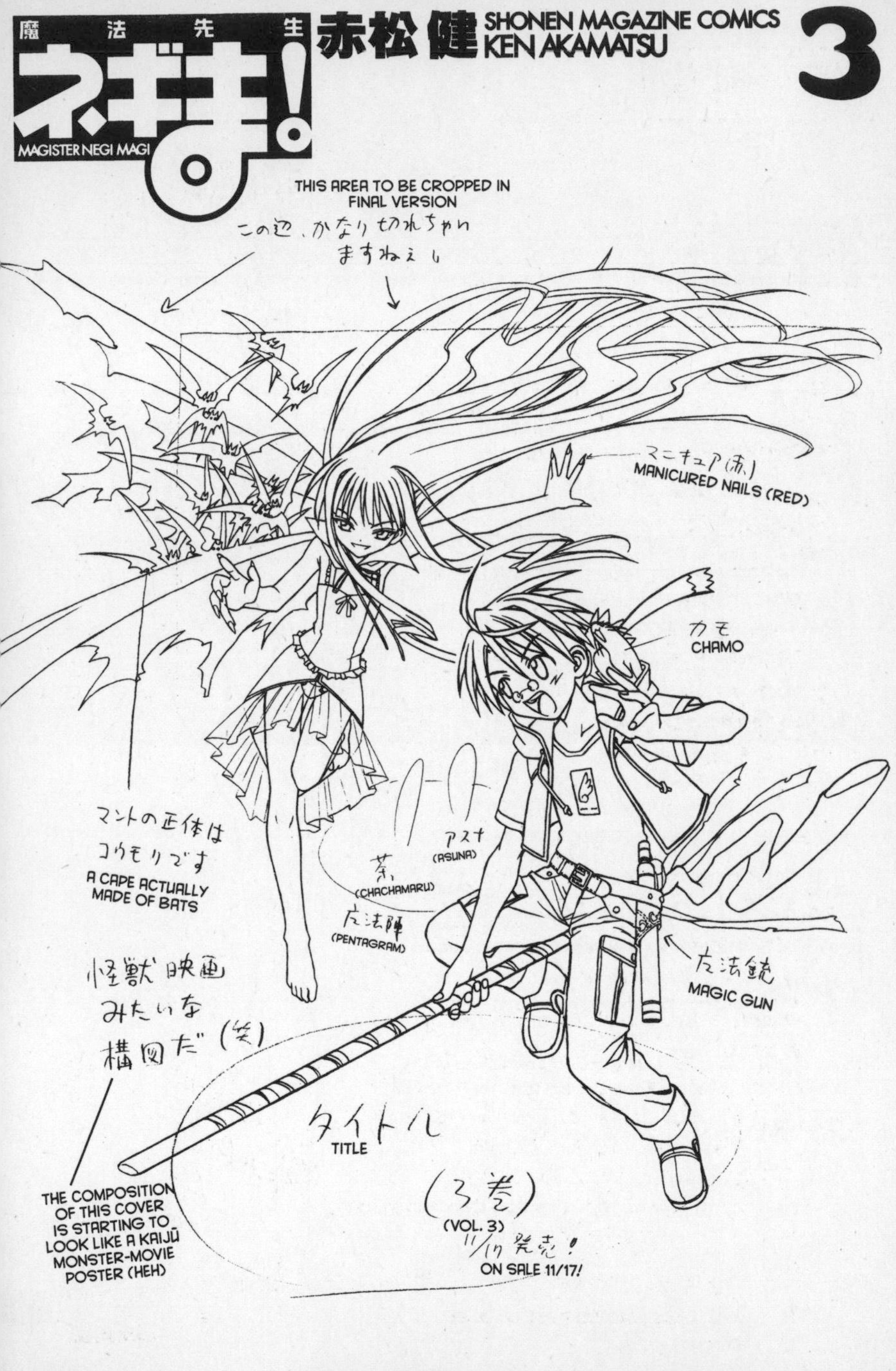

魔法先生
ネギま!
MAGISTER NEGI MAGI
赤松健
SHONEN MAGAZINE COMICS
KEN AKAMATSU
3
THIS AREA TO BE CROPPED IN FINAL VERSION
この辺、かなり切れちゃいますねぇ
マニキュア(赤)
MANICURED NAILS (RED)
カモ
CHAMO
マントの正体はコウモリです
A CAPE ACTUALLY MADE OF BATS
アスナ
(ASUNA)
茶
(CHACHAMARU)
魔法陣
(PENTAGRAM)
魔法銃
MAGIC GUN
怪獣映画みたいな構図だ(笑)
THE COMPOSITION OF THIS COVER IS STARTING TO LOOK LIKE A KAIJŪ MONSTER-MOVIE POSTER (HEH)
タイトル
TITLE
(3巻)
(VOL. 3)
11/17発売!
ON SALE 11/17!

キャラ解説

CHARACTER PROFILE

⑳ 長瀬 楓 （忍者？）

⑳ KAEDE NAGASE (NINJA?)

こういう細目のおとぼけキャラは、ぜひ

I HAD A REAL URGE TO INCLUDE A CHARACTER WITH

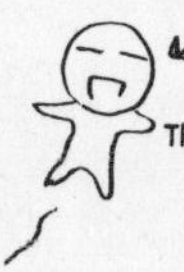

欲しかったわけです。（笑）

THIN EYES LIKE THESE (HEH). IN KAEDE'S CASE, I

かえでの場合、「おとぼけ」の他に

WANTED TO EMPHASIZE THE SEEMING "VAPIDITY" RIGHT

「やさしさ」、「強さ」が内包されていて、なかなかの好キャラに

ALONG WITH THE "KINDNESS" AND "STRENGTH" OF THE CHARACTER. SHE'S TURNED OUT TO BE A PRETTY

なりましたね。

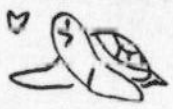

GOOD CHARACTER, I THINK.

人気投票でも上位です！

SHE'S CLIMBING THE POPULARITY POLLS!

双子と仲が良いようで、ついでに散歩部にも誘われた模様。

FRIENDLY WITH THE TWINS, SHE JOINED THE WALKING CLUB AT THEIR REQUEST. FOR A THIRD-YEAR JUNIOR-HIGH

中3のくせに巨乳をほこり。(^^;)

STUDENT, HER BREASTS ARE EXCEPTIONALLY LARGE.... (^^;)

スタイルも最強なのですが、

HER FIGURE'S AMAZING AND

成績はひじょ〜に悪いです。

HER GRADES ARE AMAZINGLY BAD

（でもそれが良い?!）

(WHICH COULD VERY WELL BE THE BASIS OF HER POPULARITY...).

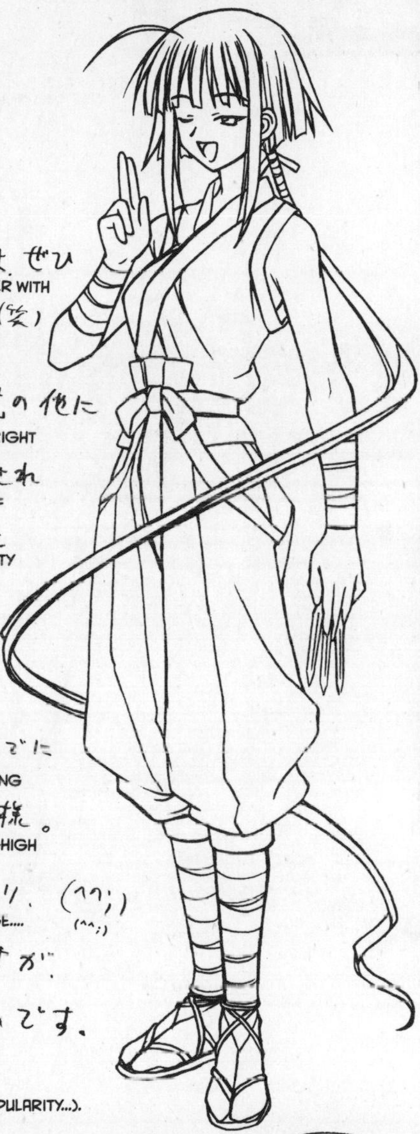

では4巻でお会いしましょう！

SEE YOU AGAIN IN VOL. 4!

赤松

(AKAMATSU)

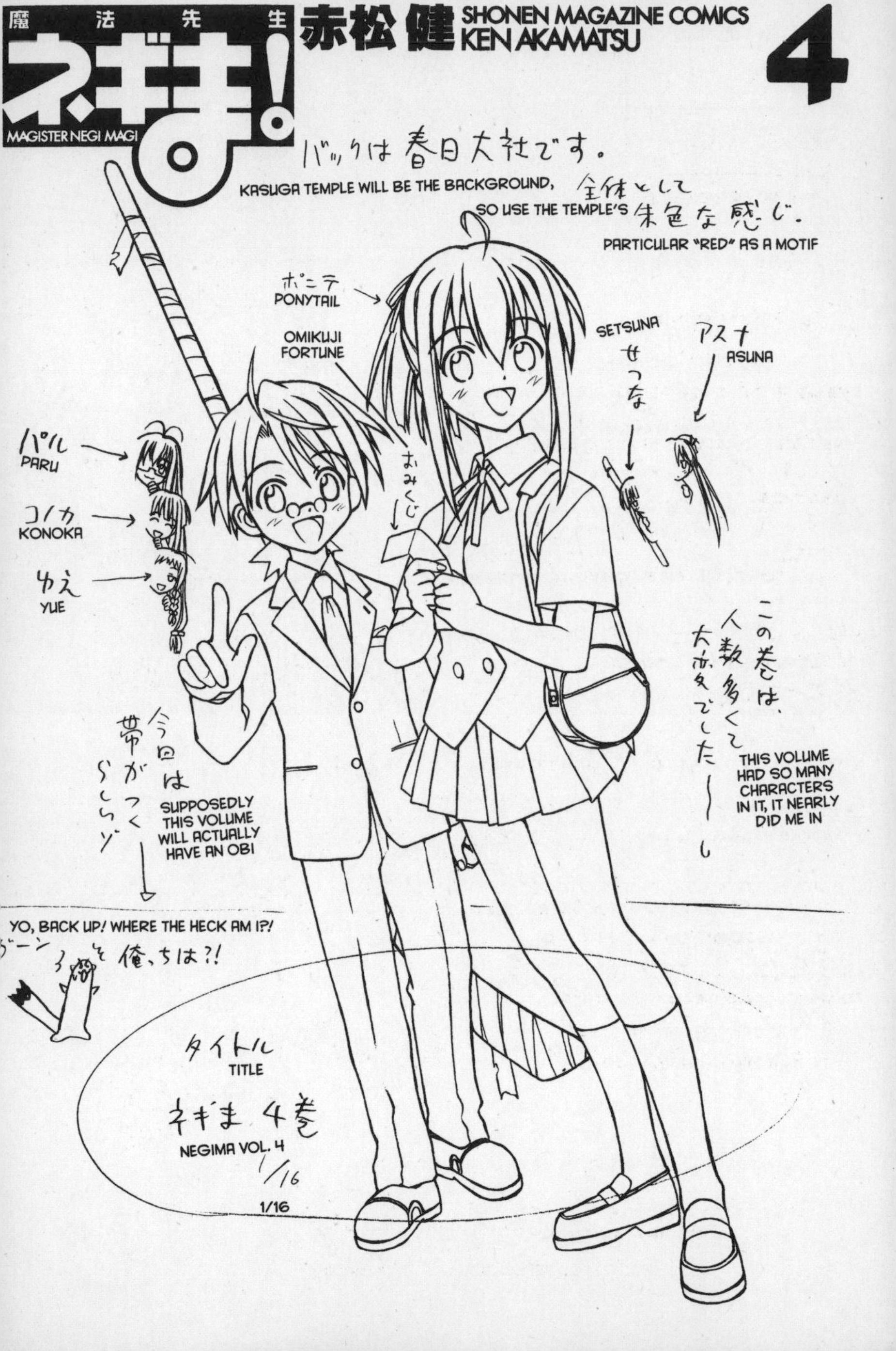
魔法先生
ネギま!
MAGISTER NEGI MAGI
赤松 健
SHONEN MAGAZINE COMICS
KEN AKAMATSU
4
バックは春日大社です。
KASUGA TEMPLE WILL BE THE BACKGROUND,
全体として朱色な感じ。
SO USE THE TEMPLE'S
PARTICULAR "RED" AS A MOTIF
ポニテ
PONYTAIL
OMIKUJI
FORTUNE
SETSUNA
せつな
アスナ
ASUNA
パル
PARU
コノカ
KONOKA
ゆえ
YUE
おみくじ
この巻は人数多くて大変でした〜し
THIS VOLUME HAD SO MANY CHARACTERS IN IT, IT NEARLY DID ME IN
今回は帯がつくらしいゾ
SUPPOSEDLY THIS VOLUME WILL ACTUALLY HAVE AN OBI
YO, BACK UP! WHERE THE HECK AM I?!
ガーン
俺っちは?!
タイトル
TITLE
ネギま 4巻
NEGIMA VOL. 4
1/16
1/16

キャラ解説

CHARACTER PROFILE

⑮ 桜咲刹那

⑮ SETSUNA SAKURAZAKI

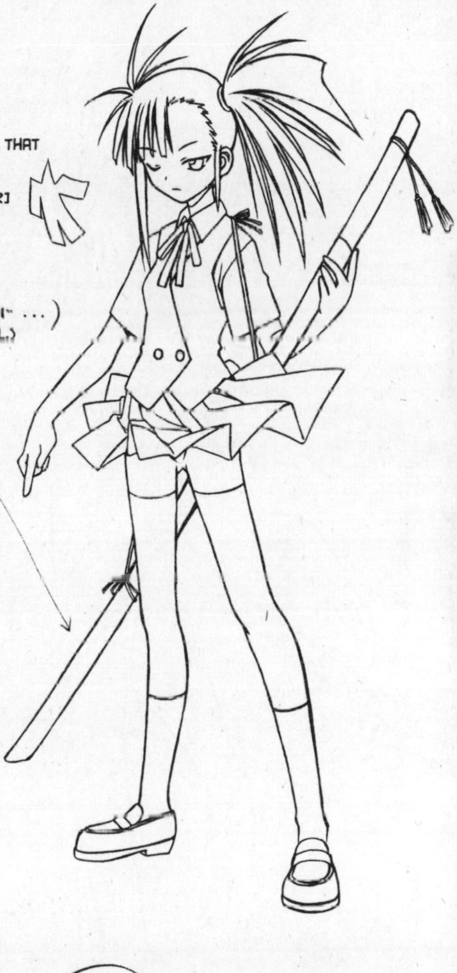

あの神鳴流ということで、
SEEING AS SHE IS FROM THE SHINMEI SCHOOL, CAN IT BE THAT
やはりモトコと関係あるので
SHE'S SOMEHOW CONNECTED TO [LOVE HINA CHARACTER]
しょうか?!
MOTOKO?!

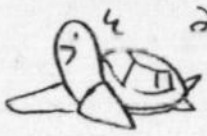
DWAH?!

(本編にも小さくそれらしき影が…)
(SOMETHING IN THE STORY ALLUDES TO THIS, AS WELL.)

使っている刀は「夕凪(ゆうなぎ)」という
SETSUNA'S SWORD IS NAMED
名前です。
"YŪNAGI"
かなりのワザモノらしいです。
(AND IT'S A PRETTY GOOD ONE, TOO, OR SO I'M TOLD).

胸ぺったんこの上に
KIND OF FLAT-CHESTED AND ALWAYS IN BIKE
スパッツということで、今は
SHORTS, SHE MAY BE LACKING A BIT IN THE
いくぶん色気不足ですが、
SEX-APPEAL DEPARTMENT NOW, BUT IN THE
将来はきっと美人になりそう。
FUTURE SHE COULD TURN OUT TO BE A REAL
がんばれセツナ！
LOOKER. HANG IN THERE, SETSUNA!

では、次の5巻で
お会いしましょ～♪
OKAY, THEN! SEE YOU IN VOL. 5!

赤松
(AKAMATSU)

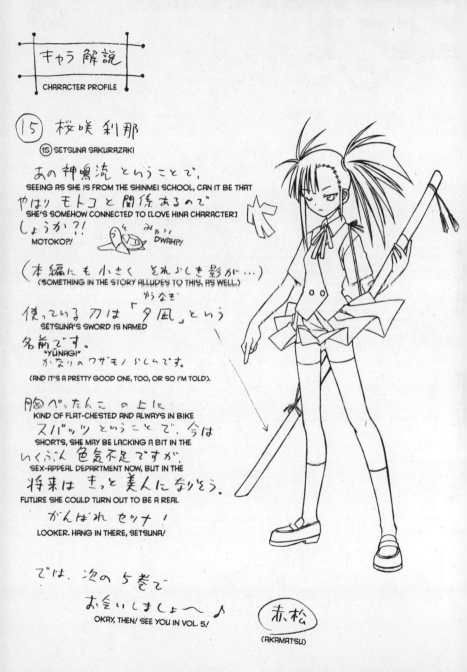

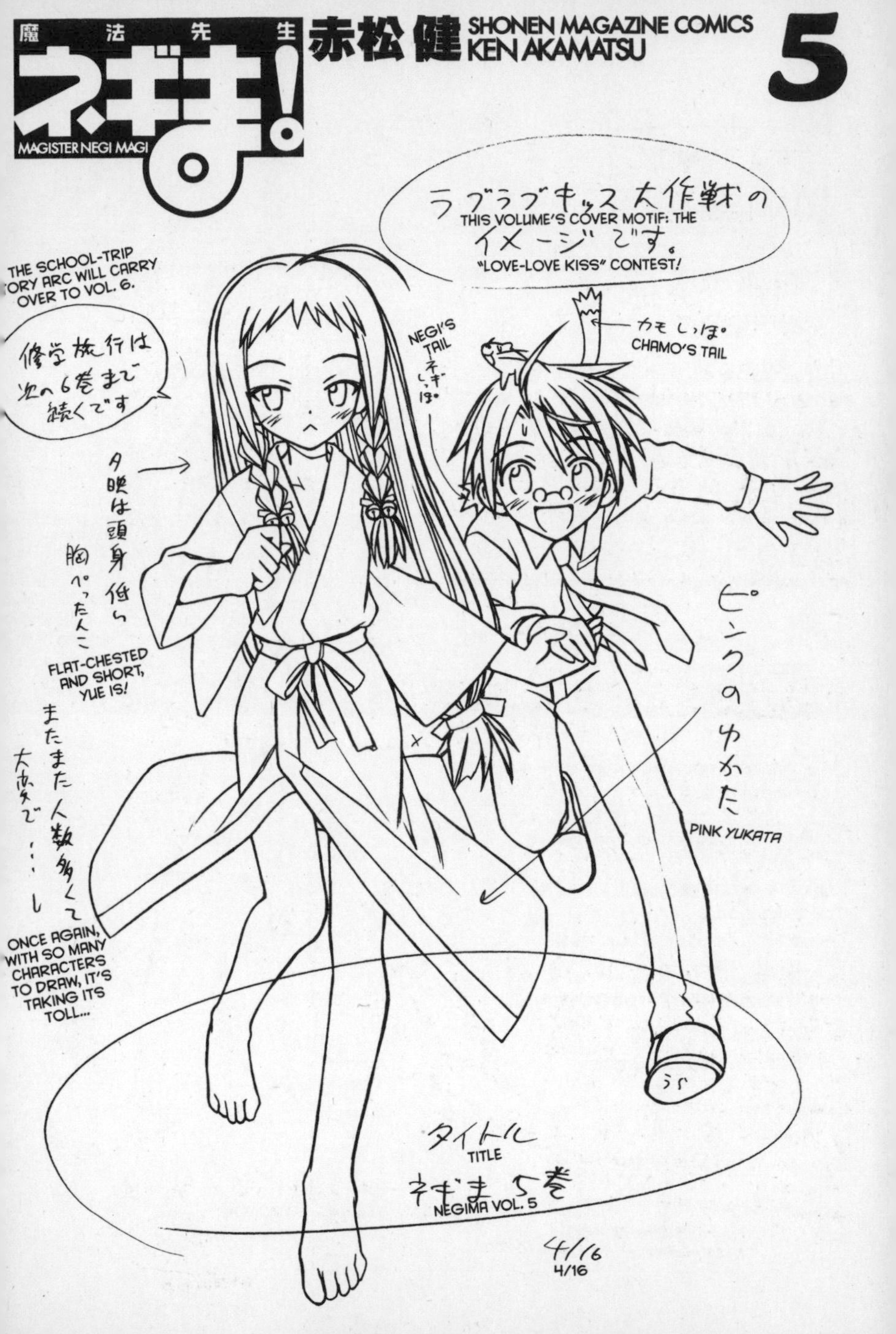

魔法先生
ネギま!
MAGISTER NEGI MAGI
赤松健
SHONEN MAGAZINE COMICS
KEN AKAMATSU
5
ラブラブキッス大作戦のイメージです。
THIS VOLUME'S COVER MOTIF: THE "LOVE-LOVE KISS" CONTEST!
THE SCHOOL-TRIP ORY ARC WILL CARRY OVER TO VOL. 6.
修学旅行は次の6巻まで続くです
NEGI'S TAIL
ネギしっぽ
カモしっぽ
CHAMO'S TAIL
夕映は頭身低ら 胸ぺったんこ
FLAT-CHESTED AND SHORT, YUE IS!
またまた人数多くて大変で…し
ONCE AGAIN, WITH SO MANY CHARACTERS TO DRAW, IT'S TAKING ITS TOLL...
ピンクのゆかた
PINK YUKATA
タイトル
TITLE
ネギま5巻
NEGIMA VOL. 5
4/16
4/16

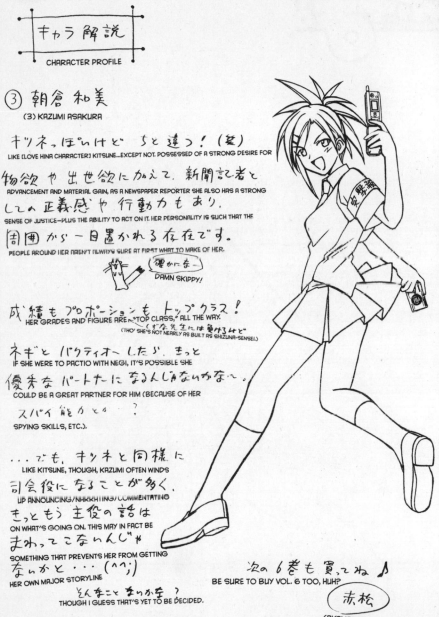

キャラ解説

CHARACTER PROFILE

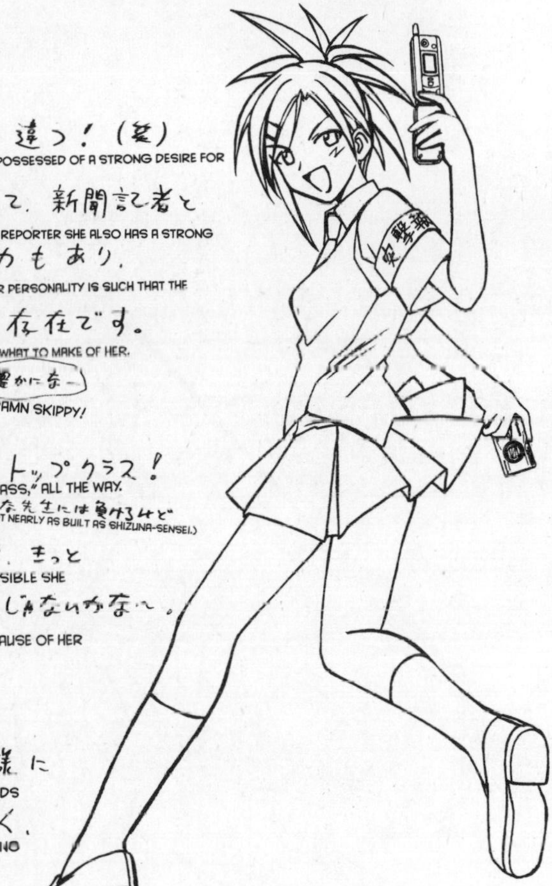

③ 朝倉 和美

(3) KAZUMI ASAKURA

キツネっぽいけど ちと違う! (笑)
LIKE [LOVE HINA CHARACTER] KITSUNE...EXCEPT NOT. POSSESSED OF A STRONG DESIRE FOR
物欲や出世欲にかえて、新聞記者と
ADVANCEMENT AND MATERIAL GAIN, AS A NEWSPAPER REPORTER SHE ALSO HAS A STRONG
しての正義感や行動力もあり。
SENSE OF JUSTICE—PLUS THE ABILITY TO ACT ON IT. HER PERSONALITY IS SUCH THAT THE
周囲から一目置かれる存在です。
PEOPLE AROUND HER AREN'T ALWAYS SURE AT FIRST WHAT TO MAKE OF HER.

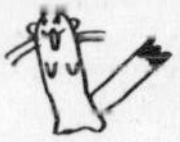

(確かにな一)
DAMN SKIPPY!

成績もプロポーションもトップクラス!
HER GRADES AND FIGURE ARE "TOP CLASS," ALL THE WAY.
(しずな先生には負けるけど
(THO' SHE'S NOT NEARLY AS BUILT AS SHIZUNA-SENSEI.)

ネギとパクティオーしたら、きっと
IF SHE WERE TO PACTIO WITH NEGI, IT'S POSSIBLE SHE
優秀なパートナーになるんじゃないかなー。
COULD BE A GREAT PARTNER FOR HIM (BECAUSE OF HER
スパイ能力とか…?
SPYING SKILLS, ETC.).

…でも、キツネと同様に
LIKE KITSUNE, THOUGH, KAZUMI OFTEN WINDS
司会役になることが多く、
UP ANNOUNCING/NARRATING/COMMENTATING
きっともう主役の話は
ON WHAT'S GOING ON. THIS MAY IN FACT BE
まわってこないんじゃ
SOMETHING THAT PREVENTS HER FROM GETTING
ないかと…(^^;)
HER OWN MAJOR STORYLINE
そんなことないかな?
THOUGH I GUESS THAT'S YET TO BE DECIDED.

次の6巻も買ってね♪
BE SURE TO BUY VOL. 6 TOO, HUH?

赤松
(AKAMATSU)

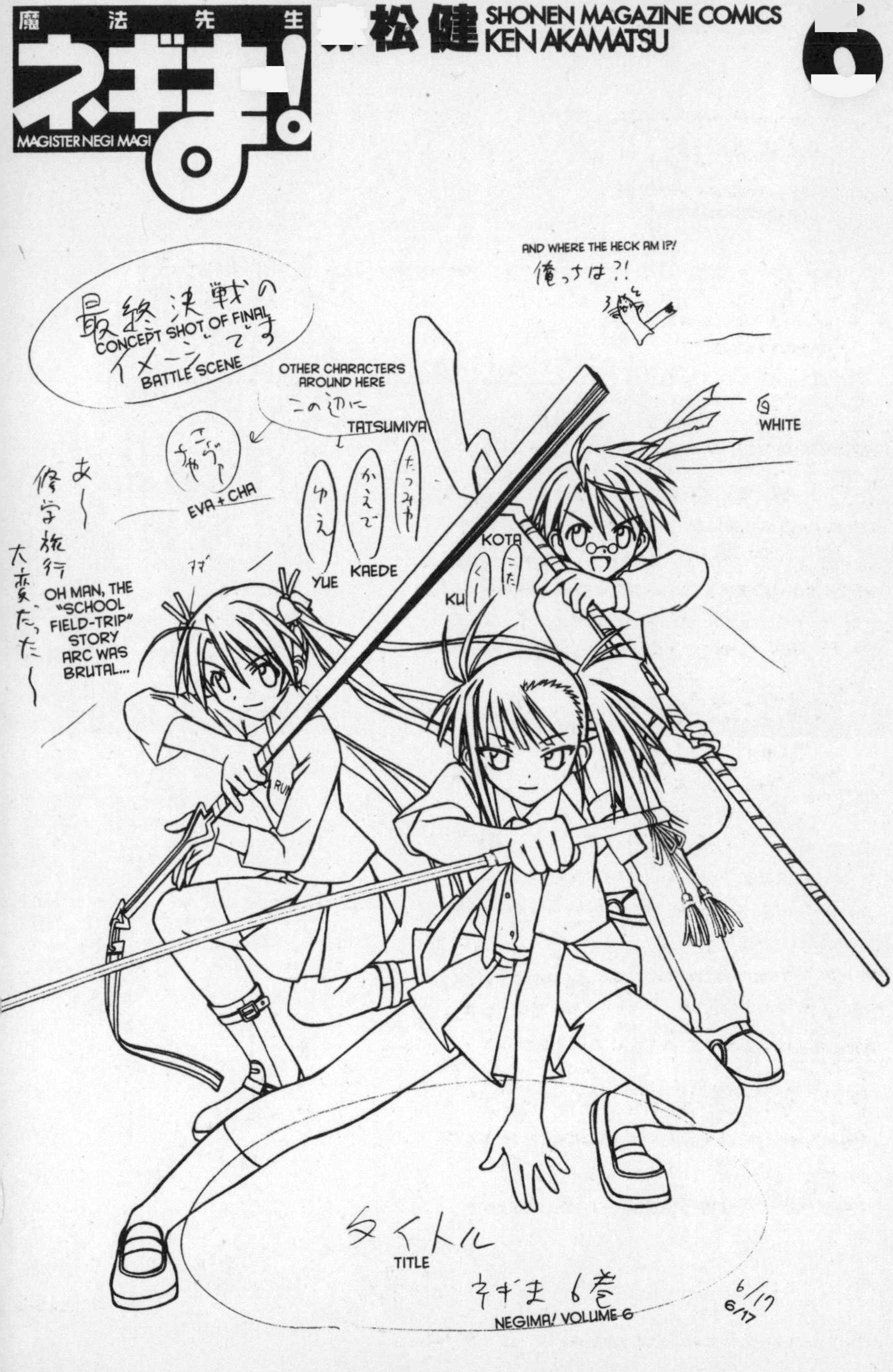
魔法先生
ネギま!
MAGISTER NEGI MAGI
松健
SHONEN MAGAZINE COMICS
KEN AKAMATSU
AND WHERE THE HECK AM I?!
俺っちは?!
最終決戦のイメージです
CONCEPT SHOT OF FINAL BATTLE SCENE
OTHER CHARACTERS AROUND HERE
この辺に
白
WHITE
TATSUMIYA
たつみや
かえで
ゆえ
EVA + CHA
あ~修学旅行大変だった~
OH MAN, THE "SCHOOL FIELD-TRIP" STORY ARC WAS BRUTAL...
YUE
KAEDE
こた
KOTA
くー
KU
タイトル
TITLE
ネギま 6巻
NEGIMA! VOLUME 6
6/17
6/17

キャラ解説
CHARACTER PROFILE

⑬ 近衛木乃香
⑬ KONOKA KONOE

アスナ

コノカは「ヒロインの親友」として
CREATED AS "BEST FRIEND OF THE HEROINE (ASUNA),"

設定されたクラスメートで、最初は
KONOKA WAS NOT INITIALLY INTENDED TO PLAY A

それほど重要な役ではなかったの
MAJOR PART IN THE STORY FOR SOME REASON NOW,

ですが… 今ではなぜか大活躍!!
THOUGH, HER ROLE'S REALLY BEEN EXPANDED!!

第3回キャラ人気投票ではアスナより
IN THE THIRD "CHARACTER POPULARITY POLL,"
上だったり…
SHE RANKED HIGHER THAN ASUNA

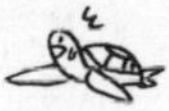

いや、私も好きなキャラですが
I KINDA LIKE HER MYSELF, OF COURSE...

声優は野中藍サン。しーぽん〜
THE VOICE-ACTOR FOR THE CHARACTER IS AI NONAKA...YES,

はんなり〜まったり〜な感じが
SHI'IPON. THE KIND YET LAID-BACK AND WARM QUALITY TO HER

ぴったりです。CDきいてね!
VOICE IS PERFECT. PLEASE LISTEN TO THE DRAMA CD*!

今後も、出番は多いはず。
I IMAGINE WE'LL BE SEEING A LOT OF KONOKA IN THE STORY

頼むぞコノカ!!
FROM NOW ON. WE'RE COUNTING ON YOU, KONOKA!!

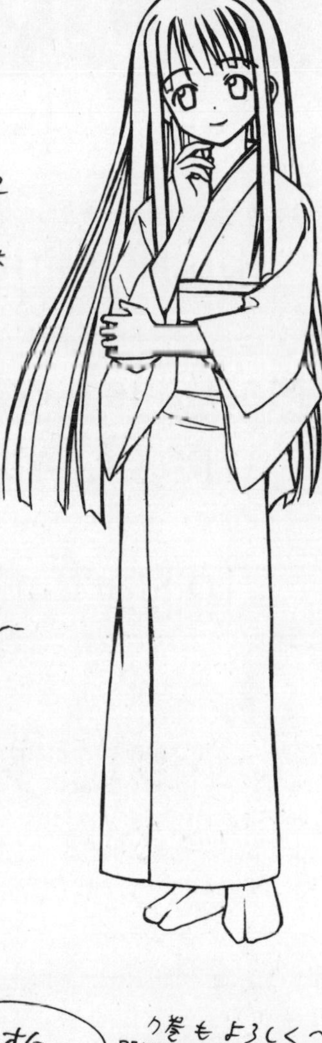

赤松
AKAMATSU

7巻もよろしく〜♡
BE WATCHING FOR VOLUME 7, OKAY?

*ONLY AVAILABLE IN JAPAN. SORRY, FOLKS!

TOMARE!

[STOP!］

You're going the wrong way!

Manga is a completely different type of reading experience.

To start at the *beginning*, go to the *end*!

That's right! Authentic manga is read the traditional Japanese way—from right to left. Exactly the *opposite* of how American books are read. It's easy to follow: Just go to the other end of the book, and read each page—and each panel—from right side to left side, starting at the top right. Now you're experiencing manga as it was meant to be.